# Decoding Tourist Behavior in the Digital Era:

## Insights for Effective Marketing

Norhidayah Azman
*Management and Science University, Malaysia*

Marco Valeri
*Niccolò Cusano University, Italy*

Ahmad Albattat
*Management and Science University, Malaysia*

Amrik Singh
*Lovely Professional University, India*

IGI Global
Publishing Tomorrow's Research Today

Published in the United States of America by
    IGI Global
    701 E. Chocolate Avenue
    Hershey PA, USA 17033
    Tel: 717-533-8845
    Fax:  717-533-8661
    E-mail: cust@igi-global.com
    Web site: https://www.igi-global.com

Library of Congress Cataloging-in-Publication Data


CIP PENDING

ISBN13:  9798369339725
EISBN13:  9798369339732


Vice President of Editorial: Melissa Wagner
Managing Editor of Acquisitions: Mikaela Felty
Managing Editor of Book Development: Jocelynn Hessler
Production Manager: Mike Brehm
Cover Design: Phillip Shickler


British Cataloguing in Publication Data
A Cataloguing in Publication record for this book is available from the British Library.

All work contributed to this book is new, previously-unpublished material.
The views expressed in this book are those of the authors, but not necessarily of the publisher.

# Table of Contents

# Detailed Table of Contents

**Chapter 1**
*Ridhima Sharma, Vivekananda Institute of Professional Studies-TC,*
*India*

The study's overarching goal is to show how technological development significantly affects the decision-making process of tourists. In order to better understand how cognitive technologies, namely AI applications, factor into humans' decision-making processes, this study reviews relevant literature and stresses the need for new theoretical frameworks. The theoretical frameworks and approaches used were examined, and a future view impacted by substantial technological advancement was provided, through a thorough analysis and integration of diverse literature. As digital technology and cyber-physical systems become intrinsic parts of a tourist's identity, technological development considerably impacts the decision-making processes of visitors. Considering the future of cyber-physical-human systems, the article lays the groundwork for a new theoretical framework in the area of tourist decision-making. As new forms of AI improve human intelligence, this paper shows how tourism decision-making theory works and why a paradigm shift is necessary.

## Chapter 2

*Karan Berry, Symbiosis International University (Deemed), India*
*Ankit Shukla, Rajamangala University of Technology, Thanyaburi,*
*Thailand*
*Amrik Singh, Lovely Professional University, India*
*Pratik Satpute, MIT World Peace University, India*

The advent of digital technology has dramatically changed the way people travel, affecting their information searches, itineraries, decisions and experiences shared on social media sites like Twitter, Instagram and Facebook, to assist prospective travellers. Besides highlighting the impact of digital technologies such as social media, online booking platforms, mobile applications and augmented virtual reality, this chapter also examines various aspects of tourist behaviour in the digital age through recent developments, and relevant case studies. It also provides insights into how tourist destinations and businesses can adjust themselves to meet the shifting demands and patterns of travel. This meticulous overview interconnects "tourist behaviour" and the "digital era" to reveal how the development of mobile and internet-based technology has changed the travel and tourism sector.

## Chapter 3

*Jatin Thakur, Lovely Professional University, India*
*Pooja Kansra, Lovely Professional University, India*
*Shad Ahmad Khan, University of Buraimi, Oman*

The rapid advancement of digital technology has profoundly transformed the tourism industry, giving rise to a new breed of traveller the digital traveller. This tech-savvy and hyper-connected demographic demands personalized, seamless, and instantaneous experiences throughout their journey. This chapter delves into the evolving landscape of digital tourism, exploring the key characteristics and behaviours of today's digital travellers. By decoding their preferences and expectations, the chapter identifies effective marketing strategies that resonate with this group. The research highlights the importance of leveraging big data analytics, artificial intelligence, and social media platforms to create tailored marketing campaigns that enhance engagement and foster loyalty. Additionally, the chapter examines the role of mobile technology, virtual reality, and user-generated content in shaping travel decisions.

## Chapter 4

*Bassam Samir Al-Romeedy, Faculty of Tourism and Hotels, University
of Sadat City, Egypt*
*Amrik Singh, School of Hotel Management and Tourism, Lovely
Professional University, India*

In today's digital era, the tourism industry is undergoing a major transformation as it shifts from traditional marketing techniques to data-driven strategies that leverage the vast amounts of digital information generated by travelers. This chapter delves into how the digital footprints left by travelers—such as search histories, social media interactions, online bookings, and mobile app usage—can be effectively utilized to craft personalized and impactful marketing campaigns. It covers the entire process, from the collection and management of these digital traces to their analysis, emphasizing the importance of advanced technologies like artificial intelligence and big data analytics in converting raw data into actionable insights. These insights empower tourism businesses to anticipate traveler behavior, customize marketing messages, and engage with customers in a more personalized and meaningful manner.

## Chapter 5

*Busenur Can, Çanakkale Onsekiz Mart University, Turkey*
*Onur Çakır, Kırklareli University, Turkey*

This chapter aims to provide tourism academics and professionals with a comprehensive understanding of influencer marketing in tourism by analyzing research findings from the last decade. In this context, the chapter investigates 82 studies' findings on influencer marketing in the tourism industry conducted between 2012 and 2023 using systematic literature review method. The results indicate that the number of studies on influencer marketing has increased exponentially since 2020. In the majority of the studies, the survey method was preferred as the data collection technique, while the topics addressed were mostly on the effects of influencers on the tourist behavior and tourists' purchasing process, followed by studies examining the content created by the influencer. The results indicate that, in general, content produced by influencers has a positive impact on consumer behavior. Therefore, it would be beneficial for tourism businesses to collaborate with influencers.

Tourism serves as a prominent illustration of the crucial role that social media has assumed in the contemporary digital age. The present study aims to examine the influence of widely used electronic platforms, namely Instagram, Facebook, WhatsApp, and TikTok, on the decision-making processes of tourists. Adopting the AIDA (Attention, Interest, Desire, Action) model as a conceptual framework, the study collects feedback from 100 participants to evaluate the impact of their social media engagement on their travel decisions. The findings demonstrate that social media exerts a substantial influence on the formation of travel preferences and the choice of destinations by effectively attracting users' attention and generating desire through well selected material and influencer marketing. Furthermore, the research investigates the application of machine learning to examine large datasets obtained from social media platforms, particularly Twitter, for the purpose of predicting tourist demand.

During outbreak crisis, the information conveyed through news media can significantly influence tourists' perceptions of risk, ultimately shaping their preventive behaviors. Previous studies have indicated that research on this influence is still insufficient and relatively new. This study investigates how exposure to news media affects risk perception and preventive behaviors among Malaysian tourists. It also explores whether risk perception mediates the relationship between news media exposure and preventive behavior. Using cross-sectional design, 250 questionnaires were collected from tourists in the Klang Valley. The analysis using the PLS-SEM technique has revealed that news media exposure and personal-level risk perception are the important predictors to explain tourist's preventive behavior during pandemic. Additionally, personal risk perception plays a significant role in mediating the relationship between news exposure and behavior. These findings offer insights for policymakers to better understand and address tourists' perceptions and behaviors during outbreaks crisis.

Objectives of the Study: The goal of this chapter is to find out the influence of AI on traveler conduct (Gopal et.al 2023), assess how tourism centered AI technology swap tourist aim, goals and ideas (Hoyer et al. 2020). Also to The research aims to recognize the influence of AI on tailored travel, ecological consciousness, and each aspect of the trip itself. Study Method/Design: The current study deploys secondary data and qualitative technique involve content analysis and in-depth interviews. Findings: From the study, it is, highlighted that AI impacts tourist conduct at various period of trip. Moreover, travel gathers abundance of memories, experiences collected by tourist, exploration of new places (Gretzel et al., 2015) On top of that inclusion of AI gives the benefit of smooth AI improves travel experience by making better ways, using less energy, and minimizing waste (Neidhardt et al ., 2015).

## Chapter 9

The integration of artificial intelligence (AI) into customer service has revolutionized various industries, with the hospitality sector being a significant beneficiary. Among AI applications, chatbots have emerged as a vital tool for enhancing customer engagement and satisfaction. This chapter explores the role of chatbots in shaping tourist behavior, focusing on a comparative analysis between Indian and Filipino travelers. Utilizing quantitative analysis through SmartPLS (Partial Least Squares Structural Equation Modeling), this seeks to decode the intricate factors influencing tourist behavior and the effectiveness of chatbots in the hospitality sectors of India and the Philippines.

## Chapter 10

*Munir Ahmad, Survey of Pakistan, Pakistan*
*Shikha Sharma, Vivekananda Institute of Professional Studies, India*

Geo-tech transforms travel with real-time traffic, weather, and attraction updates. Travelers can personalize plans for safer, more convenient journeys. Volunteered Geographic Information (VGI) empowers them further with user-generated reviews, geotagged content, check-ins, location sharing, social media posts, hashtags, vlogs, collaborative travel itineraries, community forums, and crowdsourced maps. These advancements make travel more accessible, inclusive, and enjoyable for everyone. However, VGI faces hurdles: data accuracy, information overload, privacy concerns, biased reviews, and tech dependence. To address these challenges, improved verification processes, advanced filtering options, offline features, user education on privacy, and AI-driven fraud detection are necessary to enhance the reliability and trustworthiness of VGI in travel planning.

## Chapter 11

*Harish Saini, Lovely Professional University, India*
*Pawan Kumar, Lovely Professional University, India*
*Rajesh Verma, Lovely Professional University, India*

This chapter critically examines the transformative role of social media in contemporary travel decision-making, situating its analysis within established theoretical frameworks such as the Technology Acceptance Model (TAM), Theory of Planned Behavior (TPB), and Social Influence Theory. Social media platforms—most notably Instagram, Facebook, and YouTube—are explored as pivotal in influencing destination selection, itinerary planning, and the broader experiential dimensions of tourism. The discourse delves into the complex interplay between user-generated content and destination marketing, emphasizing the emergent power dynamics facilitated by social media influencers. Furthermore, the chapter interrogates the psychological constructs of social proof, fear of missing out (FOMO), and identity construction, elucidating their profound impact on tourist behavior. The chapter concludes by identifying significant research gaps, advocating for a nuanced understanding of the implications of social media on sustainable tourism development in an increasingly digital world

**Chapter 12**

*Bassam Samir Al-Romeedy, Faculty of Tourism and Hotels, University
    of Sadat City, Egypt*
*Amrik Singh, School of Hotel Management and Tourism, Lovely
    Professional University, India*

This chapter investigates the evolving digital journey of contemporary travelers, focusing on how technology and data-driven insights have reshaped travel experiences. It explores the transition from traditional to digital platforms in travel planning, booking, and in-destination activities, emphasizing the traits of today's tech-savvy travelers. By examining consumer behavior across various groups—including millennials, Gen Z, and business travelers—the chapter highlights the growing significance of user-generated content, mobile-first experiences, and tools for real-time decision-making. It also investigates how travelers engage with digital platforms during the pre-travel phase for research and inspiration, the booking process, and the period before arrival, as well as throughout their trip and in post-travel reflections. Additionally, the chapter critically analyzes the role of data analytics, big data, AI, and machine learning in understanding and forecasting traveler behavior.

This chapter explores identity-driven tourism marketing, focusing on aligning destination branding with the values and self-expression of millennial travelers to enhance engagement and satisfaction. Millennials prioritize experiences, personal values, and digital connectivity, seeking destinations that resonate with their identities. The chapter integrates self-congruity theory, destination branding, and millennial consumer behavior to analyze travel motivations and preferences. Key concepts like authenticity, sustainability, social responsibility, and digital engagement are highlighted as crucial in creating meaningful connections. The role of social media in facilitating self-expression and community building among millennials is also discussed. Case studies illustrate successful marketing campaigns, demonstrating that aligning destination branding with millennial values is a strategic approach to engaging this influential demographic in the digital age.

# Preface

In the rapidly evolving landscape of tourism, the digital era has brought about transformative changes in how tourists interact with destinations, services, and experiences. As editors of *Decoding Tourist Behavior in the Digital Era: Insights for Effective Marketing*, we are pleased to present this comprehensive collection of scholarly works that delve into the complexities of tourist behavior in the context of digital marketing. This volume is the culmination of contributions from experts in the field, each offering unique perspectives and methodologies that advance our understanding of how tourists make decisions, engage with digital content, and influence the tourism industry.

Tourist behavior is a multifaceted phenomenon, shaped by a myriad of factors ranging from cultural influences on technological advancements. As tourists become increasingly connected and empowered through digital platforms, their behaviors have shifted, necessitating a reevaluation of traditional marketing approaches. This book seeks to bridge the gap between conventional marketing paradigms and the new realities of the digital age, providing insights that are both theoretically sound and practically relevant.

Our goal with this volume is to equip academics, industry professionals, researchers, and postgraduate students with the tools and knowledge to navigate the complexities of tourist behavior in the digital realm. The chapters within explore a wide range of topics, including the impact of digital marketing strategies on tourist decision-making, the role of social media in shaping destination perceptions, and the ways in which tourists co-create their experiences online. By examining these issues from both a theoretical and practical perspective, this book offers a holistic view of the current state of tourism marketing and its future directions.

## Chapter 1

In this chapter, we delve into the pivotal role of social media marketing in promoting products and services among small and medium-sized enterprises (SMEs) in Malaysia. Specifically, the chapter focuses on homestay operators, revealing a surprisingly low adoption rate of social media marketing within this sector. Through a rigorous cross-sectional study involving 208 operators across four Malaysian states, the research identifies key factors influencing this trend. The findings underscore the significant impact of customer and competitive pressure over perceived cost and digital skills in driving social media adoption. This chapter offers critical insights for policymakers and business owners, advocating for the strategic employment of social media marketing to enhance connectivity and market reach in a cost-effective manner.

## Chapter 2

Culinary tourism, particularly the exploration of local delicacies, plays a crucial role in attracting international tourists. This chapter investigates how digital reviews, particularly on platforms like TripAdvisor, shape tourists' perceptions of culinary destinations. Focusing on Delhi Street food, the chapter analyzes 867 reviews to identify key dimensions of tourists' culinary experiences. The results reveal that these dimensions significantly influence the destination's image among international tourists. The chapter suggests that enhancing the visibility of these dimensions in online platforms can boost a destination's appeal, and calls for further research across different geographical locations to generalize the findings.

## Chapter 3

This chapter explores the transformative impact of social media on the branding of tea destinations, emphasizing the importance of visual and interactive content in engaging tourists. Through an analysis of various social media platforms such as Instagram and Facebook, the chapter illustrates how these platforms have reshaped the branding strategies of tea destinations. Case studies highlight successful approaches that have enhanced brand visibility and engagement. Additionally, the chapter discusses the dual nature of user-generated content, weighing its potential benefits against the challenges it may pose, offering practical insights for destination marketers.

## Chapter 4

Technological development has become a significant factor in shaping tourist decision-making processes, with cognitive technologies like AI playing a central role. This chapter reviews existing literature to propose new theoretical frameworks that better account for the impact of AI on tourism decisions. The research highlights the integration of digital technology and cyber-physical systems into the tourist experience, arguing for a paradigm shift in decision-making theories. The chapter lays the groundwork for future research that will further explore the evolving role of AI in enhancing tourist decision-making.

## Chapter 5

The integration of AI in crisis management represents a significant advancement in the tourism sector. This chapter examines how contemporary AI technologies, including predictive analytics and natural language processing, can prevent and mitigate crises. It discusses the role of AI in improving communication, decision-making, and resource allocation during crises, and explores future practices that could further enhance the sector's resilience. The chapter also addresses ethical and technological challenges, offering strategies to overcome these barriers and underscoring AI's potential to revolutionize crisis management in tourism.

## Chapter 6

Digital technologies have fundamentally altered how tourists search for information, plan itineraries, and share experiences. This chapter provides a comprehensive overview of these changes, examining the impact of social media, online booking platforms, and mobile applications on tourist behavior. Through case studies and recent developments, the chapter highlights how destinations and businesses can adapt to meet the evolving demands of digital-age travelers, offering insights into the intersection of tourist behavior and digital technology.

## Chapter 7

As digital technology continues to advance, a new type of traveler has emerged—the digital traveler. This chapter explores the characteristics and behaviors of this tech-savvy demographic, emphasizing their demand for personalized, seamless, and instant experiences. By leveraging big data analytics, AI, and social media platforms, the chapter identifies effective marketing strategies tailored to the digital traveler. It also discusses the role of mobile technology, virtual reality, and user-generated content in shaping travel decisions, offering valuable insights for marketers in the digital tourism landscape.

## Chapter 8

E-commerce has emerged as a critical driver of new business opportunities within the global travel and tourism sector. This chapter presents a historical analysis of e-commerce's impact, focusing on consistent customer experiences across various channels and travel sectors. It explores the challenges posed by emerging technologies like mobile devices and GPS, advocating for a systematic assessment of their effects. The chapter concludes by emphasizing the need for the industry to proactively adapt to the evolving digital landscape to maintain competitiveness and deliver value-added services to consumers.

## Chapter 9

The rise of ICTs and Web 3.0 has revolutionized the tourism industry by enabling digital co-creation of travel experiences. This chapter explores how these technologies facilitate active tourist participation, particularly in the Malaysian tourism sector. Using the Service-Dominant logic framework, the chapter highlights the shift from traditional goods-dominant logic to a service-oriented approach, fostering a more interactive and collaborative environment. It also addresses challenges in data management and organizational culture, offering insights into the opportunities for innovative and sustainable tourism development.

## Chapter 10

In the digital age, the tourism industry is transitioning from traditional marketing techniques to data-driven strategies that leverage vast amounts of digital information. This chapter delves into how travelers' digital footprints—such as search histories, social media interactions, and online bookings—can be harnessed to create personalized marketing campaigns. Emphasizing the importance of advanced technologies like AI and big data analytics, the chapter outlines the process of converting raw data into actionable insights, empowering businesses to engage with customers in more meaningful ways.

## Chapter 11

Digital technology holds the potential to revolutionize visitor experiences at cultural heritage sites. This chapter examines how technologies like augmented reality, virtual reality, and mobile applications can create immersive and interactive experiences that deepen visitors' understanding. By integrating multimedia and digital storytelling, the chapter explores how these technologies can enhance the accessibility and impact of heritage narratives, while also addressing challenges related to digital divides, authenticity, and implementation. The chapter provides a comprehensive analysis of recent case studies, illustrating the potential of digital innovations to promote cultural heritage and support sustainable tourism practices.

## Chapter 12

This chapter provides a comprehensive analysis of influencer marketing in the tourism industry, drawing on research findings from the past decade. By systematically reviewing 82 studies conducted between 2012 and 2023, the chapter highlights the exponential growth of influencer marketing research, particularly since 2020. The findings suggest that influencer-generated content positively impacts tourist behavior and purchasing decisions. The chapter underscores the strategic value of collaboration with influencers for tourism businesses and provides recommendations for effective influencer marketing practices.

## Chapter 13

Social media has become a powerful tool in shaping tourist decision-making processes. This chapter explores how platforms like Instagram, Facebook, and Tik-Tok influence travel preferences and destination choices through the AIDA model. By collecting feedback from 100 participants, the chapter demonstrates how social media engagement drives attention, interest, desire, and action among tourists. The chapter also examines the application of machine learning to analyze large datasets from social media, offering insights into predicting tourist demand and behavior.

Editors

**Norhidayah Azman**
*Management and Science University, Malaysia*

**Marco Valeri**
*Niccolò Cusano University, Italy*

**Ahmad Albattat**

*Management and Science University, Malaysia*

**Amrik Singh**

*Lovely Professional University, India*

# Chapter 1
# Analysis of Technological Advancements and Their Impact on Tourist Decision-Making

**Ridhima Sharma**

*Vivekananda Institute of Professional Studies-TC, India*

## ABSTRACT

*The study's overarching goal is to show how technological development significantly affects the decision-making process of tourists. In order to better understand how cognitive technologies, namely AI applications, factor into humans' decision-making processes, this study reviews relevant literature and stresses the need for new theoretical frameworks. The theoretical frameworks and approaches used were examined, and a future view impacted by substantial technological advancement was provided, through a thorough analysis and integration of diverse literature. As digital technology and cyber-physical systems become intrinsic parts of a tourist's identity, technological development considerably impacts the decision-making processes of visitors. Considering the future of cyber-physical-human systems, the article lays the groundwork for a new theoretical framework in the area of tourist decision-making. As new forms of AI improve human intelligence, this paper shows how tourism decision-making theory works and why a paradigm shift is necessary.*

DOI: 10.4018/979-8-3693-3972-5.ch001

# INTRODUCTION

Research has shown that tourists' approaches to planning and executing vacations have been significantly impacted by the rise of information technology (Hamid et al., 2021). Many societal and cultural shifts occur as a result of interactions between users and AI and digital applications. A number of studies have shown that recommender systems, social media, mobile apps, and artificial intelligence agents all have a role in how people decide to plan their trips (Jain et al., 2021). Rather than the more modern categories of techno human tourists, theoretical frameworks have traditionally been developed using data from pre-Millennials. According to (Pizzi et al., 2021), digital technology has a major impact on modern consumer behaviors. When it comes to the distinct functions played by humans and artificial agents in the formation of the tourist decision-making process, neither the data science emphasis nor the socio-psychological approach have been investigated in tandem (Qahtan et al., 2023). The one model that deviates from this rule is the new general model of tourist decision making (NGMTDM) (Novera et al., 2022). It ignores the fact that visitors and AI apps might benefit each other in their interactions. This study aims to provide a future view by demonstrating the importance of technological advancement in affecting visitors' decision-making process. It makes it easier to create a complex decision-making framework, which is important since tourists have a lot of access to the knowledge of digital tourism ecosystems (Ruiz et al., 2022) and because human-AI convergence is coming soon (Cepeda et al., 2022).

There have been a number of technological advances in the last several decades. According to Pizzi8 et al. (2019), the tourism sector is being greatly affected by new technologies like virtual assistants, drones, and augmented reality apps (e.g., avatars). These technologies are also influencing location-based digital services. Models derived from consumer research have become the most popular in the literature on visitor choice. Prior to the 2000s, when most digital technologies were either nonexistent or in their experimental stages, these technologies were developed (Novera et al., 2022). The choice-set technique, the theory of planned behavior, and the expected utility theory are the most popular theoretical frameworks utilized in tourism research. Despite their rational foundations, these ideas often fail to account for the far-reaching consequences of technological upheavals. To account for the complex digital information environments that visitors engage with, Cepeda et al. (2022) proposed a dual-system model that takes into account both the analytical and intuitive systems. When it comes to decision-making, however, NGMTDM's binary assumptions don't take into account the immediate and interactive role of human intelligence (Suraña et al., 2024). This is especially true when it integrates with advanced forms of AI (like bots and recommender systems) (Ismail & Yusof, 2023). In order to understand how technologically advanced generations behave as a result of revolutionary technological developments, a new theoretical framework for tourist decision-making is required (Sigala, 2018). This framework should incorporate various decision-making agents, such as autonomous devices or extensions to humans.

## LITERATURE REVIEW

Technological developments, especially the rise of the Internet, have had a profound impact on how the tourism industry uses marketing strategies (Mehra 2023). Firstly, interactive media have largely replaced mass media, and database marketing has allowed businesses to more precisely target consumers who are actually interested in their products. Second, customer connections are more important than market share as a measure of a marketing strategy's success. Finally, technical expertise is more important than creativity, but customer service is now more important than sales. There have been major structural shifts in the tourist sector as a result of the recent innovations in information technology that have revolutionized company operations throughout the world. Not only have sales and distribution seen significant changes, but so have other parts of the tourist industry, such as product and service purchase, booking, and information search (Pahrudin et al., 2023).

The worldwide hospitality and tourist sectors are looking to the members of Generation Z as a potential source of future clients and tourists. Particularly in regard to the organization and planning of vacations and other forms of travel, this emerging generation varies greatly from earlier ones. The writers state that one should begin by gaining a better understanding of how they make decisions. An essential modification to the novel social decision-making regarding travel model is the incorporation of a component called the Social Evaluation of Experience. What this means is that social assessment is an ongoing and interdependent activity that occurs all through development. According to the authors, this is because, growing up in the digital age, members of Generation Z's cognitive stages are more interdependent and connected than in previous generations. No matter how much praise you receive, the authors maintain that inspiration is a necessary ingredient for success (Gulati, 2024). Consequently, it should be the first stage of the paradigm. Generation Z needs something to pique their attention to the point where they want to do something about it. During this phase of inspiration, you will have hedonistic, passionate, rapid, and spontaneous experiences. Traveling with Generation Z shouldn't be boring, but rather inspiring (Elshaer & Marzouk, 2024). People are motivated when they encounter something novel, unconventional, and different from what they're used to. Something that speaks to them on a personal level and is directly relevant to their objectives, yet in a new and different way than what they have experienced before (Zheng et al., 2024).

In the second stage, an inspiration is used to create a need. This stage's need, concern, or want is a direct outcome of the stimulus (or stimuli) experienced in the stage before. Need awareness is directly proportional to the intensity of social or economic pressures. For instance, compared to watching an unrelated commercial video, Gen Zers are more like to desire to visit a vacation spot if they see a film featuring their favorite authority figure, wordpress, or dear friend there (Gani et al., 2024). Gen Zers now understand the need for social recognition, specifically by sharing their own films and photographs on social media in the hopes of likes and shares, in addition to the want to travel. For travelers of Generation Z, it is proposed merging the two steps of information search and decision assessment into one. The innovative integrated phase is the new decision-making process's bedrock; its success is reliant on the travel app's attractiveness, usefulness, and technology (Buhalis et al., 2024). Generation Z is able to plan, contrast, and search for all accessible information simultaneously because to the convergence of technological advances, social networks, applications for mobile devices, web pages, and multi-device use habits. Every day, in addition to reviewing a plethora of service providers, researching possible vacation experiences is now intricately linked to thorough trip planning. As an example, TripPlanner is an app that can automatically scan trip confirmation emails and create a daily schedule for users, supported by push alerts and reminders. Users of Kayak and similar online booking platforms may compare airline tickets for the same locations from many suppliers, as well as choose the ideal days or times to buy them. Booking, the fourth step, is undeniably important for service providers. Here is where millennials and Gen Zers actively negotiate and finalize vacation payment details. After careful and thorough training, members of Generation Z are anticipated to have a more knowledgeable viewpoint at this stage. Consequently, they shouldn't feel as much cognitive dissonance (remorse about their decision) or risk as other generations did (Christensen et al, 2024). At this point, we anticipate a great deal of reasoning and impartiality. People no longer depend on the loyalty of brands to schedule their travels; instead, they choose the alternative that appears most reasonable after giving it some thought. The post-booking stage is expected to be longer and more involved for travelers from Generation Z. According to Paliwal et al., 2024, clients need to take into account two distinct yet interconnected realities: the procedure for booking and the actual trip experience. According to Kim et al., 2024, the post-booking stage is anticipated to significantly impact future travel decisions, service provider choices, and recommendations from peers. Gen Zers engage in a continual process called social appraisal of their experiences, in addition to the five processes listed above, according to the authors. In contrast to earlier models that included post-purchase evaluation as the final step, the authors suggest a more comprehensive real-time review that takes into account factors including application accessibility, agent friendliness, and pricing. Several mediums, such as mobile devices, the web, social media, and traditional telephones, are utilized to conduct this evaluation. This one-of-a-kind assessment is likely to be ever-changing. The content and rating might also see rapid changes from good to bad. The evaluation procedure could be affected by the incorporation of new data and the participation of third parties. Plus, there's a good chance that we can speed up the review process considerably in the near future.

Nowadays, it's not enough to just use the correct channel for marketing; marketers also need to provide details about the platform or vehicle (like Facebook vs. Instagram) and the device. The term "Digital Elite" was first used by Yesawich (2016) to describe frequent flyers who make extensive use of all three major types of digital technology: laptops, smartphones, and tablets. According to him, 80% of these individuals are busy on Facebook, 30% on Twitter, and 20% on Google+, Pinterest, YouTube, and Google+. Plus, he saw that compared to less connected people, these folks are more open to sharing their vacation stories in real time.

The travel and tourism industry faces a challenging but potentially lucrative task in appealing to Generation Z when they are still in the early stages of making decisions. This highlights the significance of marketing product innovation and consumer insight as the main forces propelling travel marketing strategies (Ivanov & Webster, 2024). A more defined target market has to be identified by smaller travel start-ups. Therefore, they need to be experts in creating, advertising, and marketing it if they want to beat out the competition and reach the right demographic of Gen Zers. Unconventional "travel product marketing strategies" need the establishment of dedicated departments within the travel and tourist industry. Marketing strategies for travel products should be developed, tested, and implemented on an ongoing basis by these business units with a focus on Gen Z customers. A company's marketing, operations, and technology departments should all be staffed by experts. Some examples of what these units may provide include a real-time stream from many vacation spots, a charity campaign, an online game, or a local event showcasing a particular activity at a designated location. Such advertising strategies for products could work better than the more conventional internet ads aimed to Generation Z. Popular, user-generated content with genuine, first-hand accounts of places that locals have visited is a major draw for this expanding group of tourists. Ads and other types of authentic rich media should tailor their strategies to the specific interests, hobbies, communities, and travel preferences of each individual customer. It is important to stay up-to-date with current trends and customize targeted social media advertisements to this generation's unique online behavior and psychographics. Commercials must feature and emphasize genuine home video, self-portraits, commercials using actual tourists, and videos shot by amateurs (Any et al., 2024).

Gen Zers place a premium on action and excitement, therefore it's crucial for web content and video ads to feature unique activities connected to the vacation spot and effectively communicate these attributes (Kannan, 2024).

Members of Generation Z often research and plan their trips using state-of-the-art mobile applications and websites; when they're ready to book, they reach out to well-known booking platforms like Expedia for the best deal. Startups in the travel industry would do well to carefully consider the demands of today's vacationers while designing, constructing, and offering customized packages (Zheng et al., 2024). The large agencies and brands will have a tough time competing with these bundles if they aren't reasonably priced and give great value. In addition, it is essential that these service providers present a transparent rationale for the set trip package prices, maybe by providing a comprehensive pricing breakdown, so that visitors can comprehend the advantages and worth of their investment. Moreover, members of Generation Z would be more than happy to tailor their vacation to their interests and budget by picking and choosing which activities to participate in. So, it's highly recommended that marketers in the travel and tourist industry pay close attention to these issues; doing so will boost their financial earnings and bring in precious, loyal customers.

## METHODOLOGY

This study was based on a thorough literature evaluation of articles published in peer-reviewed journals that dealt with topics such as social media and tourist destination planning, as well as reports of social media usage. In order to better understand how social media factors into vacation spot selection, a thorough literature review was conducted. Science Direct, Google Scholar, Emerald Insights Journals, Institutional Repository, Scopus, JSTOR, Taylor & Francis, Sage Publications, Sabinet, and ProQuest publications were among the sources referenced. Also cited were pieces from travel agencies that dealt with social media in particular. An exhaustive review of these sources was part of this data collection strategy to unearth details on social media and the decision-making process in relation to travel. Therefore, the study achieved its objectives by drawing on a thorough understanding of the literature.

# FINDINGS

## Web 2.0, Web 3.0 and Tourism 2.0

Along with new ways to search for any desired information, the proliferation of the Internet has provided users with a profusion of tools (Buhalis, 2019). Common terms for these resources include Web 2.0 apps and digital technologies. In 2004, this term was first used to describe a new way for software developers and end users to interact with the Internet. It was characterized by increased transparency, active user interaction, and the influence of network effects. (Akincilar & Dagdeviren, 2014). At that point, the idea began to circulate that the World Wide Web was more of a shared infrastructure where people could edit and maintain content rather than just create it (Li et al., 2023). When it first came online, the Internet was known as Web 1.0, and it only allowed one kind of communication—a read-only format (Bushara et al., 2023). The first wave of the World Wide Web consisted of static, long-running websites that provided static information about items and services and served only as an information display for customers. However, a new concept called Web 3.0 has arisen in the field of software development in the past several years. One problem with the strict definition of Web1.0, Web2.0, and Web 3.0 is that they don't show how the Internet has actually evolved technologically (Ren & Zheng, 2024) and they don't imply an alternative to one Internet platform. A number of Internet applications and development stages coexist, according to research by Huang et al. (2023), which highlights the need of viewing the Internet as a coherent techno-social system. Web 2.0 is defined as a network for human communication, Web 3.0 as a network for collaboration, and Web 1.0 as a cognitive network, according to the same set of writers (Dai et al., 2023). What distinguishes Web 2.0 and Web 3.0 from Web 1.0 is the fact that all users are actively involved and work together to create, utilize, and share information. The demand for and supply of tourism are greatly affected by the consumption and diffusion of Web 2.0 and Web 3.0 technologies, which is not surprising given the importance of information in the tourist business (Bozkurt, 2023). A new way of thinking about travel has evolved out of the changes made to travel-related websites in the Web 2.0 and 3.0 eras. User engagement and teamwork are encouraged and made easier by these generations (Pop et al., 2022). "The Link Between Digital Media and Making Travel Choices" is based on the idea that people can express themselves freely online about their feelings and experiences while traveling and then share this with other people (Deb et al., 2024). According to Mandić et al., 2023, travelers may have access to more personalized and relevant information by using new apps and internet platforms that are part of the Travel 2.0 movement. As a result, they can easily find the hotel or other location they are going (Šošić et al., 2024). Additionally, consumers can bypass

7

intermediaries and acquire travel-related information straight from these websites (Kusumawati et al., 2024). According to Pop et al., 2022, user-generated content is becoming increasingly important while planning a trip. In contrast, according to El Archi et al., 2023, travelers' own research is the most important factor when choosing where to vacation.

The Internet has developed into a medium where users may share their experiences in order to improve their decision-making skills, as Mohammed et al., 2023 explains. The growth of user-generated material also has a major impact on how other users make decisions when they're online.

## Future Perspective

Predicting the possible growth of technological advancement in the next several decades is an arduous endeavor (Borges et al., 2021). Data sources, data mining methodologies, and relevant behavioral research are becoming more accessible as a result of developments in a number of technical areas coming together, such as digital technology's incorporation into cognitive science (Cavalinhos et al., 2021). The outcome is a shift of power from individual visitors to groups, with the help of expert systems in smart digital systems (Wu et al., 2023). According to Singh et al. (2021), cyberphysical ecosystems are anticipated to be brought about by new AI technologies like the Internet of Everything and machine-to-machine interactions. For the rest of this century, this trend is likely to continue and maybe even intensify. According to Wang et al. (2023), the next big thing in technology will be Web 4.0, which will change the way people and machines interact by creating a new cyber-physical environment and improving their integrated real-time capabilities. Compared to the earlier Web era, when robots were involved in various stages of decision-making, there are clear differences. This new cyber, physical, and social ecology is causing a sea change in how humans fit inside it. Future decision-makers' hypostasis within the cyber-physical environment is the subject of a critical research. This would fundamentally alter the design of decision-making frameworks and models. The decision-makers' innate qualities might be enhanced by the use of artificial intelligence (AI) or intelligence augmentation (IA) in many ways, depending on the objectives, conditions, and relevant settings (Kontopoulou et al., 2023). When it comes to tourism, there are two options that seem to be rather popular:

1.  Collaborative robots (cobots), software programs, or human avatars are examples of non-embodied agents that are autonomous and individualized. Based on their enhanced cognitive intelligence capabilities, these agents will proactively and autonomously help with understanding and applying Big Data (Stylo et al., 2024 ; Pande et al., 2024).

2.  Embodied agents are people who have undergone cyber enhancement and have exoskeletons and tiny implanted gadgets. According to Huang et al. (2018), these implants can enhance one's cognitive, emotional, and sensory capacities. According to Kontopoulou et al. (2023) and Kadam & Sen, 2023, these two options will work together to make decisions in a way that is unified, parallel, and inclusive of everyone. We need to look into the major implications of both options.

## CONCLUSION

As a generation, tourists of the future will be markedly different from the present in that they will be more self-reliant, better at managing their time, and more tech-savvy. In one possible future, vacationers may delegate some of the planning tasks to their virtual selves, freeing them up to focus on more enjoyable aspects of their trip. One example is the incorporation of digital behaviors exhibited by human avatars into the provision of housing and recreational activities. These behaviors can include stated emotions, facial expressions, prior preferences, and online suggestion. In the second scenario, vacationers with cybernetic enhancements would be able to make decisions in real-time, including changing their plans or focusing on creative pursuits. Visitors can activate either scenario or both of them depending on the situation and their extended self's needs. One potential use of personal avatars is to take proactive measures when deciding which tourist spots to visit. Those working in tourism marketing would do well to educate themselves on how tourists behave when online so that they can craft social media marketing strategies with confidence. A thorough review of the relevant literature was carried out as part of the investigation. To further understand if and how travelers use social media to investigate tourist destinations and related activities, future studies should focus on collecting data from the supply side.

# REFERENCES

Akincilar, A., & Dagdeviren, M. (2014). A hybrid multi-criteria decision making model to evaluate hotel websites. *International Journal of Hospitality Management*, 36, 263–271. DOI: 10.1016/j.ijhm.2013.10.002

Any, B., Four, S., & Tariazela, C. (2024). Technology integration in tourism management: Enhancing the visitor experience. [SABDA Journal]. *Startupreneur Business Digital*, 3(1), 81–88. DOI: 10.33050/sabda.v3i1.508

Borges, A. F., Laurindo, F. J., Spínola, M. M., Gonçalves, R. F., & Mattos, C. A. (2021). The strategic use of artificial intelligence in the digital era: Systematic literature review and future research directions. *International Journal of Information Management*, 57, 102225. DOI: 10.1016/j.ijinfomgt.2020.102225

Bozkurt, A. (2023). Using social media in open, distance, and digital education. In *Handbook of open, distance and digital education* (pp. 1237–1254). Springer Nature Singapore. DOI: 10.1007/978-981-19-2080-6_73

Buhalis, D. (2019). Technology in tourism-from information communication technologies to eTourism and smart tourism towards ambient intelligence tourism: A perspective article. *Tourism Review*, 75(1), 267–272. DOI: 10.1108/TR-06-2019-0258

Buhalis, D., Efthymiou, L., Uzunboylu, N., & Thrassou, A. (2024). Charting the progress of technology adoption in tourism and hospitality in the era of industry 4.0. *EuroMed Journal of Business*, 19(1), 1–20. DOI: 10.1108/EMJB-11-2023-0310

Bushara, M. A., Abdou, A. H., Hassan, T. H., Sobaih, A. E. E., Albohnayh, A. S. M., Alshammari, W. G., Aldoreeb, M., Elsaed, A. A., & Elsaied, M. A. (2023). Power of social media marketing: How perceived value mediates the impact on restaurant followers' purchase intention, willingness to pay a premium price, and e-WoM? *Sustainability (Basel)*, 15(6), 5331. DOI: 10.3390/su15065331

Cavalinhos, S., Marques, S. H., & de Fátima Salgueiro, M. (2021). The use of mobile devices in-store and the effect on shopping experience: A systematic literature review and research agenda. *International Journal of Consumer Studies*, 45(6), 1198–1216. DOI: 10.1111/ijcs.12690

Cepeda-Pacheco, J. C., & Domingo, M. C. (2022). Deep learning and Internet of Things for tourist attraction recommendations in smart cities. *Neural Computing & Applications*, 34(10), 7691–7709. DOI: 10.1007/s00521-021-06872-0

Christensen, J., Hansen, J. M., & Wilson, P. (2024). Understanding the role and impact of Generative Artificial Intelligence (AI) hallucination within consumers' tourism decision-making processes. *Current Issues in Tourism*, 1–16. DOI: 10.1080/13683500.2023.2300032

Dai, Y., Cheng, X., & Liu, Y. (2023). Information alienation and circle fracture: Policy communication and opinion-generating networks on social media in China from the perspective of COVID-19 policy. *Systems*, 11(7), 340. DOI: 10.3390/systems11070340

Deb, S. K., Nafi, S. M., & Valeri, M. (2024). Promoting tourism business through digital marketing in the new normal era: A sustainable approach. *European Journal of Innovation Management*, 27(3), 775–799. DOI: 10.1108/EJIM-04-2022-0218

El Archi, Y., Benbba, B., Zhu, K., El Andaloussi, Z., Pataki, L., & Dávid, L. D. (2023). Mapping the nexus between sustainability and digitalization in tourist destinations: A bibliometric analysis. *Sustainability (Basel)*, 15(12), 9717. DOI: 10.3390/su15129717

Elshaer, A. M., & Marzouk, A. M. (2024). Memorable tourist experiences: The role of smart tourism technologies and hotel innovations. *Tourism Recreation Research*, 49(3), 445–457. DOI: 10.1080/02508281.2022.2027203

Gani, M. O., Roy, H., Faroque, A. R., Rahman, M. S., & Munawara, M. (2024). Smart tourism technologies for the psychological well-being of tourists: A Bangladesh perspective. *Journal of Hospitality and Tourism Insights*, 7(3), 1371–1390. DOI: 10.1108/JHTI-06-2022-0239

Gulati, S. (2024). Exploring the generational influence on social media-based tourist decision-making in India. *Information Discovery and Delivery*, 52(2), 185–196. DOI: 10.1108/IDD-11-2022-0115

Hamid, R. A., Albahri, A. S., Alwan, J. K., Al-Qaysi, Z. T., Albahri, O. S., Zaidan, A. A., Alnoor, A., Alamoodi, A. H., & Zaidan, B. B. (2021). How smart is e-tourism? A systematic review of smart tourism recommendation system applying data management. *Computer Science Review*, 39, 100337. DOI: 10.1016/j.cosrev.2020.100337

Huang, W., Bolton, T. A., Medaglia, J. D., Bassett, D. S., Ribeiro, A., & Van De Ville, D. (2018). A graph signal processing perspective on functional brain imaging. *Proceedings of the IEEE*, 106(5), 868–885. DOI: 10.1109/JPROC.2018.2798928

Huang, X. T., Wang, J., Wang, Z., Wang, L., & Cheng, C. (2023). Experimental study on the influence of virtual tourism spatial situation on the tourists' temperature comfort in the context of metaverse. *Frontiers in Psychology*, 13, 1062876. DOI: 10.3389/fpsyg.2022.1062876 PMID: 36687952

Ismail, N., & Yusof, U. K. (2023). A systematic literature review: Recent techniques of predicting STEM stream students. *Computers and Education: Artificial Intelligence*, 5, 100141. DOI: 10.1016/j.caeai.2023.100141

Ivanov, S., & Webster, C. (2024). Automated decision-making: Hoteliers' perceptions. *Technology in Society*, 76, 102430. DOI: 10.1016/j.techsoc.2023.102430

Jain, P. K., Pamula, R., & Srivastava, G. (2021). A systematic literature review on machine learning applications for consumer sentiment analysis using online reviews. *Computer Science Review*, 41, 100413. DOI: 10.1016/j.cosrev.2021.100413

Kadam, S., & Sen, S. (2023, February). Role of E-Business Enabled Smartphones in Creating Smart Travelers. In *2023 International Conference on Computer Science, Information Technology and Engineering (ICCoSITE)* (pp. 933-938). IEEE. DOI: 10.1109/ICCoSITE57641.2023.10127688

Kannan, R. (2024). Revolutionizing the Tourism Industry through Artificial Intelligence: A Comprehensive Review of AI Integration, Impact on Customer Experience, Operational Efficiency, and Future Trends. *International Journal for Multidimensional Research Perspectives, 2*(2), 01-14.

Kim, J. H., Kim, J., Kim, S., & Hailu, T. B. (2024). Effects of AI ChatGPT on travelers' travel decision-making. *Tourism Review*, 79(5), 1038–1057. DOI: 10.1108/TR-07-2023-0489

Kontopoulou, V. I., Panagopoulos, A. D., Kakkos, I., & Matsopoulos, G. K. (2023). A review of ARIMA vs. machine learning approaches for time series forecasting in data driven networks. *Future Internet*, 15(8), 255. DOI: 10.3390/fi15080255

Kusumawati, Y. A., Lasmy, L., Gasa, F. M., & Renanda, D. G. (2024). Community Development of Tourism Interest Group Malang Regency as an Effort to Optimize Tourism. [SEEIJ]. *Social Economics and Ecology International Journal*, 8(1), 74–81. DOI: 10.21512/seeij.v8i1.11490

Li, F., Larimo, J., & Leonidou, L. C. (2023). Social media in marketing research: Theoretical bases, methodological aspects, and thematic focus. *Psychology and Marketing*, 40(1), 124–145. DOI: 10.1002/mar.21746

Mandić, A., Pavlić, I., Puh, B., & Séraphin, H. (2023). Children and overtourism: A cognitive neuroscience experiment to reflect on exposure and behavioural consequences. *Journal of Sustainable Tourism*, 1–28. DOI: 10.1080/09669582.2023.2278023

Mehra, P. (2023). Unexpected surprise: Emotion analysis and aspect based sentiment analysis (ABSA) of user generated comments to study behavioral intentions of tourists. *Tourism Management Perspectives*, 45, 101063. DOI: 10.1016/j.tmp.2022.101063

Mohammed, R. T., Alamoodi, A. H., Albahri, O. S., Zaidan, A. A., AlSattar, H. A., Aickelin, U., Albahri, A. S., Zaidan, B. B., Ismail, A. R., & Malik, R. Q. (2023). A decision modeling approach for smart e-tourism data management applications based on spherical fuzzy rough environment. *Applied Soft Computing*, 143, 110297. DOI: 10.1016/j.asoc.2023.110297

Novera, C. N., Ahmed, Z., Kushol, R., Wanke, P., & Azad, M. A. K. (2022). Internet of Things (IoT) in smart tourism: A literature review. *Spanish Journal of Marketing-ESIC*, 26(3), 325–344. DOI: 10.1108/SJME-03-2022-0035

Pahrudin, P., Hsieh, T. H., Liu, L. W., & Wang, C. C. (2023). The role of information sources on tourist behavior post-earthquake disaster in Indonesia: A Stimulus–Organism–Response (SOR) approach. *Sustainability (Basel)*, 15(11), 8446. DOI: 10.3390/su15118446

Paliwal, M., Chatradhi, N., Singh, A., & Dikkatwar, R. (2024). Smart tourism: Antecedents to Indian traveller's decision. *European Journal of Innovation Management*, 27(5), 1521–1546. DOI: 10.1108/EJIM-06-2022-0293

Pande, L., & Sengupta, S. (2024, April). Digital Commerce and Big Data revolutionizing the tourism industry: A review article. In *2024 IEEE 9th International Conference for Convergence in Technology (I2CT)* (pp. 1-5). IEEE. DOI: 10.1109/I2CT61223.2024.10544348

Pizzi, G., Scarpi, D., & Pantano, E. (2021). Artificial intelligence and the new forms of interaction: Who has the control when interacting with a chatbot? *Journal of Business Research*, 129, 878–890. DOI: 10.1016/j.jbusres.2020.11.006

Pop, R. A., Săplăcan, Z., Dabija, D. C., & Alt, M. A. (2022). The impact of social media influencers on travel decisions: The role of trust in consumer decision journey. *Current Issues in Tourism*, 25(5), 823–843. DOI: 10.1080/13683500.2021.1895729

Qahtan, S., Yatim, K., Zulzalil, H., Osman, M. H., Zaidan, A. A., & Alsattar, H. A. (2023). Review of healthcare industry 4.0 application-based blockchain in terms of security and privacy development attributes: Comprehensive taxonomy, open issues and challenges and recommended solution. *Journal of Network and Computer Applications*, 209, 103529. DOI: 10.1016/j.jnca.2022.103529

Ren, M., & Zheng, P. (2024). Towards smart product-service systems 2.0: A retrospect and prospect. *Advanced Engineering Informatics*, 61, 102466. DOI: 10.1016/j.aei.2024.102466

Ruiz-Meza, J., & Montoya-Torres, J. R. (2022). A systematic literature review for the tourist trip design problem: Extensions, solution techniques and future research lines. *Operations Research Perspectives*, 9, 100228. DOI: 10.1016/j.orp.2022.100228

Singh, R., Ismail, A., Ps, S., & Singh, D. (2021). Compliance of accessibility in tourism websites: A pledge towards disability. *Journal of Hospitality and Tourism Insights*, 4(3), 263–281. DOI: 10.1108/JHTI-05-2020-0092

Šošić, M. M., Pavlić, I., & Puh, B. (2024, May). Understanding Users' Intention to Use Mobile Apps in Tourism Industry. In *2024 47th MIPRO ICT and Electronics Convention (MIPRO)* (pp. 1053-1058). IEEE.

Stylos, N., Jiang, Y., & Pergelova, A. (2024). Guest editorial: Marketing via smart technologies in hospitality and tourism. *Journal of Hospitality and Tourism Insights*, 7(3), 1285–1293. DOI: 10.1108/JHTI-07-2024-969

Suraña-Sánchez, C., & Aramendia-Muneta, M. E. (2024). Impact of artificial intelligence on customer engagement and advertising engagement: A review and future research agenda. *International Journal of Consumer Studies*, 48(2), e13027. DOI: 10.1111/ijcs.13027

Wang, B., Dane, G., & Arentze, T. (2023). A structural equation model to analyze the use of a new multi media platform for increasing awareness of cultural heritage. *Frontiers of Architectural Research*, 12(3), 509–522. DOI: 10.1016/j.foar.2023.02.001

Wu, E., & Liao, B. Y. (2023). Realization of Vitality Optimization in Traditional Village Human Settlement Environment Supported by Intelligent Sensor Technology. *International Journal of Communication Networks and Information Security*, 15(4), 78–89. DOI: 10.17762/ijcnis.v15i4.6288

Yesawich, P. (2016). The American Traveler: Emerging Lifestyles and Travel Trends.

Zheng, K., Kumar, J., Kunasekaran, P., & Valeri, M. (2024). Role of smart technology use behaviour in enhancing tourist revisit intention: The theory of planned behaviour perspective. *European Journal of Innovation Management*, 27(3), 872–893. DOI: 10.1108/EJIM-03-2022-0122

# Chapter 2
# Click, Search, Travel:
## Understanding Tourist Behaviour in the Digital Age

**Karan Berry**
https://orcid.org/0000-0002-8641-5228
*Symbiosis International University (Deemed), India*

**Ankit Shukla**
https://orcid.org/0000-0002-7646-3517
*Rajamangala University of Technology, Thanyaburi, Thailand*

**Amrik Singh**
https://orcid.org/0000-0003-3598-8787
*Lovely Professional University, India*

**Pratik Satpute**
https://orcid.org/0000-0002-1730-8090
*MIT World Peace University, India*

## ABSTRACT

*The advent of digital technology has dramatically changed the way people travel, affecting their information searches, itineraries, decisions and experiences shared on social media sites like Twitter, Instagram and Facebook, to assist prospective travellers. Besides highlighting the impact of digital technologies such as social media, online booking platforms, mobile applications and augmented virtual reality, this chapter also examines various aspects of tourist behaviour in the digital age through recent developments, and relevant case studies. It also provides insights into how tourist destinations and businesses can adjust themselves to meet the shifting demands and patterns of travel. This meticulous overview interconnects "tourist behaviour" and the "digital era" to reveal how the development of mobile and*

DOI: 10.4018/979-8-3693-3972-5.ch002

*internet-based technology has changed the travel and tourism sector.*

## INTRODUCTION

New technologies introduce new opportunities and threats to the tourism business, precisely in how people plan, book, and interact with such services. The trend of digitalization has come out as the enabling factor for increasing the competitive edge of the tourism businesses at a global scale because it reduces operational processes and improves engagements with clients through proper targeting and analytics (Rhena et al., 2024). On the other hand, the emergence of mobile devices and virtual technologies has changed the way tourists organize their trips by offering them customized and pre-travel experience matching the needs of today's customers (Prajapat & R, 2024). Furthermore, the coupling of technology with booking engine and AI has simplified the entire travel process whereby appropriate recommendations are offered with less human input. As the sector adapts to these changes, it faces an even more dynamic landscape as customer's preferences change, accelerating the need for continuous change and the application of strategies cantered on digitalization of the travel industry (Kumar & Sharma, 2024). Overall, the digital transformation has not only improved operational efficiency but also improved the travel experience itself. The introduction of digital technologies has also changed the techniques of making travel arrangements, making people more satisfied as well as improving the work of those concerned with the operations. The addition of online booking facilities has made it easy for clients to plan their trips and book resorts in a simpler client-friendly way than before (Atasheva et al. 2024). More recently, technological advancements including artificial intelligence (AI), the Internet of Things (IoT) and mobile apps have simplified the whole process of arranging for travel by providing tailored services and swift action to customers. In addition, it has also improved the travel fun since the user can now see a virtual reality of examples of the various destinations and types of rooms available (Tandafatu et al. 2024). Therein, it should be reminded that there are still some issues to be tackled, such as better policies along with the inclusion of such technologies into the existing tourism frameworks. This implies that the advent of technology has not only simplified booking processes but has in fact changed and shaped the various factors of purchase intention of the customers, in turn enhancing the competitiveness and innovations in the tourism sector. Knowing the relationship of OTSA, TR, OPI, faith and e-loyalty in which tourism exists digitally is important for the success in the industry. Studies show that, OTSA is found to be influential in increasing OPI, which is unsurprisingly fuelled primarily by stickiness and interactivity (Shariffuddin et al., 2023). It is different case with regards to OPI that is more slowly achieved due to the impact of TR, which is more felt in its construct of innovation. Furthermore, when OPI is at a peak, trust appeared to have an adverse effect on e-loyalty, showing that in order to increase loyalty, trust must be properly managed. Trust emerges as an important moderating component. Digital tourism's growth story, in detail, signifies changes in technology incorporating the latest features such as Virtual Reality (VR), Augmented Reality (AR), and Artificial Intelligence (AI), attributes which are really changing traveller's experience and even the business models present in the industry. The development process has resulted in predicting an increase in travel-related digital revenues that are forecasted to reach fun away close to USD 613 billion along with more than 5 million new job opportunities most likely within the next 10 years (Sivarethinamohan, 2023). The tools integration contributed to the disruption of people's travel patterns, improved the authoring of the information, and turned the social media towards place marketing. Yet, the studies have found that there is a lack of attention to maintaining true qualities of tourism experiences in the digital age which calls for more studies in this area (Gunawan et al., 2024). Potential developments include continued innovations of the digital environment, the relevance of blockchain to secure payments, and the need for a variety of stakeholders to work together if the tourism industry is to evolve sustainably. To sum up, the digital transformation introduces both concerns and opportunities for the industry and so, such implications require further examination and adapted. Many facets of daily life have undergone radical change with the arrival of the digital age, including how people view travel and tourism. Since the introduction of digital technologies, visitor behaviour has changed dramatically, standing in stark contrast to traditional settings. In the past, travellers tended to consume information more passively because they relied largely on travel professionals and printed publications. On the other hand, the emergence of digital platforms has given travellers the ability to independently organize their travels, instantly share their experiences, and impact others through social media user-generated content (Barbosa & Medaglia, 2019). Studies reveal the significant influence that internet advertising and social media have on tourists' behavioural intentions, especially when it comes to choosing their destinations (Armutcu et al., 2023). One way to analyse changes in behaviour over time in tourism is to look at how visitors engage with digital environments through the idea of a "digital pattern of life" (Mikhailov et al., 2020). Travellers are now more demanding, knowledgeable, and involved as a result of this change. As a result of this change, travellers are now more demanding, knowledgeable, and involved in an environment of collaboration that fosters interaction and expression. Despite these developments, the literature emphasizes the need for more study, especially in contexts with varying cultural perspectives, to completely comprehend the effects of these technological advances on traveller behaviour.

## Evolution & Influence of Digital Technology

The tourism industry is affected by the development of digital technologies, enabling both operational efficiency and customer contact (Cöster2009). The COVID-19 pandemic has boosted massively the dispersion of travel services over digital platforms, and such a trend was already well established as destinations are evaluated by would be travellers based on their online footprint (El Mattichi et al., 2024). ICT revolutionized the sector; new technologies were used, such as electronic reservation systems and virtual tours which served both for customization and interactivity of users (Kuzman et al., 2024). In addition, digital tools contribute to the development of sustainable tourism and facilitate contact between travellers with an environmental vocation as demonstrated by the platform for ecological events like Ecobnb that supports trips designed in absolute respect (El Archi et al., 2023). Nonetheless, despite these advancements presenting numerous advantages, challenges persist in comprehending the specific requirements of diverse traveller demographics, such as halal tourism, where digital innovations can augment cultural engagement and accessibility (Azam et al., 2024). In summary, the incorporation of digital technologies is transforming tourism, propelling growth, and encouraging sustainability, albeit with persistent challenges in user adaptation and market segmentation (Deputat et al., 2024).

Technological advancements such as online booking platforms, virtual and augmented reality (VR & AR), the Internet of Things have made travel planning nearly frictionless while providing personalized itineraries with real-time notifications. Combination of these technologies in the process has developed processes resulted with sustainable travel practices by promoting green, eco-friendly alternatives (Farid et al., 2023). In addition, the digital era has transformed tourists' decision-making systems that have been supported by online information aggregators and social media, which play important roles in influencing destinations choices (Vila et al., 2045). However, they face challenges such as the need for stronger regulatory frameworks and a more seamless integration of technology with pre-existing tourism infrastructures (Tandafatu et al., 2024). The tourism-related digitalisation, overall, represents a shift to increased adaptability and organisation of tourist services, which in turn reflects the consumer–oriented behaviour due to changing expectations for them (Barbu et al., 2023). Tourism businesses use artificial intelligence (AI) and big data analytics to give customers tailored experiences, which serve as a foundation level for customer satisfaction and operational efficiencies. Web-based information systems have also changed how travellers can access, plan and book trips in a more convenient (not to mention flexible) manner. It also helps service providers to establish a better communication channel between tourists and themselves, catering with the rising expectations of today's travellers. However, obstacles remain, particularly in achieving coherence between tourism service providers and technology developers, which is crucial for optimizing the advantages of digital advancements. Ultimately, the ongoing digital transformation in tourism not only enhances the travel experience but also cultivates a competitive environment that necessitates continual adaptation and innovation.

Globalization and tech advances have an impact on today's tourist behaviour. They create a longing to customize and experience extraordinary travel. As tourism links more with global growth, travellers want unique offerings that break from the norm. This highlights how crucial personalization and tech are in the hospitality world (Majeed et al. 2020). The growth of information and communication tech has changed the scene. It backs new ideas like digital booking platforms and online tours. These boost productivities and make customers happier (Kuzman et al. 2024). What's more, millennials love tech and prefer places rich in culture. They seek one-of-a-kind experiences instead of typical vacations (Roy & Jasrotia 2024). In sum, the interaction between globalization and technology is redefining tourist expectations and behaviours, necessitating a strategic response from the tourism sector to accommodate the shifting demands of consumers (Gupta et al., 2022). Digital technologies like social media and online booking systems, have transformed the mechanisms by which tourists select destinations, highlighting the critical role of online information and peer influence in their decision-making processes (Vila et al., 2024). Additionally, these technological advancements empower tourists, particularly millennials, to actively participate in the co-creation of their experiences, resulting in an increased demand for innovative and personalized services (Golja & Paulišić, 2021). The integration of AI and other smart technologies is changing how decisions are made showing a shift to more complex interactions between tech systems and what people want (Stylos 2019). But while these advances boost competitiveness and sustainability in tourism, they also bring challenges. Businesses need to keep up with fast-changing customer expectations and avoid relying too much on tech (Golja & Paulišić, 2021). In general, how globalization and technology work together plays a big role in shaping how tourists behave today. At the same time, globalization links economies more closely affecting what consumers like and how tourist spots market themselves. This leads to unique tourism options that cater to different interests while balancing global trends and local culture preservation. Also, using new tech not improves service but makes tourist products more attractive helping them compete better worldwide. Yet, it's still tricky to make sure these improvements match up with sustainable practices, as today's travellers often prefer eco-friendly choices. As a result, the mix of globalization and technology is key to reshaping how tourists behave and what they expect in today's world.

## Search for Information and Decision-Making

User-generated content (UGC), reviews, and influencer marketing tactics have a big impact on travel choices shaping future travellers' thoughts and feelings. Studies show that people often prefer UGC, like travel blogs and vlogs, to standard marketing materials from destination marketing organizations (DMOs). They see UGC as more believable and relatable (Jog & Alcasoas, 2023). Gen Z trusts UGC more than content from social media influencers (SMIs) (Ghaly 2023). Influencer credibility is key; while they can sway hotel preferences, travellers check multiple sources before making up their minds (Guo, 2023). A thorough review highlights the importance of teamwork between SMIs and DMOs to boost engagement and trust. Good partnerships can use the strengths of both UGC and influencer marketing to help people make travel decisions (Saini et al. 2023). To sum up, combining UGC and influencer credibility is crucial to create effective travel marketing plans (Santos et al. 2024). The success of influencer marketing in the travel industry stems from its ability to create emotional ties with potential customers. Research shows that travel influencers who highlight travel-related emotions in their stories get more people involved, which suggests that emotional connection is key to their success (Son & Park, 2024). Also, the interesting and eye-catching content that influencers make on platforms like TikTok, has a big impact on younger people's desire to travel, which underlines the emotional effects of influencer marketing (Asri et al. 2024). What's more when influencer content matches what their audience values, it increases engagement and makes people want to travel more, which supports the idea that emotional connections are crucial for marketing strategies to work well (Rajput & Gandhi, 2024). But it's important to remember that influencers might lose credibility when they share personal information that doesn't relate to what they're experts in, which could weaken the emotional bond they're trying to build (Leite et al. 2023). To sum up putting all these findings together shows how vital emotional engagement is in influencer marketing for the travel industry. The shift from old-school info sources to social media in tourism marks a big change in how travellers get info and make choices. Social media has become a top tool for shaping tourist decisions changing how the industry markets itself. Travellers now rely on social media platforms for info, with many trusting user content like reviews and photos to guide their travel plans (Okonkwo et al. 2015). Social media marketing lets tourism businesses talk straight to potential customers, which boosts brand awareness and trust (Öz, 2015). These days, travellers play a key role in telling destination stories using social media to share experiences and sway their friends' choices (Hays 2013). Platforms like Instagram and TikTok, with their visual storytelling power, help destinations create appealing images and emotional ties with travellers. While social media opens up lots of chances, it also brings challenges like managing reputation and handling crises, which means tourism businesses need to be strategic (Andzani, 2024). In spite of the benefits afforded by social media, there exists an argument asserting that traditional sources retain value, especially for comprehensive information and expert insights, thereby suggesting a prospective coexistence of both information channels within the tourism domain (Andjelic et al., 2024). The transformation of tourism marketing and information sharing brought on by social media comes with worries about the trustworthiness of that information and the risk of spreading inaccuracies, possibly harming travellers' choices and experiences.

Online reviews and recommendations have a big effect on how people plan their trips. They shape how consumers act and make choices. Studies show that how trustworthy, good, and detailed these reviews are sways what travellers pick and plan to do. People use online reviews as key guides when making choices. How much they trust the reviews is a big part of whether they use them. Things like how good the info is and how much they trust the website have a big impact on if they'll buy something (Wang & Weng, 2024). Research shows that differences in tourist route features change how often users give recommendations. This shows why we need detailed high-quality reviews. Smart systems using Natural Language Processing (NLP) look at review data to suggest destinations on. This makes trip planning easier. These systems can group possible destinations based on what past tourists experienced. This cuts down on the work travellers need to do to make smart choices. Travellers, particularly those seeking adaptable travel options, demonstrate heightened empowerment when utilizing online travel reviews, which are shaped by both informational and normative social influences. While online reviews significantly enhance travel preparation, it is crucial to acknowledge that not all reviews are regarded uniformly. Aspects such as emotional tone and the credibility of the reviewer can also influence consumer perceptions, indicating a complex interplay in the utilization of reviews during travel decision-making.

## Influencer Marketing and Destination Selection

Travellers' destination choices are heavily influenced by influencer marketing, especially when it comes to actual content and interest posted on social media The aforementioned influence is seen across demographics and geographies, highlighting the importance of influencers and tourist involvement is the cornerstone of strategic partnership. As travellers often want to experience the same activities as influencers, this increases their interest in the destinations they promote (Mqwebu, 2024). The authenticity of suggestions made by influential people is paramount; Empirical research suggests that constructive interactions between influencers and their audiences can significantly influence travel intentions. Research shows that the effectiveness of influencer marketing in choosing a location varies greatly across cultures. For example, Brazilian and German millennials exhibit different responses to influencer-generated content, shaped by their respective social norms and cultural perspectives (Seibel, 2021). In particular, influencers on TikTok have found evidence of stimulating the interest of young travellers by offering attractive destinations and unique experiences, thereby influencing travel preferences (Asri et al., 2024). The advent of social media has changed the way individuals identify destinations, as these platforms have emerged as influencing marketing tools. The information disseminated on such platforms has a direct impact on consumer decision-making processes (Rajput & Gandhi, 2024). Despite the proven effectiveness of influencer marketing to boost tourism, concerns have emerged about the false creation of destination image and surpassing the carrying capacity of a tourist place, necessitating a judicious implementation approach et al., 2024). The credibility of influencers, which encompasses dimensions such as trustworthiness, similarity, and attractiveness, directly influences both destination brand trust (DBT) and destination purchase intention (DPI) (Najar et al., 2024). One of the past study revealed that improved trust was associated with higher levels of DBT, which acts as a mediator in the relationship between influencer credibility and DPI, emphasizing the critical importance of influencer in effective marketing strategies (Tsai & Hsin, 2023). Postings by influential people can create deeper emotional connections, increasing the perceived value of a destination and encouraging travel intentions. The effectiveness of influencer marketing is uneven across generational groups, with particular ideas influencing where they are preferred among generations X, Y, and Z (Zorlu & Candan, 2023). Understanding these generational differences allows marketers to tailor their strategies to specific demographic segments. Conversely, despite the formidable power of influencer marketing, its effectiveness may be compromised by oversaturation or a lack of authenticity, resulting in consumer scepticism. Thus, fostering genuine engagement emerges as a critical factor for sustained effectiveness.

A variety of case studies exemplify the successful application of this methodology across diverse geographical regions.

Ningxia, China: The Ningxia Culture and Tourism Department deployed influencers to markedly enhance tourism traffic and economic returns, thereby demonstrating the efficacy of digital marketing strategies in fostering local culture and attractions (Ma, 2024).

Libya: Although still at an embryonic stage, certain travel agencies have initiated collaborations with influencers on platforms such as Instagram, striving to navigate the complexities associated with political instability while advancing Libyan tourism (Asan & Yolal, 2022).

TikTok Influence: Research suggests that TikTok influencers exert a considerable influence on the travel motivations of youth, with visually compelling content stimulating interest in travel among younger populations (Asri et al., 2024).

Collaborative Campaigns: Case studies featuring partnerships between travel agencies and influencers, such as those with the Korea Tourism Organization and Visit Dubai, underscore the significance of strategic communication and engagement in enhancing tourism promotion (Alkan, 2023).

While these instances illustrate the potential of influencer marketing in the realm of tourism, persistent challenges exist, particularly in the identification of appropriate influencers and the assessment of campaign efficacy, as evidenced in the context of Libya (Asan & Yolal, 2022).

## Post-Trip Online Experience Sharing

Social media has emerged as an integral part of the tourism experience, enabling individuals to disseminate travel information before, during, and after their trip. Sharing has been shown to reduce negative effect and increase positive outcomes, culminating in overall positive evaluations (Lin & Rasoolimanesh, 2024). Social media use by tourists is characterized by generational and gender variations, with observer differences noted in practices related to trip preparation, information acquisition, and research formation (Hysa et al and colleagues, 2022). The act of sharing the story through social media helps enhance the visitor experience, making it more in-depth and memorable. These shared experiences not only enhance the intrinsic value of travel but also serve as important information for potential travellers, influencing their decision-making processes.

Tourists are increasingly involved via social media channels in sharing their travel experiences, inspired by the motivations and distinctive characteristics of destinations. Sharing activities not only increases personal satisfaction but also has a big impact on regional tourism as well. Often, altruistic goals, such as the desire to help fellow human beings, coupled with personal interests and discoveries, influence how they share on online social networks. The act of sharing experiences with others, also enhances the overall travel satisfaction (Wong et al., 2024) was published. Social media acts as an important marketing device for tourism businesses, enabling them to communicate effectively with potential customers and promote their offerings (Teixeira et al., 2019). Tourists often share images, reviews and narratives, which are influential information for potential travellers, informing their decision-making processes. Various forms of social media cater to specific type of travel experiences, and enable tourists to share information which meets a prospective traveller. While the benefits of sharing experiences through social media are obvious, it is argued that too much sharing can compromise the authenticity of travel experiences, resulting in artificial travel images rather than real photos. Positive online experiences have a positive impact on location choice, while negative experiences tend to decrease options (Sultan et al., 2019). Tourist-generated stories contribute significantly to destination images, often avoiding traditional brands. Information shared on social media, especially generated by participants, has a positive impact on destination brand awareness, which subsequently raises perceptions of service quality and natural attributes is increased (Dedeoğlu et al., 2020). Digital reputation management is increasingly important in the travel industry, as customers' perceptions on platforms such as Booking.com and TripAdvisor greatly influence the success of hotel brands Destination management organizations can use a variety of strategies to research and motivated have been used to meet the challenges posed by users.

Mobile technology has enabled tourists to access information, plan and access places with unprecedented ease. Mobile technology has dramatically changed the way travellers behave, and the way the tourism industry works. Travellers can now access information, customize events, and shop with unprecedented convenience; thanks to smartphones and tablets (Çınar, 2020). Continuous communication for these devices improves communication between service providers and visitors. International travellers now use mobile phones for itinerary scheduling, social media communication, and other activities, and rely less on traditional travel agents (Rusdi et al., 2022). Mobile applications were confirmed to be well suited especially for tourism as they can improve the visitor experience on travel sites and change how content is accessed and processed. Past research shows that travellers have become more digitally savvy when seeking out nature-based experiences, and want to stay connected with their known. Understanding these emerging trends is important in order to develop successful coping strategies for the tourism industry. Mobile apps have become increasingly important in travel planning, offering a variety of features designed to help travellers in their endeavours. These apps can provide users with travel recommendations, hotel and restaurant recommendations, and information relevant tourist attractions. Some projects emphasize the plurality of transport systems, combining public transport integration and carpooling to increase transport efficiency in urban areas (Dimokas et al., 2018). User-generated content, including online travel reviews, plays an important role in this process, significantly changing the decision-making process of travellers The findings suggest that smartphone apps optimized for the travel planning process are of particular interest to younger population and passport holders show little impact on reducing, however, they significantly increase the chances of moving to other destinations (Jamal & Habib, 2019). In summary, mobile applications are changing the way individuals plan and participate in travel experiences. The proliferation of travel infrastructure has had a profound impact on tourist behaviour and experiences. Research shows that smartphones and mobile applications can dramatically change visitors' activities and emotional responses, thereby increasing safety and enhancing social interaction (Dias & Afonso, 2021). Travel apps are increasingly used for planning and decision making, with users demonstrating creativity and specificity in their use

(Tavitiyaman et al., 2021). Factors determining the acceptability of these applications include perceived usefulness, ease of use, and compatibility. Self-efficacy has an indirect effect on adoption through outcome expectations, whereas social norms were not found to be a significant predictor. Tourists use travel apps to access information and services effortlessly, making their travels easier. The proliferation of smartphones and high-speed wireless networks has shown great interest in using mobile applications to enhance tourist experience. Mobile travel apps (MTAs) have grown exponentially, offering a variety of functionality aimed at providing travel experience has been great for. Real-time enhancements are also included (Sia et al., 2022), which enables users to compare prices, reserve services and access travel information (Camilleri et al., 2023). For China, leading applications such as Ctrip and Qunar dominate the market. The adoption of MTAs is driven by factors such as information quality, source reliability, and efficiency, which, in turn, affect users' perceptions of usefulness and intentions to continue using them (Camilleri et al., 2023). The improved functionality of smartphones has fundamentally changed the way individuals navigate and understand travel planning and tourist travel. However, challenges associated with MTA development include technical capital, precision of spatial operations, and privacy concerns (Sia et al., 2022). Moving forward, MTAs have the potential to facilitate collaborative and sustainable transportation decisions. Location-based services (LBS) in the tourism industry have advanced in integrating individual features, enhancing the tourist experience. These applications offer suggestions of attractions, accommodations, and activities that match users' preferences, current location, and context. The use of translational web technologies can improve the relevance and accuracy of information to users. Individual LBS applications consider variables such as time, weather, and user profiles to determine customized information. Some programs are able to establish their business strategy by combining social resources with targeted advertising (Barragáns-Martínez & Costa-Montenegro, 2015). To overcome the deficiencies of unreliable mobile and communication networks, modular software platform systems are proposed for audio-visual production designed for their own features in navigation apps Compared to a standard LBS that provides all users with the same information, these new features aim to better meet the needs of individual users.

In the context of information overload, Ojha & Mishra's (2018) study examined the impact of tailored recommendations on tourist satisfaction. Researchers proposed a novel approach that combines data filtering and criteria decision making to identify travel destinations that suit passenger interests. This approach aims to address the challenges associated with optimal policy recommendations for the travel industry. The authors argue that their framework effectively addresses the issue of data redundancy, which can make it difficult and time-consuming for passengers to choose destinations that match their preferences. It is expected that the proposed framework will provide increased tourist satisfaction by providing attractive and customized recommendations. Ultimately, the researchers hypothesize that this increase in satisfaction may contribute to improved tourism. Their study shows that the proposed methodology is successful in solving the identified problems. Mobile payments are becoming increasingly popular in the tourism industry as they provide convenience for customers. Research on the barriers, enablers and mechanisms of adoption of mobile payments in travel retention has shown interesting results contrary to the popular belief (Hameed et al., 2022). To meet the expectations of Chinese tourists, destination players, especially in Southeast Asia, have aggressively introduced mobile payment facilities (Tangit & Law, 2020). The analysis of mobile payment applications has been studied from the perspective of suppliers, customers and policy makers in the hospitality and tourism industry, as well as recommendations for practitioners. Furthermore, the concept of multiple interface encounters enabling passengers to sort, book, access and pay for a variety of travel options through a single platform promises to radically change the travel experience, possibly saving money and increasing the sales of service providers.

## The Future of Virtual Reality and Augmented Reality in Tourism

Virtual reality (VR) and augmented reality (AR) technologies assume increasing importance in tourism and hospitality research, providing enhanced marketing strategies, heritage preservation and premium tourism experiences. Recently, scholarly research has defined important research areas, including VR tourism marketing, in the context of heritage preservation. Experimental, post-pandemic- VR use is also included (Wut & Ng, 2024). The development of this technology is accelerating, as mobile AR applications are now common in scholarly investigations, while wearable devices continue to be scrutinized (Moro et al., 2019). There has been a remarkable increase in the use of VR and AR in areas such as tourism management, marketing, and education. Research has focused on users' subjective experiences, examining the motivations, perceptions and effects associated with VR/AR usage (Wei, 2019). Possible avenues for research include theoretical development, cross-cultural analysis, and examination of prevailing influences on consumer responses to VR/AR technologies (Wut & Ng, 2024). Furthermore, the concept of interactive platforms, which make it easier for passengers to prepare, book, earn and receive rewards on different modes of travel through a single platform, has the potential to dramatically change the travel experience, which can save costs for providers and enhance service market. Virtual reality (VR) and augmented reality (AR) represent emerging technologies that are transforming tourism by enhancing the visitor experience, and transforming marketing channels. Recent academic research has identified important areas of focus, including VR tourism marketing, AR applications in heritage sites, post-pandemic VR use behaviour, and enhancing the overall tourism experience (Wut & Ng, 2024). These technologies provide interactive maps, historical perspectives and hydraulic models of tourist destinations (Jiman & Kulal, 2023). Scholarly research has examined the motivations, perceptions, and effects of user experiences associated with VR/AR, highlighting the positive effects that promote industry adoption (Wei, 2019). Text mining analysis of the existing literature revealed key themes in journal articles and conference proceedings, and provided a comprehensive overview of the development of the field over the last two decades (Loureiro et al., 2020). Future research avenues are expected to include theoretical development, multicultural studies, and applicability research on consumer responses to VR/AR applications. The use of virtual reality (VR) and augmented reality (AR) technologies in healthcare and education raises significant ethical concerns. These include issues related to user privacy, data security, and functionality that can revolutionize user experience (Ramirez et al., 2020). Although VR and AR have proven effective in a variety of medical applications, such as rehabilitation for autism spectrum disorders and interventional surgery, there are challenges in terms of cybersecurity and cost is still available (Ray et al., 2024). Ethical considerations extend to patient consent, subject autonomy, and the need for users and manufacturers to adhere to ethical standards and regulations (Pawar & Pawar, 2024). The intrusive nature of this technology also raises concerns about physical safety and potential unintended consequences. To address these issues, several researchers have proposed ethical guidelines and codes of conduct for VR/AR applications, emphasizing the importance of technological innovation and ethical responsibility emphasis on balance (Pawar & Pawar, 2024).

## CONCLUSION

The digital age has dramatically changed tourism, changing the fundamental way travellers take and destinations, make informed choices and deliver their experiences. As new technologies evolve, the ways in which individuals plan, save and engage with travel is becoming more complex and interconnected. From initial motivation to post-travel intent, digital devices and platforms now play a key role in influencing every aspect of the passenger journey Distinctive change especially in terms of tourist behaviour and the increased reliance on digital resources for travel-related information. Social media platforms, travel blogs and online searches have emerged as key for a number of travellers seeking destination information and support These changes have empowered consumers by providing more information at their fingertips, and thus more informed decision making has become easier. Nevertheless, obstacles such as rich content and the challenge of reliable identification play a role simultaneously.

Mobile technology has further enhanced the convenience and accessibility of travel, allowing visitors to plan, book and navigate their trips in real time. The proliferation of mobile applications and location-based services has enriched the travel experience, providing personalized recommendations and real-time assistance tailored to individual preferences, along with the integration of mobile payment systems, which has facilitated the creation of linkage between businesses and tourists. Virtual and augmented reality technologies are beginning to have a profound impact on tourist behaviour, creating immersive experiences for those who want to move the route requires destinations before the actual visit. As this technology gains widespread adoption, the impact on tourism is expected to expand, creating new opportunities for destinations to connect with prospective visitors. Online booking platforms provide travel solutions for passengers to compare prices, read reviews and make reservations. Competition between service providers on these platforms has intensified, leading to increases in service quality and customer service. At the same time, however, there has been a simultaneous concern about the commodification of travel experiences and the pressure on destinations to continue to attract digitally literate tourists.

As the tourism industry adapts in response to technological advances, it is important for stakeholders like tourism agencies, destination marketers and policymakers to understand and adapt to the changing tourist behaviour while simultaneously addressing concurrent challenges to ensure a sustainable and inclusive approach towards the tourism industry. Despite the many benefits of digital development, there are challenges and ethical considerations to consider. For example, the digital divide remains a key issue, with some communities and demographic groups experiencing limited access to digital tools and the internet facility. This divide can exacerbate differences in tourist experiences, and restrict opportunities for specific people. In essence, the digital epoch offers both prospects and obstacles for the tourism industry. The role of mobile applications, GPS technologies and location-based services in enhancing tourist experience and shaping behaviour patterns is also highlighted in this chapter; but, it is equally important to consider the ethical implications and importance of reducing the digital divide. All of these have changed the way travellers connect with the global landscape, making travel more efficient, personalized and efficient.

# REFERENCES

Akanfe, O., Lawong, D., & Rao, H. R. (2024). Blockchain technology and privacy regulation: Reviewing frictions and synthesizing opportunities. *International Journal of Information Management*, 76, 102753. DOI: 10.1016/j.ijinfomgt.2024.102753

Alkan, Z. (2023). Influencers and Travel Agencies in the Focus of Influencer Communication: An Evaluation of Brand Collaborations. In *Women's Empowerment Within the Tourism Industry* (pp. 203-220). IGI Global.

Alves de Castro, C., O'Reilly Dr, I., & Carthy, A. (2021). Social media influencers (SMIs) in context: A literature review. *Journal of Marketing Management*, 9(2), 59–71.

Andjelic, S., Milutinovic, O., Gajic, A., & Arsic, M. (2024). The influence of traditional and modern communication technologies on consumer attitudes. *Social Informatics Journal*, 3(1), 23–30. DOI: 10.58898/sij.v3i1.23-30

Andzani, D., Virgin, D., & Setijadi, N. (2024). Peran media sosial dalam membangun citra destinasi pariwisata yang menarik. [Jurnal Ilmiah Manajemen Bisnis dan Inovasi Universitas Sam Ratulangi]. *JMBI UNSRAT*, 11(1), 188–195. DOI: 10.35794/jmbi.v11i1.53212

Armutcu, B., Tan, A., Amponsah, M., Parida, S., & Ramkissoon, H. (2023). Tourist behaviour: The role of digital marketing and social media. *Acta Psychologica*, 240, 104025. DOI: 10.1016/j.actpsy.2023.104025 PMID: 37741033

Asan, K., & Yolal, M. (2022). Travel influencers and influencer marketing in tourism. In *Handbook on Tourism and Social Media* (pp. 365–380). Edward Elgar Publishing. DOI: 10.4337/9781800371415.00037

Asri, M. A. Z. M., Ahmad, S. Y., Sawari, S. S. M., & Zakaria, N. F. (2024). Social media influencers and the effect on travel motivation among youth. *journal of tourism, hospitality and environment management (jthem)*, 9(36).

Atasheva, D., Sarsenbayev, A., & Kulbayeva, A. (2024). Innovation and Application of Digitalization in the Formation of the Image of a smart hotel. *Eurasian Science Review An International Peer-Reviewed Multidisciplinary Journal*, 2(2), 128–133. DOI: 10.63034/esr-56

Azam, M. S. E., Muflih, B. K., & Al Haq, M. A. (2024). Intersection Between Modern Technologies and Halal Tourism: Exploring the Role of Digital Innovation in Enhancing Muslim Travellers' Experience. *The Journal of Muamalat and Islamic Finance Research*, 16-31.

Barbosa, D. P., & Medaglia, J. (2019). Tecnologia digital, turismo e os hábitos de consumo dos viajantes contemporâneos. *Marketing & Tourism Review*, 4(2), 1–33.

Barbu, C. A., Popa, A., & Zaharia, R. M. (2023). The Use of Digital Technologies in Tourism Management. *Ovidius University Annals. Economic Sciences Series*, 23(2), 394–401.

Barragáns-Martínez, A. B., & Costa-Montenegro, E. (2015). Adding personalization and social features to a context-aware application for mobile tourism. In *Hospitality, travel, and tourism: Concepts, methodologies, tools, and applications* (pp. 467–480). IGI Global. DOI: 10.4018/978-1-4666-6543-9.ch028

Barykin, S. Y., Kapustina, I. V., Kirillova, T. V., Yadykin, V. K., & Konnikov, Y. A. (2020). Economics of digital ecosystems. *Journal of Open Innovation*, 6(4), 124. DOI: 10.3390/joitmc6040124

Bieser, J. C., & Hilty, L. M. (2018). Assessing indirect environmental effects of information and communication technology (ICT): A systematic literature review. *Sustainability (Basel)*, 10(8), 2662. DOI: 10.3390/su10082662

Camilleri, M. A., Troise, C., & Kozak, M. (2023). Functionality and usability features of ubiquitous mobile technologies: The acceptance of interactive travel apps. *Journal of Hospitality and Tourism Technology*, 14(2), 188–207. DOI: 10.1108/JHTT-12-2021-0345

Çınar, K. (2020). Role of mobile technology for tourism development. In *The emerald handbook of ICT in tourism and hospitality* (pp. 273–288). Emerald Publishing Limited. DOI: 10.1108/978-1-83982-688-720201017

Dedeoğlu, B. B., Van Niekerk, M., Küçükergin, K. G., De Martino, M., & Okumuş, F. (2020). Effect of social media sharing on destination brand awareness and destination quality. *Journal of Vacation Marketing*, 26(1), 33–56. DOI: 10.1177/1356766719858644

Del Vecchio, P., Malandugno, C., Passiante, G., & Sakka, G. (2022). Circular economy business model for smart tourism: The case of Ecobnb. *EuroMed Journal of Business*, 17(1), 88–104. DOI: 10.1108/EMJB-09-2020-0098

Deputat, M., Podolian, M., Zhupnyk, V., Terletska, K., & Gorishevskyy, P. (2024). Evolution of information systems and technologies in the hospitality and tourism sector: a historical perspective. *Multidisciplinary Science Journal*, 6.

Dias, S., & Afonso, V. A. (2021). Impact of mobile applications in changing the tourist experience. *European Journal of Tourism. Hospitality and Recreation*, 11(1), 113–120. DOI: 10.2478/ejthr-2021-0011

Dimokas, N., Kalogirou, K., Spanidis, P., & Kehagias, D. (2018, July). A mobile application for multimodal trip planning. In *2018 9th International Conference on Information, Intelligence, Systems and Applications (IISA)* (pp. 1-8). IEEE. DOI: 10.1109/IISA.2018.8633665

El Archi, Y., Benbba, B., Kabil, M., & Dávid, L. D. (2023). Digital Technologies for Sustainable Tourism Destinations: State of the Art and Research Agenda. *Administrative Sciences*, 13(8), 184. DOI: 10.3390/admsci13080184

El Mattichi, F., Elabbadi, A., Hmioui, A., & Barhmi, A. (2024). Exploring Sustainability in Tourism Marketing Through Digital and Social Networks: A Literature Review. *Promoting Responsible Tourism with Digital Platforms*, 213-230.

Fanni, S. C., Febi, M., Aghakhanyan, G., & Neri, E. (2023). Natural language processing. In *Introduction to Artificial Intelligence* (pp. 87–99). Springer International Publishing. DOI: 10.1007/978-3-031-25928-9_5

Farid, S., Boudia, M. A., & Mwangi, G. (2023). Revolutionizing Tourism: Harnessing the Power of IoT in Smart Destinations. *Journal of Digital Marketing and Communication*, 3(2), 91–99. DOI: 10.53623/jdmc.v3i2.360

Ghaly, M. (2023). The influence of user-generated content and social media travel influencers credibility on the visit intention of Generation Z. *Journal of Association of Arab Universities for Tourism and Hospitality*, 24(2), 367–382. DOI: 10.21608/jaauth.2023.218047.1477

Golja, T., & Paulišić, M. (2021). Managing-technology enhanced tourist experience. *Management*, 26(1), 63–95. DOI: 10.30924/mjcmi.26.1.5

Gunawan, H., Udin, U., & Rahayu, M. K. P. (2024). Research trends on the impact of digital transformation on the development of the tourism industry: A bibliometric analysis. *Multidisciplinary Reviews*, 7(5), 2024090. DOI: 10.31893/multirev.2024090

Guo, P. (2023). Exploring the Effects of Social Media Influencer on Consumers Hotel Decision in China. *Lecture Notes in Education Psychology and Public Media*, 4(1), 1158–1166. DOI: 10.54254/2753-7048/4/2022843

Gupta, S., Sufi, T., & Kumar Gautam, P. (2022). Role of Technological Transformation in Shaping Millennials' Travel Behaviour: A Review. 2022 *10th International Conference on Reliability, Infocom Technologies and Optimization (Trends and Future Directions)* (ICRITO). https://doi.org/DOI: 10.1109/ICRITO56286.2022.9965175

Hameed, I., Mubarik, M. S., Khan, K., & Waris, I. (2022). Can your smartphone make you a tourist? Mine does: Understanding the consumer's adoption mechanism for mobile payment system. *Human Behavior and Emerging Technologies*, 2022(1), 4904686. DOI: 10.1155/2022/4904686

Hays, S., Page, S. J., & Buhalis, D. (2013). Social media as a destination marketing tool: Its use by national tourism organisations. *Current Issues in Tourism*, 16(3), 211–239. DOI: 10.1080/13683500.2012.662215

Hysa, B., Zdonek, I., & Karasek, A. (2022). Social media in sustainable tourism recovery. *Sustainability (Basel)*, 14(2), 760. DOI: 10.3390/su14020760

Irfan, M., Malik, M. S., & Zubair, S. K. (2022). Impact of vlog marketing on consumer travel intent and consumer purchase intent with the moderating role of destination image and ease of travel. *SAGE Open*, 12(2), 21582440221099522. DOI: 10.1177/21582440221099522

Jamal, S., & Habib, M. A. (2019). Investigation of the use of smartphone applications for trip planning and travel outcomes. *Transportation Planning and Technology*, 42(3), 227–243. DOI: 10.1080/03081060.2019.1576381

Jiman, J., & Kulal, S. M. (2023, December). Augmented Reality (AR) And Virtual Reality (VR) Applications In Tourism: Embracing Emerging Technologies For Improved Tourist Experiences In Malaysian Tourism Industry. In *International Conference On Digital Advanced Tourism Management And Technology* (Vol. 1, No. 2, pp. 188-199). DOI: 10.56910/ictmt.v1i2.34

Jog, D. R., & Alcasoas, N. A. (2023). Travel decision making through blogs and vlogs: An empirical investigation on how user-generated content influences destination image. *Turyzm/Tourism, 33*(2), 19-28.

Kumar, S., & Sharma, A. (2024). An Era Of Digital Transformation In The Hospitality & Tourism Sector. *Educational Administration: Theory and Practice*, 30(4), 9422–9427.

Kuzman, B., Petkovic, B., & Milovancevic, M. (2024, July). Information and communication technology in tourism. In *Tourism International Scientific Conference Vrnjačka Banja-TISC* (Vol. 8, No. 1, pp. 75-86).

Leite, F. P., Pontes, N., & Schivinski, B. (2024). Influencer marketing effectiveness: Giving competence, receiving credibility. *Journal of Travel & Tourism Marketing*, 41(3), 307–321. DOI: 10.1080/10548408.2024.2317748

Lin, Z., & Rasoolimanesh, S. M. (2024). Sharing tourism experiences in social media: A systematic review. *Anatolia*, 35(1), 67–81. DOI: 10.1080/13032917.2022.2120029

Loureiro, S. M. C., Guerreiro, J., & Ali, F. (2020). 20 years of research on virtual reality and augmented reality in tourism context: A text-mining approach. *Tourism Management*, 77, 104028. DOI: 10.1016/j.tourman.2019.104028

Ma, S. (2024). A Study on the Impact of Influencers on the Tourism Industry in Ningxia, China. *Journal of Social Sciences and Economics*, 3(1), 55–65. DOI: 10.61363/qk9rqv23

Majeed, S., Zhou, Z., Lu, C., & Ramkissoon, H. (2020). Online tourism information and tourist behaviour: A structural equation modeling analysis based on a self-administered survey. *Frontiers in Psychology*, 11, 599. DOI: 10.3389/fpsyg.2020.00599 PMID: 32373008

Mikhailov, S., Kashevnik, A., & Smirnov, A. (2020, June). Tourist behaviour analysis based on digital pattern of life. In *2020 7th International Conference on Control, Decision and Information Technologies (CoDIT)* (Vol. 1, pp. 622-627). IEEE. DOI: 10.1109/CoDIT49905.2020.9263945

Moro, S., Rita, P., Ramos, P., & Esmerado, J. (2019). Analysing recent augmented and virtual reality developments in tourism. *Journal of Hospitality and Tourism Technology*, 10(4), 571–586. DOI: 10.1108/JHTT-07-2018-0059

Mouha, R. A. R. A. (2021). Internet of things (IoT). *Journal of Data Analysis and Information Processing*, 9(02), 77–101. DOI: 10.4236/jdaip.2021.92006

Mqwebu, B. (2024). Impact of Social Media Influencers on Tourist Destination Choices and Expenditure in South Africa. *Journal of Hospitality and Tourism*, 4(1), 57–68. DOI: 10.47672/jht.1979

Naab, T. K., & Sehl, A. (2017). Studies of user-generated content: A systematic review. *Journalism*, 18(10), 1256–1273. DOI: 10.1177/1464884916673557

Najar, A. H., Wani, I. S., & Rather, A. H. (2024). Impact of Social Media Influencers Credibility on Destination Brand Trust and Destination Purchase Intention: Extending Meaning Transfer Model? *Global Business Review*, •••, 09721509241225354. DOI: 10.1177/09721509241225354

Ojha, A. C., & Mishra, J. (2018, December). Interest-Satisfaction Estimation Model for Point-of-Interest Recommendations in Tourism. In *2018 International Conference on Information Technology (ICIT)* (pp. 172-177). IEEE. DOI: 10.1109/ICIT.2018.00044

Okonkwo, E. E., Eyisi, A., & Ololo, N. (2015). Social media platforms and their contributions to tourism development and promotion in Nigeria. *Nsukka Journal of the Humanities*, 23(2), 103–117.

Öz, M. (2015). Social media utilization of tourists for travel-related purposes. *International Journal of Contemporary Hospitality Management*, 27(5), 1003–1023. DOI: 10.1108/IJCHM-01-2014-0034

Patel, A., & Jain, S. (2021). Present and future of semantic web technologies: A research statement. *International Journal of Computers and Applications*, 43(5), 413–422. DOI: 10.1080/1206212X.2019.1570666

Pawar, V. V., & Pawar, D. (2024). Augmented reality in medical education: Exploring ethical considerations. *Oral Oncology Reports*, 9, 100208. DOI: 10.1016/j.oor.2024.100208

Prajapat, D. K., & R, D. K. (2024). Revolutionizing Tourism through Technology the Digital Transformation of Travel and Tourism. *International Journal of Research Publication and Reviews*, 5(2), 3643–3648. DOI: 10.55248/gengpi.5.0224.0626

Rajput, A., & Gandhi, A. (2024, March). Influencer Voices: Exploring How Recommendations Drive Tourism Intent. In *2024 International Conference on Automation and Computation (AUTOCOM)* (pp. 586-592). IEEE. DOI: 10.1109/AUTOCOM60220.2024.10486181

Ramirez, E. J., Tan, J., Elliott, M., Gandhi, M., & Petronio, L. (2020, December). An ethical code for commercial VR/AR applications. In *International Conference on Intelligent Technologies for Interactive Entertainment* (pp. 15-24). Cham: Springer International Publishing.

Ray, S., Tawar, S., Singh, N., & Singh, G. (2024). Transition toward Technological Transformation: Challenges of Implementing Virtual Reality and Augmented Reality in the Health Sector. *Journal of Marine Medical Society*, 26(2), 161–164.

Rhena, J., Kraugusteeliana, K., & Hamzar, . (2024). Embracing Digitalization in Tourism: Strategic Approaches for Global Competitiveness in the Digital Economy Era. *Indo-Fintech Intellectuals: Journal of Economics and Business*, 4(2), 461–472. DOI: 10.54373/ifijeb.v4i2.1282

Roy, P., & Jasrotia, A. (2024). An Insight into the Behaviour of Tech-Savvy Millennial Travellers: A Global Perspective. *Tourist Behaviour and the New Normal*, I, 173–184. DOI: 10.1007/978-3-031-45848-4_10

Rusdi, J. F., Abu, N. A., Salam, S., Gusdevi, H., Hardi, R., & Nugraha, D. G. (2022, November). An international tourist behaviour on mobile smartphone usage. In *AIP Conference Proceedings* (Vol. 2658, No. 1). AIP Publishing. DOI: 10.1063/5.0106824

Saini, H., Kumar, P., & Oberoi, S. (2023). Welcome to the destination! Social media influencers as cogent determinant of travel decision: A systematic literature review and conceptual framework. *Cogent Social Sciences*, 9(1), 2240055. Advance online publication. DOI: 10.1080/23311886.2023.2240055

Santos, S., Ferreira, S., & Vasconcelos, M. (2024, May). User-Generated Content in Tourism: Could it Impact Brand Equity and Intention to Visit? In *European Conference on Social Media* (Vol. 11, No. 1, pp. 235-242). DOI: 10.34190/ecsm.11.1.2271

Seibel, G. (2021). The impact of influencer marketing on destination choice-A quantitative study among Brazilian and German millennials. *RCMOS-. Revista Científica Multidisciplinar o Saber*, 1(3), 41–150. DOI: 10.51473/rcmos.v1i1.2021.44

Shariffuddin, N. S. M., Azinuddin, M., Yahya, N. E., & Hanafiah, M. H. (2023). Navigating the tourism digital landscape: The interrelationship of online travel sites' affordances, technology readiness, online purchase intentions, trust, and E-loyalty. *Heliyon*, 9(8), e19135. DOI: 10.1016/j.heliyon.2023.e19135 PMID: 37636344

Sia, P. Y. H., Saidin, S. S., & Iskandar, Y. H. P. (2023). Systematic review of mobile travel apps and their smart features and challenges. *Journal of Hospitality and Tourism Insights*, 6(5), 2115–2138. DOI: 10.1108/JHTI-02-2022-0087

Sivarethinamohan, R. (2023, July). Exploring the Transformation of Digital Tourism: Trends, Impacts, and Future Prospects. In *2023 International Conference on Digital Applications, Transformation & Economy (ICDATE)* (pp. 260-266). IEEE. DOI: 10.1109/ICDATE58146.2023.10248691

Son, H., & Park, Y. E. (2024). A deep understanding of influencer marketing in the tourism industry: A structural analysis of unstructured text. *Current Issues in Tourism*, ●●●, 1–11. DOI: 10.1080/13683500.2024.2368152

Stylos, N. (2019). Technological evolution and tourist decision-making: A perspective article. *Tourism Review*, 75(1), 273–278. DOI: 10.1108/TR-05-2019-0167

Sultan, M. T., Sharmin, F., & Xue, K. (2019). Sharing tourism experience through social media: Consumer's behavioral intention for destination choice. *The Age (Melbourne, Vic.)*, 20(72), 34.

Tandafatu, N. K., Ermilinda, L., & Darkel, Y. B. M. (2024). Digital Transformation in Tourism: Exploring the Impact of Technology on Travel Experiences. *International Journal of Multidisciplinary Approach Sciences and Technologies*, 1(1), 55–64. DOI: 10.62207/w3vsg352

Tangit, T. M., & Law, R. (2021). Mobile Payments, Chinese Tourists, and Host Residents: Are Destination Stakeholders Prepared to Facilitate Mobile Payments? In *Information and Communication Technologies in Tourism 2021:Proceedings of the ENTER 2021 eTourism Conference,January 19–22, 2021* (pp. 210-215). Springer International Publishing.

Tavitiyaman, P., Qu, H., Tsang, W. S. L., & Lam, C. W. R. (2021). The influence of smart tourism applications on perceived destination image and behavioral intention: The moderating role of information search behavior. *Journal of Hospitality and Tourism Management*, 46, 476–487. DOI: 10.1016/j.jhtm.2021.02.003

Teixeira, R. M., Andreassi, T., Köseoglu, M. A., & Okumus, F. (2019). How do hospitality entrepreneurs use their social networks to access resources? Evidence from the lifecycle of small hospitality enterprises. *International Journal of Hospitality Management*, 79, 158–167. DOI: 10.1016/j.ijhm.2019.01.006

Torres-Moraga, E., & Barra, C. (2023). Does destination brand experience help build trust? Disentangling the effects on trust and trustworthiness. *Journal of Destination Marketing & Management*, 27, 100767. DOI: 10.1016/j.jdmm.2023.100767

Tsai, C. M., & Hsin, S. P. (2023). The Influence of Influencer Marketing on the Consumers' Desire to Travel in the Post-Pandemic Era: The Mediation Effect of Influencer Fitness of Destination. *Sustainability (Basel)*, 15(20), 14746. DOI: 10.3390/su152014746

Vila, N. A., Cardoso, L., El Archi, Y., & Brea, J. A. F. (2024). The Role of Digital Technology and Sustainable Practices in Tourists' Decision Making. In *Promoting Responsible Tourism With Digital Platforms* (pp. 36–59). IGI Global. DOI: 10.4018/979-8-3693-3286-3.ch003

Wang, E. S. T., & Weng, Y. J. (2024). Influence of social media influencer authenticity on their followers' perceptions of credibility and their positive word-of-mouth. *Asia Pacific Journal of Marketing and Logistics*, 36(2), 356–373. DOI: 10.1108/APJML-02-2023-0115

Wei, W. (2019). Research progress on virtual reality (VR) and augmented reality (AR) in tourism and hospitality: A critical review of publications from 2000 to 2018. *Journal of Hospitality and Tourism Technology*, 10(4), 539–570. DOI: 10.1108/JHTT-04-2018-0030

Wong, J. W. C., Lai, I. K. W., & Wang, S. (2024). How social values gained from sharing travel experiences influence tourists' satisfaction: Moderated mediation effect of onsite mobile sharing behaviour. *Asia Pacific Journal of Marketing and Logistics*. Advance online publication. DOI: 10.1108/APJML-10-2023-1060

Wut, T. M., & Ng, M. L. P. (2024). Virtual reality and augmented reality of tourism research: A review and research agenda. *Journal of Quality Assurance in Hospitality & Tourism*, •••, 1–24. DOI: 10.1080/1528008X.2024.2338774

Zorlu, Ö., & Candan, T. (2023). The impact of social media influencers on destination preferences: A cross-generation comparison. *Journal of Tourism Leisure and Hospitality*, 5(1), 53–61. DOI: 10.48119/toleho.1229922

## ADDITIONAL READING

Armutcu, B., Tan, A., Amponsah, M., Parida, S., & Ramkissoon, H. (2023). Tourist behaviour: The role of digital marketing and social media. *Acta Psychologica*, 240, 104025. DOI: 10.1016/j.actpsy.2023.104025 PMID: 37741033

Ho, P. T., Ho, M. T., & Huang, M. L. (2024). Understanding the impact of tourist behavior change on travel agencies in developing countries: Strategies for enhancing the tourist experience. *Acta Psychologica*, 249, 104463. DOI: 10.1016/j.actpsy.2024.104463 PMID: 39180834

Hussain, T., Wang, D., & Li, B. (2024). Exploring the impact of social media on tourist behavior in rural mountain tourism during the COVID-19 pandemic: The role of perceived risk and community participation. *Acta Psychologica*, 242, 104113. DOI: 10.1016/j.actpsy.2023.104113 PMID: 38171191

Li, N., Meng, F., & Martin, D. (2023). The influence of travel photo editing on tourists' experiences. *Tourism Management*, 98, 104762. DOI: 10.1016/j.tourman.2023.104762

Marchesani, F., Masciarelli, F., & Ceci, F. (2024). Digital trajectories in contemporary cities: Exploring the interplay between digital technology implementation, the amplitude of social media platforms, and tourists inflow in cities. *Cities (London, England)*, 146, 104749. DOI: 10.1016/j.cities.2023.104749

Wong, C. U. I., Ren, L., Ma, C., & Lam, J. F. I. (2024). What do today's Chinese tourists expect from tour guides? A mixed-method approach to understanding the evolving guide roles. *Journal of Hospitality and Tourism Management*, 59, 102–115. DOI: 10.1016/j.jhtm.2024.04.002

Zhou, C., & Huang, M. (2024). The persuasive effects of voice characteristics embedded in paid tour guide audio on tourist purchase decisions based on deep learning. *Journal of Hospitality and Tourism Management*, 60, 313–321. DOI: 10.1016/j.jhtm.2024.08.007

Zhou, Q., Sotiriadis, M., & Shen, S. (2023). Using TikTok in tourism destination choice: A young Chinese tourists' perspective. *Tourism Management Perspectives*, 46, 101101. DOI: 10.1016/j.tmp.2023.101101

## KEY TERMS AND DEFINITIONS

**Blockchain Technology (BT):** Blockchain technology constitutes a distributed record-keeping system which securely records transactions over an ensemble of computers (Akanfe et al., 2024). It began to be a basis for Bitcoin and has since discovered applications in a variety of industries.

**Destination Brand Trust (DBT):** Destination brand trust is an important factor in fostering visitor loyalty and affecting repeat visitation intentions, which are influenced by brand, location, and visitor characteristics, alongside brand characteristics having the greatest impact (Torres-Moraga & Barra, 2023).

**Destination Purchase Intention (DPI):** Destination Purchase Intention (DPI) is affected by a number of factors, including thought destination attractiveness, social networking influencers, and creative marketing strategies. Destination attractiveness, competitive edge, and convenience all have a significant impact on students' interest and pleasure in purchasing (Irfan et al., 2022).

**Digital Ecosystems:** Digital ecosystems are complicated self-organizing systems that resemble biological ecosystems but use networking and communication technologies to tackle particular application fields (Barykin et al., 2020).

**Ecobnb:** Ecobnb is a network-based tourism business that exemplifies the intersection of circular economy rules as well as smart tourism (Del Vecchio et al., 2022). It represents a shift in the tourism industry toward environmentally friendly and innovative business models that use digital technologies to generate value while also promoting environmental responsibility.

**Information and Communication Technologies (ICTs):** Information and communication technologies (ICT) is a broad range of technologies that allow for the development, accessibility, storage, dissemination, and manipulation of information (Bieser & Hilty, 2018).

**Internet of Things (IoT):** The Internet of Things (IoT) is an online community of physical objects equipped with software, sensors, and network connectivity that can gather and share data with no any human involvement (Mouha, 2021).

**Natural Language Processing (NLP):** Natural Language Processing (NLP) is a field of computer science and artificial intelligence that studies the interaction of computers as well as human languages (Fanni et al., 2023).

**Semantic Web Technologies:** Semantic Web Technologies (SWT) enhance the current web by providing machine-interpretable semantics towards data, allowing clever software systems as well as automated analysis. Ontologies and metadata are important components that help with representation of knowledge and machine understanding (Patel & Jain, 2021).

**Social Media Influencers (SMIs):** Social media influencers encompass individuals who have large followings on platforms such as YouTube, Instagram, and Facebook and promote branded products and services to their followers (Alves de Castro et al., 2021).

**User Generated Content (UGC):** User-generated content (UGC) encompasses an extensive variety of media and creative work types created or significantly co-created by individuals outside of traditional professional settings (Naab & Sehl, 2017).

# Chapter 3
# Decoding the Digital Traveller:
## Effective Marketing Strategies for Engaging Today's Tech-Savvy and Connected Tourists

**Jatin Thakur**
https://orcid.org/0009-0005-9089-0303
*Lovely Professional University, India*

**Pooja Kansra**
https://orcid.org/0000-0003-2229-0662
*Lovely Professional University, India*

**Shad Ahmad Khan**
https://orcid.org/0000-0001-7593-3487
*University of Buraimi, Oman*

## ABSTRACT

*The rapid advancement of digital technology has profoundly transformed the tourism industry, giving rise to a new breed of traveller the digital traveller. This tech-savvy and hyper-connected demographic demands personalized, seamless, and instantaneous experiences throughout their journey. This chapter delves into the evolving landscape of digital tourism, exploring the key characteristics and behaviours of today's digital travellers. By decoding their preferences and expectations, the chapter identifies effective marketing strategies that resonate with this group. The research highlights the importance of leveraging big data analytics, artificial intelligence, and social media platforms to create tailored marketing campaigns that enhance engagement and foster loyalty. Additionally, the chapter examines the role of mobile*

DOI: 10.4018/979-8-3693-3972-5.ch003

*technology, virtual reality, and user-generated content in shaping travel decisions.*

## I. INTRODUCTION

The digital era has transformed the travel industry and traveller behaviour, particularly among millennials and digital natives. Modern travellers are increasingly autonomous, connected, and informed, using digital platforms to plan trips, share experiences, and influence others (Barbosa & Medaglia, 2020). Millennials, as digital natives, have significantly impacted tourism marketing strategies due to their technological proficiency, price sensitivity, and preference for mobile applications and social media (Starcevic & Konjikusic, 2018; Kumar et al., 2022). The rise of digitally enabled tourists has led to changes in how travel experiences are recorded, shared, and exhibited online, necessitating adaptations in industry infrastructure (Andrade & Mason, 2009). Digital natives, in particular, are at the forefront of these transformations, navigating a fragmented online travel market and utilizing user-generated content alongside traditional services (Gasser & Simun, 2010). This shift has reshaped the role of travel agents and empowered consumers to interact directly with travel services. Over half of travellers in Poland reported using modern technologies for transport, with a significant portion intending to adopt them in the future (Rosa, 2023). Digital nomads blend remote work with travel, facilitated by advancements in communication technologies and a desire for financial independence (Mancinelli, 2022). Discussions among digital nomads highlight the importance of destination reviews and emotional needs, reflecting a shift in travel motivations (Xiao & Lutz, 2024). Digital travel applications can stimulate interest in destinations, as evidenced by studies showing that virtual experiences can enhance the intention to visit places like Mexico (Tjostheim & Waterworth, 2023).

Understanding digital travellers is crucial in today's tourism landscape, as their behaviors and preferences are significantly shaped by technology. This comprehension aids businesses and destinations in tailoring their offerings to meet the evolving demands of this demographic. The digital era has transformed the behavior of modern travellers, particularly millennials and Generation Z, who are highly dependent on technology for trip planning and experiences (Setiawan et al., 2018). Digital nomadism exemplifies a shift in mobility, where professionals work while traveling, highlighting the interplay between work and leisure in travel choices (Hannonen, 2022). The integration of digital technology in decision-making processes has transformed how tourists select destinations, with online information and social media playing pivotal roles (Vila et al., 2024). Research identifies distinct profiles of digital tourists based on their technology use, revealing varying behaviours and expectations that can inform marketing strategies (Reverte & Solis, 2019). Digital travellers, particularly Digital Natives, play a crucial role in shaping the modern travel landscape. This generation, which has grown up with digital technologies, is at the forefront of transformations in how travel information and services are accessed and utilized (Vercic & Vercic, 2013; Autenrieth, 2014). The emergence of the Internet travel market has enabled these travellers to interact directly with travel services, bypassing traditional intermediaries like travel agents. Moreover, the rise of user-created travel information highlights a significant shift in resource utilization, as peer-generated content increasingly influences travel decisions (Gasser & Simun, 2010). Social media has become a vital source of information for travellers, with substantial representation in search engine results for travel-related queries, further emphasizing its relevance in the digital travel domain (Xiang & Gretzel, 2020). Tourism businesses must adapt their marketing strategies to cater to these tech-savvy consumers, focusing on digital marketing techniques, smartphone compatibility, and social media engagement (Ra iu & Purcărea, 2015; Starcevic & Konjikušić, 2018). The rise of digital travelers has led to a shift away from traditional marketing methods, with millennials preferring mobile applications, digital influencers, and personalized experiences that can be shared instantly on social networks (Paula, 2015). The future of digital tourism involves emerging technologies like virtual reality, augmented reality, and artificial intelligence, which are revolutionizing travel experiences and destination marketing (Sivarethinamohan, 2023). Space tourism and ocean depth tourism are anticipated to become new frontiers, with companies like Virgin Galactic and SpaceX leading the way (Dubey, 2017). As the industry evolves, personalization, sustainability, and seamless digital experiences will become increasingly important, necessitating collaboration among stakeholders to meet the changing demands of digital travelers (Sivarethinamohan, 2023).

*Table 1. Timeline of Digital Travelling*

| Era | Year | Authors | Description |
|---|---|---|---|
| **1980s-1990s: The Dawn of Online Travel** | 1980 | (Labunska et al., 2022) (Wang, 2010) | Introduction of Global Distribution Systems (GDS) like Sabre and Amadeus, primarily used by travel agents for booking flights and accommodations. |
| | 1990 | (Vinod, 2024) (Cheung, 2012) | Launch of Expedia and Travelocity, among the first online travel agencies (OTAs), allowing travellers to book flights and hotels online. |

continued on following page

*Table 1. Continued*

| Era | Year | Authors | Description |
|---|---|---|---|
| **2000s:**<br>**The Rise of OTAs and Travel Search Engines** | 2001 | (Alaimo et al., 2020)<br>(Tuominen, 2011) | Launch of TripAdvisor, which revolutionized travel with user-generated reviews and ratings. |
| | 2004 | (Yang & Hsu, 2016) | Google introduces Google Maps, making navigation and location-based services more accessible. |
| | 2008 | (Dolnicar, 2021) | Launch of Airbnb, changing the landscape of accommodation by offering peer-to-peer lodging options. |
| **2010s:**<br>**Mobile Revolution and Social Media Influence** | 2010 | (Gon, 2020) | Instagram is launched, becoming a key platform for travel inspiration and sharing experiences. |
| | 2013 | (Schneider, 2017) | Launch of Uber and other ride-sharing apps, offering convenient transportation options in cities worldwide. |
| | 2015 | (Buhalis & Cheng, 2019) | Introduction of chatbots and AI-powered assistants by OTAs, providing personalized travel recommendations and booking assistance. |
| **2020s:**<br>**The Era of Hyper-Personalization and Immersive Experiences** | 2020 | (Zhu & Cheng, 2021)<br>(Zhang & Qiu, 2022) | COVID-19 accelerates the adoption of virtual tours and online travel experiences, with platforms like Airbnb offering virtual experiences. |
| | 2021 | (Guo et al., 2024) | AI and big data are increasingly used for hyper-personalized travel recommendations, offering tailored experiences based on user behaviour and preferences. |
| | 2022 | (Balasubramanian et al., 2022)<br>(Bigne & Maturana, 2022) | Growing integration of Augmented Reality (AR) and Virtual Reality (VR) in travel, allowing travelers to preview destinations and accommodations before booking. |

Source: Author's Construction Based on Review of Literature

## II. REVIEW OF LITERATURE

### 1. Evolution of the Digital Traveller: From Web to Mobile

The evolution of digital travel has transformed the tourism industry, shifting from traditional travel agents to tech-savvy travellers who plan and share their experiences online (Barbosa & Medaglia, 2020). The emergence of smartphones, social networks, and geolocation devices has empowered travellers to become more autonomous and collaborative (Barbosa & Medaglia, 2020). This digital transformation has given rise to the "tourist 3.0" or "Adprosumer," presenting new challenges and opportunities for law and economics (Granell, 2018). The integration of technologies like virtual reality, augmented reality, and artificial intelligence has revolutionized travel planning and experiences (Sivarethinamohan, 2023). Wearable technology devices, such as smartwatches and augmented reality glasses, are further enhancing the travel experience by providing real-time information and transforming destination management (Conyette, 2015). However, this digital environment also raises concerns about trust, security, and consumer protection, necessitating adaptations in legal frameworks and increased education for travelers (Granell, 2018).

## 2. The Role of Social Media in Travel Decision-Making

Social media plays a crucial role in travel decision-making processes, influencing travelers at various stages of trip planning (Dwityas & Briandana, 2017; Chilembwe & Gondwe, 2020). These platforms serve as valuable sources of information, allowing users to access user-generated content, peer recommendations, and real-time advice (Sharma, 2022). Studies have shown that social media is predominantly used during the information search stage and for post-trip experience sharing (Matikiti-Manyevere, 2019). The interactive nature of social media enables travelers to make more informed choices and optimize their travel experiences (Sharma, 2022). Research indicates that 92% of travelers make bookings or modify travel plans based on social media alerts (Chilembwe & Gondwe, 2020). Furthermore, social media sites are now considered among the most reliable sources of information, second only to recommendations from family and friends (Matikiti-Manyevere, 2019). This trend highlights the importance for tourism businesses to maintain an active presence on social media platforms to connect with potential customers.

## 3. Personalization in Digital Travel Marketing

Personalization in digital travel marketing leverages artificial intelligence (AI) and machine learning to create tailored experiences for travellers based on their individual preferences and behaviours (Ivanova & Vovchanska, 2023; Bhaskaraputra et al., 2022). This approach allows travel companies to offer more meaningful journeys and improve customer service, potentially increasing competitiveness (Ivanova & Vovchanska, 2023). Personalization strategies include segmentation, retargeting, and customized advertising (Ivanova & Vovchanska, 2023; Phillips-Wren & Wygant, 2010). However, the personalization-privacy paradox presents a challenge, as travelers weigh the benefits of personalized content against privacy concerns (Lei et al., 2022). Successful implementation of personalization involves understanding customer data, measuring relevant metrics, and delivering customized experiences (Phillips-Wren & Wygant, 2010). As technology advances, personalization in travel marketing is expected to integrate further into mobile applications, platforms, and voice assistants, offering innovative ways for travelers to plan and experience their trips (Ivanova & Vovchanska, 2023).

## 4. Impact of Mobile Apps on the Traveler's Journey

Mobile apps have significantly impacted travelers' journeys across all phases, from inspiration to post-travel (Cunha, 2019). These apps influence how tourists plan, experience, and share feedback about their trips, particularly among tech-savvy Millennials (Cunha, 2019). The adoption of travel apps is driven by users' innovation and individuality, with favorable usage attitudes leading to positive usage intentions (Rajora, 2022). Activity theory provides a framework for analyzing the impact of specific apps on travel behavior, highlighting the importance of examining individual applications rather than broad ICT categories (Ettema, 2017). Apps like WhatsApp and travel feedback tools have diverse effects on travel, with varying degrees of intentionality and potential for further development (Ettema, 2017). The growing reliance on mobile devices has made travel apps increasingly important for tasks such as checking hotel status, converting currencies, and accessing location-based services (Schaefer, 2016).

## 5. Virtual Reality (VR) and Augmented Reality (AR) as Emerging Tools in Travel Marketing

Virtual Reality (VR) and Augmented Reality (AR) have emerged as powerful tools in tourism marketing, offering innovative ways for businesses to engage with consumers (Ulusoy, 2024). These technologies provide immersive experiences, enhancing accessibility and marketing strategies in the tourism industry (Ozdemir, 2021). VR and AR applications in tourism span various sectors, including hotels, restaurants, and travel providers, demonstrating their versatility and impact (Ulusoy, 2024; Nayyar et al., 2018). While these technologies offer benefits such as reduced marketing costs, gamification strategies, and personalized product development, they also face challenges like high implementation costs and potential security issues (Ozdemir, 2021). Over the past two decades, research on VR and AR in tourism has evolved, with studies focusing on planning, marketing, education, and preservation (Loureiro et al., 2020; Nayyar et al., 2018). As these technologies continue to advance, they are expected to play an increasingly significant role in shaping the future of tourism marketing and experiences.

## III. CHARACTERISTICS OF THE DIGITAL TRAVELLER

### 1. Tech-Savvy and Connected

Digital travellers are deeply integrated into the digital ecosystem, with smart-phones, tablets, and laptops serving as their primary tools for planning and experiencing travel. They rely on apps, social media, and online platforms for real-time updates, information, and communication (Pencarelli, 2020). This constant connectivity enables them to stay informed, make quick decisions, and share their experiences instantly with a global audience.

### 2. Personalization Expectations

Modern digital travellers have high expectations for personalized services and experiences. They prefer travel solutions tailored to their preferences, such as custom itineraries, targeted offers, and recommendations based on past behaviours (Yang et al., 2023). This expectation is driven by their interaction with advanced algorithms and AI tools that suggest personalized content in other aspects of their digital life, making them accustomed to receiving individualized attention (Shin, 2020).

### 3. Social Media Influence

Social media plays a pivotal role in influencing the decisions of digital travellers. Platforms like Instagram, Facebook, and Pinterest are not just sources of inspiration but also powerful tools for decision-making (Dimitriou & AbouElgheit, 2019). User-generated content, reviews, and influencer endorsements heavily shape where, when, and how digital travellers choose to explore. The visual appeal of destinations and experiences shared by peers and influencers can significantly impact their travel choices (Barbe & Neuburger, 2021).

### 4. On-the-Go Planning

Unlike traditional travellers who planned trips well in advance, digital travellers are more spontaneous. They often make travel decisions on the go, relying on real-time information and mobile apps to adjust their plans (Tanti & Buhalis, 2017). This flexibility is facilitated by access to instant booking options, live updates on transportation, accommodation availability, and dynamic recommendations based on their current location (Tavana et al., 2020).

These characteristics define the modern digital traveller, making it essential for marketers to adapt strategies that cater to their connected, personalized, and on-the-go lifestyle.

*Figure 1. Characteristics of the Digital Traveller*

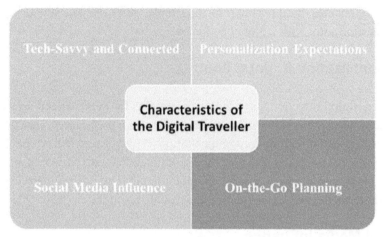

*Source: Author's Construction Based on Review of Literature*

## IV. DIGITAL TOOLS AND PLATFORMS IN TOURISM MARKETING

### 1. Social Media Platforms

Social media platforms such as Instagram, Facebook, and TikTok have become central to engaging digital travellers. These platforms are used not only for inspiration but also for sharing travel experiences (Kalinic & Vujicic, 2022). Instagram, with its visual appeal, allows travellers to explore destinations through photos and videos, often leading to spontaneous travel decisions (Egger, 2019). Facebook offers community-based engagement, where travellers can join groups, participate in discussions, and read reviews (Pham & Tran, 2014). TikTok, with its short, engaging videos, is increasingly influencing younger travellers by showcasing unique destinations and travel hacks (Cheng et al., 2023). The interactive nature of these platforms enables marketers to create campaigns that resonate with specific audience segments, driving higher engagement and conversion rates.

## 2. Travel Apps and Websites

Apps like Airbnb, TripAdvisor, and Google Travel are essential tools for modern travellers, influencing their decisions at every stage of the journey. Airbnb provides access to unique accommodations, often preferred by those seeking personalized and local experiences (Li et al., 2019). TripAdvisor offers a wealth of user-generated reviews and rankings, helping travellers make informed choices about hotels, restaurants, and activities (Garner & Kim, 2022). Google Travel consolidates information on flights, accommodations, and itineraries, offering a seamless planning experience (Dumbliauskas et al., 2017). These platforms also integrate features like real-time updates, price comparisons, and personalized recommendations, making them indispensable for digital travellers.

## 3. AI and Chatbots

AI-driven chatbots are increasingly being used in tourism marketing to provide real-time customer service and personalized recommendations (Antony & Kannan, 2024). These chatbots can handle inquiries, make bookings, and offer tailored suggestions based on a traveller's preferences and past behaviour. For instance, a chatbot might recommend a specific hotel or tour based on the traveller's search history and preferences (Khneyzer et al., 2024). The 24/7 availability of chatbots ensures that travellers receive immediate assistance, enhancing customer satisfaction and streamlining the booking process.

## 4. Influencer Marketing

Influencers play a significant role in promoting destinations and experiences to digital travellers. By sharing their travel experiences on social media, influencers can create a sense of authenticity and trust that traditional advertising often lacks (Pop et al., 2021). They can showcase lesser-known destinations, niche experiences, and local cultures, encouraging their followers to explore beyond popular tourist spots (Bastrygina et al., 2024). Marketers collaborate with influencers to reach targeted demographics, creating campaigns that align with the influencer's style and audience

(Ozuem & Willis, 2022). This strategy is particularly effective in reaching younger travellers who rely heavily on social media for travel inspiration and advice.

These digital tools and platforms are crucial in shaping the travel decisions and experiences of today's tech-savvy tourists, making them central to effective tourism marketing strategies.

*Figure 2. Social Media Engagement Funnel*

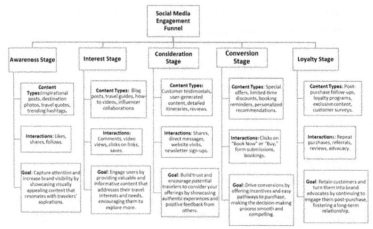

*Source: Author's Construction Based on Review of Literature*

## V. EFFECTIVE MARKETING STRATEGIES FOR DIGITAL TRAVELERS

1.  Personalization through Data Analytics

Businesses can leverage big data to create personalized marketing campaigns tailored to the preferences and behaviours of individual travellers (Vecchio et al., 2018). By analysing data from past bookings, searches, social media interactions, and demographic information, companies can deliver targeted ads, personalized emails, and customized recommendations (Minazzi, 2015). This not only increases the relevance of marketing messages but also enhances the overall customer experience, leading to higher engagement and conversion rates.

2.  Content Marketing

Content is king in the digital age, especially for attracting and engaging digital travellers. Creating high-quality, visually appealing content that resonates with travellers' aspirations and interests is crucial (Ghaderi et al., 2023). This includes blog posts, travel guides, videos, and social media posts that highlight destinations, experiences, and travel tips. Storytelling plays a significant role in content marketing, helping brands connect with their audience on an emotional level (Kang et al., 2020). The content should be not only informative but also shareable, encouraging travellers to engage with and distribute it across their networks.

3. User-Generated Content (UGC)

Encouraging travellers to share their experiences online—whether through social media posts, reviews, or photos—can significantly boost a brand's visibility and credibility (Barreto et al., 2020). UGC serves as authentic, real-world endorsements of a brand, often carrying more weight with potential customers than traditional advertising. Marketers can amplify UGC by featuring it on their own platforms, creating a sense of community and trust (Daugherty et al., 2008). Running campaigns that incentivize UGC, such as photo contests or hashtag challenges, can further increase participation and brand exposure.

4. SEO (Search Engine Optimization) and SEM (Search Engine Marketing)

Optimizing content for search engines is essential to capturing the attention of digital travellers who rely heavily on search engines for travel planning. SEO (Search Engine Optimization) ensures that content ranks high in organic search results, making it more likely to be discovered by potential travellers (Konidaris & Koustoumpardi, 2017). SEM (Search Engine Marketing), which includes paid search ads, can complement SEO efforts by targeting specific keywords and demographics (Panchal et al., 2021). Effective use of SEO and SEM can drive traffic to a brand's website or social media channels, increasing the chances of conversion.

5. Virtual Reality (VR) and Augmented Reality (AR)

VR and AR are cutting-edge technologies that can create immersive and interactive experiences, attracting digital travellers who seek innovative and engaging ways to explore destinations (Rane et al., 2023). VR can offer virtual tours of hotels, resorts, and tourist attractions, allowing travellers to experience a destination before booking (McLean & Barhorst, 2021). AR can enhance the in-destination experience, providing real-time information, navigation, and interactive elements through smartphones or AR glasses (Han et al., 2019). These technologies not only captivate potential travellers but also differentiate a brand in a competitive market.

These strategies are essential for effectively engaging today's tech-savvy and connected travellers, ensuring that marketing efforts are not only visible but also relevant and impactful.

## VI. FUTURE TRENDS IN MARKETING TO DIGITAL TRAVELERS

Digital marketing is transforming the tourism industry, with emerging technologies disrupting traditional approaches (Mpotaringa & Tichaawa, 2021). Future trends include artificial intelligence, block chain, and big data, with augmented reality showing particular promise in tourism (Kostin, 2018). Marketers must adapt to these changes, offering personalized experiences across multiple channels and devices to remain competitive (Paula, 2015). Millennials, as digital natives, are driving this transformation. They are technologically proficient, price-sensitive, and rely heavily on social media and digital influencers for travel decisions (Starcevic & Konjikusic, 2018). To effectively reach these digital travellers, tourism organizations need to adopt integrated approaches to revenue management, focus on lifetime customer value, and provide engaging experiences in travellers' preferred languages and plat-forms (Paula, 2015). Understanding and adapting to these digital trends is crucial for tourism marketers to succeed in the evolving digital landscape (Mpotaringa & Tichaawa, 2021). There is a growing demand for eco-friendly travel options, with consumers increasingly seeking responsible tourism practices (Suryani, 2024). Trav-elers are prioritizing authentic local experiences, which startups are capitalizing on by offering tailored services that meet these desires (Krupenna, 2022). Leveraging social media influencers is becoming a vital strategy for destinations to reach diverse audiences effectively. The use of analytics for targeted campaigns is enhancing marketing effectiveness, allowing for precise audience engagement (Mustafa et al., 2024). While these trends indicate a shift towards a more integrated and personalized approach to marketing, challenges such as data privacy and the need for sustainable practices remain critical considerations for the industry moving forward.

## VII. CONCLUSION

As the travel industry continues to evolve in the digital age, understanding and effectively engaging the modern digital traveler has become crucial for success. Today's travelers are tech-savvy, constantly connected, and demand personalized experiences that cater to their unique preferences and needs. To capture the attention of these travelers, businesses must leverage a combination of data-driven personalization, compelling content, and innovative technologies like AI, VR, and AR.

The policy implications emphasize the need for regulations that protect consumer data privacy while allowing businesses to leverage big data for personalized marketing. Policies should promote transparency in how data is collected and used, ensuring travellers' trust. Additionally, guidelines for ethical marketing practices, particularly in influencer marketing and UGC (User-Generated Content), are crucial to prevent misleading content. Environmental policies that promote sustainable tourism need to be in sync with marketing approaches that meet the increasing interest in eco-friendly travel to ensure the long term sustainability of the industry.

Social media platforms and user-generated content play a vital role in shaping travel decisions, with influencers driving significant impact. At the same time, the importance of optimizing content for search engines and utilizing mobile apps and websites cannot be overstated, as these tools guide travellers through every stage of their journey, from inspiration to booking. Looking ahead, the future of travel marketing will be shaped by trends such as AI and machine learning, block chain technology, and a growing emphasis on sustainability. Businesses that adapt to these trends and embrace the changing landscape will not only attract and retain digital travellers but also build stronger, more sustainable brands.

In conclusion, the key to successfully engaging today's digital travellers lies in a holistic approach that combines technology, personalization, and ethical considerations. By staying attuned to the needs and behaviours of these travellers, businesses can create meaningful connections that drive both customer satisfaction and long-term success.

# REFERENCES

Alaimo, C., Kallinikos, J., & Venegas, E. V. (2020). *Platform Evolution: A Study of TripAdvisor*. Scholarspace.manoa.hawaii.edu. DOI: 10.24251/HICSS.2020.672

Andrade, S. C., & Mason, H. (2009). Digital Imaging Trek: A Practical Model for Managing the Demand of the Digitally Enabled Traveller. In Pease, W., Michelle, M., & Cooper, M. (Eds.), *Information and Communication Technologies in Support of the Tourism Industry* (pp. 475–498). IGI Global., DOI: 10.4018/978-1-60566-088-2.ch027

Antony, P., & Kannan, R. (2024). Revolutionizing the Tourism Industry through Artificial Intelligence: A Comprehensive Review of AI Integration, Impact on Customer Experience, Operational Efficiency, and Future Trends. *International Journal for Multidimensional Research Perspectives, 2*(2), 01-14. https://www.ch andigarhphilosophers.com/index.php/ijmrp/article/view/115

Autenrieth, U. (2014). The "Digital Natives" present their children – An analysis of the increasing (self-) visualization of family and childhood in online environments. *Studies in Communication Sciences*, 14(2), 99–107. DOI: 10.1016/j.scoms.2014.12.006

Balasubramanian, K., Kunasekaran, P., Konar, R., & Sakkthivel, A. M. (2022). Integration of Augmented Reality (AR) and Virtual Reality (VR) as Marketing Communications Channels in the Hospitality and Tourism Service Sector. In O. Adeola, R. E. Hinson, & A. M. Sakkthivel (Eds.), *Marketing Communications and Brand Development in Emerging Markets Volume II* (pp. 55–79). Springer International Publishing. DOI: 10.1007/978-3-030-95581-6_3

Barbe, D., & Neuburger, L. (2021). Generation Z and Digital Influencers in the Tourism Industry. In Stylos, N., Rahimi, R., Okumus, B., & Williams, S. (Eds.), *Generation Z Marketing and Management in Tourism and Hospitality.*, DOI: 10.1007/978-3-030-70695-1_7

Barbosa, D. P., & Medaglia, J. (2020). Tecnologia digital, turismo e os hábitos de consumo dos viajantes contemporâneos. *Marketing & Tourism Review*, 4(2). Advance online publication. DOI: 10.29149/mtr.v4i2.5394

Barreto, J. J., Rubio, N., Campo, S., & Molinillo, S. (2020). Linking the online destination brand experience and brand credibility with tourists' behavioral intentions toward a destination. *Tourism Management*, 79, 104101. DOI: 10.1016/j.tourman.2020.104101

Bastrygina, T., Lim, W. M., Jopp, R., & Weissmann, M. A. (2024). Unraveling the power of social media influencers: Qualitative insights into the role of Instagram influencers in the hospitality and tourism industry. *Journal of Hospitality and Tourism Management*, 58, 214–243. DOI: 10.1016/j.jhtm.2024.01.007

Bhaskaraputra, A., Sutojo, F., Ramadhan, A. N., & Gunawan, A. A. S. (2022). Systematic Literature Review on Solving Personalization Problem in Digital Marketing using Machine Learning and Its Impact. *IEEE Xplore*, 178–182, 178–182. Advance online publication. DOI: 10.1109/iSemantic55962.2022.9920387

Bigne, E., & Maturana, P. (2022). Does Virtual Reality Trigger Visits and Booking Holiday Travel Packages? *Cornell Hospitality Quarterly*, 64(2), 193896552211023. DOI: 10.1177/19389655221102386

Buhalis, D., & Cheng, E. S. Y. (2019). Exploring the Use of Chatbots in Hotels: Technology Providers' Perspective. In Neidhardt, J., & Worndl, W. (Eds.), *Information and Communication Technologies in Tourism 2020* (pp. 231–242)., DOI: 10.1007/978-3-030-36737-4_19

Cheng, W., Tian, R., & Chiu, D. K. W. (2023). Travel vlogs influencing tourist decisions: Information preferences and gender differences. *Aslib Journal of Information Management*, 76(1), 86–103. Advance online publication. DOI: 10.1108/AJIM-05-2022-0261

Cheung, W. (2012, June 4). *Trends in Travel Technology*. Handle.net. http://hdl.handle.net/10214/3696

Chilembwe, J. M., & Gondwe, F. W. (2020). Role of Social Media in Travel Planning and Tourism Destination Decision Making. In Ramos, C. M. Q., de Almeida, C. R., & Fernandes, P. O. (Eds.), *Handbook of Research on Social Media Applications for the Tourism and Hospitality Sector* (pp. 36–51). IGI Global., DOI: 10.4018/978-1-7998-1947-9.ch003

Conyette, M. (2015). 21 Century Travel using Websites, Mobile and Wearable Technology Devices. *Athens Journal of Tourism*, 2(2), 105–116. DOI: 10.30958/ajt.2-2-3

Cunha, M. (2019). The tourism journey, from inspiration to post-travel phase, and the mobile technologies. *African Journal of Hospitality, Tourism and Leisure*, 8(5). https://www.ajhtl.com/uploads/7/1/6/3/7163688/article_1_vol_8_5__2019_portugal.pdf

Daugherty, T., Eastin, M. S., & Bright, L. (2008). Exploring Consumer Motivations for Creating User-Generated Content. *Journal of Interactive Advertising*, 8(2), 16–25. DOI: 10.1080/15252019.2008.10722139

Dimitriou, C. K., & AbouElgheit, E. (2019). Understanding generation Z's travel social decision-making. *Tourism and Hospitality Management*, 25(2), 311–334. DOI: 10.20867/thm.25.2.4

Dolnicar, S. (2021). *Airbnb before, during and after COVID-19*. The University of Queensland., DOI: 10.14264/ab59afd

Dubey, A. K. (2017). Future Technology and Service Industry: A Case study of Travel and Tourism Industry. *Global Journal of Enterprise Information System*, 8(3), 65. DOI: 10.18311/gjeis/2016/15742

Dumbliauskas, V., Grigonis, V., & Barauskas, A. (2017). Application of Google-based Data for Travel Time Analysis: Kaunas City Case Study. *PROMET - Traffic&Transportation*, 29(6), 613–621. DOI: 10.7307/ptt.v29i6.2369

Dwityas, N., & Briandana, R. (2017). Social Media in Travel Decision Making Process. *International Journal of Humanities and Social Science*, 7(7). https://www.ijhssnet.com/journals/Vol_7_No_7_July_2017/24.pdf

Egger, K. (2019). Bachelor Thesis *Instagram's Impact on Destination Choice in Tourism: A critical perspective*. https://www.kaernten-digital.at/files/content/04-News/Bildung/20201123_Digitalisierungsstipendium%20-%20Online%20Verleihung/EGGER%20Kathrin_Bachelorarbeit.pdf

Ettema, D. (2017). Apps, activities and travel: An conceptual exploration based on activity theory. *Transportation*, 45(2), 273–290. DOI: 10.1007/s11116-017-9844-5

Garner, B., & Kim, D. (2022). Analyzing user-generated content to improve customer satisfaction at local wine tourism destinations: An analysis of Yelp and TripAdvisor reviews. *Consumer Behavior in Tourism and Hospitality*, 17(4), 413–435. DOI: 10.1108/CBTH-03-2022-0077

Gasser, U., & Simun, M. (2010). Digital Lifestyle and Online Travel: Looking at the Case of Digital Natives. In Conrady, R., & Buck, M. (Eds.), *Trends and issues in global tourism 2010* (pp. 83–89). Springer Nature., DOI: 10.1007/978-3-642-10829-7_11

Ghaderi, Z., Beal, L., Zaman, M., Hall, C. M., & Rather, R. A. (2023). How does sharing travel experiences on social media improve social and personal ties? *Current Issues in Tourism*, 1–17. DOI: 10.1080/13683500.2023.2266101

Gon, M. (2020). Local experiences on Instagram: Social media data as source of evidence for experience design. *Journal of Destination Marketing & Management*, 19, 100435. DOI: 10.1016/j.jdmm.2020.100435

Granell, V. B. (2018). The tourist 3.0 or adprosumer: a new challenge for the law and the economy. *International Journal of Tourism Law Ridetur*, 2(2), 47–73. DOI: 10.21071/ridetur.v2i2.11518

Guo, Q., Mu, L., & Lou, S. (2024). Revolutionizing travel experiences: An in-depth analysis of intelligent booking systems and behavioral patterns. *Intelligent Decision Technologies*, 18(2), 1–18. DOI: 10.3233/IDT-230625

Han, D.-I. D., Weber, J., Bastiaansen, M., Mitas, O., & Lub, X. (2019). Virtual and Augmented Reality Technologies to Enhance the Visitor Experience in Cultural Tourism. In tom Dieck, M. C., & Jung, T. (Eds.), *Augmented Reality and Virtual Reality* (pp. 113–128). Springer Cham., DOI: 10.1007/978-3-030-06246-0_9

Hannonen, O. (2022). Towards an Understanding of Digital Nomadic Mobilities. *Transfers*, 12(3), 115–126. DOI: 10.3167/TRANS.2022.120310

Ivanova, L., & Vovchanska, O. (2023). Marketing technologies of personalization in tourism based on artificial intelligence. *Business and Management, 39*(4). Advance online publication. Eastern Europe: Economy. DOI: 10.32782/easterneurope.39-4

Kalinic, C., & Vujicic, M. D. (2022). Social Media Analytics: Opportunities and Challenges for Cultural Tourism Destinations. In Oliveira, L. (Ed.), *Digital Communications, Internet of Things, and the Future of Cultural Tourism* (pp. 385–410). IGI Global., https://www.igi-global.com/chapter/social-media-analytics/295514 DOI: 10.4018/978-1-7998-8528-3.ch021

Kang, J., Hong, S., & Hubbard, G. T. (2020). The role of storytelling in advertising: Consumer emotion, narrative engagement level, and word-of-mouth intention. *Journal of Consumer Behaviour*, 19(1), 47–56. DOI: 10.1002/cb.1793

Khneyzer, C., Boustany, Z., & Dagher, J. (2024). AI-Driven Chatbots in CRM: Economic and Managerial Implications across Industries. *Administrative Sciences*, 14(8), 182–182. DOI: 10.3390/admsci14080182

Konidaris, A., & Koustoumpardi, E. (2017). The Importance of Search Engine Optimization for Tourism Websites. In V. Katsoni & K. Velander (Eds.), *Springer Proceedings in Business and Economics* (pp. 205–218). Springer Cham; Researchgate. DOI: 10.1007/978-3-319-67603-6_15

Kostin, K. (2018). Foresight of the global digital trends. *Strategic Management*, 23(2), 11–19. DOI: 10.5937/StraMan1801011K

Krupenna, I. (2022). Marketing digital tools from startup projects in the tourism and travel industry. *Proceedings of Scientific Works of Cherkasy State Technological University Series Economic Sciences*, 67(67), 24–31. DOI: 10.24025/2306-4420.67.2022.278790

Kumar, N. P., Dubey, N. S., & Kumar, A. (2022). A Review on Smart and Intelligent Techniques for Digital Tourism. *International Journal of Scientific Research in Computer Science Engineering and Information Technology*, 8(6), 617–624. DOI: 10.32628/CSEIT228651

Labunska, S., Zyma, O., & Sushchenko, S. (2022). The use of information systems as a way to ensure interaction between small and big tourism enterprises. *Access Journal - Access to Science, Business. Innovation in the Digital Economy*, 3(1), 16–28. DOI: 10.46656/access.2021.3.1(2)

Lei, S. S. I., Chan, I. C. C., Tang, J., & Ye, S. (2022). Will tourists take mobile travel advice? Examining the personalization-privacy paradox. *Journal of Hospitality and Tourism Management*, 50, 288–297. DOI: 10.1016/j.jhtm.2022.02.007

Li, J., Hudson, S., & So, K. K. F. (2019). Exploring the customer experience with Airbnb. *International Journal of Culture, Tourism and Hospitality Research*, 13(4), 410–429. DOI: 10.1108/IJCTHR-10-2018-0148

Loureiro, S. M. C., Guerreiro, J., & Ali, F. (2020). 20 years of research on virtual reality and augmented reality in tourism context: A text-mining approach. *Tourism Management*, 77, 104028. DOI: 10.1016/j.tourman.2019.104028

Mancinelli, F. (2022). Digital Nomads. In Buhalis, D. (Ed.), *Encyclopedia of Tourism Management and Marketing* (pp. 957–960). Edward Elgar Publishing., https://www.elgaronline.com/display/book/9781800377486/b-9781800377486.digital.nomads.xml DOI: 10.4337/9781800377486.digital.nomads

Manyevere, R. M., & Kruger, M. (2019). The role of social media sites in trip planning and destination decision-making processes. *African Journal of Hospitality, Tourism and Leisure*, 8(5). https://www.ajhtl.com/uploads/7/1/6/3/7163688/article_3_vol_8_5__2019_cut.pdf

McLean, G., & Barhorst, J. B. (2021). Living the Experience Before You Go . . . but Did It Meet Expectations? The Role of Virtual Reality during Hotel Bookings. *Journal of Travel Research*, 61(6), 004728752110283. DOI: 10.1177/00472875211028313

Minazzi, R. (2015). *Social Media Marketing in Tourism and Hospitality*. Springer International Publishing., DOI: 10.1007/978-3-319-05182-6

Mpotaringa, M. C., & Tichaawa, T. (2021). Tourism Digital Marketing Tools and Views on Future Trends: A Systematic Review of Literature. *African Journal of Hospitality, Tourism and Leisure*, 10(2), 712–726. DOI: 10.46222/ajhtl.19770720-128

Raji, M. A., Olodo, H. B., Oke, T. T., Addy, W. A., Ofodile, O. C., & Oyewole, A. T. (2024). Digital marketing in tourism: A review of practices in the USA and Africa. *International Journal of Applied Research in Social Sciences*, 6(3), 393–408.

Nayyar, A., Mahapatra, B., Nhuong Le, D., & Suseendran, G. (2018). Virtual Reality (VR) & Augmented Reality (AR) technologies for tourism and hospitality industry. *International Journal of Engineering & Technology, 7*(2.21), 156. DOI: 10.14419/ijet.v7i2.21.11858

Ozdemir, M. A. (2021). Virtual Reality (VR) and Augmented Reality (AR) Technologies for Accessibility and Marketing in the Tourism Industry. In C. Eusebio, L. Teixeira, & M. J. Carneiro (Eds.), *ICT Tools and Applications for Accessible Tourism* (pp. 277–301). IGI Global. DOI: 10.4018/978-1-7998-6428-8.ch013

Ozucm, W., & Willis, M. (2022). Influcnccr Markcting. In Ozucm, W., & Willis, M. (Eds.), *Digital Marketing Strategies for Value Co-creation* (pp. 209–242). Springer Nature., DOI: 10.1007/978-3-030-94444-5_10

Panchal, A., Shah, A., & Kansara, K. (2021). Digital Marketing - Search Engine Optimization (SEO) and Search Engine Marketing (SEM). *International Research Journal of Innovations in Engineering and Technology, 5*(12).

Paula, M. (2015). Digital Tourism on the Way to Digital Marketing Success. *Holistic Marketing Management Journal, 5*(2), 30–37. https://ideas.repec.org/a/hmm/journl/v5y2015i2p30-37.html

Pencarelli, T. (2020). The digital revolution in the travel and tourism industry. *Information Technology & Tourism*, 22(3), 455–476. DOI: 10.1007/s40558-019-00160-3

Pham, Q. T., & Tran, T. L. (2014). Customer engagement in a Facebook brand community: An empirical study on travel industry in Vietnam. *2014 IEEE 6th International Conference on Adaptive Science & Technology (ICAST)*, 1–9. DOI: 10.1109/ICASTECH.2014.7068121

Pop, R. A., Saplacan, Z., Dabija, D. C., & Alt, M. A. (2021). The Impact of Social Media Influencers on Travel decisions: The Role of Trust in Consumer Decision Journey. *Current Issues in Tourism*, 25(5), 823–843. DOI: 10.1080/13683500.2021.1895729

Rajora, P. (2022). The impact of mobile applications on tourist behavior in national capital region. *International Journal of Research in Finance and Management*, 5(2), 321–328. DOI: 10.33545/26175754.2022.v5.i2d.258

Rane, N., Choudhary, S., & Rane, J. (2023, October 31). *Sustainable tourism development using leading-edge Artificial Intelligence (AI), Blockchain, Internet of Things (IoT), Augmented Reality (AR) and Virtual Reality (VR) technologies.* Social Science Research Network. DOI: 10.2139/ssrn.4642605

Reverte, F. G., & Solis, D. L. (2019). We Are All Digital Tourists, but Are All Digital Tourists the Same? In de Luna, I. R., Bertran, À. F., Masllorens, J. L., & Cabanillas, F. L. (Eds.), *Sharing Economy and the Impact of Collaborative Consumption* (pp. 263–277). IGI Global., DOI: 10.4018/978-1-5225-9928-9.ch014

Rosa, G. (2023). Digital Traveler: The Use of Modern Information Technologies in Passenger Transport. *European Research Studies*, 26(3), 275–288. DOI: 10.35808/ersj/3211

Schaefer, C. (2016, June 2). Toward Building a Mobile App Experience to Support Users' Mobile Travel Needs. *Proceedings of the 2016 ACM SIGMIS Conference on Computers and People Research.* SIGMIS-CPR '16: 2016 Computers and People Research Conference. DOI: 10.1145/2890602.2906193

Schneider, H. (2017). Uber and Society. *Innovation in Society*, 55–78. DOI: 10.1007/978-3-319-49514-9_3

Setiawan, B., Trisdyani, N. L. P., Adnyana, P. P., Adnyana, I. N., Wiweka, K., & Wulandani, H. R. (2018). The Profile and Behaviour of "Digital Tourists" When Making Decisions Concerning Travelling Case Study: Generation Z in South Jakarta. *Advances in Research*, 17(2), 1–13. DOI: 10.9734/AIR/2018/43872

Sharma, R. (2022). Influence of social media in travel decision making. *REST Journal on Data Analytics and Artificial Intelligence*, 1(3), 42–50. DOI: 10.46632/jdaai/1/3/6

Shin, D. (2020). User Perceptions of Algorithmic Decisions in the Personalized AI System:Perceptual Evaluation of Fairness, Accountability, Transparency, and Explainability. *Journal of Broadcasting & Electronic Media*, 64(4), 1–25. DOI: 10.1080/08838151.2020.1843357

Sivarethinamohan, R. (2023, July 14). Exploring the Transformation of Digital Tourism: Trends, Impacts, and Future Prospects. *2023 International Conference on Digital Applications, Transformation & Economy (ICDATE).* DOI: 10.1109/ICDATE58146.2023.10248691

Starcevic, S., & Konjikusic, S. (2018). Why millenials as digital travelers transformed marketing strategy in tourism industry. *Tourism International Scientific Conference Vrnjačka Banja,* 3(1), 221–240. http://www.tisc.rs/proceedings/index.php/hitmc/article/view/12

Suryani, W. (2024). New Trends in Consumer and Tourism Marketing Science. In Tarnanidis, T. K., & Sklavounos, N. (Eds.), *New Trends in Marketing and Consumer Science*. IGI Global. DOI: 10.4018/979-8-3693-2754-8.ch015

Tanti, A., & Buhalis, D. (2017). The influences and consequences of being digitally connected and/or disconnected to travellers. *Information Technology & Tourism*, 17(1), 121–141. DOI: 10.1007/s40558-017-0081-8

Tavana, M., Mousavi, S. M. H., Mina, H., & Salehian, F. (2020). A dynamic decision support system for evaluating peer-to-peer rental accommodations in the sharing economy. *International Journal of Hospitality Management*, 91, 102653. DOI: 10.1016/j.ijhm.2020.102653

Tjostheim, I., & Waterworth, J. A. (2023). Digital Travel – A Study of Travellers' Views of a Digital Visit to Mexico. *Information Technology and Systems*, 1, 185–194. DOI: 10.1007/978-3-031-33258-6_17

Tuominen, P. (2011). *The Influence of TripAdvisor Consumer-Generated Travel Reviews on Hotel Performance*. Uhra.herts.ac.uk. https://uhra.herts.ac.uk/handle/ 2299/7612

Ulusoy, S. (2024). The use of augmented reality (ar) and virtual reality (vr) in tourism marketing. *Bulletin of Dulaty University*, 14(2), 212–225. DOI: 10.55956/XRLV7458

Vecchio, P. D., Mele, G., Ndou, V., & Secundo, G. (2018). Creating value from Social Big Data: Implications for Smart Tourism Destinations. *Information Processing & Management*, 54(5), 847–860. DOI: 10.1016/j.ipm.2017.10.006

Vercic, A. T., & Vercic, D. (2013). Digital natives and social media. *Public Relations Review*, 39(5), 600–602. DOI: 10.1016/j.pubrev.2013.08.008

Vila, N. A., Cardoso, L., Archi, Y. E., & Fraiz, A. (2024). The Role of Digital Technology and Sustainable Practices in Tourists' Decision Making. In Archi, Y. E., Benbba, B., David, L. D., & Cardoso, L. (Eds.), *Promoting Responsible Tourism With Digital Platforms* (pp. 36–59). IGI Global., DOI: 10.4018/979-8-3693-3286-3.ch003

Vinod, B. (2024). Origins of Online Travel Agencies. In *Mastering the Travel Intermediaries* (pp. 329–341). Springer Nature., DOI: 10.1007/978-3-031-51524-8_10

Wang, Z. (2010). A preliminary study of the Global Distribution Systems (GDS'). *IEEE Xplore*, 60–63, 60–63. Advance online publication. DOI: 10.1109/ ICIME.2010.5478307

Wren, G. P., & Wygant, J. (2010). Influencing Consumer Decisions Through Personalization. *Proceedings of F 15th IFIP WG8.3 International Conference, ISBN 978-1-60750-576-1*, 152–162.

Xiang, Z., & Gretzel, U. (2020). Role of Social Media in Online Travel Information Search. *Tourism Management*, 31(2), 179–188. DOI: 10.1016/j.tourman.2009.02.016

Xiao, Y., & Lutz, C. (2024). Wayfarers in Cyberspace: A Temporal Investigation of Digital Nomads Based on Liquid Modernity Theory. *Journal of Travel Research*, 0(0), 00472875231224242. Advance online publication. DOI: 10.1177/00472875231224242

Yang, S.-Y., & Hsu, C.-L. (2016). A location-based services and Google maps-based information master system for tour guiding. *Computers & Electrical Engineering*, 54, 87–105. DOI: 10.1016/j.compeleceng.2015.11.020

Yang, X., Zhang, L., & Zhou, F. (2023). Personalized Tourism Recommendations and the E-Tourism User Experience. *Journal of Travel Research*, 63(5), 1183–1200. Advance online publication. DOI: 10.1177/00472875231187332

Zhang, J., & Qiu, H. (2022). Window to the Destination: Tourists' Local Experience via "Online Experiences" on Airbnb Amid the Pandemic. In Stienmetz, J. L., Rosell, B. F., & Massimo, D. (Eds.), *Information and Communication Technologies in Tourism 2022* (pp. 310–315)., DOI: 10.1007/978-3-030-94751-4_28

Zhu, J., & Cheng, M. (2021). The rise of a new form of virtual tour: Airbnb peer-to-peer online experience. *Current Issues in Tourism*, 25(22), 1–6. DOI: 10.1080/13683500.2021.2016662

# Chapter 4
# From Data to Destination:
## How Digital Traces Can Be Transformed Into Targeted Marketing Campaigns for Tourists

**Bassam Samir Al-Romeedy**

*Faculty of Tourism and Hotels, University of Sadat City, Egypt*

**Amrik Singh**
https://orcid.org/0000-0003-3598-8787
*School of Hotel Management and Tourism, Lovely Professional University, India*

## ABSTRACT

*In today's digital era, the tourism industry is undergoing a major transformation as it shifts from traditional marketing techniques to data-driven strategies that leverage the vast amounts of digital information generated by travelers. This chapter delves into how the digital footprints left by travelers—such as search histories, social media interactions, online bookings, and mobile app usage—can be effectively utilized to craft personalized and impactful marketing campaigns. It covers the entire process, from the collection and management of these digital traces to their analysis, emphasizing the importance of advanced technologies like artificial intelligence and big data analytics in converting raw data into actionable insights. These insights empower tourism businesses to anticipate traveler behavior, customize marketing messages, and engage with customers in a more personalized and meaningful manner.*

DOI: 10.4018/979-8-3693-3972-5.ch004

# INTRODUCTION

The tourism industry has experienced a significant transformation in recent years, largely due to the widespread adoption of digital technologies. Traditional marketing approaches, once the foundation of tourism promotion, are increasingly being replaced by data-driven strategies that utilize the vast digital information generated by contemporary travelers. This shift is part of a broader trend across various industries, where the ability to collect, analyze, and utilize data has become a key competitive advantage. In tourism, the digital footprints left by travelers—often referred to as digital traces—provide valuable insights that can be leveraged to develop highly targeted and effective marketing campaigns (Gaafar & Al-Romeedy, 2024a; Singh et al., 2023).

Digital traces refer to the data left behind by travelers during their interactions with digital platforms, such as searching for destinations, booking accommodations, using travel apps, and sharing experiences on social media. These traces include search histories, social media activities, and app usage, which collectively provide insights into traveler behavior, preferences, and decision-making processes. For tourism businesses, analyzing and utilizing these digital traces is essential for creating personalized and effective customer engagement strategies (Al-Romeedy & Hashem, 2024; Nix & Decker, 2023).

The significance of data in modern tourism marketing is immense. As consumers become increasingly accustomed to personalized experiences in various areas of their lives—such as online shopping, streaming services, and social media—there is a growing expectation that their travel experiences will also be customized to suit their preferences. This expectation has fueled the rise of data-driven marketing, where insights derived from digital traces are used to craft campaigns that resonate with specific segments of the travel market. By analyzing these digital footprints, marketers can detect trends, anticipate future behaviors, and deliver content that is not only relevant but also highly personalized, thereby boosting engagement and driving higher conversion rates (Chaffey & Smith, 2022; Juska, 2021).

The transition from data to destination is not without its obstacles. The vast amount of data generated by travelers can be daunting, and the processes involved in collecting, managing, and analyzing this data demand advanced tools and specialized expertise. Moreover, using personal data for marketing purposes introduces ethical dilemmas, especially concerning privacy and consent. Marketers must carefully balance the need to respect individuals' privacy with the goal of leveraging data for effective marketing strategies (Rachmad, 2024; Gaafar & Al-Romeedy, 2024b).

Despite these hurdles, the potential of data-driven marketing in the tourism sector is significant. When digital traces are skillfully converted into targeted marketing campaigns, the advantages are evident: heightened customer engagement, improved conversion rates, stronger brand loyalty, and a more personalized experience for travelers. In other industries, data-driven approaches have already demonstrated their value, with companies using sophisticated analytics to optimize their marketing efforts and achieve impressive outcomes. The tourism industry, with its abundant data sources and varied customer base, is especially well-suited to benefit from these strategies (Das, 2021; Visser et al., 2021).

The evolution of technology is pivotal in harnessing the potential of digital traces. Tools like AI, machine learning, and big data analytics empower tourism businesses to efficiently process vast datasets, identify patterns, and generate actionable insights with remarkable precision and speed. These technologies also enable real-time marketing, allowing businesses to adapt to travelers' needs and preferences as they change. The ability to predict traveler behavior and deliver personalized marketing messages at the optimal time and through the most effective channels is a transformative advantage for the industry, providing a substantial competitive edge (Al-Romeedy, 2024b; Sultan et al., 2023).

This chapter explores the conversion of digital traces into actionable marketing strategies, focusing on data collection and analysis methodologies, translating insights into marketing actions, and addressing challenges in data-driven tourism marketing. It highlights the importance of leveraging digital footprints to create personalized and impactful campaigns, emphasizing that mastering data-driven marketing is essential for tourism businesses and destination management organizations to stay competitive in the digital market. The chapter aims to equip stakeholders with the knowledge and tools needed to effectively utilize digital data for more successful marketing efforts and stronger connections with modern travelers.

## Digital Traces in Tourism

Digital traces consist of the data and information individuals generate through their interactions with digital platforms. In tourism, these traces arise from travelers' online activities, producing a variety of data points that can be analyzed to reveal insights into tourist behavior and preferences. Understanding these digital traces is crucial for mapping the modern traveler's journey and crafting marketing strategies that align with their needs (Al-Romeedy, 2024a, b). Social media platforms such as Facebook, Instagram, Twitter, and TikTok are significant sources of these digital traces. Travelers frequently share their experiences, post photos, check in at various locations, and interact with travel-related content. This activity provides valuable data on popular destinations, brand interactions, and engaging content. Additionally, social media offers insights into the sentiments and emotions linked to travel experiences, which are essential for gauging consumer satisfaction and expectations (Meyer & Schroeder, 2023; Zhang et al., 2024).

Search engines such as Google, Bing, and Yahoo! play a crucial role for tourists seeking information and planning their trips. The queries tourists enter, such as "best beach destinations," "cheap flights to Paris," or "family-friendly hotels," reveal valuable details about their intentions, preferences, and interests. By analyzing these search behaviors, tourism businesses can gain insights into what potential customers are searching for, detect emerging travel trends, and enhance their online visibility through search engine marketing (SEM) and search engine optimization (SEO) (Kingsnorth, 2022; Meyer & Schroeder, 2023). Additionally, online booking platforms, including OTAs like Expedia and Booking.com, and direct booking websites for airlines, hotels, and tour operators, gather extensive data on booking behaviors. This data includes information on booking dates, lead times, price sensitivity, preferred accommodation types, and travel durations. Understanding these booking patterns enables businesses to tailor their offers and promotions to match tourist behaviors (Fawns et al., 2023; Sultan et al., 2023).

The interaction of tourists with a destination's or business's website is another crucial type of digital trace. Metrics such as page views, time spent on specific pages, click-through rates, and conversion rates reveal which content or services attract the most attention, where users tend to exit, and which site elements are most effective in driving bookings or inquiries. As well, many travelers rely on mobile apps for various aspects of their trips, including booking accommodations, navigating destinations, discovering local attractions, and managing travel itineraries. Data collected from app usage—such as user preferences, in-app behavior, and location information—provides real-time insights into tourists' on-the-go needs and behaviors, facilitating timely and personalized marketing interventions (Al-Romeedy, 2024a; Juska, 2021).

Digital traces offer immense value to the tourism industry by providing a detailed and dynamic view of traveler behavior that traditional data sources cannot match. In an industry where understanding and anticipating consumer preferences is critical for competitiveness, the ability to analyze and leverage these digital footprints is a significant advantage. By examining digital traces, tourism businesses can effectively segment their market, identifying distinct traveler groups based on their online behaviors. This segmentation enables the creation of highly personalized marketing messages and offers tailored to specific segments, such as luxury travelers, budget-conscious tourists, or adventure seekers. Personalization enhances the likelihood of engagement and conversion, as travelers receive content that aligns with their interests and needs (Ohme et al., 2024; Zhang et al., 2024).

The real-time nature of digital traces allows businesses to respond swiftly to shifts in traveler behavior or preferences. For instance, if search data shows a sudden spike in interest for a specific destination or type of experience, businesses can quickly adapt their marketing strategies to leverage this trend. This responsiveness is vital in the dynamic tourism industry, where trends can rapidly emerge and change (Das, 2021; Gaafar & Al-Romeedy, 2024b). Digital traces are also instrumental in enhancing the overall customer experience. By understanding what tourists seek at each stage of their journey—whether it's inspiration during the planning phase or information while traveling—businesses can offer more relevant content, recommendations, and services. This approach not only boosts customer satisfaction but also fosters loyalty, as travelers are more inclined to return to a brand that understands and meets their needs (Chaffey & Smith, 2022; Deiss & Henneberry, 2020).

Moreover, digital traces are essential for grasping the intricate and evolving behaviors of modern tourists. In an era where travelers increasingly use digital platforms to plan, book, and share their travel experiences, these traces provide valuable insights into their preferences, motivations, and decision-making processes. Analyzing digital traces reveals what drives tourist behavior, such as trending destinations from search queries or brand perceptions from social media interactions. Booking data sheds light on factors like price sensitivity, preferred travel times, and booking patterns, which are crucial for developing effective marketing strategies (Khang et al., 2024; Singh et al., 2023).

Analyzing digital traces helps forecast travel trends and preferences, such as a growing interest in sustainable travel, allowing businesses to adjust their offerings to meet emerging demands. By understanding tourists' values and expectations through their digital footprints—generated across search engines, social media, booking platforms, and apps—businesses can refine products and services to align with customer expectations, resulting in higher satisfaction and repeat business (Juska, 2021; Buitrago-Ropero et al., 2023; Nix & Decker, 2023; Al-Romeedy & Hashem, 2024).

Besides, social media and online booking platforms play crucial roles in capturing detailed data on tourists' preferences, influences, and travel behaviors. Engagements like likes, shares, and posts reflect tourists' perceptions, while booking platforms gather insights into practical travel decisions. Mobile apps used during travel offer real-time data on tourist behavior, aiding businesses in delivering timely services. Additionally, tourism-related websites act as key touchpoints for content engagement and bookings. By analyzing these digital interactions, tourism businesses can better understand the traveler's journey, enabling them to craft effective marketing strategies and enhance customer experiences (Holsinger, 2023; Gaafar & Al-Romeedy, 2024a; Kingsnorth, 2022; Fawns et al., 2023).

## SOURCES OF DIGITAL TRACES

Digital traces in the tourism sector are derived from a range of online activities and interactions that travelers engage in throughout their journey, from the initial planning stages to the period after their trip. These digital footprints provide crucial insights into traveler behaviors, preferences, and decision-making patterns, which can be utilized to enhance marketing strategies and service delivery. The following is an examination of the main sources of digital traces within the tourism industry (Zhang et al., 2024; Al-Romeedy, 2024b; Das, 2021):

A- Social media interactions

***Content sharing and engagement***: Social media platforms such as Facebook, Instagram, Twitter, TikTok, and Pinterest are significant sources of digital traces. Travelers use these platforms to share their experiences, upload photos, write reviews, and interact with travel-related content. These activities generate various data points, including likes, comments, shares, and hashtags. Analyzing this data can reveal trends in popular destinations, activities, and overall consumer sentiment. For example, a rise in Instagram posts tagged with a particular destination can signal its growing appeal among certain groups (Khang et al., 2024; Buitrago-Ropero et al., 2023; Juska, 2021).

***Influencer and brand interactions***: Social media also plays a crucial role in the interaction between travelers and influencers or brands. When travelers follow and engage with travel influencers, they leave digital traces that reflect their interests and preferences. Additionally, interactions with branded content, such as promotional posts or sponsored advertisements, provide insights into which marketing messages are effectively capturing audience attention (Al-Romeedy & Hashem, 2024; Meyer & Schroeder, 2023).

B- Search engine queries

***Search behavior and intent***: Search engines such as Google, Bing, and Yahoo! are essential tools for travelers when they begin planning their trips. The search queries they enter, such as "top family resorts," "adventure travel spots," or "affordable flights to Europe," provide clear insights into their travel goals and preferences. By analyzing these search terms, businesses can gain a better understanding of what potential customers are seeking, spot emerging travel trends, and optimize their content to rank well in relevant search results (Fawns et al., 2023; Gaafar & Al-Romeedy, 2024a).

*Paid search and SEO analytics*: In addition to organic search behavior, data from paid search campaigns (PPC) and SEO efforts offer valuable digital traces. Metrics such as click-through rates (CTR), keyword performance, and conversion rates from search ads provide insights into the effectiveness of search strategies. Analyzing these metrics allows marketers to evaluate and refine their targeting strategies to better match user intent (Sultan et al., 2023; Holsinger, 2023; Ohme et al., 2024).

C- Online Bookings

*Booking platforms and behavior*: Online Travel Agencies (OTAs) such as Expedia, Booking.com, and Airbnb, as well as direct booking sites for airlines, hotels, and tour operators, collect a wealth of data on booking behaviors. This data includes details about when travelers make their bookings (lead time), the devices they use (desktop vs. mobile), their choices (room type, amenities, flight class), and their sensitivity to prices. Such information is crucial for understanding the factors that impact travel decisions and for customizing offers and promotions to align with booking patterns (Zhang et al., 2024; Singh et al., 2023).

*Abandoned bookings and re-engagement*: Data from abandoned bookings, where travelers begin but do not complete a reservation, provide significant insights into potential obstacles in the booking process. This data can reveal issues such as pricing concerns, lack of information, or technical problems, helping businesses identify barriers to conversion. Strategies to address these challenges might include sending reminder emails or offering special discounts to encourage users to finalize their bookings (Buitrago-Ropero et al., 2023; Gaafar & Al-Romeedy, 2024b).

D- Mobile App Usage

*In-trip engagement and real-time data:* Travelers increasingly rely on mobile apps for various needs during their trips, such as navigation, discovering local attractions, booking last-minute services, and managing itineraries. The data collected from these app interactions provides real-time insights into travelers' preferences and behaviors while they are traveling. For instance, location-based data can highlight which attractions are frequently visited, while in-app searches can reveal the types of services travelers are actively seeking at that moment (Khang et al., 2024; Al-Romeedy, 2024b).

*Personalization and notifications*: Mobile apps offer valuable opportunities for personalized marketing through features like push notifications and in-app messaging. The data generated from these interactions—such as click-through rates on notifications and responses to in-app promotions—enables businesses to refine their marketing strategies and understand which types of offers are most engaging to users (Das, 2021; Juska, 2021; Deiss & Henneberry, 2020).

E- Website Visits

*User interaction and behavior*: Websites are essential for travelers to research, compare, and book travel services. The digital traces from these interactions include metrics such as page views, time spent on specific pages, navigation paths, and conversion actions like making a booking or subscribing to a newsletter. Analyzing these traces helps businesses identify which content or services are most engaging and where users might be dropping off before completing their intended actions (Al-Romeedy & Hashem, 2024; Sultan et al., 2023; Meyer & Schroeder, 2023).

*A/B testing and optimization:* Websites also gather data through A/B testing, where different versions of a webpage are compared to determine which one performs better in terms of user engagement and conversions. The insights gained from these tests reveal user preferences, such as which headlines, images, or calls-to-action are most effective, allowing businesses to continuously refine and enhance their website's performance (Chaffey & Smith, 2022; Al-Romeedy, 2024a).

## DATA COLLECTION AND PRIVACY CONCERNS

## Methods for Collecting Digital Traces Ethically

*Ethical considerations in digital data collection*: In the digital age, gathering digital traces is essential for understanding tourist behavior and tailoring marketing strategies. However, ensuring that this data is collected ethically is crucial for maintaining trust and adhering to legal standards. Ethical data collection practices involve transparency, obtaining informed consent, and safeguarding user privacy (Buitrago-Ropero et al., 2023; Khang et al., 2024).

*Cookies and web analytics*: A common method for collecting digital traces is through cookies—small text files placed on a user's device by a website. Cookies monitor user activities such as page visits, clicks, and session duration, providing insights into user preferences and behaviors. Ethical use of cookies involves informing users about their use and obtaining consent before placing cookies. This is typically managed through cookie consent banners that allow users to opt in or out of non-essential cookies, including those for marketing or analytics. Web analytics tools, like Google Analytics, also collect data on user demographics, traffic sources, and conversion rates. Ensuring these tools are configured to anonymize data and respect privacy settings is essential (Kingsnorth, 2022; Holsinger, 2023; Fawns et al., 2023).

*Informed consent and transparency*: Informed consent is fundamental to ethical data collection. Tourists must be clearly informed about what data is being collected, how it will be used, and who will have access to it. This information is usually provided through privacy policies or terms of service agreements, which users must acknowledge before their data is collected. Transparent communication about data practices fosters trust and ensures that users make informed decisions regarding their privacy. Additionally, allowing users to opt out of data collection or delete their data enhances ethical data practices (Ohme et al., 2024; Gaafar & Al-Romeedy, 2024a).

*Voluntary data sharing*: Encouraging voluntary data sharing is another ethical approach. Businesses can offer incentives, such as discounts or personalized services, in return for travelers willingly sharing their preferences or travel plans. This approach ensures that data is collected with the user's full knowledge and consent, often resulting in more accurate and relevant information. It is important, however, that the value exchange is clear and users fully understand what they are agreeing to share (Singh et al., 2023; Zhang et al., 2024).

## Methods for Managing and Organizing Large Datasets

## Managing and Organizing Digital Traces

The vast amounts of data generated from digital traces require effective management and organization to be valuable. Proper data management involves using reliable storage solutions and integrating data efficiently to ensure it is accessible, secure, and analyzable (Meyer & Schroeder, 2023; Das, 2021).

*Data storage solutions*: Handling large datasets necessitates scalable and secure storage solutions. Cloud storage is a popular choice due to its flexibility, scalability, and cost-effectiveness. Providers such as Amazon Web Services (AWS), Google Cloud Platform, and Microsoft Azure offer storage options that handle large volumes of data, with features for encryption, backup, and disaster recovery to safeguard against data loss or breaches. For organizations requiring more control over their data, on-premise storage solutions are an alternative. These involve setting up physical servers for local data storage, often incorporating advanced security measures to protect sensitive information (Gaafar & Al-Romeedy, 2024b; Nix & Decker, 2023; Sultan et al., 2023).

*Data integration practices*: Integrating data from diverse sources into a unified dataset is essential for comprehensive analysis. In tourism, where data comes from various platforms like social media, booking engines, and mobile apps, data integration tools such as ETL (Extract, Transform, Load) platforms are used. These tools extract data from multiple sources, transform it into a consistent format, and load it into a centralized data warehouse or database. Effective data integration ensures all relevant data is available for analysis, providing a holistic view of tourist behavior. Metadata management, which documents the data's source, structure, and usage, is also crucial for maintaining data quality and accuracy (Al-Romeedy & Hashem, 2024; Zhang et al., 2024; Fawns et al., 2023).

*Data cleansing and preparation*: Before analysis, data often needs to be cleansed and prepared. Data cleansing involves correcting errors such as duplicate records, missing values, or inconsistencies in formatting to ensure data accuracy and quality. Data preparation may also include aggregating data, normalizing it for consistency, or anonymizing it to protect user privacy. Common tools for this stage include SQL databases, data cleaning software like OpenRefine, and data preparation platforms such as Talend (Das, 2021; Deiss & Henneberry, 2020; Buitrago-Ropero et al., 2023; Nix & Decker, 2023).

## Legal and Ethical Considerations in Data Collection

As the use of digital traces becomes more prevalent, addressing legal and ethical issues is crucial for safeguarding user privacy and maintaining trust (Ohme et al., 2024; Gaafar & Al-Romeedy, 2024a).

*GDPR and data protection regulations*: The General Data Protection Regulation (GDPR) is a leading data protection law in the European Union, setting rigorous standards for personal data handling. It requires that personal data be collected and processed legally, transparently, and for specific purposes. Organizations must ensure data security, avoid retaining data longer than necessary, and obtain explicit user consent. Additionally, users must have the right to access and delete their data, and data breaches must be reported within 72 hours. Similar laws exist in other regions, such as the California Consumer Privacy Act (CCPA) in the United States, which provides rights related to personal information. Adhering to these regulations is essential for legal and ethical data management (Juska, 2021; Meyer & Schroeder, 2023).

*Data anonymization and minimization*: Protecting user privacy often involves anonymizing or minimizing data collection. Anonymization entails removing personal identifiers to prevent individual identification, using techniques like data masking, pseudonymization, and aggregation. Data minimization involves gathering only the data necessary for specific purposes. By limiting data collection and ensuring it is anonymized, organizations can mitigate privacy risks and adhere to legal standards (Kingsnorth, 2022; Buitrago-Ropero et al., 2023; Holsinger, 2023).

*Ethical use of data*: Ethical considerations extend beyond legal compliance. Data should be used to benefit individuals, respect their rights, and avoid exploitation. Practices that manipulate or target users in an invasive or coercive manner are deemed unethical. Organizations must be transparent about data usage and avoid deceptive or misleading practices. Upholding ethical standards helps build user trust and enhances organizational reputation (Meyer & Schroeder, 2023; Al-Romeedy, 2024a).

## ANALYZING DIGITAL TRACES

## Tools and Technologies for Analyzing Tourist Digital Behavior

The rapid technological advancements have empowered the tourism industry to harness the vast amounts of data generated from tourist interactions. Understanding this digital behavior involves using sophisticated analytical techniques to transform raw data into actionable insights. Key technologies crucial to this analytical process include AI, machine learning, sentiment analysis, and data visualization tools (Al-Romeedy, 2024b; Khang et al., 2024).

*Artificial intellig*ence (**AI**): AI plays a pivotal role in analyzing digital traces, enabling the processing of large datasets to uncover insights that manual methods might miss. AI algorithms can simultaneously analyze data from diverse sources like social media, search queries, and booking platforms to provide a holistic view of tourist behavior. For instance, AI can identify patterns in search behavior, recognize popular destinations, and forecast future travel trends. Additionally, AI-driven tools like natural language processing (NLP) can analyze text data from reviews and social media to understand the context and sentiment of tourist feedback. This helps businesses assess traveler satisfaction, pinpoint potential issues, and refine marketing strategies (Ohme et al., 2024; Singh et al., 2023; Deiss & Henneberry, 2020).

*Machine learning*: As a subset of AI, machine learning excels in detecting patterns within large datasets and making predictions based on these patterns. By training models on historical data, machine learning can predict tourist behaviors, such as booking preferences or seasonal trends. For example, analyzing past booking data enables machine learning models to forecast which types of accommodations will be popular during specific seasons or among certain demographics. These models continually improve their predictions as they process more data, offering increasingly accurate insights crucial for adapting to the dynamic tourism industry (Al-Romeedy & Hashem, 2024).

*Sentiment analysis*: This specialized text analysis technique assesses the emotional tone of user-generated content, including social media posts, reviews, and comments. Sentiment analysis tools evaluate the language used by tourists to gauge whether their experiences are positive, negative, or neutral. This insight is valuable for understanding customer satisfaction and identifying areas for improvement. For example, sentiment analysis can highlight common complaints about a destination or service, allowing businesses to address these issues proactively. Monitoring sentiment over time also helps track the impact of customer experience improvements and adjust strategies as needed (Meyer & Schroeder, 2023; Fawns et al., 2023).

*Data visualization tools*: Effective data management is complemented by visualization tools such as Tableau, Power BI, and Google Data Studio, which transform complex data into intuitive visual formats like charts, graphs, and heat maps. These visualizations simplify the identification of trends, comparisons between segments, and communication of findings to stakeholders. For instance, a heat map can illustrate tourist foot traffic in a destination, highlighting popular areas and identifying opportunities for targeted marketing (Kingsnorth, 2022; Juska, 2021; Al-Romeedy, 2024a).

## Identifying Patterns and Trends in Tourist Preferences Through Digital Traces

Analyzing digital traces is pivotal for uncovering patterns and trends in tourist preferences, which can guide the development of more effective marketing strategies and offerings. By understanding these patterns, tourism businesses can tailor their approaches to better meet the evolving needs of travelers (Khang et al., 2024; Singh et al., 2023).

*Behavioral patterns*: Digital traces offer insights into tourist behaviors from initial searches to final bookings. For instance, analyzing search queries may reveal recurring interests, such as a demand for adventure tourism or cultural experiences during specific times of the year. Identifying these patterns enables businesses to align marketing efforts with peak interest periods, promoting relevant experiences and increasing booking potential (Das, 2021; Gaafar & Al-Romeedy, 2024b).

*Temporal trends*: Seasonal trends are well-known, but digital data allows for the identification of more nuanced temporal patterns. For example, spikes in interest for certain destinations around holidays or special events can be detected. By aligning marketing campaigns with these periods of increased interest, businesses can enhance their visibility and appeal. Additionally, analyzing annual data helps anticipate demand changes, allowing businesses to adjust offerings, such as introducing new packages or discounts during off-peak times to attract more visitors (Kingsnorth, 2022; Zhang et al., 2024).

*Preference shifts*: Over time, tourist preferences evolve due to changing societal values, economic conditions, or emerging trends. Continuous analysis of digital traces helps businesses stay informed about these shifts. For example, if data shows a growing interest in sustainable travel, businesses can highlight eco-friendly options in their marketing. Conversely, a rising demand for technology-driven experiences, such as virtual tours, suggests an investment in such technologies might be beneficial (Gaafar & Al-Romeedy, 2024a; Rachmad, 2024).

*Cross-platform behavior*: Tourists engage with multiple digital platforms throughout their travel journey. Analyzing how they transition between platforms—such as starting with a search engine, moving to social media, and finalizing bookings on an OTA website—reveals crucial behavioral insights. Understanding this cross-platform behavior helps businesses identify key touchpoints and create integrated, multi-channel marketing strategies that guide tourists seamlessly from search to booking (Visser et al., 2021; Ohme et al., 2024).

By leveraging these insights, tourism businesses can enhance their marketing strategies, improve customer engagement, and better meet the evolving needs of travelers.

## Segmentation of Tourists Based on Digital Behavior

Segmentation is a key technique for dividing a broader market into more defined groups based on specific characteristics or behaviors. When applied to digital traces, segmentation allows businesses to target and personalize marketing strategies effectively, enhancing engagement and customer satisfaction (Nix & Decker, 2023; Sultan et al., 2023).

*Behavioral segmentation*: This approach categorizes tourists based on their actions, such as search behavior, booking patterns, and in-trip activities. For example, tourists searching for luxury accommodations can be segmented separately from budget-conscious travelers. This distinction allows businesses to tailor marketing efforts with targeted offers: luxury travelers might receive exclusive experience promotions, while budget travelers are targeted with cost-effective options (Holsinger, 2023; Al-Romeedy & Hashem, 2024).

*Demographic segmentation*: Grouping tourists based on demographic factors like age, gender, income, or family status provides insights into broad trends within these groups. For instance, younger travelers might prefer mobile apps and social media, whereas older travelers might lean towards traditional websites and email communications. By understanding these preferences, businesses can optimize their digital strategies and communication channels for different demographic groups (Deiss & Henneberry, 2020; Meyer & Schroeder, 2023; Singh et al., 2023; Holsinger, 2023).

*Psychographic segmentation*: This method goes beyond demographics and behavior to explore tourists' attitudes, values, and lifestyles. Analyzing digital interactions and content preferences can reveal underlying motivations. For example, eco-conscious travelers who value sustainability can be segmented from adventure seekers who prioritize thrill-based experiences. This segmentation allows businesses to craft personalized campaigns that align with each segment's values, enhancing engagement and loyalty (Chaffey & Smith, 2022; Al-Romeedy, 2024b; Gaafar & Al-Romeedy, 2024b).

*Geographic segmentation*: Dividing tourists based on their location (e.g., country, region, city) helps tailor marketing strategies to different markets. Preferences and behaviors can vary significantly across regions. For instance, tourists from different countries may have distinct destination preferences or activity choices. Analyzing location data and search behavior enables businesses to customize their marketing to address the specific needs of each geographic area (Juska, 2021; Khang et al., 2024; Audy Martínek et al., 2023; Das, 2021).

***Engagement-based segmentation***: This type categorizes tourists by their interaction level with a brand or destination. Highly engaged users might frequently interact with social media content, participate in loyalty programs, and make repeat bookings, while less engaged users might only occasionally visit the website. Segmenting based on engagement levels allows businesses to create targeted strategies to nurture leads, re-engage inactive users, or reward loyal customers with exclusive offers (Ohme et al., 2024; Kingsnorth, 2022).

Leveraging digital traces for segmentation enables tourism businesses to understand and address the diverse needs of their audiences more effectively. By applying behavioral, demographic, psychographic, geographic, and engagement-based segmentation techniques, businesses can craft targeted, personalized marketing strategies that enhance customer experience and drive growth in the competitive tourism industry.

## TRANSFORMING DATA INTO INSIGHTS

The enormous volume of data created by tourists through their digital activities presents significant opportunities for tourism companies. The real benefit of this data is realized when it is converted into practical insights that can guide marketing efforts and improve the overall visitor experience. This transformation of raw data into useful insights involves several steps: data cleaning, analysis, and interpretation. These steps are crucial for making better decisions and planning strategically (Meyer & Schroeder, 2023; Fawns et al., 2023).

## Converting Raw Data Into Actionable Insights for Marketing

The process of transforming raw data into actionable insights begins with collecting diverse digital traces, including search queries, social media interactions, booking patterns, and mobile app usage. This raw data is often extensive, unstructured, and complex, necessitating systematic handling to become useful. The initial phase involves data cleaning and preprocessing to eliminate inaccuracies, inconsistencies, and irrelevant information, ensuring that the data is accurate, complete, and suitable for analysis (Sultan et al., 2023; Al-Romeedy, 2024a). After cleaning, the data is organized into a structured format to facilitate analysis. This may include categorizing the data into different segments such as demographics, behavioral patterns, or geographic regions. Structured data is typically managed using tools like SQL databases, data warehouses, and data lakes, which enable efficient storage, retrieval, and analysis (Visser et al., 2021; Deiss & Henneberry, 2020).

The next phase involves applying analytical techniques to derive meaningful insights. This could include descriptive analytics, which summarizes historical data to highlight trends and patterns, or diagnostic analytics, which investigates the causes behind specific behaviors or outcomes. For instance, descriptive analytics might uncover peak booking times for a destination, while diagnostic analytics could reveal the drivers behind these trends, such as promotional efforts, seasonal events, or favorable weather conditions (Buitrago-Ropero et al., 2023; Gaafar & Al-Romeedy, 2024a; Singh et al., 2023; Nix & Decker, 2023).

These insights can then be translated into actionable marketing strategies. For example, if data indicates a high demand for eco-friendly accommodations, a tourism business might create a campaign emphasizing its sustainability efforts and green offerings. Conversely, if travelers from a specific region are found to book last-minute trips, the business might target these customers with special last-minute deals and promotions (Das, 2021; Zhang et al., 2024; Chaffey & Smith, 2022). Effective data visualization is essential at this stage, as it aids marketers and decision-makers in interpreting complex data and identifying key trends. Tools like heat maps, bar charts, and trend lines can represent data in a clear, intuitive way, simplifying the communication of findings and guiding strategic decisions (Al-Romeedy & Hashem, 2024; Juska, 2021).

## Predictive Modeling to Forecast Tourist Behavior and Preferences

Predictive modeling is a valuable technique that enables tourism businesses to anticipate future tourist behavior and preferences based on historical data. By utilizing machine learning algorithms and statistical models, predictive analytics can uncover patterns and trends to forecast how tourists are likely to act in the future (Fawns et al., 2023; Rachmad, 2024). The predictive modeling process starts with selecting relevant data points that significantly influence tourist behavior. These might include past booking history, search queries, social media interactions, demographic details, and economic factors. Machine learning algorithms, such as regression models, decision trees, and neural networks, are then trained on this historical data to understand the relationships between these variables and the desired outcomes, such as future booking decisions, preferred destinations, or spending habits (Ohme et al., 2024; Deiss & Henneberry, 2020; Nix & Decker, 2023).

Once trained, the model can predict future behavior. For instance, it might use a tourist's previous search patterns and booking history to forecast their next destination or accommodation preference. This allows businesses to proactively adjust their marketing strategies, product offerings, and pricing to align with the anticipated needs and preferences of their audience (Al-Romeedy, 2024b; Singh et al., 2023; Audy Martínek et al., 2023). Predictive modeling also helps in identifying potential risks and opportunities. For example, a model might forecast a downturn in bookings for a particular destination due to economic conditions, prompting businesses to adjust their marketing strategies or explore alternative revenue sources. Conversely, it might highlight a rising trend in a new travel niche, such as wellness tourism, encouraging businesses to create targeted marketing campaigns to exploit this emerging opportunity (Al-Romeedy, 2024a; Sultan et al., 2023).

In addition to long-term forecasting, predictive modeling is useful for real-time decision-making. For instance, real-time predictive analytics can process data from mobile apps, social media, and web traffic to identify travelers currently planning trips and predict their preferences based on their current activities. This enables businesses to provide personalized offers and recommendations at optimal moments, thereby increasing the chances of conversion (Meyer & Schroeder, 2023; Buitrago-Ropero et al., 2023).

## Examples of Key Insights That Can Be Derived From Digital Traces

Digital traces offer a rich source of information that, when analyzed effectively, can provide crucial insights into tourist behavior and preferences. These insights are essential for crafting marketing strategies, developing products, and enhancing customer engagement. Here are some key insights that can be obtained from analyzing digital traces (Gaafar & Al-Romeedy, 2024b; Holsinger, 2023):

*Popular destinations*: By examining search queries, social media activity, and booking patterns, businesses can pinpoint which destinations are favored by different traveler segments. For instance, a surge in searches for "beach vacations" during winter may signal a strong interest in tropical destinations during this season. This insight allows businesses to tailor their marketing efforts to highlight beach destinations and promote relevant travel packages during peak times (Khang et al., 2024; Kingsnorth, 2022; Ohme et al., 2024).

***Booking patterns***: Analyzing booking windows helps determine when travelers are likely to book their trips relative to their travel dates. Some may book well in advance, while others prefer last-minute deals. Understanding these patterns allows businesses to fine-tune their pricing strategies, offer targeted promotions, and manage resources more effectively. For example, last-minute travelers can be targeted with urgent offers, while early bookers might receive loyalty discounts or personalized suggestions (Juska, 2021; Khang et al., 2024).

***Travel preferences***: Digital traces can reveal tourists' preferences for various travel experiences, such as luxury versus budget accommodations, adventure versus relaxation activities, or solo versus family travel. These preferences can be deduced from the content tourists interact with on social media, their accommodation choices, and their online searches for activities. This understanding enables businesses to align their marketing messages and product offerings with the specific interests of different customer segments (Sultan et al., 2023; Chaffey & Smith, 2022).

***Spending behavior***: Insights into tourists' spending habits can be derived from online transactions, booking data, and customer feedback. For example, some traveler segments may be inclined to spend more on luxury experiences, while others might prioritize budget-friendly options. This information assists businesses in devising pricing strategies, creating tiered product offerings, and designing targeted promotions to cater to various spending levels (Das, 2021; Gaafar & Al-Romeedy, 2024a).

***Customer satisfaction and issues***: Sentiment analysis of reviews, social media comments, and customer feedback can provide a clear picture of tourist satisfaction and pinpoint common issues. For example, recurring complaints about long wait times or inadequate customer service might indicate areas needing improvement. Conversely, positive feedback about certain aspects, such as high-quality accommodations or a smooth booking process, can highlight strengths to be emphasized in marketing efforts (Kingsnorth, 2022; Meyer & Schroeder, 2023).

## The Role of Real-Time Data in Adapting Marketing Strategies

In the rapidly evolving tourism sector, real-time data is crucial for businesses to adjust their marketing strategies swiftly. Real-time data provides immediate insights as events occur, allowing businesses to react quickly to shifting conditions, emerging trends, and customer preferences (Zhang et al., 2024; Nix & Decker, 2023).

*Adaptive marketing*: Real-time data supports adaptive marketing, enabling businesses to modify their messaging, promotions, and content based on current trends and consumer behavior. For example, if real-time data reveals a sudden rise in interest for a specific destination due to a significant event or favorable weather, businesses can promptly launch targeted campaigns to leverage this trend. Similarly, if a competitor introduces a promotion, real-time insights allow a business to respond with a counteroffer or supplementary service, ensuring it stays competitive (Al-Romeedy, 2024a).

*Customized experiences*: Real-time data is vital for creating personalized experiences for customers. By analyzing data from mobile apps, websites, and social media as it comes in, businesses can identify tourists actively planning their trips and offer them tailored recommendations, deals, and content. For instance, if a tourist searches for flights to a particular destination, a travel company can immediately send personalized hotel suggestions or activity ideas for that location. This level of customization enhances engagement and improves the overall customer experience (Buitrago-Ropero et al., 2023; Fawns et al., 2023).

*Dynamic pricing*: Real-time data facilitates dynamic pricing strategies, where prices are adjusted based on current demand, availability, and other variables. For example, during peak travel seasons or when inventory is scarce, prices can be raised to maximize revenue. Conversely, during off-peak periods or when demand is lower, prices can be reduced to attract more bookings. Real-time data ensures that these price adjustments are made swiftly and accurately, optimizing revenue while keeping the business competitive (Gaafar & Al-Romeedy, 2024b).

*Crisis management*: Real-time data is essential for managing crises in the tourism industry. Whether dealing with natural disasters, political instability, or health emergencies, real-time insights enable businesses to monitor the situation as it unfolds and communicate effectively with customers. For example, if a natural disaster impacts a popular destination, real-time data can be used to update travelers about the situation, offer alternative options, and provide support. This proactive approach helps maintain customer trust and mitigates the crisis's impact on the business (Audy Martínek et al., 2023; Sultan et al., 2023; Ohme et al., 2024).

# The Role of Predictive Analytics in Anticipating Future Tourist Behaviors

Predictive analytics is a valuable tool that empowers tourism businesses to foresee future tourist behaviors and make proactive, data-driven decisions. By examining historical data and recognizing patterns, predictive analytics models can forecast future tourist actions, enabling businesses to anticipate trends and address customer needs before they emerge.

*Demand forecasting*: Predictive analytics is crucial for forecasting demand in tourism. By evaluating past booking data, search trends, and market dynamics, predictive models can estimate future demand for specific destinations, experiences, and accommodations. For instance, if historical data suggests a rising interest in eco-friendly lodgings, predictive analytics can help businesses prepare by adjusting their inventory, pricing, and marketing strategies to meet this anticipated demand (Al-Romeedy & Hashem, 2024).

*Customer lifetime value (CLV)*: Predictive analytics can estimate CLV, which measures the total revenue expected from a customer throughout their relationship with the business. By identifying customers who are likely to be the most valuable long-term, businesses can focus their marketing efforts and resource allocation more effectively. For example, high-CLV customers might receive tailored loyalty programs or exclusive offers to encourage repeat engagement (Gaafar & Al-Romeedy, 2024a).

*Churn prediction*: Predictive analytics helps identify tourists who may be at risk of churning, or ending their relationship with the brand. By analyzing changes in customer behavior, such as reduced engagement or shifts in purchasing patterns, predictive models can flag those likely to disengage. This enables businesses to implement targeted retention strategies, such as personalized offers or enhanced customer service, to mitigate churn and preserve loyalty (Meyer & Schroeder, 2023; Das, 2021).

*Product development*: Predictive analytics can guide product development by spotting emerging trends and customer preferences. For example, if data indicates increasing interest in wellness travel, a business might create new health-focused travel packages. By predicting future trends, businesses can innovate and offer new products that align with evolving customer expectations, gaining a competitive advantage (Nix & Decker, 2023; Singh et al., 2023).

*Marketing optimization*: Predictive analytics aids in refining marketing strategies by forecasting the effectiveness of various campaigns and channels. For example, models can analyze previous campaign performance to identify which marketing channels are most likely to convert specific tourist segments. This allows businesses to allocate their marketing budget more efficiently, focusing on the most effective channels and strategies (Zhang et al., 2024; Holsinger, 2023; Ohme et al., 2024).

Converting data into actionable insights involves analyzing digital traces, predicting future behaviors, and deriving strategies that inform marketing efforts. Utilizing AI, machine learning, sentiment analysis, and predictive analytics, tourism businesses can gain a deep understanding of tourist behavior, anticipate future trends, and make informed decisions that enhance customer experiences and drive growth. Real-time data is vital for adapting to current conditions, while predictive analytics enables businesses to proactively meet the evolving needs of their customers.

## DESIGNING TARGETED MARKETING CAMPAIGNS

The digital age has dramatically transformed marketing strategies, shifting from broad, generic approaches to more personalized, data-driven tactics. Targeted marketing involves crafting messages specifically tailored to the unique preferences, behaviors, and needs of distinct consumer segments. In the tourism sector, where consumer preferences are varied and constantly evolving, targeted marketing has proven far more effective than traditional methods. This shift is driven by the extensive data generated through tourists' digital interactions, enabling businesses to develop highly personalized and relevant marketing campaigns (Visser et al., 2021; Khang et al., 2024; Deiss & Henneberry, 2020).

### Principles of Targeted Marketing and How Data-Driven Insights Can Enhance Campaign Effectiveness

At its core, targeted marketing involves dividing a broad market into smaller, more specific segments based on distinct characteristics such as demographics, behavior, or interests, and then crafting marketing messages tailored to each segment. This approach aims to enhance the consumer experience, driving higher engagement, loyalty, and conversion rates (Kingsnorth, 2022; Chaffey & Smith, 2022).

*Market segmentation*: Effective segmentation is the foundational principle of targeted marketing. By examining data from digital interactions—such as search activity, social media engagement, booking patterns, and demographic details—businesses can identify distinct tourist groups with similar traits. For instance, one segment might include young adventure enthusiasts who frequently search for extreme sports and outdoor activities, while another might comprise affluent travelers interested in high-end accommodations and gourmet dining. Understanding these segments enables businesses to customize their messaging and offerings to align with the specific preferences and needs of each group (Al-Romeedy, 2024b; Sultan et al., 2023).

*Personalization*: Personalization is crucial to targeted marketing. After seg-menting the market, businesses can leverage data-driven insights to craft tailored marketing messages that address the unique interests and desires of each segment. For example, a personalized email campaign could feature adventure tourism op-tions for the adventure seekers segment and luxury spa packages for the affluent travelers segment. Personalization involves more than just using the recipient's name; it requires delivering content that resonates with the individual's specific preferences, travel history, and future intentions (Juska, 2021; Buitrago-Ropero et al., 2023; Fawns et al., 2023).

*Relevance and timing*: Ensuring that marketing messages are relevant and timely is another key principle of targeted marketing. For example, a traveler who recently searched for flights to a tropical destination may be more inclined to respond to a marketing message promoting beachfront hotels or local attractions in that area. Timing is particularly important in tourism, where factors like seasonality, special events, and last-minute deals can influence decisions. By using real-time data, businesses can deliver messages that align with the traveler's current stage in the decision-making process, thus increasing the chances of conversion (Chaffey & Smith, 2022; Visser et al., 2021; Kingsnorth, 2022).

*Data-driven decision making*: Data-driven insights are essential for effective targeted marketing. Continuous analysis of digital traces allows businesses to refine their strategies based on performance metrics. Techniques such as A/B testing can compare the effectiveness of different marketing messages, while predictive analytics can anticipate which campaigns will resonate with specific segments. This iterative approach ensures that marketing efforts are optimized for maximum impact, leading to improved return on investment (ROI) and greater customer satisfaction (Gaafar & Al-Romeedy, 2024b).

## Designing Personalized Marketing Campaigns Based on Digital Traces

Personalization in marketing has become a fundamental strategy, particularly in the tourism industry where experiences are uniquely personal and diverse. Lever-aging digital traces—from search history and social media interactions to booking behavior and in-destination activities—allows businesses to craft highly relevant and engaging marketing campaigns.

*Understanding the customer journey*: Effective personalization begins with mapping out the customer journey and identifying key touchpoints where digital traces are generated. The journey typically includes inspiration (exploring desti-nations), planning (gathering details and booking), and post-trip phases (sharing experiences). By analyzing data from each stage, businesses can engage travelers more effectively. For instance, if a traveler searches for family-friendly destinations during the planning phase, businesses can target them with content highlighting family-friendly accommodations and activities (Deiss & Henneberry, 2020; Al-Romeedy, 2024a; Das, 2021).

*Dynamic content personalization*: This technique involves tailoring content based on user behavior, preferences, and real-time interactions. For example, a tourism website might display luxury hotel options to users who have previously searched for such accommodations, while budget travelers might see affordable options. Similarly, personalized email marketing can include recommendations based on recent searches or bookings (Gaafar & Al-Romeedy, 2024a; Chaffey & Smith, 2022).

*Leveraging behavioral data*: Behavioral data, such as interactions with websites or apps, offers insights into traveler preferences and intentions. If a user frequently views pages related to outdoor activities, they likely have an interest in adventure tourism. Businesses can use this information to send targeted emails featuring adventure packages or display relevant ads. This approach increases the relevance of marketing messages and enhances user experience (Sultan et al., 2023; Ohme et al., 2024; Singh et al., 2023; Khang et al., 2024).

*Geo-targeted campaigns*: Geo-targeting delivers content based on a traveler's geographic location, which can be especially useful in tourism. For example, a hotel chain might promote local attractions or dining options based on the traveler's current location or interests. Additionally, real-time geo-targeted offers, like discounts on nearby attractions or last-minute hotel deals, can effectively drive engagement (Al-Romeedy & Hashem, 2024; Meyer & Schroeder, 2023; Audy Martínek et al., 2023).

*Predictive personalization*: Predictive personalization uses predictive analytics to anticipate traveler interests based on past behavior. By identifying patterns, businesses can suggest relevant destinations, activities, or services. For instance, if a traveler often books wellness retreats, predictive analytics might recommend spa packages or yoga retreats in new locations. This proactive approach enhances customer experience and boosts conversion rates by providing timely, relevant content (Holsinger, 2023; Nix & Decker, 2023).

# The Effectiveness of Targeted vs. Traditional Marketing Approaches

The transition from traditional to targeted marketing reflects the growing need for more precise, relevant, and efficient approaches in reaching today's digital consumers. Here's a closer look at the key benefits of targeted marketing over traditional methods:

*Relevance and engagement*: Targeted marketing excels in delivering messages that are tailored to specific audience segments. Unlike traditional marketing, which often uses a one-size-fits-all approach that may not resonate with everyone, targeted marketing utilizes data to craft personalized content that aligns with individual preferences and needs. This tailored approach increases the likelihood of engagement, as consumers are more likely to interact with content that speaks directly to their interests and desires (Visser et al., 2021; Gaafar & Al-Romeedy, 2024b).

*Efficiency and ROI*: Targeted marketing improves efficiency by focusing efforts on the most relevant audience segments rather than attempting to reach a broad, less interested audience. This reduces waste and enhances return on investment (ROI). For example, a traditional TV commercial might reach millions but only appeal to a small subset interested in the product. In contrast, targeted online ads can be directed at specific segments, such as those searching for luxury vacations, resulting in higher conversion rates and reduced acquisition costs (Holsinger, 2023; Kingsnorth, 2022).

*Measurability and optimization*: Targeted marketing offers superior measurability and optimization capabilities compared to traditional methods. Traditional marketing metrics like reach and frequency provide limited insight into campaign effectiveness. Targeted marketing, however, allows for detailed tracking of metrics such as click-through rates, conversion rates, and customer lifetime value. This data-driven approach enables continuous optimization, where businesses can test various messages, offers, and channels, and refine strategies based on performance (Gaafar & Al-Romeedy, 2024b; Al-Romeedy & Hashem, 2024).

*Building customer relationships*: Targeted marketing fosters stronger, long-term customer relationships by delivering relevant and personalized content. This approach helps build trust and loyalty, as consumers feel understood and valued. Traditional marketing methods often focus on immediate sales and broader reach, which can overlook the importance of ongoing customer engagement. In contrast, targeted marketing aims to address individual needs, resulting in deeper engagement and improved customer retention over time (Deiss & Henneberry, 2020; Kingsnorth, 2022).

## Techniques for Personalizing Marketing Messages Based on Tourist Profiles and Preferences

Personalization has become central to effective targeted marketing, particularly in the tourism industry, where individualized experiences are highly valued. By harnessing data from digital interactions, businesses can tailor their marketing strategies to better meet the specific needs and preferences of tourists.

*Segmentation and profiling*\*\*: Personalization begins with segmenting the audience and developing detailed profiles based on data such as demographics, booking history, search behavior, and social media interactions. For instance, segments might include frequent last-minute travelers or eco-conscious vacationers. These profiles help in crafting targeted marketing messages that align with each segment's unique characteristics, ensuring that the content is relevant and engaging (Al-Romeedy, 2024a; Ohme et al., 2024; Singh et al., 2023; Das, 2021).

*Dynamic content creation*: Dynamic content adapts in real-time based on a user's profile and behavior. For example, travel websites can display tailored offers and recommendations based on past searches and bookings. A luxury traveler might see premium hotel options, while a budget traveler might be presented with affordable accommodations and local discounts. This approach extends to email marketing, where personalized recommendations and offers are tailored to the recipient's recent interactions (Gaafar & Al-Romeedy, 2024a; Meyer & Schroeder, 2023; Sultan et al., 2023).

*Behavioral triggering*: This technique involves sending personalized messages based on specific actions, such as abandoned bookings or extensive research on a destination. For instance, an automated reminder email with an incentive could be sent if a user leaves a booking process incomplete. Behavioral triggering ensures timely and relevant engagement, increasing the likelihood of conversion (Ohme et al., 2024; Al-Romeedy & Hashem, 2024).

*Personalized recommendations*: By analyzing past behavior, businesses can suggest tailored destinations, activities, and accommodations. For example, a user frequently searching for outdoor adventures might receive recommendations for adventure tours, while a history enthusiast might see suggestions for cultural experiences. These personalized recommendations enhance user experience and engagement by helping tourists discover options that align with their interests (Gaafar & Al-Romeedy, 2024a; Visser et al., 2021).

*Geo-targeting and location-based offers*: Geo-targeting uses a tourist's geographic location to personalize marketing messages. Mobile apps can send real-time offers or recommendations based on a user's current location, such as discounts at nearby attractions or dining options. Geo-targeting can also be applied in online ads, ensuring that the content is relevant to the user's current context (Al-Romeedy & Hashem, 2024; Chaffey & Smith, 2022; Fawns et al., 2023).

*Multi-channel personalization*: A multi-channel approach ensures that personalized content is consistent across various platforms, including emails, social media, websites, and mobile apps. This strategy reinforces brand identity and provides a cohesive experience for the tourist, regardless of how they interact with the brand. Consistency across channels maximizes the effectiveness of personalized marketing efforts (Zhang et al., 2024; Sultan et al., 2023; Khang et al., 2024; Ohme et al., 2024).

Effective targeted marketing hinges on personalization, which is achieved through careful segmentation, dynamic content, behavioral triggering, personalized recommendations, geo-targeting, and multi-channel strategies. By leveraging detailed data insights, businesses can create highly relevant and engaging marketing campaigns that resonate with individual tourists, ultimately enhancing customer experience and driving business growth.

## CONCLUSION AND RECOMMENDATIONS

The chapter emphasizes the revolutionary impact of digital traces on marketing strategies within the tourism industry. By examining the diverse digital footprints left by tourists—such as search engine queries, social media interactions, booking patterns, and mobile app usage—tourism businesses can gain profound insights into traveler behaviors, preferences, and needs. This data-driven methodology facilitates the development of highly targeted and personalized marketing campaigns, which are not only more relevant and engaging but also far more effective than traditional, broad-based approaches.

To maximize the benefits of digital traces, tourism businesses and destinations should consider several strategic recommendations. First, investing in sophisticated data analytics tools, such as AI and machine learning, is crucial. These tools can accurately analyze and interpret digital data, converting raw information into actionable insights. They allow businesses to predict tourist behavior, tailor marketing messages, and optimize campaigns in real-time, thereby enhancing the effectiveness and efficiency of marketing efforts. Second, it is vital to proactively address privacy and data security issues. This involves implementing strong data protection measures, ensuring adherence to regulations like GDPR, and adopting transparent data practices to build consumer trust. Third, businesses should explore innovative technologies like blockchain and virtual reality. Blockchain can offer a secure and transparent method for managing digital traces, while VR can provide immersive, personalized experiences that deeply engage consumers.

Looking forward, the environment of data-driven marketing in the tourism sector is set to evolve rapidly. With advancing technology, the integration of real-time data, hyper-personalization, and ethical AI will become increasingly crucial. Tourism businesses that embrace these trends will be well-positioned to cater to the rising expectations of tech-savvy consumers who demand seamless and personalized experiences. Additionally, as sustainability gains prominence among both consumers and the industry, there will be a heightened focus on utilizing digital data to encourage responsible travel behaviors and support environmental initiatives. In summary, effectively leveraging digital traces for marketing not only improves business outcomes but also fosters a more responsive, sustainable, and customer-centric tourism industry.

# REFERENCES

Al-Romeedy, B. (2024a). Tomorrow's Travel Companion: The Role of Artificial Intelligence in Shaping the Future of Tourism. In Hashem, T., Albattat, A., Valeri, M., & Sharma, A. (Eds.), *Marketing and Big Data Analytics in Tourism and Events* (pp. 162–182). IGI Global., DOI: 10.4018/979-8-3693-3310-5.ch010

Al-Romeedy, B. (2024b). Unlocking the Power of Data: Exploring the Dynamic Role of MKIS in Revolutionizing Tourism Marketing. In Hashem, T., Albattat, A., Valeri, M., & Sharma, A. (Eds.), *Marketing and Big Data Analytics in Tourism and Events* (pp. 183–204). IGI Global., DOI: 10.4018/979-8-3693-3310-5.ch011

Al-Romeedy, B., & Hashem, T. (2024). From Insight to Advantage: Harnessing the Potential of Marketing Intelligence Systems in Tourism. In Hashem, T., Albattat, A., Valeri, M., & Sharma, A. (Eds.), *Marketing and Big Data Analytics in Tourism and Events* (pp. 80–98). IGI Global., DOI: 10.4018/979-8-3693-3310-5.ch005

Audy Martínek, P., Caliandro, A., & Denegri-Knott, J. (2023). Digital practices tracing: Studying consumer lurking in digital environments. *Journal of Marketing Management*, 39(3-4), 244–274. DOI: 10.1080/0267257X.2022.2105385

Buitrago-Ropero, M., Ramírez-Montoya, M., & Laverde, A. (2023). Digital footprints (2005–2019): A systematic mapping of studies in education. *Interactive Learning Environments*, 31(2), 876–889. DOI: 10.1080/10494820.2020.1814821

Chaffey, D., & Smith, P. (2022). *Digital marketing excellence: planning, optimizing and integrating online marketing.* Routledge. DOI: 10.4324/9781003009498

Das, S. (2021). *Search engine optimization and marketing: A recipe for success in digital marketing.* Chapman and Hall/CRC. DOI: 10.1201/9780429298509

Deiss, R., & Henneberry, R. (2020). *Digital marketing for dummies.* John Wiley & Sons.

Fawns, T., Ross, J., Carbonel, H., Noteboom, J., Finnegan-Dehn, S., & Raver, M. (2023). Mapping and tracing the postdigital: Approaches and parameters of post-digital research. *Postdigital Science and Education*, 5(3), 623–642. DOI: 10.1007/s42438-023-00391-y

Gaafar, H., & Al-Romeedy, B. (2024a). Bridging the Digital Divide: Unleashing the Power of Big Data Analytics for Touristic Destination Promotion. In Hashem, T., Albattat, A., Valeri, M., & Sharma, A. (Eds.), *Marketing and Big Data Analytics in Tourism and Events* (pp. 17–37). IGI Global., DOI: 10.4018/979-8-3693-3310-5.ch002

Gaafar, H., & Al-Romeedy, B. (2024b). Data Fusion for Destination Success: Exploring the Integration of MKIS and BDA in Marketing Touristic Destinations. In Hashem, T., Albattat, A., Valeri, M., & Sharma, A. (Eds.), *Marketing and Big Data Analytics in Tourism and Events* (pp. 38–60). IGI Global., DOI: 10.4018/979-8-3693-3310-5.ch003

Holsinger, B. (2023). *On Parchment: Animals, Archives, and the Making of Culture from Herodotus to the Digital Age.* Yale University Press. DOI: 10.12987/9780300271485

Juska, J. (2021). *Integrated marketing communication: advertising and promotion in a digital world.* Routledge. DOI: 10.4324/9780367443382

Khang, A., Gujrati, R., Uygun, H., Tailor, R., & Gaur, S. (2024). *Data-Driven Modelling and Predictive Analytics in Business and Finance: Concepts, Designs, Technologies, and Applications.* CRC Press. DOI: 10.1201/9781032618845

Kingsnorth, S. (2022). *Digital marketing strategy: an integrated approach to online marketing.* Kogan Page Publishers.

Meyer, E., & Schroeder, R. (2023). *Knowledge machines: Digital transformations of the sciences and humanities.* Mit Press.

Niininen, O. (2022). *Contemporary issues in digital marketing.* Taylor & Francis.

Nix, A., & Decker, S. (2023). Using digital sources: The future of business history? *Business History*, 65(6), 1048–1071. DOI: 10.1080/00076791.2021.1909572

Ohme, J., Araujo, T., Boeschoten, L., Freelon, D., Ram, N., Reeves, B., & Robinson, T. (2024). Digital trace data collection for social media effects research: APIs, data donation, and (screen) tracking. *Communication Methods and Measures*, 18(2), 124–141. DOI: 10.1080/19312458.2023.2181319

Rachmad, Y. (2024). *Digital Marketing Theories: From Gimmicks to Loyalty.* PT. Sonpedia Publishing Indonesia.

Singh, S., Rajest, S., Hadoussa, S., Obaid, A., & Regin, R. (2023). *Data-driven decision making for long-term business success.* IGI Global. DOI: 10.4018/979-8-3693-2193-5

Sultan, M., Scholz, C., & van den Bos, W. (2023). Leaving traces behind: Using social media digital trace data to study adolescent wellbeing. *Computers in Human Behavior Reports*, 10, 100281. DOI: 10.1016/j.chbr.2023.100281

Visser, M., Sikkenga, B., & Berry, M. (2021). *Digital marketing fundamentals: From strategy to ROI.* Taylor & Francis. DOI: 10.4324/9781003203650

Zhang, W., Xie, J., Zhang, Z., & Liu, X. (2024). Depression detection using digital traces on social media: A knowledge-aware deep learning approach. *Journal of Management Information Systems*, 41(2), 546–580. DOI: 10.1080/07421222.2024.2340822

# Chapter 5
# The Impact of Influencer Marketing on Tourist Behavior and Tourism Marketing:
## A Systematic Literature Review

**Busenur Can**
https://orcid.org/0009-0002-4771-9840
*Çanakkale Onsekiz Mart University, Turkey*

**Onur Çakır**
*Kırklareli University, Turkey*

## ABSTRACT

*This chapter aims to provide tourism academics and professionals with a comprehensive understanding of influencer marketing in tourism by analyzing research findings from the last decade. In this context, the chapter investigates 82 studies' findings on influencer marketing in the tourism industry conducted between 2012 and 2023 using systematic literature review method. The results indicate that the number of studies on influencer marketing has increased exponentially since 2020. In the majority of the studies, the survey method was preferred as the data collection technique, while the topics addressed were mostly on the effects of influencers on the tourist behavior and tourists' purchasing process, followed by studies examining the content created by the influencer. The results indicate that, in general, content produced by influencers has a positive impact on consumer behavior. Therefore, it would be beneficial for tourism businesses to collaborate with influencers.*

DOI: 10.4018/979-8-3693-3972-5.ch005

# INTRODUCTION

Tourism marketing has undergone a significant transformation over the last decade, largely driven by the emergence of influencer marketing and social media as a powerful tool for promoting tourism destinations and tourism businesses. The widespread use of social media has led to the emergence of a user group known as influencers (Stoldt et al., 2019). These individuals play an active role on social media platforms not only as information receivers but also as informers. Influencers have the ability to influence the thoughts and behaviors of their followers through the content they share (Iwashita, 2019). With the spread of social media, people can now reach influencers directly or indirectly. This rapid access to social media and the internet has facilitated the rapid spread of information, including advertisements and various content shared by influencers (Avcı & Bilgili, 2020). In fact, being an influencer on social media has become the main job for some individuals. In recent years, the importance of influencer marketing has increased with the development of digital technologies in the tourism sector (Marvick & Boyd, 2011). Social media platforms, virtual reality experiences and interactive content have made it easier for tourists to discover and share their travel experiences in advance and gain more in-depth knowledge about destinations. This has increased the opportunities for tourism businesses to use influencer marketing effectively. Overall, the impact of social media and influencers has greatly influenced the way people acquire and share information in today's digital age (Bognar et al., 2019).

Influencers on popular social media platforms such as Facebook, Instagram and Twitter have a significant impact on social media users. These influencers collaborate with individuals or organizations to promote their recognition, increase their popularity, reach their target audience and ultimately generate more sales. They achieve these goals by producing content such as photos, videos, articles, and stories on social media channels and sharing them with a large number of followers (Bokunewics & Shulman, 2017). Additionally, influencers can expand their reach beyond their own followers by purchasing sponsored advertisements. This allows them to reach a wider audience and increase their influence (Pop et al., 2022). Overall, influencers play a crucial role in social media marketing by using their influence and content creation capabilities to help individuals and organizations achieve their goals. In addition, due to the high number of followers and supported by the purchasing power of their followers; influencers can spread advertisements to a wide audience. The reach of ads can increase depending on the number of people interested in making a purchase. Research shows that 50% of internet users follow and trust influencers, indicating that they have a positive influence on users during the buying process.

Social media influencers also have a significant impact on the tourism industry. Tourism businesses and destination management organizations (DMO's) collaborate with influencers to promote their products and services. However, it is important for tourism professionals to be aware of some considerations when working with influencers (Rudeloff & Egbert, 2023). One such consideration is to ensure that the influencer's followers are aligned with the target audience of the business. If the influencer's followers are not interested in tourism, the money paid to the influencer may be wasted (Pop et al., 2022). Image quality is also very important. The images and videos that tourism businesses offer to influencers should have high-resolution content and accurately reflect reality (Martínez-Sala et al., 2019). To achieve this, businesses and DMO's can seek the help of professional photographers. Businesses and DMO's may also find it useful to invite influencers to their establishments and destinations; and offer them free vacation services for the sake of credibility. The influencer's satisfaction with the tourism products and services advertised can lead to sincere behavior that can positively influence their followers on social media. As a result, influencers' followers may be more willing to purchase (Martínez-López et al, 2019).

According to the Customer Journey model, influencers have a significant impact on decision-making and purchasing processes. Individuals start their journey when they feel the need or desire to purchase a product or service (Pop et al., 2022). Social media users who encounter content produced by influencers may develop a desire to buy. The next step is the information search phase, where people look for various details about the product or service they want to buy. Influencers' social media posts can provide informative content, making it easier for people to access the necessary information. This is especially true for destination marketing, as influencer posts help individuals gather information about a particular destination prior to a visit (Bognar et al., 2019). People then evaluate alternatives by comparing different options. Finally, the purchase stage takes place and influencer-generated content plays an important role in encouraging people to make a purchase. In sum, influencers have the potential to directly influence every stage of the buying process, emphasizing their importance in today's consumer market (Pop et al., 2022).

While anecdotal evidence suggests that influencer marketing can generate significant excitement and increase visitor numbers to destinations, scientific data on its effectiveness and wider impacts on destination branding, tourist perceptions and economic outcomes is still emerging. Despite the growing popularity of influencer marketing in the tourism industry, a comprehensive understanding of its impact on tourism destinations and businesses is still needed. This study aims to fill this gap by conducting a systematic analysis of the effects of influencer marketing on tourist behavior and tourism marketing. In this context, this section analyzes the studies on influencer marketing in the tourism sector between 2012 and 2023. Both Turkish and English studies were analyzed using a systematic literature review method. The keywords 'influencer marketing', 'content created by influencers', 'tourism', 'tourism marketing' and 'destination marketing' were used in the literature review. Through a systematic review of 82 studies in the relevant literature, this research provides insights into how influencer marketing affects tourists' perceptions and decision-making processes. Furthermore, the study explores the role of influencer marketing in tourism management and marketing strategies and illuminates the best approaches as well as potential drawbacks for destination marketers.

In conclusion, the aim of this systematic review is to enhance knowledge about the function of influencer marketing in the management and marketing of tourism destinations and tourism businesses. By synthesizing and analyzing existing research findings, this study aims to provide academics and industry professionals with insights into various aspects of influencer marketing in tourism by consolidating and evaluating 82 previous research findings.

## 1. CONCEPTUAL FRAMEWORK

### 1.1. Definition and Importance of Influencer Marketing Concept

With the increasing number of people using social media, using social media platforms has become a daily event. The effective use of social media has paved the way for marketing to be carried out in online channels (Marvick & Boyd, 2011). For this reason, influencers have emerged who promote products and services, prepare and share advertisements on online channels. The concept of influencer is defined as someone who attracts a large number of followers on social media and becomes a source of advice for them (Vrontis et al., 2021). The content produced by influencers on social media aims to gain the favor of their followers, inform them and, most importantly, influence them. For businesses, reaching consumers is a difficult and costly task. In our age, TV or newspaper advertisements are not as popular as in previous years. Therefore, social media and influencer marketing can be more advantageous than traditional marketing. Some of these advantages are the rapid spread of the message in the content due to the high number of followers of influencers, the target audience of influencers, and the lack of distribution fee in terms of cost (Bayuk & Aslan, 2019, p. 178). Businesses that want to use the power of influencers on social media can collaborate with influencers and add them to their marketing network for a certain fee, and they can seize an opportunity to deliver their products and services to consumers in a short way (Harrigan et al., 2021). In this way, businesses can present the messages they want to convey to the audience they want (for example, if they want to reach young people, they can choose influencers who appeal to the young audience) and the advertisements they want to present in a sincere, reliable, effective and fast way. Tourism businesses can also benefit from influencer marketing (Pop et al., 2022). Iwashita (2019) defines influencer marketing as 'one of the marketing methods in which information about products and services is spread through influencers who create social impact, leading to increased awareness and interest in the market'. Businesses and DMO's can promote their touristic products by collaborating with influencers who have followers suitable for their target audience. When influencers provide positive information about the tourism business and the touristic products they produce, it can encourage their followers to buy (Pop et al., 2022). In this respect, it can be said that the advantages of influencer marketing are undeniably valuable, and the preference of influencers in content marketing can take tourism businesses to the upper levels.

Influencers are often confused with traditional celebrities. Influencers are famous people, but the fact that they work for their followers and answer their questions are some of the features that distinguish influencers from other celebrities (Can & Koz, 2018). When influencers increase their number of followers and share content that has an impact on their followers, they can be even more recognizable than traditional celebrities. The effects of influencers on their followers can be explained by source credibility, source attraction and costumer journey theories.

According to the source credibility theory, the effectiveness of the message to the target audience is related to the reputation of the person or business that wants to deliver the message. According to this theory, the message can only be received and effective by recipients who accept the reputation and personality of the sender (Hovland & Weiss, 1951). Based on this theory, it can be said that influencers being reputable people can leave a good impression on their followers. Similar to the source credibility theory, there is also the source attraction theory. According to this theory, the image of the advertiser is important for buyers. Here, we can consider the advertiser as influencers and the buyers as their followers. According to the theory, the attractiveness or well-groomed appearance of influencers can increase their influence on their followers (Baker & Churchill, 1977). According to the customer journey theory, the buying process works in 6 stages. These are desire, information search, alternative evaluation, making purchasing decision, post-purchase satisfaction and experience sharing (Pop et al., 2022). In fact, this model is fully compatible with influencer marketing. People who are pushed to buy by influencers also follow these steps.

## 1.2. Evaluating Long and Short Term Effects and Sustainability of İnfluencer Marketing

In the current digital age, many brands have found influencer marketing to be an effective strategy for reaching their target audiences. The long-term success of this approach depends on the continued effectiveness of influencers, which is closely tied to their credibility and relationship with their followers. While influencer collaborations can yield short-term benefits, their long-term impact hinges on the careful selection of influencers and strategic management of these partnerships. It is important to consider the potential risks of choosing the wrong influencer or failing to maintain their influence over time, as they could potentially hinder a brand's goals and harm its reputation. To maximize the potential of influencer marketing, brands may wish to approach these partnerships with a long-term perspective, continuously monitoring and adjusting their strategies as needed.

In order to implement a successful and sustainable influencer marketing strategy, businesses may collaborate with influencers, whether short-term or long-term. The financial resources allocated by businesses for the engagement of influencers can serve as a determining factor in the duration of such collaborations. When establishing a budget for influencers, it is essential to recognize that there are no fixed prices. Each influencer may request disparate fees, necessitating an evaluation of each influencer individually (Glenister, 2021). Nevertheless, it would be erroneous to assume that businesses will necessarily achieve their desired outcomes when engaging in influencer marketing. The selection of an inappropriate influencer or the influencer's inability to effectively promote the brand at the desired level can impede businesses' ability to achieve their desired outcomes (Brown & Hayes, 2008).

Short-term collaborations with influencers are characterized by a rapid pace of interaction and a focus on immediate outcomes. If a business seeks to expand its customer base, increase sales, and enhance brand awareness in a relatively short period of time, it may opt for a short-term influencer marketing strategy. An alternative approach is to initially enter into short-term agreements with influencers with whom the business has no prior experience (Backaler, 2018). Furthermore, short-term agreements with influencers are typically less costly than long-term partnerships. The greater the number of potential customers exposed to product advertisements, the greater the likelihood of an increase in purchases. Nevertheless, there are also disadvantages associated with short-term influencer marketing (Table 1). Furthermore, the influencer may not adopt the product in short-term collaborations, which may result in a lack of sincerity in the promotion of the brand. Moreover, in the context of short-term collaborations, influencers may lack sufficient information about the product in question. When customers possess comprehensive knowledge about a product, they are more likely to make prompt purchasing decisions. The exposure of customers to short-term advertisements may result in them becoming less attentive to them. Additionally, businesses may lose the influencers with whom they have established a positive working relationship when they engage with them for a limited duration (Nandi, 2022).

Long-term influencer marketing is defined as a long-term contractual agreement between a business entity and an influencer. As a result of their prolonged engagement with businesses, influencers may eventually assume the role of brand ambassadors, internalizing the brand in question (Nandi, 2022). Furthermore, when influencers enter into long-term agreements with businesses, they may perceive greater financial stability, as they can anticipate a reliable source of income over an extended period. This may facilitate the sharing of more sincere and authentic content by influencers (Turku, 2023). In light of these considerations, it can be posited that long-term agreements are mutually beneficial for both businesses and influencers. It is crucial for businesses and influencers to cultivate a constructive dialogue and establish mutual trust in order to ensure the success of long-term collaborations. Nevertheless, long-term influencer marketing, like short-term collaboration, also presents certain disadvantages (Backaler, 2018). It is incumbent upon businesses to exercise careful and meticulous management in their long-term collaborations with influencers. This places a significant responsibility on the business. Such circumstances may result in a loss of interest and engagement between the business and the influencer. In such instances, it may be beneficial for businesses to consider taking brief intermissions in their collaborations with influencers (von Mettenheim & Wiedman, 2021). The assessment of long-term impact in influencer marketing is a more challenging undertaking than that of short-term measurements. It is recommended that businesses measure customer loyalty over an extended period of time. In the context of long-term collaborations, businesses are typically constrained to working with a limited number of influencers. In the context of short-term collaborations, businesses are afforded the opportunity to engage with a greater number of influencers (Santigo & Castelo, 2020). This may entail reaching a greater number of followers. In this context, the objectives of the business become evident. If the business aims to reach a broader audience, it can collaborate with short-term, dependable influencers. Alternatively, if it seeks to promote its product to a particular target demographic, it can enter into long-term agreements with influencers (Nadanyiova, 2020). However, a potential drawback is that long-term collaborations necessitate more frequent communication with influencers, which can be time-consuming (Turku, 2023) (Table 1).

*Table 1. Comparison of Long-term vs. Short-term Influencer Marketing*

| | Long-term Influencer Marketing | Short-term Influencer Marketing |
|---|---|---|
| **Advantages** | Influencers who build long-term relationships with brands are more likely to produce content that is both intimate and authentic, thereby enhancing brand loyalty (Turku, 2023). | Businesses can achieve rapid increases in sales and brand awareness through short-term collaborations with influencers (Backaler, 2018). |
| | Influencers who engage in long-term collaborations with businesses tend to feel a greater sense of security, fostering a more stable partnership (Turku, 2023). | These brief engagements provide businesses with an opportunity to evaluate influencers they have not previously partnered with, allowing for a trial period before committing to a longer-term relationship (Backaler, 2018). |
| | Businesses tend to retain influencers whom they trust, ensuring consistent brand representation over time (Nandi, 2022). | Short-term contracts with influencers tend to be more cost-effective, making them a financially attractive option for many companies (Nandi, 2022). |
| | Long-term collaborations enable businesses to deliver targeted advertisements to specific audiences, potentially increasing the effectiveness of their marketing efforts (Nadanyiova, 2020). | This approach allows businesses to collaborate with a larger number of influencers within a limited timeframe compared to long-term partnerships (Nadanyiova, 2020). |
| **Disadvantages** | By focusing on long-term deals with a select group of influencers, businesses may limit the reach of their advertising campaigns, as fewer people are exposed to their products (Turku, 2023). | However, customers may only have fleeting exposure to the influencer's advertisements in short-term collaborations, which can reduce the overall impact of the campaign (Nandi, 2022). |
| | Long-term collaborations necessitate ongoing communication between businesses and influencers, which can be time-consuming and may result in inefficiencies for both parties. | Influencers may not fully embrace or understand the products they are promoting in short-term collaborations, leading to less authentic and persuasive endorsements (Nandi, 2022). |
| | Businesses must implement careful and strategic policies in long-term partnerships, which can present significant challenges and require sustained effort (von Mettenheim & Wiedman, 2021). | Businesses risk losing valuable connections with influencers when engagements are short-lived, potentially missing out on long-term benefits. |
| | Assessing the impact of influencer marketing in long-term collaborations can be challenging, as it is difficult to quantify the effectiveness of these partnerships over extended periods (Santigo and Castelo, 2020). | Brief advertising exposure may cause customers to disregard the promotional content altogether (Nandi, 2022). |

There are advantages and disadvantages inherent to both forms of influencer marketing. The most crucial factor is the objective a company is trying to achieve. Organizations may engage in long- or short-term collaborations with influencers that align with their strategic goals. For those aiming to achieve tangible outcomes in a relatively short timeframe, a shorter collaboration may be more suitable. However, for those who wish to maintain brand visibility and retain the trust of influential individuals, a longer-term strategy of influencer marketing may be more beneficial.

# METHODOLOGY

## 2.1. Study Design

In this study, a systematic literature review was used. A systematic literature search is a technique used in the social sciences to examine studies in a field and to learn the contributions of these studies to the literature (Chu et al., 2020; Maggiore et al., 2022, p. 2749). The steps used in this study are as follows; (1) Identifying literature using online databases and academic search engines to identify studies that have made scientific contributions about influencers. (2) Screening to delete studies that are not included in the purpose of the study. (3) Selecting among the studies that are suitable for the purpose of the study, determining whether they really fit the desired purpose. (4) Sorting the identified studies by subject before conducting a deep research on the studies. (5) In-depth review and reporting of the identified studies. As a result of the search, 82 studies were found. These studies were analyzed in terms of year, method, subject, sample and results.

## 2.2. Data Collection

The following databases were used to examine the studies conducted to examine the effects of the content produced by influencers on the behavior of tourists on social media: Google Scholar, Science Direct, Scopus, EBSCO, Proquest, Web of Science and YÖK National Thesis Center. In order to be inclusive, both English and Turkish studies were reviewed. While examining the studies, a meticulous study was carried out to be reproducible. The following keywords were selected to examine the studies on the targeted topic: 'influencer marketing', 'content created by influencers', 'tourism', 'tourism marketing'. Online research was then conducted on the identified databases using these keywords. During the research, only studies specific to a particular topic were focused on. All studies published between 2012 and 2023 that examine the effects of influencers' content on consumer (tourist) behavior on social media were collected and content analysis method was applied.

## 2.3. Inclusion and Exclusion Criteria

The literature was systematically reviewed to ensure validity, reliability and reproducibility (Xiao & Watson, 2019; Maggiore et al., 2022). Rigorous steps were taken to eliminate studies. When screening the studies, we focused on the following questions: 'does the study investigate the specific topic, i.e. the relationship between the content produced by influencers on social media and tourists' behavior'. Studies that met this criterion were included in this systematic literature review, while studies that did not meet this criterion were excluded from the systematic literature review. Another exclusion criterion was that the studies were published outside the years 2012-2023.

## 2.4. Data Analysis

A coding table was created in the study. At this stage of the study, the literature between 2012 and 2023 was coded and categorized by first determining the number of studies, distribution by years, methods used in the studies, data collection tools, theories used, main topics of the studies, and authors of the studies. Afterwards, a deeper examination was made and the studies were separated according to their subjects and the studies were classified in 5 categories: the year of the study, the name of the study, the authors, the method (design, data collection tool, analysis and methods) and the results and findings of the study.

## 3. FINDINGS

## 3.1. Systematic Analysis of Studies on the Content Produced by Influencers on Social Media

As a result of the analysis of the studies on the content produced by influencers on social media, it was determined that there was one study in 2012, four studies in 2022 and 43 studies in 2023 (Figure 1). Accordingly, it is understood that in 2023, studies on influencers were emphasized compared to other years. As can be seen in Figure 1, the number of studies on this subject increased after 2015 and reached its peak in 2023.

*Figure 1. Distribution of studies on content created by influencers by years*

## 3.2. Findings Regarding the Methods of Studies Conducted on the Content Produced by Influencers on Social Media

When examining studies on influencer marketing in tourism, it was found that 41 studies used quantitative research methods and 41 studies used qualitative research methods (Table 2). These results indicate that both methods are used equally. However, when compared to 2022 and previous years, it was determined that quantitative methods were used more frequently, while the use of qualitative methods increased in 2023.

*Table 2. Research methods used in studies on the content produced by influencers*

| Research Method | n | % |
|---|---|---|
| Quantitative | 41 | 50.0 |
| Qualitative | 41 | 50.0 |
| Total | 82 | 100 |

In terms of data collection techniques, more than half of the studies conducted in the last 10 years have preferred the use of surveys (43), followed by content analysis (12), literature review (10), conceptual analysis (9), interviews (7), and experiments (3) (Table 3).

*Table 3. Data collection tools used in studies on the content produced by influencers*

| Data Collection Tool | n | % |
|---|---|---|
| Questionnaire | 43 | 51,19% |
| Content analysis | 12 | 14,29% |
| Literature review | 10 | 11,90% |
| Conceptual | 9 | 10,71% |
| Interviews | 7 | 8,33% |
| Experimental | 3 | 3,57% |
| Total | 84* | 100 |

\* Although there are 82 studies in total, the fact that the total data collection tools are more is due to the fact that two data collection tools were used in two studies.

## 3.3. Theories Used in Studies Conducted on the Content Produced by Influencers on Social Media

Upon examining the theories presented in the relevant literature between 2012 and 2023, a total of 25 theories were identified. The most frequently utilized theory was the source credibility theory. followed by uses and gratifications, planned behavior, and social comparison theories (Table 4).

*Table 4. Theories used in studies on the content produced by influencers*

| 1 | Source credibility theory | 6 |
|---|---|---|
| 2 | Uses and gratifications theory | 2 |
| 3 | Theory of planned behavior | 2 |
| 4 | Social comparison theory | 2 |
| 5 | Customer Journey Theory | 1 |
| 6 | Persuasion theory | 1 |
| 7 | Business-to-business (B2B) marketing theory | 1 |
| 8 | Strauss-Howe Generational Theory | 1 |
| 9 | Endorsement theory | 1 |
| 10 | Social media marketing theory | 1 |
| 11 | Associative-network memory theory | 1 |
| 12 | Behavioral decision theory | 1 |
| 13 | Cognitive dissonance theory | 1 |
| 14 | Conspicuous consumption theory | 1 |
| 15 | Social impact theory | 1 |
| 16 | Parasocial interaction theory | 1 |
| 17 | Marketing funnel theory | 1 |
| 18 | Gad (2000) four-dimensional model | 1 |
| 19 | Modern entrepreneurship theory | 1 |
| 20 | Theory of contextual cue diagnosticity | 1 |
| 21 | Moral responsibility theory | 1 |
| 22 | Signaling Theory | 1 |
| 23 | Willing identification | 1 |
| 24 | Balance theory | 1 |
| 25 | Human Brand Theory | 1 |

## 3.4. Subjects of the Studies Conducted on the Content Produced by Influencers on Social Media

The studies discussed in this part of the research are classified according to their subjects. The studies were carried out on 3 main topics: the impact of the content produced by influencers on tourists' purchasing intention, analysis of the content produced by influencers, and other studies on the content produced by influencers. Studies on the content produced by social media influencers have primarily focused on its impact on the purchasing behaviors of tourists (40), followed by the analysis of the contents produced by influencers (32) and other topics (10) (such as the relationship between influencer marketing and business performance (2), tourists' attitudes towards influencers and the content they produce (5) and tourists' trust in influencers and the content they produce (3) (Table 5). When examining the literature, most studies were found to be focused on the effect of influencer-generated content on tourists' purchase intention, and the fewest studies were found to be focused on analyzing the relationship between influencer-generated content and business performance. Therefore, further research is needed to investigate the relationship between influencer content and business performance.

*Table 5. Topics Covered in Studies Conducted Regarding Content Produced by Influencers on Social Media*

| Subject | n | % |
|---|---|---|
| 1) The effect of the content produced by influencers on tourists' purchasing intention/purchasing process | 40 | 48.78% |
| 2) Analysis of the content produced by influencers | 32 | 39.02% |
| 3) Other | 10 | 12.19% |
| Total | 82 | 100 |

## 4. FINDINGS ON THE SUBJECTS EXAMINED IN THE STUDIES

The studies are categorized according to their subjects. A total of 82 studies were discussed in 3 categories. These are the effects of the content produced by influencers on tourists' purchasing intention, analysis of the content produced by influencers and other categories. The other category includes studies on the relationship between the content produced by influencers and the performance of businesses, the trust of tourists in influencers and the content they produce, and the attitude of tourists towards influencers and the content they produce (Table 5).

## 4.1. The Impact of Content Produced by Influencers on Tourists' Purchasing Intention

Table 5 shows that 40 studies have investigated the effect of influencer-produced content on tourists' purchasing intentions. Overall, the majority of studies indicate a positive impact of such content on the purchasing process. Additionally, the study results suggest that influencer recommendations carry more weight than friend recommendations or accommodation prices. It has been revealed that interest in influencers is increasing, and they can help eliminate tourists' doubts about accommodation establishments. Influencers' sincerity, reliability, and interesting content have an impact on tourists, making it easier for them to decide to buy.

However, several studies have found that the content produced by influencers has little to no significant effect on tourists' purchasing intentions (Demir, 2018; Aslan & Öziç, 2020; Hıra & Karabulut, 2021). As a result, tourists may be skeptical of influencers (Şahin, 2020), leading to a contradiction regarding their trustworthiness. Therefore, further research is necessary to examine trust in influencers.

The impact of influencer content on purchase intention has been the subject of research in four areas: the impact of influencers on tourists' brand attitude and awareness towards tourism businesses, the impact of the number of followers an influencer has on tourists' choice of tourism business and destination, and their intention to revisit. The studies recommend that influencers be sincere towards their followers and produce engaging content. In order to increase their influence, it is recommended that influencers respond to messages from their followers. This can lead to greater persuasiveness when it comes to encouraging tourists to make purchases (see Table 6).

*Table 6. Topics and Authors Covered in Studies Conducted on the Effect of Content Produced by Influencers on Tourists' Purchasing Intention*

| Subject | Findings | Suggestions | Sources |
|---|---|---|---|
| **The impact of content produced by influencers on tourists' purchasing intention** | Research has shown that influencers are more influential than friend recommendations and accommodation prices when it comes to making travel decisions. Additionally, the popularity of influencers is on the rise, as they help to alleviate tourists' concerns about accommodation/travel options. | In order to be effective, influencers should be sincere with their followers and create engaging content. It is also important for influencers to respond to messages from their followers. This can help to increase the likelihood of tourists making a purchase. | Kalpaklıoğlu, 2015; Demir, 2018; Can & Saldamlı, 2018; Karadeniz, 2019 Saldamlı, 2019; Semiz & Zengin, 2019 Avcı & Yıldız, 2019; Bognar, Puljic & Kadezabek, 2019; Şahin, 2020; Canöz, Gülmez & Eroğlu, 2020; Aslan Çetin & Öziç, 2020; Avcı & Bilgili, 2020; Theocharis & Papaioannou, 2020; Wonseok et al., 2020; Hıra & Karabulut, 2021; Gürkan & Ulema, 2021; Yetimoğlu & Uğurlu, 2021; Sesar et al., 2021; Belanche et al., 2021; Seibel, 2021; Han & Chen, 2021; Deegan, 2021; Ďaďová & Soviar, 2021; Zhang & Huang, 2022; Masuda et al., 2022; Güneş, Ekmekçi & Tan, 2022; Pop et al., 2022; Erdoğan, 2023; Haseki, 2023; Gümüş & Kızılırmak, 2023; Yavuz & Sağlam, 2023; Köprülü & Turhan, 2023; Sarıoğlu, 2023; Lou et al., 2023; Ao et al., 2023; Ooi et al., 2023; Khan et al., 2023; Conde & Casais, 2023; Kim & Park, 2023; Filieri et al., 2023. |

continued on following page

*Table 6. Continued*

| Subject | Findings | Suggestions | Sources |
|---|---|---|---|
| **Desire** | It has been found that influencers can influence purchasing decisions and encourage tourists to buy. The content produced by influencers is particularly effective in creating desire during the purchasing process. | To create demand, it is recommended that influencers share interesting and colorful images and videos. Businesses can advertise to influencers to create demand among their followers and have them create special discount codes for their followers. | Şahin, 2020; Pop et al., 2022. |
| **Information Search** | It was found that influencers are primarily followed to be entertained, to stay informed, and to satisfy followers' curiosity. Additionally, trust in influencers has been found to impact the information search stage. | During the information search stage, it is advisable for influencers to use hashtags to influence their followers. The content produced by influencers should not be incomplete and short, and businesses collaborating with influencers should partner with those who provide up-to-date information. | Semiz & Zengin, 2019; Bognar, Puljic & Kadezabek, 2019; Martinez-López et al., 2019; Ďaďová & Soviar, 2021; Pop et al., 2022. |
| **Alternative Assessment** | Influencer posts have been found to be effective when tourists are evaluating alternatives during the purchase process. | To stand out during the alternative evaluation process, it is recommended that influencers create engaging posts. However, it is important to avoid subjective evaluations and maintain a clear, objective language. Businesses collaborating with influencers may request the use of hashtags such as 'most prestigious hotel' when sharing. | Pop et al., 2022. |

continued on following page

*Table 6. Continued*

| Subject | Findings | Suggestions | Sources |
|---|---|---|---|
| **Purchase** | Studies have shown that influencer content can positively impact the purchasing stage. However, there are also studies in the literature that suggest otherwise. | Tourism operators may benefit from reliable influencers, who can gain the trust of their followers. Businesses should follow surveys about influencers and work with those who suit their needs. | Kalpaklıoğlu, 2015; Demir, 2018; Can & Saldamlı, 2018; Karadeniz, 2019 Saldamlı, 2019; Semiz & Zengin, 2019 Avcı & Yıldız, 2019; Bognar, Puljic & Kadezabek, 2019 Canöz, Gülmez & Eroğlu, 2020; Aslan Çetin & Öziç, 2020; Avcı & Bilgili, 2020; Theocharis & Papaioannou, 2020; Wonseok et al., 2020; Hıra & Karabulut, 2021; Gürkan & Ulema, 2021; Yetimoğlu & Uğurlu, 2021; Sesar et al., 2021; Belanche et al., 2021; Seibel, 2021; Han & Chen, 2021; Deegan, 2021 Zhang ve Huang, 2022; Masuda et al., 2022; Güneş, Ekmekçi & Tan, 2022; Pop et al., 2022; Erdoğan, 2023; Haseki, 2023; Gümüş & Kızlırmak, 2023; Yavuz ve Sağlam, 2023; Köprülü & Turhan, 2023; Sarıoğlu, 2023; Lou et al., 2023; Ao et al., 2023; Ooi et al., 2023; Khan et al., 2023; Conde & Casais, 2023; Kim & Park, 2023; Filieri et al., 2023. |

111

### 4.1.1. Desire Creation

Tourists may use social media to research holiday options or purchase tourism products. Influencers' posts can influence their decisions. Tourists who are exposed to the images and videos in the content produced by influencers may be more likely to make a purchase. Businesses and DMOs can collaborate with influencers to advertise to their target audiences and increase their desire to buy. Based on the studies conducted by Şahin (2020) and Pop et al. (2022), it has been determined that influencer-generated content stimulates tourists' desire. As per the recommendations of these studies, businesses can advertise to influencers to create demand among their followers. Additionally, they can offer special discount codes to the influencers' followers, which the influencers can share with their audience (Table 6).

### 4.1.2. Information Search

After the desire to purchase the touristic product is aroused in social media users, tourists search for information about the relevant products on the internet. Influencers' posts can be particularly helpful in this regard, as they often provide informative texts and visuals. This allows potential buyers to obtain the necessary information without having to physically visit the destination or product they are interested in. The studies indicate that people follow influencers to obtain information, and trust in influencers is a key factor in their effectiveness in providing information (Semiz & Zengin, 2019; Bognar, Puljic & Kadezabek, 2019; Martínez-López et al., 2019; Ďaďová & Soviar, 2021; Pop et al., 2022). Studies recommend that influencers use hashtags to influence their followers during the information search stage. The content produced by influencers should not be short or incomplete. Businesses collaborating with influencers should work with those who share up-to-date information (Table 6).

### 4.1.3. Alternative Assessment

Tourists evaluate alternatives by comparing prices and features of products or destinations after obtaining the necessary information. Tourists want to access information quickly and accurately. Therefore, influencers should share clear and objective information. The study results suggest that influencer-generated content is effective during the alternative evaluation phase (Pop et al., 2022). To stand out in the alternative evaluation process, influencers are advised to create interesting posts. Businesses collaborating with influencers can request the use of hashtags such as 'this is the most prestigious hotel' when sharing (Table 6).

### 4.1.4. Purchase

After considering various options, tourists can choose the product that best meets their needs and desires. When making a purchase decision, they may prioritize features such as product quality, location, and comfort. Studies have shown that influencer-generated content has a positive impact on persuading tourists to make a purchase. Table 5 shows that tourism operators should use trustworthy influencers, and influencers should gain the trust of their followers. Businesses should follow surveys about influencers and work with those who are a good fit for them (Table 6).

## 4.2. Studies Conducted to Analyze the Content Produced by Influencers

There are 32 studies analyzing the content produced by influencers (Table 7). It has been determined that the contents produced by influencers have an impact on consumers through the E-WOM method (Sarıışık & Özbay, 2012; Dhun & Dangi, 2023; Simay et al., 2023) and thus increase product and service sales (Bokunewics & Shulman, 2017). It has also been determined that the content produced by influencers has a positive effect on increasing brand awareness and purchasing frequency, that influencers are important and valuable within the scope of brand promotion, that they can deliver brands to large audiences, that businesses go to branding through influencers, and that tourists discover businesses thanks to influencers (Ergun, Bayrak & Doğan, 2019; Martínez-Sala et al., 2019; Serra & Gretzel, 2020; Xu et al., 2021; Bilgin, 2023; Mero et al., 2023; Han et al., 2023; Xie & Feng, 2023; Borges- Tiago et al., 2023). It is important for influencers to produce interesting and abundant visual content, to choose images that are especially colorless, and to include animals in the images in order to increase the number of followers and reach large audiences (Xu et al., 2021; Ergun, Bayrak & Doğan, 2019; Abell & Biswas, 2023). Influencers' content containing visuals about businesses may also attract the attention of tourists. Influencers with content including elements of humor in their content, giving importance to appearance, and originality of the content also increase the effectiveness of the messages intended to be given (Barta et al. 2023; Deng & Jiang, 2023; Vassey et al., 2023; Arnesson, 2023).

Chatzigeorgiou (2017), one of the studies conducted within the scope of analyzing the content produced by influencers, found a negative relationship between the number of followers and the attitudes of social media users, that is, he determined that the number of followers does not affect other users. Wies et al. (2023) determined that as the number of followers of influencers increases, interaction first increases and then gradually decreases. Additionally, it has been revealed that traditional marketing cannot be applied to small businesses, while influencer marketing has become a valuable asset for the tourism industry. Additionally, it has been found that some posts made by influencers for the purpose of showing off can have negative effects on the psychological and physical health of their followers (Hudders & Lou, 2023). This is one of the negative aspects of influencer marketing. Pradhan et al. (2023) determined that influencers were seen as morally irresponsible.

According to studies, it is recommended that influencers increase their number of followers and reveal their true identities on social media. It is recommended that businesses collaborate with influencers with high follower numbers (Table 7).

*Table 7. Subjects of the Studies Conducted to Analyze Content Produced by Influencers*

| Subject | Findings | Suggestions | Sources |
|---|---|---|---|
| **Analysis of content produced by influencers** | It has been determined that as the number of followers of influencers increases, their interaction first increases and then gradually decreases. Additionally, it has been revealed that traditional marketing cannot be applied to small businesses, while influencer marketing has become a valuable asset for the tourism industry. It has also been found that some posts made by influencers to show off can have negative effects on the psychological and physical health of their followers. | Influencers should aim to grow their audience and disclose their true identity on social media. Businesses should work with influencers who have a large number of followers. | Sarışık & Özbay, 2012; Bokunewics & Shulman, 2017; Chatzigeorgiou, 2017; Ge & Gretzel, 2018; Ergun, Bayrak & Doğan, 2019; A-M Martínez-Sala et al., 2019; Gedik, 2020 ;Serra ve Gretzel, 2020; Xu et al., 2021; Kocabay & Öymen, 2023; Sönmez, 2023; Akyol & Atabey, 2023; Bilgin, 2023; Hudders & Lou, 2023; Mero et al., 2023; Barta et al., 2023; Han et al., 2023; Pradhan et al., 2023; Gamage & Ashill, 2023; Abell ve Biswas, 2023; Wies et al., 2023; Dhun & Dangi, 2023; Xie & Feng, 2023; Vanninen et al., 2023; Bhattacharya, 2023; Deng & Jiang, 2023; Vassey et al., 2023; Chen et al., 2023; Barbosa et al., 2023; Arnesson, 2023; Simay et al., 2023; Borges-Tiago et al., 2023. |
| **Studies examining videos shared by influencers** | It has been determined that influencers can increase product and service sales, create new fans, and generate site visits and YouTube views on social media platforms. | Tourists often discover businesses through influencers. Therefore influencers' content should be interesting and informative, with detailed information about the destination's natural beauty and fun activities. It is important to avoid short videos and instead focus on creating longer, more detailed videos. | Bokunewics & Shulman, 2017; Xu et al., 2021; Akyol & Atabey, 2023; Gamage & Ashill, 2023; Xie & Feng, 2023; Vanninen, 2023; Vassey et al., 2023; Chen et al.,2023; Simay et al., 2023 |

continued on following page

*Table 7. Continued*

| Subject | Findings | Suggestions | Sources |
|---|---|---|---|
| **Studies examining photos shared by influencers** | Influencer marketing has been shown to deliver better ROI than branded content or direct advertising when marketed correctly. Additionally, colorless images containing animals have been shown to have a positive effect on follower interactions. Furthermore, there is a significant relationship between the number of likes and comments from followers. It has been determined that influencers are important and valuable for brand promotion and can reach large audiences. The results indicate that businesses use influencers for branding. | Influencers are advised to include a variety of interesting photos in their content to increase their number of followers. It is also recommended to include animal images as they tend to attract attention. | Ge & Gretzel, 2018; Ergun, Bayrak & Doğan, 2019; Martínez-Sala et al., 2019; Serra & Gretzel, 2020; Kocabay & Öymen, 2023; Akyol & Atabey, 2023; Barta et al., 2023; Gamage & Ashill, 2023; Abell & Biswas, 2023; Wies et al., 2023; Xie & Feng, 2023; Vanninen et al., 2023; Bhattacharya, 2023; Deng & Jiang, 2023; Vassey et al., 2023; Barbosa et al., 2023; Arnesson et al., 2023; Simay et al., 2023 |

### 4.2.1. Studies Examining Videos

Studies available in the literature have analyzed the content produced by influencers by examining Facebook, Twitter, Instagram and YouTube platforms. Studies examining videos are in the minority compared to studies with photo analysis (Table 6). According to these studies, it has been determined that influencers sharing videos about the relevant product or destination in the content they produce has a positive effect on their followers (Bokunewics & Shulman, 2017; Xu et al., 2021; Akyol & Atabey, 2023; Gamage & Ashill, 2023; Xie & Feng, 2023; Vanninen, 2023; Vassey et al., 2023; Chen et al., 2023; Simay et al., 2023). Studies have shown that tourists learn about businesses through influencers. In addition, it is recommended that the videos shared by influencers should not be short, the information in the videos should be detailed, and the natural beauties and fun activities of the destination should be included in the videos (Table 7).

### 4.2.2. Studies Examining Photos Shared by Influencers

There are many studies in the literature examining the content produced by influencers in various social media channels (Table 7). Influencers adding photos to the content they produce attracts the attention of tourists. According to studies, influencers' production of accurate and comprehensive content can push tourists into the purchasing process (Gretzel, 2018; Ergun, Bayrak & Doğan, 2019; Martínez-Sala et al., 2019; Serra & Gretzel, 2020; Kocabay & Öymen, 2023; Akyol & Atabey, 2023; Barta et al., 2023; Gamage & Ashill, 2023; Abell & Biswas, 2023; Wies et al., 2023; Xie & Feng, 2023; Vanninen et al., 2023; Bhattacharya, 2023; Deng & Jiang, 2023; Vassey et al., 2023; Barbosa et al., 2023; Arnesson et al., 2023; Simay et al., 2023). According to studies, influencers are recommended to share lots of interesting photos in their content in order to increase their number of followers. While sharing photos, it is also recommended to share animal images as they attract attention (Table 7).

### 4.3. Other Studies Conducted on the Content Produced by Influencers

There are 10 other studies conducted on influencer marketing in tourism. Among these studies, there are two studies examining the relationship between the content produced by influencers and the performance of businesses, three studies on the trust of tourists in influencers and the content they produce, and five studies on the attitude of tourists towards influencers and the content they produce (Table 8). According to studies, it is recommended that influencers use real accounts instead of fake accounts. It is also recommended that influencers clearly express their areas of expertise in their content and add them to their profile articles.

*Table 8. Topics and Authors Covered in Other Studies on Content Produced by Influencers*

| Subject | Findings | Suggestions | Sources |
|---|---|---|---|
| **Other Studies on Influencers** | It has been determined that the level of interest of influencers in the product and the interaction effect of tourists affects the attitude towards advertising and the intention of electronic word-of-mouth communication, that trust in influencers increases the desire to seek information, that travel agencies actively use social media accounts, and that influencers provide great advantages to businesses in terms of recognition. In addition, it has been determined that users are interested in influencers close to themselves or their areas of expertise. | Influencers should use authentic accounts instead of fake ones. Additionally, they should clearly state their areas of expertise in their content and profile articles. | Avcılar et al., 2018; Martínez-López et al., 2019; Akdeniz & Kömürcü, 2021; Öztürk, 2023; Demirağ, 2023; Lou et al., 2023; Younis, 2023; Malik et al., 2023; Rudeloff & Egbert, 2023; Chen et al., 2023. |
| **The Relationship between the Content Produced by Influencers and the Performance of Businesses (2)** | It has been determined that travel agencies constantly use social media channels and do not ignore the benefits that influencers provide them. It has been determined that it would be beneficial for DMO's to cooperate with influencers and supporters. | In order to create a positive impact on their followers, it is recommended that influencers actively utilize their all different types of social media accounts. This can also benefit businesses that collaborate with influencers. | Akdeniz & Kömürcü, 2021; Rudeloff & Egbert, 2023. |
| **Tourists' Trust in Influencers and the Content They Produce (3)** | Research has shown that trust in influencers is more likely to decrease due to the perceived commercial nature of their posts rather than the influencer's perceived control over the content. Additionally, the credibility of influencers is positively impacted by their physical attractiveness, social attractiveness, and attitudinal similarity. | Presenting yourself professionally and being courteous is important for influencers. Businesses should collaborate with influencers who are perceived as trustworthy by their followers. | Martínez-López et al., 2019; Demirağ, 2023; Younis, 2023. |
| **Tourists' Attitudes Towards Influencers and the Content They Produce (5)** | Using new digital innovations and technologies, such as ai assited social media accounts, can have a more persuasive impact on tourists' attitudes. | Influencers should keep up with social media innovations and use artificial intelligence applications when sharing content. This will attract the attention of tourists. | Avcılar et al., 2018; Öztürk, 2023; Lou et al., 2023; Malik et al., 2023; Chen et al., 2023. |

### 4.3.1. Studies on the Relationship between the Content Produced by Influencers and the Performance of Businesses

Looking at the results of studies conducted on this subject, it has been determined that travel agencies actively use social media platforms (Akdeniz & Kömürcü, 2021). However, the influence of influencers on social media is not surprising for businesses and DMO's. Thanks to influencers appealing to large audiences, businesses and DMO's can find the opportunity to make their products shine more easily. It has also been determined that influencers benefit businesses and DMO's if they cooperate with businesses and DMO's (Rudeloff & Egbert, 2023). According to studies, it is recommended that influencers use their social media accounts actively (Table 8).

### 4.3.2. Studies on Tourists' Trust in Influencers and the Content They Produce

Considering the results of the studies conducted on this subject, it has been determined that trust in influencers has a positive effect on the purchasing process and persuading tourists to purchase. In addition, it has been found that influencers' being attractive, social and sincere has a positive effect on their credibility (Martínez-López, 2019; Demirağ, 2023; Younis, 2023). Studies suggest that influencers should pay attention to their self-care in order to increase their reliability. According to studies, it is recommended that influencers be well-groomed and treat their followers politely. It is recommended that businesses collaborate with influencers who are perceived as trustworthy by their followers (Table 8).

### 4.3.3. Studies on Tourists' Attitudes Towards Influencers and the Content They Produce

Based on the studies conducted, it has been determined that influencers' interest in the product and tourists' interaction have a positive effect on attitude towards advertising and intention for electronic word of mouth communication (Avcılar and Demirgüneş, 2018). On the basis of this, it can be concluded that tourists in general have a positive point of view towards influencers. Studies have shown that users perceive fake influencer accounts as unnatural (Lou et al., 2023; Malik et al., 2023). In this regard, it would be more appropriate for influencers to establish sincere relationships with their followers and to share posts from accounts that state their identities in order to create a positive impact on their followers. It has been determined that identity prestige is important for influencers (Öztürk, 2023).

Influencers' areas of expertise help to attract their target audience. They share content based on their interests and can answer their followers' questions. A study has shown that social media users are interested in influencers who are similar to them or have expertise in their fields (Chen et al., 2023). It is recommended that influencers keep up with social media innovations. Influencers should keep up with social media innovations and utilize artificial intelligence applications when sharing content to capture the attention of tourists (Table 8).

## 5. CONCLUSION AND RECOMMENDATIONS

In the tourism industry, advertising and promotion of touristic products are crucial for businesses and DMOs to reach their target audiences. Influencers on social media have a significant impact and can help promote touristic products. When selecting an influencer to collaborate with, businesses and DMOs should consider the influencer's areas of expertise. It is crucial that the influencer possesses areas of expertise and creates content that resonates with the target audience of businesses and DMOs.

This study first defines the concept of influencers and their importance in influencer marketing, as well as their cooperation with tourism businesses and DMOs. The analysis of how influencers have been discussed in tourism literature over the past eleven years was conducted using the systematic literature review technique. A total of 82 studies were examined in terms of their methods, analysis techniques, main subject of research, and results. The studies were found to be focused on three main topics.

Since 2012, most studies have focused on the effect of influencer-produced content on tourists' purchasing intentions (40), followed by studies analyzing the content (videos/photos/blogs etc.) (32). From 2012 to 2017, most studies analyzed influencer-produced content. After 2017, the focus shifted to the impact of such content on purchasing intentions. After analyzing the results of these studies, it has been determined that influencers can significantly impact purchasing intention by creating and promoting content for businesses.

Upon analyzing the results, it is evident that the content created by influencers from 2012 to 2018 had minimal impact on tourists. However, since 2018, it has been determined that influencer-generated content is more effective than recommendations from friends in terms of its effect on purchasing intention and brand awareness, and has a positive impact on tourists' purchasing frequency. Therefore, it can be concluded that the influence of influencers on tourists has increased in recent years.

Based on the study results, influencers can expand their audience and promote their products and services by being sincere to their followers, creating original and interesting content, and partnering with businesses for sweepstakes. Additionally, high-resolution images used in their content can also influence tourists. The study results suggest that consumers find the number of followers and interactions with followers, such as comments and likes, of influencers on their social media accounts attractive. Influencers can increase their number of followers by producing interesting content. Therefore, it is important for influencers to consider this element in order to reach a wider audience.

The results of studies on the effects of the content produced by influencers on tourists and businesses after 2019 have yielded more positive results compared to previous years. In general, studies have determined that influencers' content production has a positive relationship with tourists and businesses. In this regard, it will be beneficial for businesses to cooperate with influencers in terms of branding. Thanks to the content produced by influencers, businesses have a high return on investment opportunity. As for tourists; They found the content produced by influencers very useful when planning travel. Tourists benefit from the content produced by influencers before, during and after the purchasing process.

Between 2020 and 2022, studies were conducted to measure the trust in influencers. In these studies, a significant relationship was determined between trust in influencers and tourists' purchasing intention. In 2023, studies on influencers and the content they produce have accelerated. In 2023, the issue of interaction between influencers and consumers has come to the fore. According to the recommendations of the studies examined, it is necessary to reveal the importance of influencer marketing with more research.

This study analyzes research conducted on the impact of influencer marketing on tourists' behavior and tourism marketing since 2012. It fills a gap in the literature by providing a comprehensive overview of the studies in this field and their results. By taking a relational perspective among studies on influencers since 2012, it offers a more precise understanding of their aims and outcomes.

When collaborating with influencers, businesses and DMOs should ensure that the influencers they choose are a good fit for their target audience. It is important to consider the character of the influencers, the content they share on social media, the realism of their advertisements, and the size of their audience, as measured by the number of followers they have (Katamnaa, 2020, p. 60). Additionally, it is crucial for influencers to be reliable (Maggiore et al., 2022, p. 19). In this way, influencers' posts can have a greater impact on consumers. Businesses and DMOs that value these suggestions can encourage purchasing behavior through influencer marketing.

It will be advantageous for influencers, tourists, businesses and DMO's to be sincere towards their followers, produce original content, produce interesting content and offer raffles in cooperation with businesses. Thus, they can appeal to larger audiences and have the opportunity to promote themselves and their products and services. In addition, the high resolution images used by influencers in the content they produce may also have an impact on tourists. The number of followers of influencers on their social media accounts and their interactions with tourists, such as comments and likes, may be perceived as attractive for tourists. In addition, including animal images in the content produced by influencers can increase the attractiveness of influencers' posts. For example, when we think of the Hagia Sophia Mosque in Istanbul, cats come to mind. Using cat images in the content produced here can increase the likeability of the content. The use of technological innovations in the content produced by influencers can also affect tourists.

Despite the current prominence of influencer marketing, questions remain regarding its long-term viability and the potential long-term effects of this marketing area. Short-term influencer marketing represents a specific branch of marketing that is characterized by an immediate and transient interaction with the influencer (Backaler, 2018). Short-term influencer marketing may be an optimal choice for businesses seeking to achieve results in a relatively short timeframe, such as enhancing brand awareness or sales (Gross & von Wangenheim, 2019). Alternatively, businesses that have not previously engaged with influencers may also opt for a short-term influencer marketing strategy (Backaler, 2018). Moreover, as businesses engage with influencers over an extended period, they may find themselves allocating a greater proportion of their marketing budget to this activity. In light of these considerations, businesses may also opt to engage with influencers on a short-term basis (Santiago & Castelo, 2020).

Short-term influencer marketing has both advantages and disadvantages. One significant drawback is that influencers may lack comprehensive knowledge of the advertised product or service (Nandi, 2022). Additionally, short-term collaborations can hinder effective communication between businesses and influencers. The expedited nature of short-term campaigns may reduce their efficacy, as both parties may rush the advertising process. Social media users are also more likely to ignore ads presented within a brief timeframe. Long-term collaborations are more advantageous for several reasons. They provide influencers with security, enabling them to adopt the brand and produce more authentic and enthusiastic content. Consequently, businesses may achieve greater gains from sustained influencer partnerships (Turku, 2023).

Although long-term influencer marketing offers considerable advantages, it also poses certain challenges in terms of sustainability and efficacy. The establishment and preservation of robust relationships with influencers hinges on effective communication and a mutual respect for one another (Breves et, al., 2019). Nevertheless, the lack of careful management in long-term partnerships may result in burnout among influencers. It is therefore important to allow for regular breaks, to ensure diversity of content and to offer fair remuneration. It is essential to ensure the provision of creative and topical content in order to circumvent the phenomenon of content fatigue and to maintain relevance for the target audience. It is recommended that influencers and brands adopt a responsive approach to social media trends, adapting their strategies in a timely manner. Furthermore, the alignment of brand and influencer values serves to preserve authenticity. In addition, it is challenging to quantify the long-term impact of influencer marketing (von Mettenheim & Wiedman, 2021). It is crucial to monitor brand loyalty, customer lifetime value, and referral rates. The combination of qualitative and quantitative data allows for the calculation of an effective return on investment (ROI). Moreover, the establishment of clear contractual agreements is essential to safeguard the rights of both parties. In terms of legal and ethical considerations, it is vital to adhere to relevant laws, maintain transparency, and uphold authenticity. Ethical partnerships and fair remuneration foster positive long-term outcomes. Cost and budget allocation should be conducted in a prudent manner, with meticulous planning and the measurement of long-term ROI (Backaler, 2018; Turku, 2023). In summation, it is imperative to consider a number of critical issues in order to develop a successful long-term influencer marketing strategy. These include, but are not limited to, relationship management, measurement and return on investment (ROI), consistency, risk management, legal and ethical considerations, cost and budget allocation. These elements contribute to the long-term value of brands by enhancing sustainability and effectiveness.

In the study, studies covering subjects other than the content produced by influencers were excluded. Subsequently, studies related to the subject were analyzed in depth and their main features were emphasized. When the literature is examined, the majority of studies are on the effect of the content produced by influencers on tourists' purchasing intention. However, there are 2 studies on the performance of businesses in the content produced by influencers (Akdeniz & Kömürcü, 2021; Rudeloff & Egbert, 2023), and a total of 3 studies on the trust of tourists in influencers and the content they produce (Martínez-López et al., 2019; Demirağ, 2023; Younis, 2023). Further research on these topics may be useful to fill the gap in the literature.

In summary, influencer marketing has positive effects on the tourism industry, but there are also studies in the literature that conclude that influencers are not effective. More work needs to be done on this subject in order to eliminate this contradiction.

# REFERENCES

Abell, A., & Biswas, D. (2023). Digital engagement on social media: How food image content influences social media and influencer marketing outcomes. *Journal of Interactive Marketing*, 58(1), 1–15. DOI: 10.1177/10949968221128556

Akdeniz, A., & Kömürcü, S. (2021). Evaluation of social media accounts of travel agencies: A research on the relations of travel agencies operating in Izmir with social media influencers. *International Journal of Contemporary Tourism Research*, 5(Special Issue), 98–115. DOI: 10.30625/ijctr.956026

Akyol, Z., & Atabey, Z. (2023). Personal Brand Building Process on Social Media: A Review of Twitter Phenomenons. *Afyon Kocatepe University Journal of Social Sciences*, 25(3), 929–944. DOI: 10.32709/akusosbil.1248420

Añaña, E., & Barbosa, B. (2023). Digital Influencers Promoting Healthy Food: The Role of Source Credibility and Consumer Attitudes and Involvement on Purchase Intention. *Sustainability (Basel)*, 15(20), 15002. DOI: 10.3390/su152015002

Ao, L., Bansal, R., Pruthi, N., & Khaskheli, M. B. (2023). Impact of social media influencers on customer engagement and purchase intention: A meta-analysis. *Sustainability (Basel)*, 15(3), 2744. DOI: 10.3390/su15032744

Arnesson, J. (2023). Influencers as ideological intermediaries: Promotional politics and authenticity labour in influencer collaborations. *Media Culture & Society*, 45(3), 528–544. DOI: 10.1177/01634437221117505

Avcı, İ., & Yıldız, E. (2019). The effects of influencers' credibility, attractiveness and expertise on brand attitude, purchase intention and electronic word-of-mouth marketing: Instagram example. *Kocaeli University Journal of Social Sciences*, 2(38), 85–107.

Avcılar, M. Y., Külter Demirgüneş, B., & Açar, M. F. (2018). Examining the effects of using social media influencers as product endorsers in Instagram ads on attitudes towards the ad and e-wom intention. *Journal of Marketing and Marketing Research*, 21, 1–27.

Avci, E., & Bilgili, B. (2020). The effect of the characteristics of the social media phenomenon on the followers' intention to visit a destination. *Journal of Tourism and Recreation*, 2(1), 83–92.

Backaler, J. (2018). *Digital Influence: Unleash the Power of Influencer Marketing to Accelerate Your Global Business*. Palgrave Macmillan. DOI: 10.1007/978-3-319-78396-3

Baker, M. J., & Churchill, G. A. Jr. (1977). The impact of physically attractive models on advertising evaluations. *JMR, Journal of Marketing Research*, 14(4), 538–555. DOI: 10.1177/002224377701400411

Barta, S., Belanche, D., Fernández, A., & Flavián, M. (2023). Influencer marketing on TikTok: The effectiveness of humor and followers' hedonic experience. *Journal of Retailing and Consumer Services*, 70, 103149. DOI: 10.1016/j.jretconser.2022.103149

Bayuk, M. N., & Aslan, M. (2019). Influencer Marketing. *The Journal of Academic Social Science*, 75(75), 173–185. DOI: 10.16992/ASOS.14033

Belanche, D., Casaló, L. V., Flavián, M., & Ibáñez-Sánchez, S. (2021). Understanding influencer marketing: The role of congruence between influencers, products and consumers. *Journal of Business Research*, 132, 186–195. DOI: 10.1016/j.jbusres.2021.03.067

Bhattacharya, A. (2023). Parasocial interaction in social media influencer-based marketing: An SEM approach. *Journal of Internet Commerce*, 22(2), 272–292. DOI: 10.1080/15332861.2022.2049112

Bilgin, B. (2023). Influencer Marketing from a Digital Entrepreneurship Perspective. Master's Thesis.

Bognar, Z. B., Puljic, N. P., & Kadezabek, D. (2019). Impact of influencer marketing on consumer behaviour. *Economic and Social Development: Book of Proceedings*, 301-309.

Bokunewicz, J. F., & Shulman, J. (2017). Influencer identification in Twitter networks of destination marketing organizations. *Journal of Hospitality and Tourism Technology*, 8(2), 205–219. DOI: 10.1108/JHTT-09-2016-0057

Borges-Tiago, M. T., Santiago, J., & Tiago, F. (2023). Mega or macro social media influencers: Who endorses brands better? *Journal of Business Research*, 157, 113606. DOI: 10.1016/j.jbusres.2022.113606

Breves, P. L., Liebers, N., Abt, M., & Kunze, A. (2019). The perceived fit between instagram influencers and the endorsed brand: How influencer–brand fit affects source credibility and persuasive effectiveness. *Journal of Advertising Research*, 59(4), 440–454. DOI: 10.2501/JAR-2019-030

Brown, D., & Hayes, N. (2008). *Influencer marketing*. Routledge. DOI: 10.4324/9780080557700

Canöz, K., Gülmez, Ö., & Eroğlu, G. (2020). Influencer marketing, the rising star of marketing: A research to determine the purchasing behavior of influencer followers. *Journal of Selçuk University Vocational School of Social Sciences*, 23(1), 73–91.

Chatzigeorgiou, C. (2017). Modelling the impact of social media influencers on behavioural intentions of millennials: The case of tourism in rural areas in Greece. *Journal of Tourism* [JTHSM]. *Heritage & Services Marketing*, 3(2), 25–29.

Chen, L., Yan, Y., & Smith, A. N. (2023). What drives digital engagement with sponsored videos? An investigation of video influencers' authenticity management strategies. *Journal of the Academy of Marketing Science*, 51(1), 198–221. DOI: 10.1007/s11747-022-00887-2

Chen, W. K., Silaban, P. H., Hutagalung, W. E., & Silalahi, A. D. K. (2023). How Instagram influencers contribute to consumer travel decision: Insights from SEM and fsQCA. *Emerging Science Journal*, 7(1), 16–37. DOI: 10.28991/ESJ-2023-07-01-02

Conde, R., & Casais, B. (2023). Micro, macro and mega-influencers on instagram: The power of persuasion via the parasocial relationship. *Journal of Business Research*, 158, 113708. DOI: 10.1016/j.jbusres.2023.113708

Çetin, F. A., & Öziç, N. (2020). The effect of Instagram influencers on purchasing in integrated marketing communication. *Journal of Business Research*, 12(1), 157–172.

Ďaďová, I., & Soviar, J. (2021). The application of online marketing tools in marketing communication of the entities with the tourism offer in 2020 in Slovakia. *Transportation Research Procedia*, 55, 1791–1799. DOI: 10.1016/j.trpro.2021.07.170

Deegan, O. (2021). # Influenced: The Impact of Influencer Marketing on the Travel and Tourism Industry of Ireland. A qualitative study (Doctoral dissertation, Dublin Business School).

Demir, S. (2019). The impact of the perception of memorable tourism experiences across generations on post-purchase behavior. Master's Thesis.

Demirağ, F. (2023). The Impact of Influencer Characteristics on Consumers' Behavioral Intentions. *Dumlupınar University Journal of Social Sciences*, 77, 219–233.

Deng, F., & Jiang, X. (2023). Effects of human versus virtual human influencers on the appearance anxiety of social media users. *Journal of Retailing and Consumer Services*, 71, 103233. DOI: 10.1016/j.jretconser.2022.103233

Dhun & Dangi, H. K. (2023). Influencer marketing: Role of influencer credibility and congruence on brand attitude and eWOM. *Journal of Internet Commerce*, 22(sup1), S28-S72.

Egbert, S., & Rudeloff, C. (2023). Employees as corporate influencers: Exploring the impacts of parasocial interactions on brand equity and brand outcomes. *International Journal of Strategic Communication*, 17(5), 439–456. DOI: 10.1080/1553118X.2023.2231922

Erdoğan, M. (2023). The Effect of Phenomenon on the Purchasing Behavior of Generation Z: The Example of Female Students of Istanbul Esenyurt University. *Ordu University Social Sciences Institute Journal of Social Sciences Research, 13*(3), 3033-3050.

Ergun, N., Bayrak, R., & Doğan, S. (2019). A qualitative research on Instagram, an important marketing channel for tourism marketing. *Journal of Current Tourism Research*, 3(1), 82–100.

Femenia-Serra, F., & Gretzel, U. (2020). Influencer marketing for tourism destinations: Lessons from a mature destination. In *Information and Communication Technologies in Tourism 2020: Proceedings of the International Conference in Surrey, United Kingdom, January 08–10, 2020* (pp. 65-78). Springer International Publishing.

Filieri, R., Acikgoz, F., Li, C., & Alguezaui, S. (2023). Influencers' "organic" persuasion through electronic word of mouth: A case of sincerity over brains and beauty. *Psychology and Marketing*, 40(2), 347–364. DOI: 10.1002/mar.21760

Gamage, T. C., & Ashill, N. J. (2023). # Sponsored-influencer marketing: Effects of the commercial orientation of influencer-created content on followers' willingness to search for information. *Journal of Product and Brand Management*, 32(2), 316–329. DOI: 10.1108/JPBM-10-2021-3681

Ge, J., & Gretzel, U. (2018). Emoji rhetoric: A social media influencer perspective. *Journal of Marketing Management*, 34(15-16), 1272–1295. DOI: 10.1080/0267257X.2018.1483960

Gedik, Y. (2020). A rising trend in social media: A conceptual evaluation on influencer marketing. *Pamukkale University Journal of Business Research*, 7(2), 362–385.

Glenister, G. (2021). *Influencer Marketing Strategy: How to create successful influencer marketing*. Kogan Page Publishers.

Gross, J., & von Wangenheim, F. (2022). Influencer Marketing on Instagram: Empirical Research on Social Media Engagement with Sponsored Posts. *Journal of Interactive Advertising*, 22(3), 289–310. DOI: 10.1080/15252019.2022.2123724

Gümüş, D., & Kızılırmak, I. (2023). The Effect of Recall Marketing on Customer Behavior and Satisfaction. *Yaşar University E-Journal*, 18(72), 380–404.

Güneş, E., Ekmekçi, Z., & Taş, M. (2022). The effect of trust in social media influencers on pre-purchase behavior: A research on Generation Z. *Turkish Journal of Tourism Research*, 6(1), 163–183.

Gürkan, A. S., & Ulema, Ş. (2021). The Effect of Snobism on Tourism Demand: A Research on Instagram Users Living in Nişantaşı. *Journal of Turkish Tourism Research*, 4(4), 3249–3262.

Han, J., & Chen, H. (2022). Millennial social media users' intention to travel: The moderating role of social media influencer following behavior. *International Hospitality Review*, 36(2), 340–357. DOI: 10.1108/IHR-11-2020-0069

Han, X., Wang, L., & Fan, W. (2023). Cost-effective social media influencer marketing. *INFORMS Journal on Computing*, 35(1), 138–157. DOI: 10.1287/ijoc.2022.1246

Harrigan, P., Daly, T. M., Coussement, K., Lee, J. A., Soutar, G. N., & Evers, U. (2021). Identifying influencers on social media. *International Journal of Information Management*, 56, 102246. DOI: 10.1016/j.ijinfomgt.2020.102246

Haseki, M. İ. (2023). *Phenomen Marketing. Accounting and marketing issues in theory and practice*. Crop.

Hıra, M., & Karabulut, A. N. (2021). The Effect of Influential Marketing Practices on Brand Equity and Purchase Intention: A Research on Gastronomy Tourism. *International Journal of Contemporary Tourism Research*, 5(2), 116–128. DOI: 10.30625/ijctr.1022806

Hovland, C. I., & Weiss, W. (1951). The influence of source credibility on communication effectiveness. *Public Opinion Quarterly*, 15(4), 635–650. DOI: 10.1086/266350

Hudders, L., & Lou, C. (2023). The rosy world of influencer marketing? Its bright and dark sides, and future research recommendations. *International Journal of Advertising*, 42(1), 151–161. DOI: 10.1080/02650487.2022.2137318

Iwashita, M. (2019, July). Trend of influencer marketing and future required functions. 20th IEEE/ACIS International Conference on Software Engineering, *Artificial Intelligence, Networking and Parallel/Distributed Computing* (SNPD) (pp. 2-2). IEEE.

Jantcsh, J. (2008). Let's Talk: Social Media for Small Businesses. https://ducttapemarketing.com/the-definition-of-social-media

Kalpaklıoğlu, N. Ü. (2015). The effect of e-wom as a marketing communication element on the choice of tourism products. *Maltepe University Faculty of Communication Journal, 2*(1), 66-90.

Kaplan, A., & Haenlein, M. (2010). Users of The World, Unite! The Challenges and Opportunities of Social Media. *Business Horizons*, 53(1), 59–68. DOI: 10.1016/j.bushor.2009.09.003

Karadeniz, I. (2019). The effect of social media users' perceptions of travel influencer advertisements on attitude and destination choice. Master's thesis, Trakya University, Institute of Social Sciences.

Kaya, A. (2020). Consumption And Perceptual Obsoletion In The Digital Age: A Study Through Social Media Phenomena. *Academic Sensitivities*, 7(13), 169–191.

Khan, S. W., Shahwar, D., & Khalid, S. (2023). Unlocking the Potential of YouTube Marketing Communication: The Effects of YouTube Influencer Attributes on Millennials' Purchase Intention in Pakistan. *Annals of Social Sciences and Perspective*, 4(1), 65–76. DOI: 10.52700/assap.v4i1.184

Kim, D. Y., Park, M., & Kim, H. Y. (2023). An influencer like me: Examining the impact of the social status of Influencers. *Journal of Marketing Communications*, 29(7), 654–675. DOI: 10.1080/13527266.2022.2066153

Kocabay, N., & Öymen, G. (2023). Phenomenon Activism: A Research on Environmental Phenomena. *Üsküdar University. Journal of Social Sciences*, 16.

Köprülü, O., & Turhan, M. (2023). Effects of Influencer Marketing on Consumers' Purchasing Behavior: Bursa Province Example. *Fiscaoeconomia*, 7(2), 1158–1177.

Liu, S., Aw, E. C. X., Tan, G. W. H., & Ooi, K. B. (2023). Virtual Influencers as the Next Generation of Influencer Marketing: Identifying Antecedents and Consequences. In *Current and Future Trends on Intelligent Technology Adoption* (Vol. 1, pp. 23–39). Springer Nature Switzerland. DOI: 10.1007/978-3-031-48397-4_2

Lou, C., Taylor, C. R., & Zhou, X. (2023). Influencer marketing on social media: How different social media platforms afford influencer–follower relation and drive advertising effectiveness. *Journal of Current Issues and Research in Advertising*, 44(1), 60–87. DOI: 10.1080/10641734.2022.2124471

Maggiore, G., Lo Presti, L., Orlowski, M., & Morvillo, A. (2022). In the travel bloggers' wonderland: Mechanisms of the blogger–follower relationship in tourism and hospitality management–a systematic literature review. *International Journal of Contemporary Hospitality Management*, 34(7), 2747–2772. DOI: 10.1108/IJCHM-11-2021-1377

Malik, A. Z., Thapa, S., & Paswan, A. K. (2023). Social media influencer (SMI) as a human brand–a need fulfillment perspective. *Journal of Product and Brand Management*, 32(2), 173–190. DOI: 10.1108/JPBM-07-2021-3546

Martínez-López, F. J., Anaya-Sánchez, R., Esteban-Millat, I., Torrez-Meruvia, H., D'Alessandro, S., & Miles, M. (2020). Influencer marketing: Brand control, commercial orientation and post credibility. *Journal of Marketing Management*, 36(17-18), 1805–1831. DOI: 10.1080/0267257X.2020.1806906

Martínez-Sala, A. M., Monserrat-Gauchi, J., & Segarra-Saavedra, J. (2019). The influencer tourist 2.0: From anonymous tourist to opinion leader. *Revista Latina de Comunicación Social*, (74), 1344–1365. DOI: 10.4185/RLCS-2019-1388en

Marwick, A., & Boyd, D. (2011). To See and Be Seen: Celebrity Practice on Twitter. *Convergence (London)*, 17(2), 139–158. DOI: 10.1177/1354856510394539

Masuda, H., Han, S. H., & Lee, J. (2022). Impacts of influencer attributes on purchase intentions in social media influencer marketing: Mediating roles of characterizations. *Technological Forecasting and Social Change*, 174, 121246. DOI: 10.1016/j.techfore.2021.121246

Mero, J., Vanninen, H., & Keränen, J. (2023). B2B influencer marketing: Conceptualization and four managerial strategies. *Industrial Marketing Management*, 108, 79–93. DOI: 10.1016/j.indmarman.2022.10.017

Nadanyiova, M., Gajanova, L., Majerova, J., & Lizbetinova, L. (2020) Influencer marketing and its impact on consumer lifestyles. In Forum Scientiae Oeconomia (Vol. 8, No. 2, pp. 109- 120).

Nandi, S. (2022). Short-term vs long-term influencer marketing campaigns. Available at: https://www.getsaral.com/academy/short-term-vs-long-term-influencer -marketing-campaigns Accessed on: 04.08.2024.

Öztek, M., Yerden, N. K., Çolak, E., & Sarı, E. (2021). A content analysis on the role of social media in phenomenon marketing and the fashion industry. (62), 1053-1077.

Öztürk, O. (2023). A Study to Determine the Relationships Between Phenomenon Stickiness and Its Antecedents. *Business and Economics Research Journal*, 14(1), 123–140.

Pop, R. A., Săplăcan, Z., Dabija, D. C., & Alt, M. A. (2022). The impact of social media influencers on travel decisions: The role of trust in consumer decision journey. *Current Issues in Tourism*, 25(5), 823–843. DOI: 10.1080/13683500.2021.1895729

Pradhan, D., Kuanr, A., Anupurba Pahi, S., & Akram, M. S. (2023). Influencer marketing: When and why gen Z consumers avoid influencers and endorsed brands. *Psychology and Marketing*, 40(1), 27–47. DOI: 10.1002/mar.21749

Saldamlı, A., & Can, İ. I. (2018). A New Trend in Marketing: Hatırlı Marketing–A Study on Consumers' Accommodation Preferences, 2nd International Future of Tourism Innovation, *Entrepreneurship and Sustainability Congress*, 698-707.

Saldamlı, A., & Özen, F. (2019). The effect of promotional marketing on consumer purchasing decisions in food and beverage businesses. *Journal of Tourism Theory and Research*, 5(2), 327–339.

Santiago, J. K., & Castelo, I. M. (2020). Digital influencers: An exploratory study of influencer marketing campaign process on instagram. *Online Journal of Applied Knowledge Management*, 8(2), 31–52. DOI: 10.36965/OJAKM.2020.8(2)31-52

Sarıışık, M., & Özbay, G. (2012). A Literature Review on Electronic Word of Mouth Communication and Applications in the Tourism Industry. *International Journal of Management Economics and Business*, 8(16), 1–22.

Sarıoğlu, C. İ. (2023). The Effect of Influencer Source Credibility and Brand Attitude on Purchase Intention. *Journal of Human and Social Sciences Research*, 12(2), 912–937.

Seçer, A., & Boğa, M. (2017). The impact of social media on consumers' food purchasing behavior. *KSÜ Journal of Natural Sciences*, 20(4), 312–319.

Seibel, G. (2021). The impact of influencer marketing on destination choice-A quantitative study among Brazilian and German millennials. *RCMOS-. Revista Científica Multidisciplinar o Saber*, 1(3), 41–150. DOI: 10.51473/rcmos.v1i1.2021.44

Semiz, B. B., & Zengin, E. (2019). Examining The Role Of Social Media Phenomena On The Purchasing Decision Process. B*usiness & Management Studies. International Journal (Toronto, Ont.)*, 7(5), 2325–2347.

Sesar, V., Hunjet, A., & Kozina, G. (2021). Influencer marketing in travel and tourism: literature review. *Economic and social development: book of proceedings*, 182-192.

Simay, A. E., Wei, Y., Gyulavári, T., Syahrivar, J., Gaczek, P., & Hofmeister-Tóth, Á. (2023). The e-WOM intention of artificial intelligence (AI) color cosmetics among Chinese social media influencers. *Asia Pacific Journal of Marketing and Logistics*, 35(7), 1569–1598. DOI: 10.1108/APJML-04-2022-0352

Sonmez, I. C. (2023). A Different Source of Social Change in Media History Studies: Social Media Phenomena. In *New Media Studies. Language, Image, Phenomena, Technology, Disinformation* (pp. 91–110). Özgür Yayın Dağıtım Ltd. Şti.

Stoldt, R., Wellman, M., Ekdale, B., & Tully, M. (2019). Professionalizing and profiting: The rise of intermediaries in the social media influencer industry. *Social Media + Society*, 5(1), 2056305119832587. DOI: 10.1177/2056305119832587

Şahin, E. (2020). Self-presentation of popular doctors in personal branding: Practices of using Instagram accounts. In E. Eroğlu, & B. Taşdelen. *Communication Studies and Media Studies in the Digital Age,* (p 42). Education.

Theocharis, D., & Papaioannou, E. (2020). Consumers' responses on the emergence of influencer marketing in Greek market place. *International Journal of Technology Marketing*, 14(3), 283–304. DOI: 10.1504/IJTMKT.2020.111543

Turku, N. (2023). *The consumer perception of short-term and long-term influencer marketing campaigns on Instagram and their effect on consumer brand awareness.* [Master's Thesis, Abo Academy University]. https://www.doria.fi/bitstream/handle/10024/187327/turku_niklas.pdf?sequence=2&isAllowed=y

Vassey, J., Valente, T., Barker, J., Stanton, C., Li, D., Laestadius, L., & Unger, J. B. (2023). E-cigarette brands and social media influencers on Instagram: A social network analysis. *Tobacco Control*, 32(e2), e184–e191. DOI: 10.1136/tobaccocontrol-2021-057053 PMID: 35131947

Von Mettenheim, W., & Wiedmann, K. P. (2021). The role of fashion influencers' attractiveness: A gender-specific perspective. *Communication Research and Practice*, 7(3), 263–290. DOI: 10.1080/22041451.2021.2013087

Vrontis, D., Makrides, A., Christofi, M., & Thrassou, A. (2021). Social media influencer marketing: A systematic review, integrative framework and future research agenda. *International Journal of Consumer Studies*, 45(4), 617–644. DOI: 10.1111/ijcs.12647

Wies, S., Bleier, A., & Edeling, A. (2023). Finding goldilocks influencers: How follower count drives social media engagement. *Journal of Marketing*, 87(3), 383–405. DOI: 10.1177/00222429221125131

WonSeok, B., DongHwan, C., & Reddy, N. S. (2020). Investigating the effect of creating shared value on the performance of partner companies and social performance. , 20(4), 131-144.

Xie, Q., & Feng, Y. (2023). How to strategically disclose sponsored content on Instagram? The synergy effects of two types of sponsorship disclosures in influencer marketing. *International Journal of Advertising*, 42(2), 317–343. DOI: 10.1080/02650487.2022.2071393

Xu, J., Qu, L., & Zhang, G. (2022). Governing social eating (chibo) influencers: Policies, approach and politics of influencer governance in China. *Policy and Internet*, 14(3), 525–540. DOI: 10.1002/poi3.318

Yavuz, D., & Sağlam, M. (2023). Examining the Effect of Phenomenon Characteristics on Repeat Purchase, Word of Mouth Communication and Intention to Pay More. *Süleyman Demirel University Visionary Magazine*, 14(37), 296–313.

Yetimoğlu, S., & Uğurlu, K. (2020). Influencer marketing for tourism and hospitality. In *The emerald handbook of ICT in tourism and hospitality* (pp. 131–148). Emerald Publishing Limited. DOI: 10.1108/978-1-83982-688-720201009

Younis, D. (2024). Social Inclusion portrayal on TikTok and Instagram: The role of social media influencers in promoting mental health literacy, body image and self-esteem. *Journal of Media and Interdisciplinary Studies*, 3(7), 121–140. DOI: 10.21608/jmis.2024.252107.1017

Zhang, T., & Huang, X. (2022). Viral marketing: Influencer marketing pivots in tourism–a case study of meme influencer instigated travel interest surge. *Current Issues in Tourism*, 25(4), 508–515. DOI: 10.1080/13683500.2021.1910214

# Chapter 6
# Social Media and Its Influence on Travel Decision-Making

**M. Mehataj**

*IFET College of Engineering, India*

**P. Kanimozhi**

*IFET College of Engineering, India*

**T. Ananth Kumar**

https://orcid.org/0000-0002-0494-7803

*IFET College of Engineering, India*

## ABSTRACT

*Tourism serves as a prominent illustration of the crucial role that social media has assumed in the contemporary digital age. The present study aims to examine the influence of widely used electronic platforms, namely Instagram, Facebook, WhatsApp, and TikTok, on the decision-making processes of tourists. Adopting the AIDA (Attention, Interest, Desire, Action) model as a conceptual framework, the study collects feedback from 100 participants to evaluate the impact of their social media engagement on their travel decisions. The findings demonstrate that social media exerts a substantial influence on the formation of travel preferences and the choice of destinations by effectively attracting users' attention and generating desire through well selected material and influencer marketing. Furthermore, the research investigates the application of machine learning to examine large datasets obtained from social media platforms, particularly Twitter, for the purpose of predicting tourist demand.*

DOI: 10.4018/979-8-3693-3972-5.ch006

# 1. INTRODUCTION

## 1.1 Social Media and Tourism

People today find it hard to fully appreciate the beauty of nature, take time for themselves, and relax in a peaceful place because of how fast-paced and chaotic modern life is. A place where people go to relax is called a tourist attraction because people go there to enjoy the natural beauty of the place, which can only be understood and appreciated by the human minds. In general, tourism means traveling to different places for different reasons, like for fun, business, religious reasons, or family vacations (Apriyanti, M.E et al., 2023). Tourism is sometimes linked to traveling to other countries, but in its most basic form, it means going to a different place in the same country. There have been a lot of important publications in the field of tourism in the last ten years that show how much attention has been paid to social media. A story from the study that is often used is that social media has greatly or fundamentally changed the sources of information that visitors use and the choices they make as a result. The exact definition of social media has been the subject of a lot of heated debate lately. The idea of social media changes as it grows and finds more uses (Farkić, j et al., 2023). These definitions take into account a number of important and natural traits that are often associated with social media. This includes the following things: Both "social media" and "social networking" should be included in a full analysis." Social networking applications are online services, platforms, or websites that specifically enable the establishment of social networks or relationships among individuals who have similar interests, activities, backgrounds, or real-life involvements." As of 2013b, Wikipedia says that a social networking service is "an internet-based service, platform, or website." The intentional use of social media tools to directly communicate and interact with people. This activity is commonly referred to as social networking. Within the domain of social media, platforms are typically described as "tools" or "communication channels" because of their capacity to enable the exchange, alteration, and distribution of information to a vast audience (Ellison,R.,2023). There exists a plethora of online platforms that facilitate interpersonal connections by means of social networking. Examples of these genres of websites include consumer review websites, content community websites, wikis, online forums, and social media interfaces that are location-based. The convergence of social interaction, information and communication technology, and the creation of text, images, videos, and audio has given rise to social media as a new medium for individuals to establish connections with each other. In fact, it's not just a new way to talk to people; it's a pervasive digital space that revolves around the contributions and interactions of its users. There have been more social media platforms than ever before in the past few years. It had over 1.2 billion users by the end of 2012, making it one of the most popular social networking sites. Increasingly, tourists are utilizing social media for various purposes such as conducting research, making decisions, promoting their destinations, and acquiring knowledge on how to interact with customers on these platforms (Abbasi, A.Z et al., 2023). Extensive research has demonstrated that promoting tourist products on social media is a very successful approach. Several countries acknowledge the influence of social media as a highly effective marketing instrument for global tourism. Recent research and enhancements have been implemented to optimize the use of social media by tourism enterprises. A recent literature review on the use of social media in the hotel and tourism industries captured our interest. In recent years, there has been a substantial change in both the number and diversity of published articles, as well as the focused topics of study. An essential task is to evaluate the prominent social media publications in the field of tourist research.

## 1.2 Destination Marketing

Destination marketing is becoming increasingly prevalent in online communities, where social media platforms such as Facebook, Weibo, Twitter, Instagram, and YouTube facilitate the decision-making process for individuals regarding where they would like to travel (Alzaydi, Z.M. & Elsharnouby, M.H., 2023). An increasing number of individuals are turning to social media platforms in order to make momentary choices within a destination, such as selecting a restaurant or hotel to stay at. However, scholars are currently challenging the long-established notion that social media exerts a substantial influence on the choice of destinations. Through our investigation of the influence exerted by social media on tourists' decision-making processes about their travel arrangements, we aim to enhance our comprehension of the significant influence that social media offers and the specific conditions under which it functions. To accomplish the objective, there are two different contributions that could be made. To begin, the objective is to bring attention to specific environments and/or the presence of specific circumstances at the same time. This is done in order to influence the locations that people choose to travel to through the use of social media. In addition, it was desired to identify the circumstances and elements that would render social media significantly less significant in the process of selecting a travel destination. The results of this study are contingent on the circumstances, which illustrate how the internal motivations of tourists and the external characteristics of a destination influence an individual's decision to visit that particular location (Zhou, L et al., 2024). You will gain a deeper comprehension of the ways in which social media influences the process of selecting a vacation destination as a result of reading this. To accomplish this, you will need to carefully follow each of the four distinct sections. In order to come up with clear research questions and demonstrate a number of different ways to understand decision results, we take a careful look at the research that has already been conducted on the topic of selecting a vacation destination, the ways in which travel environments are significant, and the roles that social media plays. Following that, we will provide an overview of the research methodology and data analysis that were selected that were selected. Last but not least, the findings and the subsequent discussion provide the answers to the questions posed by the research. The conclusion highlight the significant contributions that were made and provide an outline of the areas that require additional research. When it comes to how tourists obtain and make use of information, a lot has changed over the past few years, and the majority of this change can be attributed to social media (SM). The fact that social media can be used to mold one's thoughts, feelings, and experiences is a significant reason why so many people share their experiences on these platforms. Consequently, it is a goldmine of information for vacation planners. The term "social media influencer" (SMI) describes a person who has amassed a large following on social networking sites (Leite, Â et al., 2023). A relatively new breed of independent third-party endorsers known for their ability to sway public opinion through social media channels such as blogs, tweets, and more has emerged: the social media influencer (SMI). How much people trust the information is a significant factor in determining whether or not they will purchase tourist goods and whether or not they will accept the information that is produced by service-oriented marketing initiatives (SMIs). Based on the findings of previous research on trust in the travel industry, it has been determined that it is beneficial for both the peer-to-peer market and the desire of individuals to purchase tourism products online. This conclusion was reached after considering a wide range of perspectives. Researchers who investigate the ways in which social media influencers (SMIs) impact the purchasing process in the travel industry discover that this alters the travel plans of followers, making it more likely that they will visit a particular location. In this day and age, the most common way for people to obtain information is through social media. It has already been investigated by researchers how social media influencers (SMIs) influence the decisions that tourists make regarding their purchases. The purpose of these studies was to investigate a variety of topics, including trust, the customer journey, the quality of information provided about the tourist destination, and how individuals felt about advertising and the destination. Furthermore, previous research has demonstrated that social media has the potential to alter the way in which tourists express their thoughts and opinions regarding their travel experiences. People who work in the field of tourism research are constantly discussing the question of how to differentiate between a destination and a tourism product. Scholars have stated in the past that tourism products are what you get when you use travel services while you are on a trip, which eventually results in an experience that is more complicated (Holiday, S et al., 2023). Therefore, there has not been a great deal of research conducted on the factors that cause people to interact with service-oriented marketing (SMI) materials for travel destinations or on the ways in which confidence based on SMIs influences travel choices. In addition to this, social media (SM) is an important digital interface that has the potential to have a significant impact on the decisions that customers make throughout their journey, particularly at various stages of the journey. On account of these elements, there is a gap in our knowledge that needs to be filled with additional research in order to acquire a comprehensive understanding of the ways in which social media influencers impact each and every stage of the consumer engagement process. The purpose of this research is to investigate the ways in which SMI trust, which is an independent factor, influences all aspects of the travel customer journey, including the time before the purchase, the time during the decision-making process, and the time after the purchase, which is a dependent factor. In addition to this, it will investigate the role that intermediaries play at each stage of the customer journey in relation to the trustability of SMI. The customer journey encompasses all of the various ways in which a customer engages with a brand as well as all of the various experiences that they have while making a decision. We used a model based on the customer journey theory to investigate how trust in social media influencers (SMIs) influences all aspects of the decision-making process regarding travel. These aspects include your desire to travel, your search for information, your consideration of your options, your decision to make a purchase, your satisfaction with your trip, and your desire to share your experience with others. Furthermore, we investigate the manner in which the effect of the SMI trust on the subsequent stage is altered as each stage of the process progresses. People are increasingly selecting vacation or travel destinations based on audiovisual information sources rather than reading a great deal of detailed information about the destination. There are times when they choose a website based on the audiovisual content that it provides rather than selecting a website that has already been selected. Commercials, television shows, and movies were just some of the mediums that destination marketing organizations (DMOs) utilized in order to promote their respective vacation destinations. Gan et al. state that short video tourism advertising films are an excellent method for demonstrating to prospective tourists the wonderful places that can be visited for vacations (Gan J et al., 2023). Through the use of this technique, the audience is able to visualize, fantasize, and imagine themselves in a vacation destination. The visual presentation of a location in a video typically inspires viewers to want to visit that location and engage in the activities that are depicted there. Videos promoting tourism were created by multinational destination marketing organizations (DMOs) and distributed via television, YouTube, and various other websites and social networking sites in an effort to attract more people to visit their destinations. Previous research has demonstrated that young tourists have a strong desire to travel to a diverse range of locations that are home to a variety of cultures. Through the use of promotional videos for tourism advertising, travellers are able to quickly find information that is helpful to them regarding certain destinations. A previous study conducted by China Forever discovered that the promotional video for tourism advertisements had a positive impact on the perceptions of young tourists regarding China as a destination. Based on their experiences, these tourists believed that China was not only a stunning destination but also beneficial to both the environment and the culture. In their study, Lee et al. investigated the meanings of the images that were featured in two advertisements for tourism in New Zealand. The study also investigated the impact that these videos had on the individuals who participated in the study. The promotional video for Australia titled "Nothing Like Australia" has been examined and demonstrated to have contributed to the promotion of the country's tourism and brand due to the fact that it has inspired people to want to visit the country. A number of studies have been conducted to investigate the effects of videos that promote tourism, and this particular study is one of those studies (Harding-Smith, R., 2024). All of the things that we have discussed up until this point make it abundantly clear that tourism promotional advertising videos do an excellent job of promoting destinations and contribute to the expansion of the tourism industry by encouraging people to visit particular locations. In order to gain a better understanding of the ways in which videos that promote tourism influence the decisions that young adults make when they are planning their vacations, additional research needs to be conducted. In addition, this particular field of research has not been investigated in great detail up until this point. As evidence of the extent to which promotional videos in tourism advertisements influence the decisions that young adults make regarding where they will go on vacation, this study was carried out.

## 2. ROLE OF SM IN TOURISM

The term "social media" is most frequently used to refer to online communities. These communities allow users to view and share content that was generated by other users. Examples of social media include online discussion boards (like Lonely Planet Thorn Tree), websites that allow users to share videos (like YouTube), video-sharing websites (like YouTube), picture archives (like Flickr), and social networking sites (like Facebook). On these social media platforms, some individuals favor one-on-one conversations, while others feel more comfortable in settings that involve more people. In addition to gender, age, and nationality, other factors that influence an individual's engagement on social media accounts include nationality (Keerthana, R et al.,2020). In essence, electronic word of mouth, also known as the widespread dissemination of social media content across a variety of platforms, makes it possible to obtain more personalized information. Tourists have more opportunities to interact with the content and with one another as a result of the versatility and user-friendliness of social media platforms. With the help of social media, individuals are able to organize their vacations and conduct research on possible destinations. One instance that illustrates how social media can be utilized in a variety of settings is the manner in which individuals utilize it prior to, during, and after a trip. During each of these three stages, it would appear that social media plays a significant role in influencing the choices and preferences of tourists. When tourists are making plans for a trip, one of the first things they do is use social media to gather information about the trip, including general information and specifics about the trip itself. Through the use of social media, tourists can lessen the impact of post-purchase dissonance and gain a better understanding of their purchases. This can be accomplished by discussing their purchases, including their desired destinations. Due to two primary factors, it is likely that the choices of destinations will not be aligned properly. From the very beginning, there is no assurance that you will actually consume the food that you buy simply because you have purchased it. Second, it is not unusual for people to choose a vacation destination without first having the chance to "pre-test" it. This is a common practice. In the second phase, travellers will share their experiences with one another through various social media platforms. Some theories propose that people engage in this behavior in order to ensure that other individuals can indirectly benefit from the experience that the tourist has. One school of thought contends that people's perceptions of a person are altered when they see them participating in a tourist activity (Soltani Nejad, N et al.,2024). This is due to the fact that social media has evolved into a magnified version of the ideal social self-image. The use of social media to keep others informed about the whereabouts of tourists is another trend that is becoming increasingly popular. Tourists are becoming increasingly concerned about their safety and security. Tourism professionals continue to use social media to relive their trips even after they have returned home from visiting their destinations. It is not uncommon for online forums and picture archive web-sites to feature posts from a diverse range of travellers who discuss the positives and negatives of their travel experiences. Some travellers choose to do this so that they can assist other travellers with the planning of their trips, rather than doing it for themselves. Nevertheless, it is irrelevant; some travellers may even share their post-trip reflections on social media to show their appreciation. There is no question that people who are traveling use social media at any time of the day or night of the week. Utilizing social media in an efficient manner is a fantastic way to increase both individuals' interest in and knowledge of a particular location. Any location that is worth its salt is aware of how to influence the number of visitors and how to keep them coming back for more opportunities. There is a substantial amount of written material available on the subject of social media in the travel industry. However, not all of these studies have concentrated on decision-making, and the ones that have frequently only offered a cursory examination of the contexts in which decisions were actually put into action.

## 3. AIDA MODEL AND TOURIST DECISION MAKING

### 3.1 Understanding the AIDA Model

There are a variety of communication models that have been put forward to help with marketing strategy development and advertising effectiveness evaluation. The AIDA model was one of the experimental strategies that were initially considered. Researchers in the fields of marketing and advertising looked into the model after it had been suggested in psychology (Wong, S.Y et al.,2024). The AIDA paradigm is a well-known theory that provides a framework for the field of advertising and communication. People often use it to learn about the whole process, which involves people's mental reactions, the effect of marketing messages, and how media consumption behavior is affected by those messages. The components that comprise the acronym AIDA are Attention (Awareness), Interest (Desire), and Action. Beginning with the consumer's first exposure to advertising and continuing until the consumer either tests the product or decides to buy it, it lays out the transactional process of consumer buying behavior. Several mental processes take place following ad exposure, predicated on the idea that the consumer goes through four distinct phases of processing information. Attracting attention, piquing interest, creating desire, and finally taking action (i.e., buying) are the steps involved. As a result of maturation, the pool of potential candidates shrinks throughout these stages. A large number of people can become aware of a brand or product; a smaller group can become interested in the brand or product; and finally, only a small percentage of those people can make a real purchase. Those who disagree with the AIDA model contend that it exaggerates people's actions. The customer is meant to become aware of the availability of a specific service or product during the attention stage of the communication process. Here we are at the very beginning of the communication process. In the second stage, called interest, the customer provides their personal assessment of the service or product. At the initial stages of a customer's interest in a product or service, they are in the interest stage. Here, the buyer delves further into learning about the ins and outs of the service or product. Accordingly, the interest level stands in for the emotional phase, and the attention phase for the psychological stage of recognition. Numerous studies have shown that people are very receptive to media stimuli, which can increase interest in a product, brand, or service by getting them featured in the media. An interest serves as the initiating factor for the emotional stage of desire, as stated by the AIDA theory. An individual's desire to purchase a good or service is directly proportional to the level of interest they feel in it. In fact, according to the model of goal-directed behavior (MGB), desire is a key mediator between attitude and intention. Viewed from a different angle, attitude is the more important factor influencing desire than interest.

*Figure 1. AIDA modelling for social media influence in travel booking.*

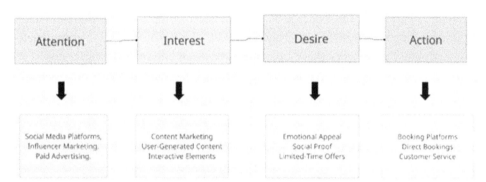

## 3.2 Application of AIDA Model

The objective of the Instagram account was to establish a long-lasting impact through meticulously curated material and enhance customer interest in making a purchase. Effective management of an Instagram account would motivate users to engage with the page. The primary factor influencing consumers' interest was their inherent motivation to visit the location that initially captured their attention. Preceding their decision to visit a certain location, consumers would acquire factual information about it. The AIDA theory incorporates four fundamental pillars: attention, interest, participation, and action. Attention can be defined as the capacity of a message to captivate individuals through the medium and structure of communication. The term "interest" denoted that when a marketer introduced the product, a consumer had acquired awareness. The emotional response a buyer undergoes after purchasing an item is referred to as "desire". The final phase, sometimes referred to as "action," indicates that consumers genuinely desire to acquire the advertised product or directly place an order for the offered item. After reviewing the content posted on the account, active Instagram users were surveyed to determine their level of interest and comprehension of the posts according to the criteria established in this study (Di Censo, G et al.,2024).

## 3.3 How Social Media Captures Attention and Drives Travel Desires

A viewer is an integral element of this inquiry. There are four distinct stages that a viewer undergoes while observing an advertisement. The main goal of an advertisement is to attract prospective clients. To effectively engage viewers, an advertising video must stimulate their interest in the product or service, which, as per this research, serves as the ultimate goal. Once the advertisement has aroused the viewer's interest, it must then convince them to use or buy the promised product. Ultimately, the viewer must decide whether or not to complete the purchase, which in this case involves physically visiting the outlet. The AIDA model is a comprehensive conceptual framework that categorizes phases of behavioral progression. The stages encompassed in this process are: (1) attracting the attention of the audience, (2) arousing their curiosity, (3) creating a willingness to acquire the product or service, and (4) inspiring a purchase. Hence, the AIDA model clarifies the influence of advertising and other forms of persuasive communication on consumer attitudes and actions. The AIDA paradigm has been widely used to assess the influence of marketing activities, such as sponsorship, advertising, promotions, and business, on the future intentions of individuals. AIDA is a conceptual framework used by tourism researchers to examine the influence of popular culture, media, films, and the Internet on travel tourist destinations. Despite the utilization of the model in these studies to achieve a more thorough comprehension of tourist behaviors, the aspects of attention, interest, desire, and action have been the primary focus, without any exploration of the causal connections among these elements. Scholars in the field of tourism have extensively studied the intentions of potential tourists to visit in the context of pop culture tourism.

## 4. INFLUENCER MARKETING IN TOURISM

### 4.1 Social Media Influencers (SMIs)

The proliferation of social media has significantly altered the decision-making process regarding vacation destinations. Before embarking on their vacation, numerous individuals conduct searches on social media platforms to locate pertinent content. Additionally, social media provides an excellent platform for them to communicate their experiences during the journey and their subsequent discoveries (Polat, E et al.,2024). The proliferation of social media influencers (SMIs) can be explicitly attributed to the growth of social media platforms. Social media influencers (SMIs) refer to prominent individuals within the online community who possess a substantial number of followers and can effectively disseminate information through their networks. Moreover, social media influencers are often perceived as relatively obscure celebrities by many individuals. Companies are increasingly prioritizing influence marketing strategies as a result of the proliferation of social media influencers (SMIs). Thus, influencer marketing has become a rather prevalent strategy in the realm of global online business. This method enables organizations to establish more intimate and dependable relationships with their clients. Influencer marketing is a marketing strategy in which companies collaborate with content creators who are capable of effectively presenting their products or services to their target audience by incorporating their own distinctive personalities into the content of the materials. Creating a favorable impression for prospective guests is facilitated by employing well-known individuals in travel destination commercials. Gretzel's (2018) research on the results of influencer marketing suggests that destinations are less likely to employ this strategy than international hotels. Destination marketing organizations (DMOs) now have a new opportunity to leverage influence marketing (IM) to enhance the appeal of a destination to visitors and optimize the power of social media (SM). This will allow them to engage with a greater number of individuals, particularly younger generations such as Millennials and Gen Z, who are more influenced by social media. Reviews and ratings on social media platforms can be a valuable resource for prospective tourists as they determine which tourist products to purchase. 88% of respondents reported that their decision regarding their vacation destination was influenced by someone, as indicated by a global survey that utilized questionnaires. This renders social media a dynamic and potent platform that enables social media influencers (SMIs) to share their travel experiences with their peers, thereby influencing the preconceived notions that potential travelers have about travel. Despite the fact that social media is an excellent tool for engaging consumers in a variety of ways, the reputation of travel agencies and destinations can be tarnished by social media influencers (SMIs). Travelers are significantly influenced by negative content when selecting a hotel or lodging facility. Additionally, the impact of negative elements is greater than that of positive ones; therefore, they could be employed as a filter to automatically exclude hotels during the decision-making process. The tourism sector's plans can be influenced by negative reviews from dissatisfied or angry consumers, which can also result in a decrease in demand for a specific destination. Additionally, social media may be a significant factor in the development of overtourism in certain regions; however, it is possible that negative electronic word of mouth could influence individuals' decisions to return.

## 4.2 Trust in SM and SMIs

Researchers in the fields of economics, social science, marketing, and organizational studies are just some of the disciplines that have investigated the concept of trust. Some authors have emphasized the multifaceted and intricate nature of trust, arguing that it is the only factor that has such a significant impact on the behavior of individuals who interact with one another and with other groups. In the realm of marketing, trust is of the utmost importance when it comes to the establishment and maintenance of fruitful long-term relationships. Both trustworthiness and dependability are essential components of the marketing strategy (Manthiou, A et al.,2024). It is important to differentiate between trust and untrustworthiness. Trust is a term that describes the accumulation of one's previous perceptual experiences that lead to untrustworthiness. Consumers tend to place a higher level of trust in information that is disseminated online by influential individuals. The reliability of the source has an impact not only on the persuasiveness of the information but also on the quality of the information itself. Trust in the hospitality and tourism industry has been the subject of extensive research conducted by eminent academics from a wide range of fields, including airlines, travel agencies, and destinations, amongst others. As a result of the multifaceted nature of trust, the concept of consumer trust in the tourism and hospitality industry has been the subject of a significant amount of research conducted by academics. "The readiness to depend on a trading partner in whom one has confidence" is the standard definition of consumer trust, according to Wang et al. (2014). This definition was developed by the American Consumer Institute. There was a strong emphasis placed on the importance of user-friendliness, website excellence, website standing, and perceived utility in the process of establishing consumers' trust in online travel websites. When it comes to making a reservation, the level of trust that customers have in hotel websites and online booking services is another factor that influences their choice. According to the findings of our investigation, the reputation of a location is one of the most significant factors in attracting customers from other locations. It has been demonstrated through research that the informative value, trustworthiness, attractiveness, and perceived similarity of the content that social media influencers (SMIs) make available to their followers are factors that influence the level of trust that influencers have in branded posts. There was also a positive correlation between the trust that audiences have in content that is endorsed by influencers and the likelihood that they will make a purchase during that time period. This trust's predictive power regarding the post's reliability is directly responsible for the increased interest that has been shown in the posts that have been made by the influencers. In situations where individuals trust one another and the information that they provide, it is possible for them to form a favorable impression of any brand. The presence of a high level of trust is linked to an increased amount of electronic word-of-mouth (eWOM), and this level of trust is further increased by positive interactions with the social media influencer (SMI) in the past. It is common for people to place more faith in social media influencers (SMIs) than they do in famous people. Encouraged followers are more likely to interact with social media influencers (SMIs), and SMIs have a greater impact on the consumers' intention to make a purchase. In spite of this, there is a wide variety of possible explanations for why the trust perceptions of customers can be harmed. In earlier studies, it was found that sponsorships have the potential to undermine the faith that consumers have in influencers. In order to assist them in making decisions that are more informed, travellers are gathering an increasing amount of significant information about their trips. Because of the proliferation of user-generated content and social media, travellers are increasingly looking to the opinions of their fellow travellers for guidance rather than official marketing claims. This trend is observed in the travel industry.

## 4.3 Role and Influence of Social Networking Sites

A significant number of vacationers look for verifiable evidence from other travelers that they have successfully planned and executed an ideal trip. When vacationers are making plans for their trips, the advice or recommendations of a personal friend or acquaintance can have a significant impact on the decisions they make. For the purpose of conducting an intriguing study on the ways in which social media influences individuals, As a result of the study, it was discovered that social relationships have a significant impact on business decisions (Bastrygina, T et al., 2024). To be more specific, 83 percent of participants share their discovery of a good deal with their friends, 90 percent of people believe what their friends say, and buyers are 300% more likely to purchase something when a friend recommends it, and they are 1000% more likely to purchase something after seeing a friend purchase it. The manner in which tourists plan, share, and create their travel experiences is significantly impacted by the influence of modern social networking sites. The statistics from a large number of different studies were compiled in order to provide support for this claim. The findings demonstrated that more than half of travelers, or 52%, altered their initial travel plans after conducting research on various social media websites. While on vacation, people engaged in a variety of activities, including the following: seventy percent of them updated their status on Facebook; seventy-six percent shared photos from their trip on a social media site; fifty-five percent liked Facebook pages that were related to their trip; and forty-six percent of travelers wrote reviews of hotels after their trip. More than half of people who use social media altered their travel plans as a result of what they saw on those sites, according to the World Travel Market Industry Report. Furthermore, more than three quarters of passengers altered their hotel reservations as a direct result of the information that they found on those websites. Research indicates that ninety percent of people who travel for leisure take photographs, and forty-five percent of those individuals share those photographs on the internet. The study investigated the ways in which social networking sites influence the behavior of travelers. I found it fascinating to learn that fifty percent of the people who took part in the survey selected their next vacation destination based on the photographs that their friends had shared with them. This study also discovered that 88 percent of the people who participated in it regularly look at the vacation photos that their friends have taken. On a regular basis, approximately forty percent to fifty percent of the participants share texts and photos, but only three percent post videos. In contrast to websites that share media or reviews, respondents are significantly more likely to share content on their own personal social media accounts (Nazlan, N.H et al., 2024). This holds true for both social media platforms. This assignment provides a concise summary of the most important findings from the research study that investigated the impact that online travel review sites have on the individuals who make use of them. As a result of reading travel reviews, individuals are influenced by them. (1) Investigate a particular location and locate information regarding the amenities that it offers. (2) Investigate each and every single alternative. (3) They should refrain from using services or visiting websites that do not cater to their preferences. (four) Make some recommendations. (5) Strengthen the safety of your travel options. You should encourage the mental process of visualizing what it is that you want to take place. Reduces the amount of risk and uncertainty to the greatest extent possible. The ease with which one can plan a trip is an improvement. There are not many studies that have directly investigated how social media influences tourists' choice of destination. This is due to the fact that the majority of studies on social media and tourism have concentrated on decisions that are on a smaller scale. The findings of sixteen studies that investigated the influence of social media on the destinations that people choose to visit are presented in Table 1. These studies provide us with valuable information regarding the ways in which social media influences the destinations that people choose to travel to. According to the findings of the study, individuals from a wide variety of nations and cultures use social media to make decisions about where they will go on vacation. As a matter of fact, not only is social media utilized, but it has also been demonstrated to have a significant impact on the geographical locations that tourists choose to visit. In spite of this, the effect was either small or not noticeable when it was discovered or discovered. A number of individuals are of the opinion that social media does not have a significant impact because the sources that were utilized in these studies are not very trustworthy. In addition, a number of studies demonstrated that social media did not have a direct impact on the decisions that tourists made; rather, it assisted in consolidating the decisions that they ended up making, thereby reducing cognitive dissonance. The fact remains that these studies have only utilized a single market segment or destination, as well as one or a few social media sites. At the end of the day, our understanding of how social media influences the decisions that tourists make regarding where they want to travel has been extremely limited, which means that it cannot be utilized in every circumstance. It is of the utmost importance to pay close attention to the circumstances in which social media is more significant. This is due to the fact that people make decisions about where they will go based on a wide variety of different circumstances and factors. Concerning this reason, there are questions that are of great significance. To begin, does the fact that attention is focused on a particular outcome, which is evident in the majority of the studies that were examined, make it more difficult to recognize and comprehend the notion of influence? To put it simply, participants who are already connected to the destination might not give much thought to the potential effects of social media (or any other platform) because they are already familiar with the location. The fact that the majority of studies concentrate on a small number of social media sites raises the question of whether or not this makes it more difficult to understand how other sites (or other communication channels) might work? To put it another way, it has been discovered that tourists obtain information about their choices of places to visit from a wide variety of sources. As a result of this, concentrating solely on one or two variables would most likely result in a smaller overall effect when the effects of many interactions are added together. The concept that social media influences the decision that tourists make regarding where to go demonstrates how significant context is. When it comes down to it, when it comes to dealing with post-purchase dissonance, tourists frequently turn to social media for information. On the other hand, the reasons that the tourist chose their destination have been largely disregarded or even intentionally minimized during the course of the discussion. According to the findings of research conducted on the topic of selecting a vacation destination, the impact of social media is likely to vary depending on the particular decision-making process that is being undertaken.

## 5. SOCIAL MEDIA INFLUENCE ACROSS TRAVEL JOURNEY

Because of the large number of people who use the internet to plan their vacations, the reviews and comments that are posted on various websites and social media sites are extremely important in determining the preferences of individuals. Social media comments have the ability to sway individuals who are looking for information about tourist destinations that they are interested in visiting or who are making their initial reservations for accommodations(Gulati, S., 2024). The number one priority for businesses that cater to tourists is to ensure that the customers they are trying to attract make reservations through social media. Visitors have the ability to access tourist attractions in the most reliable and time-efficient manner possible through the use of the internet. Through the use of the internet, individuals are able to easily find information about tourist establishments and additionally make reservations. Both the level of satisfaction that tourists have with the brand and the value that they attribute to the brand through the various promotional channels are positively impacted as a result of this phenomenon. These remarks, in addition to those that are shared on social media during the reservation process, have an impact on the credibility and brand recognition of the tourism establishment as well as the internet-using tourist. Because of this, social media has a significant influence on the process of vacation planning. The components that constitute a positive product review are recommendations and positive experiences with a product, whereas the components that constitute a negative product review are disappointments and negative experiences. As a result, it is of the utmost importance to conduct an exhaustive investigation into the repercussions of the negative product reviews. If consumers are active participants in the environment that encourages the exchange of opinions, they are more likely to encounter reviews of products that are unfavourable. When taking into consideration the fact that individuals who are dissatisfied are more likely to voice their disapproval than those who are thrilled. Currently, there is a discernible pattern of consumers giving negative feedback to products and services. For tourist businesses to effectively engage with their customers on social media, one of the most important strategies they can employ is to ask individuals to participate in hashtag campaigns on social media platforms such as Twitter, Instagram, and Facebook. Over a relatively short period of time, millions of individuals have had their shares distributed in a fair manner. For the purpose of categorizing the factors that influence social media users before, during, and after a trip, Fotis (2012) categorized social media factors. In the past, the responses took the following form: 44.5 percent of individuals who were considering going on a trip looked into other possible locations; 24.9 percent lowered their preferences regarding the destination; 30.9 percent made certain that they had chosen the appropriate location; 41.6 percent looked into things to do while they were there; and 34.4 percent looked into places to stay. 29.5% of the participants were looking for information related to entertainment, 16.5% were providing feedback on the trip, 44.1% were maintaining contact with friends, and 15% were simply exploring social media on their own. These are just some of the many things that participants did while they were on the trip. A number of people, after returning from a trip, engage in activities such as discussing the trip with their friends (78.3%), rating and reviewing the location (26.6%), and making plans for their next vacation (29.2%). When using social media, the most important thing that tour operators should keep in mind is the fact that they should be able to share information with both their existing customers and potential customers. Due to the absence of regulations regarding social media in the tourism industry, the marketing industry has been confronted with a number of ethical conundrums. In the context of social media marketing for tourist destinations, the presence of advertising materials that are inaccurate and information that is misleading may be an indication that an unethical standard is present. When it comes to the use of social media for tourist marketing, the most common unethical practices include providing information that is misleading, exaggerated, or incomplete about the products and services offered by the destination or establishment, as well as the creation of subjective comments on social networking sites by individuals who receive compensation from establishments. In addition, the utilization of social media platforms can also help to reduce the number of complaints received. Reviews that are written by individuals who have used the service directly can be a good indication of how good the service actually is. This is because the majority of tourist services are qualitative in nature. When it comes to the ethics of conducting business, however, it is abundantly clear that comments that are misleading can have a significant and detrimental effect on prospective tourists. Therefore, in accordance with the principles of business ethics, businesses should respond to both positive and negative feedback in a short amount of time and with careful consideration(Hardt, D. & Glückstad, F.K., 2024). Therefore, businesses operating in this sector are obligated to conduct themselves in an ethical manner on the numerous social media platforms that facilitate their communication and dissemination. Companies operating in this industry have a responsibility to ensure that all employees, from upper-level management to entry-level workers, adhere to the ethical standards that have been established for these applications. In the tourism industry, it is of the utmost importance for businesses and stakeholders to assimilate these ethical principles and implement them as a management strategy. In addition, users should exercise caution and verify the veracity of the content before acting on it when they are interacting with social media platforms. The tourist industry has felt the effects of the meteoric rise of the internet and technology, particularly among the demographic of people under the age of 35, which is becoming increasingly dependent on these technologies. Included in this category are mobile phones, applications for computers, and services based on the internet. Taking into consideration the current state of affairs, it is reasonable to anticipate that the tourism industry will enter a new technological age in the years to come. While developing economies are creating new demographics in order to adapt to a changing world, it is believed that businesses that cater to tourists are making effective use of the internet in order to communicate with their specific customers. Given that a significant number of individuals under the age of 35 engage in social activities on the internet on a regular basis, it is reasonable to assume that this trend has the most significant impact on the travel industry overall. When the proportion of new technologies increases, the tourism industry will inevitably experience both positive and negative effects.

## 5.1 User Generated Content (UGC)

The data collected from surveys is an essential component of the current research on tourist travel, particularly the research conducted prior to trips. This line of reasoning demonstrates that when compared to data collected directly from tourists through user-generated content (UGC), this method is not as comprehensive and requires more time to complete. User-generated content, also known as UGC, refers to the kinds of content that are produced by users of a particular platform(Li, S et al.,2024). Among the many forms of media that are included in user-generated content (UGC) are text, photographs, and videos. Within the context of a social media platform for tourism, an example of user-generated content (UGC) would be the written or visual content that users submit in order to record their travelogues. In contrast to the content that is meticulously crafted by destination marketing agencies, user-generated content (UGC) is able to capture the genuine, organic, democratic, and genuine experiences that tourists have. Employing data that users have created themselves, also known as user-generated content (UGC), is a low-cost method that can be utilized to investigate how tourists behave when they are visiting a particular location. Researchers are able to extract a wealth of information from this data that can be used to establish a correlation between the experiences of visitors and specific locations. The information that can be gleaned from user-generated content (UGC) is a treasure trove for comprehending the ways in which tourists navigate their way around various locations. In light of these findings, it is clear that user-generated content (UGC) data can be extremely valuable for intelligent destination management. Before they can benefit from this information, destination management organizations (DMOs) and other tourism organizations need to have a solid understanding of it. As a consequence of this, there are three levels of discourse that tourists engage in: pre-decision, while they are sightseeing, and after they have returned home.

## 5.2 Understanding Tourist Behavior at Different Stages of the Travel Journey

As a result of advancements in Information and Communication Technology (ICT), an increasing number of tourists are opting to share and document their travels on popular social media platforms such as Weibo, Twitter, and Ctrip. In this essay, a novel approach to conducting tourism research that is "data-driven" is demonstrated. The complex travel behavior of tourists, as well as their mental states and the emotional needs they establish for themselves during their journey, are influenced by time. The journey of a typical tourist around the world is divided into three distinct components: the pre-trip, the trip, and the post-trip. Travelers will meticulously document their experiences and observations during their vacations, and they will subsequently reflect on and discuss them upon their return home. Individuals who are traveling will conduct extensive research on the region and organize their itinerary by reviewing the recommendations of other travelers regarding the most desirable routes and destinations. In order to obtain a comprehensive understanding of the demand for tourist travel, a small group of researchers have examined the travel habits of tourists prior to, during, and after their trips. Data from social media question sets is employed to compile the critical information that vacationers require prior to their departure. By examining photo data and points of interest (POI) tags in travel blogs, we can gain a more comprehensive understanding of the landscapes that tourists prefer to view during their vacations and the manner in which they navigate the area. It is feasible to ascertain the sentiments of tourists regarding their destinations and their satisfaction with their excursions subsequent to their conclusion by reading travel blogs and attraction reviews. This implies that the proposed research framework can provide a comprehensive understanding of the behavior of tourists prior to, during, and following their trip.

**5.2.1 Pre-Trip Behavior:** There is a significant influence that social media has on the decision-making process that travelers go through before departing. Some of the places where people can find visually appealing content and read about the experiences of other people include Pinterest, Instagram, and travel blogs, to name just a few. The breathtaking locations that are highlighted by influential members of the travel industry create an atmosphere that encourages prospective tourists to plan their own adventures. The various social media platforms also provide access to a wealth of information that can be of beneficial use. When tourists are making plans for a trip, they are constantly looking for recommendations, reading reviews, and gaining as much information as they can about the real culture, attractions, and hotels in the area. In the process of making decisions regarding travel arrangements such as flights, hotels, and activities, a great number of individuals rely on the opinions of influential individuals.

Before they even leave for their trips, people spend a significant amount of time on the internet reading articles that are interesting to them and mentally planning their trips. A captivating travel narrative or an eye-popping picture of the destination is consistently ranked as one of the most powerful motivators for people to travel. As they scroll through their social media feeds, people who are traveling often fantasize about going on adventures such as hiking through verdant rainforests, exploring ancient temples, or sipping coffee at a café in Paris. People are more likely to turn their hazy interests into actionable plans when they connect with others online, which in turn encourages them to seek out travel experiences that are one of a kind.

### 5.2.2 In-Trip Behavior

Despite the fact that they are away from home, vacationers are still subject to a significant amount of influence from social media. It is possible for travelers to share their experiences with their followers and virtually bring them along with them through the use of live videos, blog posts, and real-time narratives. A greater number of individuals are engaging in independent research as a consequence of these changes, which cause people's perspectives to shift. Additionally, social media allows for the connection of locals and tourists, which opens up a world of opportunities to engage in one-of-a-kind activities, authentic dining establishments, and hidden treasures. The use of geotags and hashtags makes it simpler to locate or identify specific items. It is possible for social media to serve as a useful travel companion when you are not present. The application gives users the ability to connect with other travelers, as well as provide them with detailed information about upcoming events, directions to less well-known locations, and more. Be sure to describe these moments, such as having a dinner of street food in Bangkok or watching the sunrise over Angkor Wat, in order to make the experience of exploration more exciting. As a result of tourists documenting and sharing their experiences, they become a part of the digital fabric of the destination and become storytellers.

### 5.2.3 Post-Trip Behavior

Social media continues to be of great assistance even when you are back at your residence. When people want to remember their trips, they compile photo albums, write insightful descriptions of their experiences, and then share those albums with other people. These cherished memories contribute to the establishment of the location's reputation, which in turn attracts a greater number of visitors. TripAdvisor and Google are two examples of digital platforms that receive reviews from travelers. Negative reviews can discourage potential customers from purchasing a product or service, while positive reviews can boost the credibility of a company.

In the post-trip phase, there is more to it than simply experiencing feelings of nostalgia. Whenever something like this takes place, people's perceptions of a location shift. It is a great way for tourists to shape the reputation of the destination by talking about things like the breathtaking sunset, the one-of-a-kind street art, or the friendly locals. On social media, the one-of-a-kind travel experiences of individuals become a diverse array of travel desires, which in turn inspires others to follow in their footsteps and travel(Wei, D et al., 2024).

## 6. THEORETICAL AND PRACTICAL IMPLICATION FOR DESTINATION MARKETING

*Figure 2*. **Average number of product taken based on the number of follow-ups in social media.**

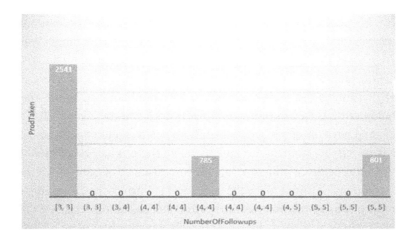

*Figure 3. Average number of children travelling on the influence of social media and number of trips taken by them.*

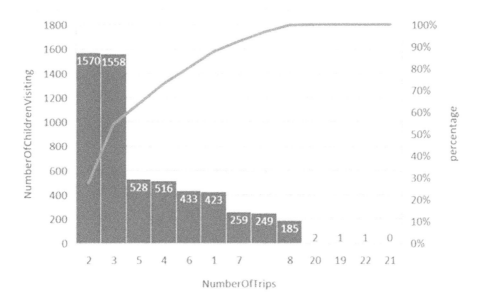

## 7. SENTIMENT ANALYSIS AND TOURISM MARKETING

In the hospitality industry, the immediate impact of a significant amount of information that is shared on social media is significant. This phenomenon is a consequence of the fact that tourists have a need to acquire knowledge about a location and to find out about the experiences that other people have had there (Singgalen, Y.A., 2024). People have the ability to post updates in real time on company websites, which can then be monitored and turned into information that is valuable to the business. It was through this channel that the visitors gained an understanding of the emotions and thoughts that were held by other purchasers. More than just booking flights and hotels, these tourists do a lot more than that, as was mentioned earlier. On top of that, they utilize social media apps and review websites to share information and write in-depth accounts of both positive and negative experiences during their travels. Customers are able to select the product or service that best meets their requirements or preferences with the assistance of online reviews, which contribute additional information to the decision-making process. A rapidly expanding field of research, sentiment analysis is a tool that can automatically evaluate the relevance of reviews as well as the semantic relationships between them. Over the past few years, sentiment analysis (SA) and opinion mining have become increasingly popular as a result of the abundance of data that has been made possible by the meteoric rise of online communities and social networks. As a consequence of this, the hotel industry has benefited from the utilization of text mining and sentiment analysis in order to extract additional information from online reviews. When referring to the process of determining the meaning of written or spoken text through the utilization of computer programs, the term "semantic analysis" (SA) is utilized. Specifically, it monitors the mental and emotional tendencies of individuals with regard to analytical sources.

*Figure 4. Implementation of sentiment analysis in social media.*

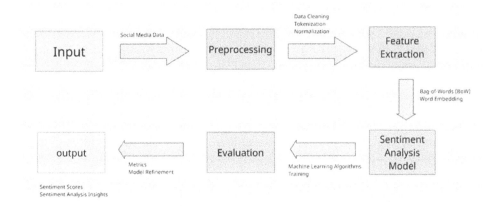

The practice of identifying moods and emotions in text sources derived from social media platforms is gaining popularity in South Africa. The amount of positive and negative sentiment towards vacation spots, hotels, and airline travel services has been measured and understood by a number of authors through the utilization of this method. The evaluation, potential, and activity model (EPA) is an important foundation that serves as a basis for evaluating both positive and negative sentiment. In addition, sentiment analysis has proven to be an important marketing tool that can be used to determine how customers will feel about a product or service in the future. It is of the utmost importance to acknowledge that online reviews have evolved into a valuable resource that enables customers to become more knowledgeable about their options. The value of these platforms lies in the fact that they enable businesses and their customers to gain knowledge from one another through the exchange of experiences and perspective.

## 7.1 Implementing Sentiment Analysis

Text analytics platforms, machine learning algorithms, and natural language processing technology are some of the tools and methodologies that can be utilized by businesses operating in the tourism industry in order to carry out sentiment analysis. A textual data set is analyzed by these programs in order to identify patterns and trends in the emotional states of individuals. In addition to this, businesses operating in the tourism industry can enhance the precision of their marketing targeting and simplify the process of customer segmentation by incorporating sentiment analysis into their customer relationship management (CRM) systems. A sentiment analysis (SA) is a methodical process that includes the following steps: identifying relevant data, collecting data from a source, classifying data according to sentiment, determining polarity, summarizing data based on sentiment, and finally writing up the results. A SA is a methodical process. The purpose of this research is to develop a method that is not only effective but also transparent and open to public scrutiny. It was decided that this particular group would be the primary supporter of the application. Following the acquisition of the data from social networks, it was processed, evaluated, and validated in order to determine the key performance indicators (KPIs) that were pertinent. By utilizing the data that was provided, a Balanced Scorecard (BSC) was subsequently developed in order to provide assistance in the process of formulating strategic decisions. It is possible to identify the steps that need to be taken in order to improve the operations of the company by utilizing this system. The use of software analytics (SA) makes it possible to automate and streamline the process of handling data in the software development process (Iswari, N.M.S et al., 2024). One of the strengths of this study is that it offered empirical evidence to support the hypothesis that supply chain management could potentially gain advantages from implementing the structural management strategy. The lack of previous research on balanced scorecards (BSCs) that combine systematic analysis (SA) and systematic planning (SP) served as the impetus for this particular scholarly investigation. This gap was discovered through a comprehensive analysis of a wide range of literature sources. When it comes to the subject of corporate strategy, there is a mountain of influential literature to choose from. For the sake of clarity, the gap that we are attempting to fill is a component of the process of developing a Balanced Scorecard (BSC), which is a tool that takes data from social media and offers strategic decision-makers a more effective method of making decisions based on these four perspectives.

## 8. FUTURE TREND IN SOCIAL MEDIA AND TOURISM MARKETING

### 8.1 Digital Content Marketing

The advancement of technology has made it possible for content to be created and shared at a rapid pace. Ideas and topics that have a strong resonance with particular target groups, such as tourists, serve as the foundation for the production of written or visual content(Sano, K et al., 2024). The term "content generation" refers to the process that is used here. Some examples of digital marketing tools include websites and social media platforms. These tools are used to disseminate digital information in a variety of formats, such as audio, video, infographics, and blogs. This can be accomplished through the utilization of websites in content marketing, which will result in a pleasant online experience with the destination brand. In order to provide an explanation for this phenomenon, the systematic categorization of online content on websites makes it possible to easily navigate and keep track of the various tourist attractions. Currently, site visitors are more likely to place their trust in promoted content on official tourism websites as opposed to posts made on social media sites. This is primarily due to the fact that the information that is available on these websites is of a higher quality. The fact that the vast majority of content on tourism websites is comprised of official destination information is a significant factor that contributes to travel and tourism. The primary goal of content marketing is to attract and keep customers by consistently producing high-quality, relevant content that has the ability to change or improve consumer behavior. This is accomplished through the production of content that is relevant to the target audience. The new trend of allowing users to create and share their own content is one that is rapidly gaining popularity and is expected to continue to do so. We anticipate a significant rise in the level of participation of consumers in the creation of digital content that can be utilized for marketing purposes in an efficient manner as a consequence of the widespread implementation of user-generated content platforms. The reason for this is that user-generated content enables users to connect with one another, plan trips, and document their everyday adventures through images, videos, blogs, and reviews. All of these things contribute to the overall quality of the travel experience.

## 8.2 Social Media Marketing

Many organizations, including for-profit businesses, nonprofit organizations, educational institutions, and government agencies, are increasingly using the term "social media marketing" to describe their promotional endeavors related to social media. There is also an increase in the amount of academic interest in the topic. The positions of "blogger," "manager of social marketing," "digital communications manager," and "social media content manager" are currently being advertised by corporations that provide consulting services. There is a high probability that new job titles will be introduced in the not too distant future. As a result of its ever-growing user base and widespread availability, social media has firmly established itself as the foundation upon which digital marketing is built.It has been observed that the number of individuals who use social media platforms such as Facebook has been rapidly increasing. The impact that social media has had on the travel industry has resulted in changes to the marketing strategies employed by the industry on both the demand and supply sides. Marketers consider social media to be an extremely efficient method of communicating with people all over the world because of its low cost, user-friendly interface, and rapid reaction to content updates and modifications. There are a great number of tourist destinations that have set up social media accounts in order to market and promote their tourist attractions. By looking at the photos and videos that their customers share, marketers can gain a great deal of insight into the behaviors of their customers. A sizeable portion of the youth demographic can be found posting and sharing media on a variety of social media platforms on a regular basis. Because of this, an increasing number of locations are offering photo opportunities, which is fantastic for the locations that people go to. It is possible to ask for feedback from customers through social media platforms, despite the fact that there are a lot of obstacles that could potentially get in the way of communication between tourist destinations and customers (Leung et al., 2019). As was mentioned earlier, social media platforms enable two-way marketing communication and provide marketers working in the tourism industry with an immediate opportunity to interact with tourists visiting their establishments. A significant number of Destination Management Organizations (DMOs) in Europe are responsible for the upkeep of official accounts on social media platforms such as Facebook, Twitter, YouTube, and Instagram. Furthermore, this lends credence to the idea that marketing strategies based on social media can be extended to encompass multiple websites. This is a significant development. When using social media, it is essential for a destination's brand to maintain its credibility in order to be successful. When official tourist destinations' social media pages are integrated with these platforms, customers are more likely to trust social media as an accurate source of information. This is because social media is constantly evolving. Social media, which is a significant source of information, exerts a significant amount of influence on the decision-making process of consumers. Social media is being used by an increasing number of people to make reservations for lodging and to organize their vacations. Whenever they are conducting research, tourists frequently look for more specific information about their trip. In spite of the fact that social media platforms provide a wealth of information to a large number of people, individuals who are traveling frequently find it challenging to sort through all of the content in order to find the specific information that they require. The anticipated rise in the utilization of hashtags is being driven by the fact that they have the capability of enhancing content organization and establishing social media as a more reliable source of information in comparison to other digital marketing methodologies. By making the content more visible, the process of finding information is simplified and therefore made easier. According to Buhalis and Sinarta (2019), hashtags make it possible to keep track of a conversation that is currently taking place and to precisely identify a topic that is either relevant or interesting. The literature that was reviewed indicates that it is anticipated that the utilization of social media for marketing purposes will continue its upward trend. There are a few social media marketing trends that are anticipated to see significant growth in popularity over the next decade. These trends include digital storytelling, travel blogging, and messenger marketing.

Facebook and WhatsApp's popularity has led to many people using the messenger for communication. Facebook and WhatsApp began as simple messaging apps but have become powerful business promotional tools. Due to their WhatsApp and Facebook use, tourists may prefer messenger marketing. According to Trunfio and Della Lucia (2019), Facebook is the best social media platform. Its strong media presence makes it a popular marketing tool. Brands can send private messages to customers and share links to audio, video, and text files on Facebook.

Travel blogs will likely help people choose a vacation spot in the future. Travel blogs cover every step of the tourist decision-making process, from researching to buying to reviewing their experiences afterward. Research indicates that travelers seek travel information before making purchases (Díaz-Meneses, 2019). This includes travel tips, weather reports, and current pricing. Travel bloggers share news, last-minute deals, and special offers to meet demand for travel advice and discounts. Díaz-Meneses (2019) states that blogging aids travelers in preparation. Travel blogs provide more information about travelers' trips, so they'll likely be read and used. Travel bloggers increasingly use personal experiences to influence decisions, resulting in increased traveler reliance on their advice (Díaz-Meneses, 2019). Marketers pay "influencers" with a large social media following to share content or blog posts. These "influencers" promote travel destinations and companies on their social media accounts to their followers and the group's target demographic. The Tuscany Destination Marketing Organization's blog tour invited media, photographers, and bloggers to follow predetermined routes and write about their adventures for their audiences. They found that travel blogs with digital storytelling—audio and visual narratives—are more engaging and encourage readers to visit the featured destinations. An et al. (2020) found that digital storytelling provides verifiable evidence of tourist experiences through visual and auditory media. Digital storytelling captures a tourist's experience, builds suspense, and lingers, triggering an overwhelming desire to travel. Influencers as travel bloggers and digital storytellers may become more popular as tourism digital marketers learn to tell compelling stories.

Smartphones have become multipurpose devices, according to Dickinson et al. smartphone users can now control when, where, and what they access. Smartphones have transformed customer information delivery. Customers can access information through an ongoing process. People can buy things, plan trips, share stories, and make financial transactions online from anywhere in the world. Many travelers use apps to maximize their vacations. Consumers want smartphone travel apps with useful features to improve their experience. Tourism professionals can use travel apps to market businesses and destinations. As smartphones become more popular, mobile marketing will become more important. Mobile marketing uses smartphones and the internet because these are the main ways customers interact with businesses. Email signatures and email marketing are increasingly used to promote services. More people check their email on the go, increasing the likelihood that promotional materials will reach their targets. Promo emails spark interest in a product or service. Clients receive email or newsletters about the latest deals, holiday packages, membership programs, and room availability from the tourism marketing database. Digiorgio (2016) says email marketing to tourists is simple, cheap, and effective for loyalty. Email is still useful for communicating with clients and getting their input on decisions. Pre-booked tourists may receive transactional emails about their bookings. Emailing clients after an excursion is also possible (Digiorgio, 2016). Giving customers the option to "opt-in" or "opt-out" of the mailing list is key to marketing. Thus, they can opt out of receiving and considering irrelevant emails. The importance of environmental protection has grown in the past decade. Emailing is appealing to eco-conscious people because it eliminates paper waste. Increasing awareness of green technology causes this. Advertising also lets users improve their mobile and desktop viewing experience. Travelers can now access trip promotions on their phones.

## 9. CONCLUSION

It is possible that we underestimate the significance of social media, its revolutionary potential, and its influence on the decisions that vacationers make. It is still common practice for businesses and tourists to use social media in order to locate local restaurants and attractions. Only in situations where all three factors are present does social media have an impact on one's choice of destination. These things occur when a potential traveler is addicted to social media, is not familiar with the location, and has a difficult time preparing for their trip. In addition to that, social media has very little influence on the planning of vacations. However, we discovered that the context either restricts or permits travel decision variables. Numerous pieces of evidence suggest that social media does not have an impact on popular tourist destinations. This lends credence to research on the relationship between social media and vacation planning, but it contradicts the hypothesis. Using a more in-depth and comprehensive analysis, this study debunks the notion that social media has an impact on the decisions that tourists make regarding their vacation destinations. This study highlights the significance of social media engagement, familiarity or novelty of the destination, and the complexity of the planning process by examining the diverse destinations that tourists chose to visit. The findings of this enhancement lend support to earlier studies that investigated the effects of social media on groups of users who share similar characteristics or locations. Recent research has demonstrated that the use of social media can enhance the appeal of destinations. Neither the tourists who were impacted nor the decision-making process that they went through is mentioned.Because tourists choose their destinations with absolute certainty, social media may have an effect on tourist destinations. It is possible for visitors who are self-assured or who are low-risk to use heuristics because some visitors experience only a mild to moderate impact. It is simpler to persuade people in situations where they are unaware of their identity and must rely on the cues provided by their surroundings. The influence of social media on public opinion demonstrates that going to unfamiliar places and making complicated preparations can cause trust to be damaged. Whenever social media is utilized, visitors will make a few decisions that are relatively minor. This research discovered two additional effects. At first, social media does not have an impact on the selection of vacation destinations. Those who are most impacted by these are tourists who are visiting new places and making a lot of decisions. People are wary of places that have been promoted. Because of this, destination managers are required to make use of social media in order to demonstrate how simple it is to plan trips and make decisions. The managers of the destination should also encourage the people who are currently visiting to post on social media about their upcoming vacations.

# REFERENCES

Abbasi, A. Z., Tsiotsou, R. H., Hussain, K., Rather, R. A., & Ting, D. H. (2023). Investigating the impact of social media images' value, consumer engagement, and involvement on eWOM of a tourism destination: A transmittal mediation approach. *Journal of Retailing and Consumer Services*, 71, 103231. DOI: 10.1016/j.jretconser.2022.103231

Alzaydi, Z. M., & Elsharnouby, M. H. (2023). Using social media marketing to pro-tourism behaviours: The mediating role of destination attractiveness and attitude towards the positive impacts of tourism. *Future Business Journal*, 9(1), 42. DOI: 10.1186/s43093-023-00220-5

Apriyanti, M. E., Subiyantoro, H., & Ratnasih, C. (2023). Focus on local cultural attraction in increasing tourist visits in Central Java Tourism Villages. *Journal Research of Social Science, Economics, and Management*, 2(11), 2645–2653. DOI: 10.59141/jrssem.v2i11.480

Bastrygina, T., Lim, W. M., Jopp, R., & Weissmann, M. A. (2024). Unraveling the power of social media influencers: Qualitative insights into the role of Instagram influencers in the hospitality and tourism industry. *Journal of Hospitality and Tourism Management*, 58, 214–243. DOI: 10.1016/j.jhtm.2024.01.007

Di Censo, G., Delfabbro, P., & King, D. L. (2024). The impact of gambling advertising and marketing on young people: A critical review and analysis of methodologies. *International Gambling Studies*, 24(1), 71–91. DOI: 10.1080/14459795.2023.2199050

Ellison, R., 2023. Strategies Behind the Communications: An Analysis of Social Media Platforms and Online Communication Channels Utilized by Agricultural Organizations in Texas.

Farkić, J., Isailovic, G., & Lesjak, M. (2023). Conceptualising tourist idleness and creating places of otium in nature-based tourism. *Academica Turistica-Tourism and Innovation Journal*, 15(1), 11–23.

Gan, J., Shi, S., Filieri, R., & Leung, W. K. (2023). Short video marketing and travel intentions: The interplay between visual perspective, visual content, and narration appeal. *Tourism Management*, 99, 104795. DOI: 10.1016/j.tourman.2023.104795

Gulati, S. (2024). Unveiling the tourist's social media cycle: Use of social media during travel decision-making. *Global Knowledge. Memory and Communication*, 73(4/5), 575–595. DOI: 10.1108/GKMC-06-2022-0134

Harding-Smith, R. 2024. Tourism Australia: an organisation made for crisis. In *Handbook on Crisis and Disaster Management in Tourism* (pp. 295-308). Edward Elgar Publishing. DOI: 10.4337/9781839105388.00025

Hardt, D., & Glückstad, F. K. (2024). A social media analysis of travel preferences and attitudes, before and during Covid-19. *Tourism Management*, 100, 104821. DOI: 10.1016/j.tourman.2023.104821

Holiday, S., Hayes, J. L., Park, H., Lyu, Y., & Zhou, Y. (2023). A multimodal emotion perspective on social media influencer marketing: The effectiveness of influencer emotions, network size, and branding on consumer brand engagement using facial expression and linguistic analysis. *Journal of Interactive Marketing*, 58(4), 414–439. DOI: 10.1177/10949968231171104

Iswari, N. M. S., Afriliana, N., Dharma, E. M., & Yuniari, N. P. W. (2024). Enhancing Aspect-based Sentiment Analysis in Visitor Review using Semantic Similarity. *Journal of Applied Data Sciences*, 5(2), 724–735. DOI: 10.47738/jads.v5i2.249

Keerthana, R., Kumar, T. A., Manjubala, P., & Pavithra, M. 2020, July. An interactive voice assistant system for guiding the tourists in historical places. In *2020 International Conference on System, Computation, Automation and Networking (ICSCAN)* (pp. 1-5). IEEE. DOI: 10.1109/ICSCAN49426.2020.9262347

Leite, Â., Lopes, S., & Rodrigues, A. (2023). Who are Portuguese followers of social media influencers (SMIs), and their attitudes towards SMIs? An exploratory study. *Management & Marketing*, 18(4), 556–576. DOI: 10.2478/mmcks-2023-0030

Li, S., Li, Y., Liu, C., & Fan, N. (2024). How do different types of user-generated content attract travelers? Taking story and review on Airbnb as the example. *Journal of Travel Research*, 63(2), 371–387. DOI: 10.1177/00472875231158588

Manthiou, A., Ulrich, I., & Kuppelwieser, V. (2024). The travel influencer construct: An empirical exploration and validation. *Tourism Management*, 101, 104858. DOI: 10.1016/j.tourman.2023.104858

Nazlan, N. H., Zhang, H., Sun, J., & Chang, W. (2024). Navigating the online reputation maze: Impact of review availability and heuristic cues on restaurant influencer marketing effectiveness. *Journal of Hospitality Marketing & Management*, 33(3), 288–307. DOI: 10.1080/19368623.2023.2246471

Nieto-Ferrando, J., Gómez-Morales, B., & Castro-Mariño, D. (2023). Audiovisual Fiction, Tourism, and Audience Studies: A Literature Review. *Review of Communication Research.*, 11, 88–126.

Polat, E., Çelik, F., Ibrahim, B., & Gursoy, D. (2024). Past, present, and future scene of influencer marketing in hospitality and tourism management. *Journal of Travel & Tourism Marketing*, 41(3), 322–343. DOI: 10.1080/10548408.2024.2317741

Sano, K., Sano, H., Yashima, Y., & Takebayashi, H. (2024). The effects of temporal distance and post type on tourists' responses to destination marketing organizations' social media marketing. *Tourism Management*, 101, 104844. DOI: 10.1016/j.tourman.2023.104844

Singgalen, Y.A., 2024. Understanding digital engagement through sentiment analysis of tourism destination through travel vlog reviews. *KLIK: Kajian Ilmiah Informatika dan Komputer, 4*(6), pp.2992-3004.

Soltani Nejad, N., Rastegar, R., & Jahanshahi, M. (2024). Tourist engagement with mobile apps of E-leisure: A combined model of self-determination theory and technology acceptance model. *Tourism Recreation Research*, 49(4), 714–725. DOI: 10.1080/02508281.2022.2100194

Wei, D., Wang, Y., Liu, M., & Lu, Y. (2024). User-generated content may increase urban park use: Evidence from multisource social media data. *Environment and Planning. B, Urban Analytics and City Science*, 51(4), 971–986. DOI: 10.1177/23998083231210412

Wong, S. Y., Ong, L. Y., & Leow, M. C. (2024). AIDA-based Customer Segmentation with User Journey Analysis for Wi-Fi Advertising System. *IEEE Access : Practical Innovations, Open Solutions*, 12, 111468–111480. DOI: 10.1109/ACCESS.2024.3424833

Zaim, I. A., Stylidis, D., Andriotis, K., & Thickett, A. (2024). Does user-generated video content motivate individuals to visit a destination? A non-visitor typology. *Journal of Vacation Marketing*, 13567667241268369. DOI: 10.1177/13567667241268369

Zhou, L., Qiu, R. T., Wang, S., Liu, A., & Wang, L. (2024). Incidental negative emotions and tourist destination preferences: A choice model during lockdown. *International Journal of Tourism Research*, 26(4), e2722. DOI: 10.1002/jtr.2722

# Chapter 7
# The Effects of News Media on Tourist Preventive Behaviors During Infectious Disease Outbreaks:
## The Mediating Effect of Risk Perception

**Noraihan Mohamad**
https://orcid.org/0000-0001-9815-7070
*Management and Science University, Malaysia*

## ABSTRACT

*During outbreak crisis, the information conveyed through news media can significantly influence tourists' perceptions of risk, ultimately shaping their preventive behaviors. Previous studies have indicated that research on this influence is still insufficient and relatively new. This study investigates how exposure to news media affects risk perception and preventive behaviors among Malaysian tourists. It also explores whether risk perception mediates the relationship between news media exposure and preventive behavior. Using cross-sectional design, 250 questionnaires were collected from tourists in the Klang Valley. The analysis using the PLS-SEM technique has revealed that news media exposure and personal-level risk perception are the important predictors to explain tourist's preventive behavior during pandemic. Additionally, personal risk perception plays a significant role in mediating the relationship between news exposure and behavior. These findings offer insights for policymakers to better understand and address tourists' perceptions and behaviors*

DOI: 10.4018/979-8-3693-3972-5.ch007

*during outbreaks crisis.*

## INTRODUCTION

The COVID-19 pandemic significantly impacted international tourism due to its close association with individuals' behaviors in public spaces. This global crisis led to variations in domestic public health policies and international travel controls implemented by authorities across different countries and regions. During a pandemic crisis, communication between authorities and the public community is essential to keep citizens updated about the risk (Lunn et al., 2020; Vanherle et al., 2023). For that reason, the media, either old or new, play a significant role for authorities and stakeholders to communicate messages related to the crisis to the public community. The public community relies on news media to obtain an important message that benefits their knowledge in terms of the current situation of the crisis as well as the instruction and guideline provided by the authorities for public safety and health. Accordingly, news media has become one of the key drivers of guidance to public community behavioral health during pandemic. However, it is vital for the media to completely understand the phenomenon or situation of the crisis in order to ensure the media content and information delivered will be beneficial for the public and authorities. For instance, social media is a new avenue for communication that offers rapid information dissemination. Due to that, social media has always been recognized as the most significant channel for individuals to seek any related and relevant information about the current situation of the crisis. Ultimately, messages conveyed by social media can be attached to promote an individual's altruistic behavior (Icoz et al., 2018; Qin & Men, 2023).

In recent years, a series of infectious disease outbreaks such as Ebola, Middle East Respiratory Syndrome coronavirus (MERS-CoV), severe acute respiratory syndrome (SARS) and H1N1 influenza around the world have shed light on the significance of effective communication strategies regarding such diseases (Oh et al., 2020). An outbreak of infectious disease is the existence of a disease that is not usually predicted in a particular community, geographical region, or time period (Oh et al., 2015). Typically, an emerging infectious disease involves rapid spreading, threatening the health of large numbers of people, and thus requires urgent action to stop the disease at the community level. Infectious disease communication is a type of emergency risk communication that is vital to public health and safety (Lunn et al., 2020). Accurate information about risk and treatment may not be readily available. During recent infectious disease outbreaks, media either traditional or new media have functioned as firsthand information channels from which the public can obtain disease-related information and exchange it with their family, friends, and neighbors in real time (Lunn et al., 2020; Oh et al., 2020).

News media, on the one hand, will affect people's risk perceptions about the crisis. On the other hand, the risk perception expanded by news media associated with the extent of subsequent preventive behaviors. Typically, in a crisis or infectious disease outbreak, news media have an important role in disseminating the risk to the public community. Sometimes, news media reporting that only aims to attract audiences tends to be very dramatic, attention seeking, and inaccurate. This case would affect the public's risk perception and their behavioral intention to prevent the disease. Indeed, the benefits of social media in crises are mixed (Lunn et al., 2020; Vanherle et al., 2023). Previous research found that messages delivered by authorities through social media during the Zika and Ebola outbreak may not be beneficial for public knowledge. Instead, they contribute to the increase of panic and uncertainty among the public (Kilgo, Yoo & Johnson, 2019). In support of that, a study by Oh et al. (2020) also found that exposure to information about MERS-CoV on social media has affected emotions, fear, and anger among the public community in South Korea.

Previous literature stated that mass media have been identified as vital shapers of the public's risk perception during an infectious disease outbreak. When they do not have knowledge about the health hazard, they tend to rely on the mass media to gather credible information and learn about risk caused by the disease (Oh et al., 2015). Previous research also found that media significantly influence public perceptions of risk issues on H1N1 flu (Oh et al., 2015), Ebola (Fung et al., 2014), and MERS-CoV (Oh et al., 2020). If only traditional media provide insufficient information related to the risk of disease, people tend to heavily use social media to obtain disease-related information (Yoo & Choi, 2019). Besides, information seeking, scanning, and gaining through media have self-relevant emotions, which are defined as transient feelings that arise from thoughts about one's life and self (Dunlop, Wakefield & Kashima, 2008). Self-relevant emotions such as fear and anger are assumed to shape individual's beliefs on how risk affects them and in turn, increase their desirable preventive behaviors (Oh et al., 2020). Findings from the study by Oh et al. (2020) showed that people's exposure on social media is positively related to self-related emotion and in turn positively associated with risk perception and preventive behavior.

From the perspective of tourism, the safety and security of tourists is classified as one of the most fundamental conditions that need to be met for discretionary or leisure travel to take place. The importance of this factor is reinforced whenever this need is compounded by natural and man-made disasters that occur in tourist destinations, as well as the impact on travel flows through the introduction of uncertainty and fear of consequences (Kapuscinski, 2014). Compared to other industries, the tourism industry is exposed to external factors based on faith and trust (Morakabati et al., 2017). Accordingly, there are many factors that will influence a tourist's travel decision making, either tangible or intangible. Travel decision making is complicated since tourists take uncertainties and risks during holiday into consideration (Alkier et al., 2023).It can be said that risk is a main factor of tourist travel decision making. In this case, the tourism destination image plays an important role in convincing the tourist's decision.

It is common that tourists are sensitive to the environment particularly regarding their safety, health, and well-being during travel. Research on tourism provides ample evidence of the fact that the tourist travel decision-making process is influenced by the presence of risk, whether real or perceived. The news media are always providing tourists with destination risk information, which raises tourists' perceived risk and consequently affects their travelling behavior. Media found the possibility to form tourist's perceptions about the destination image of countries, as well as their governments (Fan & Shahani, 2014). Parrey, Hakim, and Rather (2018) found that the media significantly established the relationship of perceived risks and destination image.

Previous research stated that the relationship between the news media, tourist's perceived risk, and their behavioral responses is infrequently studied (Kapuscinski, 2014). Study by Parrey et al. (2018) mentions the relationship between media influence and tourist perceived risk has not been thoroughly studied in the tourist travel decision-making process. In addition, the latest study by Oh et al. (2020) also stated that research about the effects of news media on risk perception and behavioral responses among the public in the case of emerging infectious diseases is still relatively new. Therefore, this study aims to examine the effect of news media exposure on Malaysian tourist preventive behavior during COVID-19 pandemic outbreak by including the predictor of personal-level risk perception as a mediating factor.

## LITERATURE REVIEW

### Preventive Behaviors

Due to the rapid spread of COVID-19, people around the world are strongly advised by the World Health Organization (WHO) to perform preventive behavior by wearing face masks, maintaining social distance, frequently washing hands, remaining at home, and self-isolating for those affected with COVID-19 virus (World Health Organization, 2020). However, the effectiveness of implementing these measures relies heavily on the public's high level of compliance and support. During infectious disease outbreaks, it is common for governments in many countries to take precautions by implementing relevant rules and regulations that must be followed by the public. The main purpose of these decisions is to control the further spread of the outbreak. Previous literature suggests that numerous factors can predict people's preventive behavior. According to a study by Lee and Shin (2023), some of these factors include perceived behavioral control, subjective norms, perceived benefits, and social stigma. Similarly, Han et al. (2023) found that individuals are more likely to alter their normal behavior to adhere to health protocols and support government regulations for controlling outbreaks if they trust and perceive the government as credible. Basically, people will engage in preventive behavior of COVID-19 when they perceive themselves at a high risk (Dawi et al., 2021; Lee & Shin 2023).

With the advent of COVID-19 outbreak disease, various means of information such as TV, magazine, newspaper, government officials, and online media are key elements that contribute to the increment of people's preventive behavior (Yıldırım & Güler, 2020). According to Rubin and Wessely (2020) and Wang et al. (2020), lack of knowledge and information disseminated by the media about an outbreak disease will increase individuals' anxiety, stress, and depression, which may affect their mental health. An individual's perception of COVID-19 significantly triggers them to be aware about the importance of preventing themselves from the threats. During COVID-19, it is common for governments around the world to utilize mass media and digital channels such as social media, mobile applications, websites, and portals to disseminate relevant information about COVID-19 to the public. It is worth to note that preventive behaviors are essential to prevent infectious disease that arise from a variety of sources, demonstrating a person who have a higher risk of infection to have a tendency to adopt the behaviors (Aschwanden et al., 2021; Dawi et al., 2021; Li & Liu, 2020).

## News Media Exposure

Mass media has been recognized as the main source of information that shapes people's risk perception particularly if they do not have solid knowledge about health hazards. When it comes to crises or infectious disease outbreaks, it is common for them to rely on mass media to obtain information and to know more about the situation which is affected by the disease (Oh et al., 2020; Wahlberg & Sjoberg, 2000; Rivera et al., 2024; Yoo & Choi, 2019). A study on newsprint media coverage focused on infectious disease outbreaks in America, such as the Zika virus and chikungunya, and their impact on the tourism industry found that the number of published articles increased during these outbreaks (Rivera et al., 2024). Emerging disease outbreaks commonly persist for extended periods. Consequently, the majority of articles published across various media platforms advise tourists to refrain from traveling to destinations, especially those severely affected by outbreaks. Additionally, there were enlightening messages on numerous media platforms about actions travelers can take to safeguard themselves from these diseases. Previous studies consistently revealed that news media exposure significantly affects people's personal-level risk perceptions and their behavioral responses towards infectious diseases such as H1N1, COVID-19, Ebola and malaria (Sell et al., 2017; Talabi & Oko-Epelle, 2024; Walter et al., 2012; Yoo et al., 2018). Nowadays, social media is considered an important platform for the public to gain and exchange information quickly as its nature allows cross interactions between different channels, provide various levels of communication, and integrate a bounty of formats such as text, audio, and image (Biradar et al., 2023). Due to that, social media is defined as a group of Internet-based applications that are developed based on the ideology and technology that allow users to interact, communicate, share ideas, content, experiences, perspectives, and information with other Internet users (Kaplan & Haenlein, 2010).

It is worth noting that media plays an important role in forming people's social experience of risk either by strengthening or weakening their risk perception (Hardt & Glückstad, 2024). Apart from obtaining risk information, it is common for individuals to interpret the information which in turn affects their risk perception and behavior. Adverse media reporting of a crisis in a specific destination can significantly influence tourists' perceptions of that destination and the creation of destination images (Huang et al., 2021). As a result, tourists are more inclined to regard these destinations as 'risky' and consequently steer clear of them. Therefore, it is important to note that, during disease outbreaks, it is crucial for the media to disseminate accurate information to travelers about the current situation. This includes suggestions for managing and preventing infection, as well as promoting responsible behavior while traveling. Key to point out, inaccurate information, fake news or misinformation has resulted in endangering community harmony, inciting violence, fostering suspicion, causing social unrest, and instigating targeted assaults on healthcare providers. During disease outbreaks, it exacerbates uncertainty and anxiety, fueling social stigma surrounding the phenomenon (Biradar et al., 2023).

Previous literature reported that inadequate information about infectious diseases such as Ebola and COVID-19 could lead to lack of people's awareness about the disease as well as increasing people's preventive behaviors (Lee et al., 2020; Suzuki et al., 2023). A study in Pakistan revealed that social media exposure is positively associated with the public's preventive behaviors towards COVID-19 (Awais & Ali, 2021). According to Dawi et al. (2021), social media has been recognized as a reliable platform to increase people's awareness about COVID-19 and adherence to the recommended preventive behaviors as stated by the government. The study indicated that social media and e-government are significant predictors of people's protective behavior. Hence, the following hypotheses are created:

Hypothesis 1: There is a significant effect between news media exposure and tourists' personal-level risk perception ($P_{12}$).

Hypothesis 2: There is a significant effect between news media exposure and tourists' preventive behaviors ($P_{13}$).

## Personal-level Risk Perception

Risk perception is a person's personal perception of how he or she generates and receives knowledge about potential in public health risk or incident (Choi et al., 2017; Yoo & Choi, 2019). Additionally, individuals' risk perception is often linked to personal factors such as gender, age, and personality (Hardt & Glückstad, 2024). Essentially, people's behavior and reactions to a crisis depend on their perception of the risks associated with it, which refers to an individual's assessment of the likelihood of negative effects resulting from the crisis. In other words, individuals with a high-risk consciousness are more likely to exhibit security-oriented behavior when choosing a tourism destination compared to those with lower risk consciousness, including preventive behavior. A result of high levels of health risk or contact with a health concern could lead people's risk perception towards prioritizing the preventive practices such as by wearing face masks during infectious disease outbreaks (Bae & Chang, 2021; Liu et al., 2021). Moreover, risk perception can even influence people's activities particularly with a person who has a greater risk perception intends to practice the preventive behaviors, whereas a person with a weaker risk perception intends to take a risk and is less likely to do preventive measures (Ding et al., 2020).

Furthermore, finding from the previous study found that risk perception was positively associated with preventive behaviors with the reason that women are more affected to have a greater level in risk perception (Reyna et al., 2021). Similarly, a study in Pakistan also revealed that a person with their self-perception toward threat in COVID-19 may form a person into practicing the self-preventive measures (Mahmood et al., 2021). It is worth noting that people who have a high-risk perception toward COVID-19 will practice adopting full preventive behaviors, while a person with a lower risk perception is less practicing the said behaviors. In addition, previous study also indicated that personal-level risk perception significantly mediates an individual's social media exposure and their intention to take preventive behaviors (Yoo et al., 2018). Therefore, the following hypotheses are created:

Hypothesis 3: There is a significant effect between tourists' personal-level risk perception and tourist preventive behaviors ($P_{23}$).

Hypothesis 4: There is a significant mediating effect of tourists' personal-level risk perception between news media exposure and tourists' preventive behaviors ($P_{12}P_{23}$).

## Research Framework

Figure 1 below illustrates the research framework, indicating the influence of exogenous constructs namely news media exposure and personal-level risk perceptions on the endogenous construct of tourist preventive behavior. In addition to its direct effect on tourist preventive behavior, the construct of personal-level risk perceptions has also been examined as a mediator in the relationship between news media exposure and tourist preventive behavior.

*Figure 1. Research Framework*

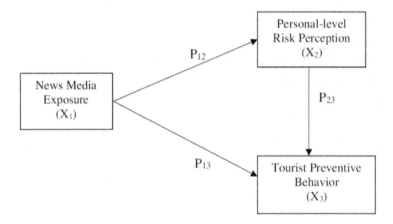

## METHODOLOGY

## Research Design and Sampling

The descriptive research design based on cross-sectional study was implemented in this study to discover the effects of respondent's social media risk information exposure towards their risk perception and preventive behavior during infectious disease outbreaks. Based on the convenience sampling technique, a total of 250 self-administered questionnaires were collected from local tourists in Klang Valley. This sample size is sufficient since it meets the threshold for several statistical sampling principles. First, in line with the "10 times rule" procedure in PLS-SEM technique, each structural path in the research model needs to be multiplied by 10 (Hair et al., 2014). Hence, the minimum number of respondents needed for this study was 30 (3 structural paths × 10). Second, studies with a large number of respondents or an unspecified population, the minimum appropriate sample size is 100 to 200 (Hair et al., 2006). Third, behavioral studies should have an appropriate sample size of 30 to 500 respondents (Roscoe, 1975). Referring to these suggestions, a total of 250 respondents were considered adequate and valid for advance analysis.

## Research Instrument-Questionnaire

The research instrument is divided into two sections. Section A covers questions about respondents' profile demographic and social media usage for information searching related to COVID-19. Section B consists of items for constructing news media exposure, personal-level risk perception, and preventive behavior. All items were adapted from previous literature and fixed into the research circumstance. Except for Section A, items for constructs in Section B were measured using a five-point Likert scale (1=strongly disagree to 5=strongly agree). First, seven items for the construct of news media exposure were retrieved from Dawi et al. (2021). Second, the construct of personal-level risk perception which consists of four items was adapted from Oh et al. (2020). Lastly, five items for tourists' preventive behavior construct were measured based on items from (S. Oh et al., 2020; Šuriņa et al., 2021). To complete the descriptive analysis, the IBM Statistical Package for Social Science (SPSS) version 22 was employed. An inferential analysis was conducted to test the research hypotheses based on Partial Least Square-Structural Equation Modelling (PLS-SEM) technique by operating SmartPLS software (Hair et al., 2014). Based on the PLS-SEM technique, the research hypotheses were tested based on the assessment procedures indicated for the reflective measurement model and structural model.

## Reflective Measurement Model Assessment

An assessment of reflective measurement model involves four main criteria, namely (1) internal consistency (Cronbach Alpha ($\alpha$) and composite reliability (CR) above 0.7); (2) reliability (factor loading ($\lambda$) above 0.708); (3) convergent validity (Average Valuation Extracted-AVE value above than 0.5); and (4) discriminant validity (cross-loading, Fornell-Larcker criteria ($\sqrt{AVE}$ value more than $r$), and the Heterotrait-Monotrait (HTMT) ratio value greater than 0.9) (Hair et al., 2014).

## Structural Model Assessment

The assessment of structural model was generated based on the evaluation of particular values, specifically the Variance Inflation Factor value less than five (VIF<5), path coefficient ($\beta$) value, standard error (SE) value, t-value greater than 1.96, p-value less than 0.05 (p<0.05), and confidence interval (CI) value at 95%. The structural model was also presented as the research conceptual framework using the beta ($\beta$) and $R^2$ values. $R^2$ was assessed to evaluate the structural model by measuring the model's predictive accuracy. To describe whether $R^2$ has a weak, moderate, or strong coefficient of determination, the values of 0.25, 0.5 and 0.7 were used as thresholds (Hair et al., 2014). Additionally, the advanced procedure of PLS-SEM for mediation analysis was employed to measure the mediation effect as suggested by Hair et al. (2014). According to Hair et al. (2014) and Garson (2016), two steps assessment should be carried out to evaluate the effect of mediation: (1) clarifying whether the indirect effects are significant; (2) verifying whether the mediation effects are partial or full. The mediating effects are present if the indirect effect is significant. On the one hand, full mediation occurs if the direct effect is not significant, but the indirect effect is significant. Conversely, if both direct and indirect effects are significant, it means that partial mediation has occurred.

## Findings

## Reflective Measurement Model Evaluation

Results discovered in Table 1 indicated that there is no issue regarding internal consistency, indicator reliability, and convergent validity of reflective constructs in the measurement model as each of the construct values met the criteria for reflective measurement model assessment. The analysis specifically found that the Cronbach alpha ($\alpha$) values, composite reliability (CR) values, factor loading values ($\lambda$), and AVE values for all constructs were well-above the thresholds. Nevertheless, there are few items with factor loading values not meeting the threshold, which are Media_2, PRisk_3, Prevent_3 and Prevent_4. These items remained in this study since the construct in which they belong to has already reached the CR and AVE values (Hair et al., 2014).

*Table 1. Reflective Measurement Model Evaluation*

| Constructs | Items | λ (>0.708) | IR (>0.501) | (α) (>0.7) | CR (>0.7) | AVE (>0.5) | Discriminant Validity |
|---|---|---|---|---|---|---|---|
| News Media Exposure | Media_1 | 0.758 | 0.575 | 0.889 | 0.913 | 0.602 | Yes |
| | Media_2 | 0.645 | 0.416 | | | | |
| | Media_3 | 0.842 | 0.709 | | | | |
| | Media_4 | 0.831 | 0.690 | | | | |
| | Media_5 | 0.796 | 0.633 | | | | |
| | Media_6 | 0.820 | 0.672 | | | | |
| | Media_7 | 0.721 | 0.520 | | | | |
| Personal-level Risk | PRisk_1 | 0.833 | 0.694 | 0.813 | 0.877 | 0.642 | Yes |
| | PRisk_2 | 0.856 | 0.733 | | | | |
| | PRisk_3 | 0.687 | 0.471 | | | | |
| | PRisk_4 | 0.819 | 0.671 | | | | |
| Preventive Behavior | Prevent_1 | 0.750 | 0.562 | 0.760 | 0.837 | 0.512 | Yes |
| | Prevent_2 | 0.813 | 0.661 | | | | |
| | Prevent_3 | 0.612 | 0.375 | | | | |
| | Prevent_4 | 0.554 | 0.307 | | | | |
| | Prevent_5 | 0.808 | 0.653 | | | | |

The evaluation of cross-loading values indicates that the discriminant validity is achieved as all indicators are loaded in their appropriate construct. In addition, the assessment towards Fornell-Larcker criteria and Heterotrait-Monotrait (HTMT) ratio also proves that this study is fit to the discriminant validity. Result exhibited in Table 2 indicates that Fornell-Larcker criteria are achieved when each construct has AVE square root value that is larger than the correlation coefficient value ($\sqrt{AVE} > r$). This indicates that the construct is unique and different from others. Table 3 demonstrates the Heterotrait-Monotrait (HTMT) ratio, and the HTMT criteria confirm that the construct is unique based on the value of the correlation coefficient between constructs that is less than 0.90 (HTMT.$_{90}$<0.90) (Hair et al., 2014).

*Table 2. Fornell-Larcker Criteria*

| Constructs | (1) | (2) | (3) |
|---|---|---|---|
| News Media Exposure (1) | **0.776** | | |
| Personal-level Risk (2) | 0.357 | **0.801** | |
| Preventive Behavior (3) | 0.391 | 0.556 | **0.715** |

Note: The values in bold are AVE square root values

*Table 3. Heterotrait-Monotrait (HTMT) Ratio*

| Constructs | (1) | (2) | (3) |
|---|---|---|---|
| News Media Exposure (1) | | | |
| Personal-level Risk (2) | 0.409 | | |
| Preventive Behavior (3) | 0.430 | 0.689 | - |

Note: $HTMT_{.90} < 0.90$

## Structural Model Assessment

The analysis revealed that all the predictive variables have VIF values less than 5 toward the endogenous variable respectively. Table 4 exhibits that the highest VIF value is shown through the relationship between predictive variables news media exposure and personal-level risk on tourists' preventive behavior (VIF=1.146).

*Table 4. Construct Collinearity Evaluation*

| Constructs | Personal-level Risk | Preventive Behavior |
|---|---|---|
| News Media Exposure | 1.000 | 1.146 |
| Personal-level Risk | - | 1.146 |
| Preventive Behavior | - | - |

Note: VIF < 5=No collinearity

## Direct Effect

Additionally, the significant estimation of predictive variables was carried out through the bootstrapping operation based on statistical t-value more than 1.96 (t>1.96). According to Hair et al. (2014), statistical t-value more than 1.96 is used to test the two-tailed hypothesis, which explains the significant value of the parameter at 0.05 (p<0.05). The analysis shows that all the predictive constructs have positive and significant direct effects on the endogenous constructs. First, the news media exposure construct found has a significant effect on tourists' personal-level risk perception (β=0.357, t=5.613, p=0.00, CI[0.232,0.484]). Second, the news media exposure construct has a significant effect on tourists' preventive behavior (β=0.221, t=3.770, p=0.00, CI[0.102, 0.335]). Third, personal-level risk perception was also found to have a significant effect on tourists' preventive behavior (β=0.447, t= 8.607, p=0.00, CI[0.365, 0.583]).

To begin, previous studies have mentioned that an individual's exposure toward social media contents positively affects their personal-level risk (Hardt & Glückstad, 2024; Vanherle et al., 2023; Yoo et al., 2018). Relatively, people have been exposed to risk information in social media incidentally while they are using it for other non-news related purposes. As a result, social media users may obtain information that could affect their perception and behavior. Results by Yoo et al. (2018) indicated that individuals who have been exposed to social media content significantly influence their personal-level risk perception. Similarly, a study by Oh et al. (2015) found that individuals who like to be exposed to news and information on social media related to Middle East Respiratory Syndrome Coronavirus (MERS-CoV) have great level perceptions of risks related to that infectious disease. Additionally, Ren et al. (2021) posit that individual's perceived severity during COVID-19 would increase as they were more likely to be exposed to traditional media. Hence, Hypothesis 1 ($P_{12}$) is accepted.

Next, results by Ren et al. (2021) also indicated that the more frequent people receive news on traditional media about infectious disease, the more frequent they tend to have preventive behaviors. Yoo et al. (2018) clearly highlight that exposure on news media particularly traditional or official media will shape people's intention to take preventive actions as the information provided is more reliable than social media. Moreover, results from a study on the impact of radio messages on the adoption of malaria prevention among Nigerians also indicate that radio messages regarding malaria prevention significantly influenced respondents' health behavior (Talabi & Oko-Epelle, 2024). Thus, Hypothesis 2 ($P_{13}$) is accepted. Nevertheless, study by Awais and Ali (2021) provide different findings where social media exposure significantly increased people's preventive behavior associated with COVID-19. Lastly, Oh et al. (2020) postulated that personal-level risk perception on infectious disease is positively associated with tourist's preventive behaviors. Similarly, Ren et al. (2021) found that individual's perceived severity positively and significantly influences their preventive behaviors related to COVID-19. Moreover, Alkier et al. (2023) as well as Garg and Kumar, (2017) have verified that tourists' decision making to visit a certain destination is affected by their personal-level risk perception. The study also indicated that tourists' personal level-risk perception is associated with information shared on media as well as socio-cultural factors. Thus, Hypothesis 3 ($P_{23}$) is accepted. Table 5 below illustrates a summary of constructs' significant assessment.

*Table 5. A Summary of Significant Assessment*

| H | Path | Relationship | β | t | P | 95%CI | Results |
|---|------|-------------|---|---|---|-------|---------|
| H1 | $P_{12}$ | News Media Exposure -> Personal-Level Risk | 0.357 | 5.613 | 0.00* | [0.232,0.484] | Accepted |
| H2 | $P_{13}$ | News Media Exposure -> Preventive Behavior | 0.221 | 3.770 | 0.00* | [0.102,0.335] | Accepted |
| H3 | $P_{23}$ | Personal-Level Risk -> Preventive Behavior | 0.447 | 8.607 | 0.00* | [0.365,0.583] | Accepted |

*p<0.05

## Indirect Effect

Personal-level risk was discovered to significantly mediate the relationship between news media exposure and tourists' preventive behavior ($\beta$=0.181, t=3.169, CI[0.102, 0.273]). The research findings revealed that news media exposure significantly affects both direct and indirect effects on tourists' preventive behavior. Hence, this study indicates that personal-level risk partially affects news media exposure and tourists' preventive behavior (Hair et al., 2014). Thus Hypothesis 4 ($P_{12}P_{23}$) is accepted. In addition, the assessment of coefficient of determination ($R^2$) was conducted as a major part of structural model evaluation. The analysis found that the construct of news media exposure explains 12.7% ($R^2$=0.127) of the variance of the endogenous personal-level risk perception construct. Moreover, news media exposure construct and personal-level risk perception jointly explain 35.2% ($R^2$=0.352) of the variance of the endogenous construct on tourist preventive behaviors. Figure 2 signifies the structural model that illustrates the effect of exogenous constructs on endogenous constructs respectively.

*Figure 2. Structural Model*

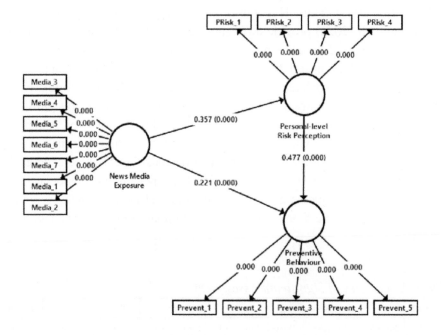

## DISCUSSION

By referring to the infectious disease outbreaks of COVID-19 as a case study, this study attempts to investigate the influence of news media exposure and personal-level risk perception towards tourist's preventive behavior when planning their trips. Previous researchers have suggested that news media will shape people's personal-level risk perception and preventive behavior during infectious disease outbreak such as MERS-CoV, H1N1 and Ebola (Abboodi et al., 2023; Fung et al., 2014; Oh et al., 2020; Oh et al., 2015; Yoo & Choi, 2019). However, there is limited study on COVID-19 which makes this study still relatively new and relevant to be investigated. Predictably, the research findings indicated that tourists' preventive behavior during infectious disease outbreaks was significantly influenced by tourist's level of exposure on news media and their risk perception towards the outbreak. Undoubtedly, during infectious disease outbreaks, mass media and social media become major sources for individuals to obtain any news and information associated with the outbreak. The findings have explained that the more individuals expose themselves to the news disseminated in media about a certain infectious disease, the higher their risk perception of that disease. This study also found that personal-level risk is a significant mediating factor between news media and tourists' preventive behavior. This finding follows prior literature, which also noted that people with high-risk perception of a certain infectious disease will enhance their practicing in terms of preventive behaviors (Choo et al., 2021; Hardt & Glückstad, 2024). This is because it is common for an individual's emotion to be affected by the news or information shared on media whether it is from the authority bodies or others. Emotions such as anger and fear also can easily shape people's risk perception and in turns increase their preventive behavior (Montazeri et al., 2023; Yıldırım et al., 2023).

Practically, this study suggests that when it comes to infectious disease outbreaks, it is crucial for the authorities to communicate and disseminate the information through official media that represent the authority's organization. This is important because besides the information shared must be clear and easy to understand by the public, it is also important to create and enhance people's trust and sense of security. In addition, unclear information will create various high-risk perceptions and emotional disruption such as uncontrolled fear and eagerness regarding the current phenomenon. Prior literature has proven that there is significant association between people's behavior and their trust towards the government. Han et al. (2023) mentioned in their study that individuals with a high level of trust in the government are more likely to exhibit a strong willingness to adhere to government procedures for controlling infectious diseases. These procedures include adopting preventive behaviors such as wearing face masks, handwashing, self-quarantining, and avoiding crowded spaces.

On the one hand, high-risk perception can help control infectious disease viruses from further spreading. On the other hand, it can make people switch to preventive behavior, which indirectly will affect the tourism industry and other industries such as economy, small and medium enterprises, food and beverages, transportation and so forth. In the context of tourism perspectives, it is crucial for authorities, including service providers and Destination Management Organizations (DMOs), to thoroughly comprehend tourists' risk perceptions of the tourism destination or product. By doing so, authorities can effectively manage any negative destination image associated with the destination or product. This is particularly important in attracting groups of tourists, especially those who are concerned about health risks (Hardt & Glückstad, 2024). Apart from that, the type of media also plays an important role in disseminating important information. In this digital era, we can't deny that most people rely more on social media channels to gain information. This is due to the fact of social media as a fast platform, which is easy to use, globalized, mobile, and open for users' feedback and engagement. It is worth saying that the synchronization and accuracy of information between prime media and social media needs to be considered carefully in order to avoid uncertainty feelings among viewers (Vanherle et al., 2023).

## CONCLUSION AND RECOMMENDATION

In conclusion, based on the research findings, the authority bodies and the policymakers are expected to have better understanding about how infectious disease outbreaks can shape people's emotion, attitude, and behavior. Apart from the managerial implications, this study also has some limitations. First, various constructs related to media can be studied as predictors of tourists' preventive behavior. However, this study only focuses on one construct, which is news media exposure. Thus, it is recommended for future research to investigate other relevant and significant predictors towards tourists' preventive behavior particularly during infectious disease outbreaks. Next, this study did not mention the sources of tourist's personal level risk specifically. News media exposure could be via prime media, authority's social media, or family and friends' social media. Thus, to provide better understanding on the effect of news media during an infectious disease outbreak, it would be captivating to investigate the specific sources of news regarding the infectious disease in order to understand the influence of specific media in shaping people's emotion and behavior. After that, data for this study only focuses on tourist's personal level-risk and preventive behavior regarding COVID-19 disease. Further studies could include tourists' perception and behavior on other infectious diseases such as influenza. Finally, future studies are encouraged to employ multilevel structural equation modelling (MSEM) technique analysis and bibliometric analysis to produce more resilient and comprehensive results than this study has, as it employs statistical technique analysis PLS-SEM to test the research model.

# REFERENCES

Abboodi, B., Pileggi, S. F., & Bharathy, G. (2023). Social networks in crisis management: A literature review to address the criticality of the challenge. *Encyclopedia*, 3(3), 1157–1177. DOI: 10.3390/encyclopedia3030084

Alkier, R., Okičić, J., & Milojica, V. (2023). Perceived safety and some other factors in tourist's decision-making process: Findings from Opatija Riviera. *Pomorstvo*, 37(1), 151–159. DOI: 10.31217/p.37.1.12

Awais, M., & Ali, F. (2021). Social Media Exposure and Preventive Behaviors against COVID-19 in Pakistan. *Journal of Media Studies*, 36(1), 23–52.

Bae, S. Y., & Chang, P. J. (2021). The effect of coronavirus disease-19 (COVID-19) risk perception on behavioral intention towards 'untact' tourism in South Korea during the first wave of the pandemic (March 2020). *Current Issues in Tourism*, 24(7), 1017–1035. DOI: 10.1080/13683500.2020.1798895

Biradar, S., Saumya, S., & Chauhan, A. (2023). Combating the infodemic: COVID-19 induced fake news recognition in social media networks. *Complex & Intelligent Systems*, 9(3), 2879–2891. DOI: 10.1007/s40747-022-00672-2 PMID: 35194546

Choo, J., Park, S., & Noh, S. (2021). Associations of covid-19 knowledge and risk perception with the full adoption of preventive behaviors in Seoul. *International Journal of Environmental Research and Public Health*, 18(22), 12102. Advance online publication. DOI: 10.3390/ijerph182212102 PMID: 34831866

Dawi, N. M., Namazi, H., Hwang, H. J., & Ismail, S. (2021). *Attitude toward protective behavior engagement during COVID-19 pandemic in Malaysia: The role of e-government and social media.* 9(March), 1–8. https://doi.org/DOI: 10.3389/fpubh.2021.609716

Dilek, S. E. (2018). The Changing Meaning of Travel, Tourism and Tourist Definitions. (Unpublished thesis). Batman Üniversitesi.

Ding, Y., Du, X., Li, Q., Zhang, M., Zhang, Q., Tan, X., & Liu, Q. (2020). Risk perception of coronavirus disease 2019 (COVID-19) and its related factors among college students in China during quarantine. *PLoS ONE, 15*(8 August), 1–13. https://doi.org/DOI: 10.1371/journal.pone.0237626

Fung, I. C. H., Tse, Z. T. H., Cheung, C. N., Miu, A. S., & Fu, K. W. (2014). Ebola and social media. *Lancet*, 384(9961), 2207. DOI: 10.1016/S0140-6736(14)62418-1 PMID: 25625391

Garg, A., & Kumar, J. (2017). The impact of risk perception and factors on tourists' decision making for choosing the destination Uttarakhand/India. *Journal of Tourism and Management Research*, 2(2), 144–160. DOI: 10.26465/ojtmr.2017229490

Garson, G. D. (2016). *Partial Least Squares: Regression and Structural Equation Models* (3rd ed.). Asheboro: Statistical Publishing Associates.

Hair, J. F., Black, W. C., Babin, B. J., Anderson, R. E., & Tatham, R. L. (2006). *Multivariate Data Analysis* (6th ed.). Pearson University Press.

Hair, J. F., Hult, G. T. M., Ringle, C. M., & Sastedt, M. (2014). *A Primer on Partial Least Squares Structural Equation Modeling (PLS-SEM)* (1st ed.). SAGE Publications, Inc.

Han, Q., Zheng, B., Cristea, M., Agostini, M., Belanger, J. J., Gutzkow, B., Kreienkamp, J., Leander, N. P., Collaboration, P. (2023). Trust in government regarding COVID-19 and its associations with preventive health behavior and prosocial behavior during the pandemic: a cross-sectional and longitudinal study. *Psychological Medicine 53*(1), 149–159. 9. https://doi.org/DOI: 10.1017/S0033291721001306

Hardt, D., & Glückstad, F. K. (2024). A social media analysis of travel preferences and attitudes, before and during Covid-19. *Tourism Management*, 100, 1–16. DOI: 10.1016/j.tourman.2023.104821

Huang, S. S., Shao, Y., Zeng, Y., Liu, X., & Li, Z. (2021). Impacts of COVID-19 on Chinese nationals' tourism preferences. *Tourism Management Perspectives*, 40(July), 1–10. DOI: 10.1016/j.tmp.2021.100895 PMID: 34642624

Icoz, O., Kutuk, A., & Icoz, O. (2018). Social media and consumer buying decisions in tourism: The case of Turkey. *Pasos (El Sauzal)*, 16(4), 1051–1066. DOI: 10.25145/j.pasos.2018.16.073

Kaplan, A. M., & Haenlein, M. (2010). Users of the world, unite! The challenges and opportunities of social media. *Business Horizons*, 53(1), 59–68. DOI: 10.1016/j.bushor.2009.09.003

Kapuscinski, G. (2014). *The effects of news media on leisure tourists' perception of risk and willingness to travel, with specific reference to events of terrorism and political instability* [Doctoral dissertation, Bournemouth University]. Repository of John Kent Institute in Tourism. https://eprints.bournemouth.ac.uk/21778/

Lee, J. J., Kang, K. A., Wang, M. P., Zhao, S. Z., Wong, J. Y. H., O'Connor, S., Yang, S. C., & Shin, S. (2020). Associations between COVID-19 misinformation exposure and belief with COVID-19 knowledge and preventive behaviors: Cross-sectional online study. *Journal of Medical Internet Research*, 22(11), 1–13. DOI: 10.2196/22205 PMID: 33048825

Lee, W. K., & Shin, S. R. (2023). Integrated factors affecting intention of COVID-19 preventive behaviors including vaccination in Korea. *Nursing Open*, 10(5), 3424–3431. DOI: 10.1002/nop2.1597 PMID: 36611182

Li, X., & Liu, Q. (2020). Social media use, eHealth literacy, disease knowledge, and preventive behaviors in the COVID-19 pandemic: Cross-sectional study on Chinese netizens. *Journal of Medical Internet Research*, 22(10), e19684. Advance online publication. DOI: 10.2196/19684 PMID: 33006940

Liu, Y., Duong, H. T., & Nguyen, H. T. (2021). Media exposure and intentions to wear face masks in the early stages of the COVID-19 outbreak: The mediating role of negative emotions and risk perception. *Atlantic Journal of Communication*, 1–14. DOI: 10.1080/15456870.2021.1951733

Lunn, P. D., Belton, C. A., Lavin, C., McGowan, F. P., Timmons, S., & Robertson, D. (2020). Using behavioral science to help fight the coronavirus: A rapid, narrative review. *Journal of Behavioral Public Administration*, 3(1), 1–37. DOI: 10.30636/jbpa.31.147

Mahmood, Q. K., Jafree, S. R., Mukhtar, S., & Fischer, F. (2021). Social Media Use, Self-Efficacy, Perceived Threat, and Preventive Behavior in Times of COVID-19: Results of a Cross-Sectional Study in Pakistan. *Frontiers in Psychology*, 12(June), 1–10. DOI: 10.3389/fpsyg.2021.562042 PMID: 34220597

Mat Dawi, N., Namazi, H., Hwang, H. J., Ismail, S., Maresova, P., & Krejcar, O. (2021). Attitude toward protective behavior engagement during COVID-19 pandemic in Malaysia: The role of E-government and social media. *Frontiers in Public Health*, 9(March), 1–8. DOI: 10.3389/fpubh.2021.609716 PMID: 33732677

Montazeri, A., Mohammadi, S., Hesari, M., Yarmohammadi, P., Bahabadi, H., Naghizadeh, M. R., Moghari, F., Maftoon, F., Tavousi, M., & Riazi, H. (2023). Exposure to the COVID-19 news on social media and consequent psychological distress and potential behavioral change. *Scientific Reports*, 13(15224), 1–10. DOI: 10.1038/s41598-023-42459-6 PMID: 37710006

Morakabati, Y., Page, S. J., & Fletcher, J. (2017). Emergency management and tourism stakeholder responses to crises: A global survey. *Journal of Travel Research*, 56(3), 299–316. DOI: 10.1177/0047287516641516 PMID: 29708106

Oh, S., Lee, S. Y., & Han, C. (2020). The effects of social media use on preventive behaviors during infectious disease outbreaks: The mediating role of self-relevant emotions and public risk perception. *Health Communication*, 1–11. DOI: 10.1080/10410236.2020.1724639 PMID: 32064932

Oh, S. H., Paek, H. J., & Hove, T. (2015). Cognitive and emotional dimensions of perceived risk characteristics, genre-specific media effects, and risk perceptions: The case of H1N1 influenza in South Korea. *Asian Journal of Communication*, 25(1), 14–32. DOI: 10.1080/01292986.2014.989240

Parrey, S. H., Hakim, I. A., & Rather, R. A. (2018). Mediating role of government initiatives and media influence between perceived risks and destination image: A study of conflict zone. *International Journal of Tourism Cities*, 1–18. https://doi.org/DOI: 10.1108/IJTC-02-2018-0019

Qin, Y. S., & Men, L. R. (2023). Exploring the Impact of Internal Communication on Employee Psychological Well-Being During the COVID-19 Pandemic: The Mediating Role of Employee Organizational Trust. *International Journal of Business Communication*, 60(4), 1197–1219. DOI: 10.1177/23294884221081838

Ren, W., Zhu, X., & Hu, Y. (2021). Differential effects of traditional and social media use on COVID-19 preventive behaviors: The mediating role of risk and efficacy perceptions. *Journal of Health Psychology*, 27(8), 1861–1874. DOI: 10.1177/13591053211003125 PMID: 33909510

Reyna, D., Rivas, Z., Lidia, M., Jaldin, L., Canaviri, B. N., Aguilar, J. P., Fabiola, L., & Ferna, A. M. C. A. (2021). Social media exposure, risk perception, preventive behaviors and attitudes during the COVID-19 epidemic in La Paz, Bolivia: A cross sectional study. *PLoS One*, 16(1), 1–12. DOI: 10.1371/journal.pone.0245859 PMID: 33481945

Rivera, E. P., Urioste-Stone, S., Rickard, L. N., Caprara, A., & Estrada, L. N. Tourists and epidemics: how news media cover the risks of Zika virus and chikungunya outbreaks in the Americas. *Current Issues in Tourism*, 1-18. https://doi.org/DOI: 10.1080/13683500.2024.2309164

Roscoe, J. T. (1975). *Fundamental Research Statistics for The Behavioral Sciences* (2nd ed.). Holt Rinehart & Winston.

Rubin, G. J., & Wessely, S. (2020). The psychological effects of quarantining a city. *BMJ*, 368, 1–2). https://doi.org/DOI: 10.1136/bmj.m313

Sell, T. K., Boddie, C., McGinty, E. E., Pollack, K., Smith, K. C., Burke, T. A., & Rutkow, L. (2017). Media messages and perception of risk for Ebola virus infection, United States. *Emerging Infectious Diseases*, 23(1), 108–111. DOI: 10.3201/eid2301.160589 PMID: 27983495

Šuriņa, S., Martinsone, K., Perepjolkina, V., Kolesnikova, J., Vainik, U., Ruža, A., Vrublevska, J., Smirnova, D., Fountoulakis, K. N., & Rancans, E. (2021). Factors related to COVID-19 preventive behaviors: A structural equation model. *Frontiers in Psychology*, 12(676521), 1–15. DOI: 10.3389/fpsyg.2021.676521 PMID: 34290652

Suzuki, T., Yamamoto, H., Ogawa, Y., & Umetani, R. (2023). Effects of media on preventive behavior during COVID-19 pandemic. *Humanities & Social Sciences Communications*, 10(58), 1–8. DOI: 10.1057/s41599-023-01554-9 PMID: 36818040

Talabi, F. O., & Oko-Epelle, L. (2024). Influence of radio messages on the awareness and adoption of malaria preventive measures among rural dwellers in South-West Nigeria. *Journalism and Media*, 5(1), 271–280. DOI: 10.3390/journalmedia5010018

Vanherle, R., Kurten, S., & Rousseau, A. (2023). How social media, news media and interpersonal communication relate to Covid-19 risk perceptions and behaviors. *European Journal of Health Communication*, 4(1), 28–50. DOI: 10.47368/ejhc.2023.102

Wahlberg, A. A., & Sjoberg, L. (2000). Risk perception and the media. *Journal of Risk Research*, 3(1), 31–50. DOI: 10.1080/136698700376699

Walter, D., Böhmer, M. M., Reiter, S., Krause, G., & Wichmann, O. (2012). Risk perception and information-seeking behavior during the 2019/10 influence A(H1N1) pdm09 pandemic in Germany. *Eurosurveillance*, 17(13), 1–8. DOI: 10.2807/ese.17.13.20131-en PMID: 22490383

Wang, C., Pan, R., Wan, X., Tan, Y., Xu, L., Ho, C. S., & Ho, R. C. (2020). Immediate psychological responses and associated factors during the initial stage of the 2019 coronavirus disease (COVID-19) epidemic among the general population in China. *International Journal of Environmental Research and Public Health*, 17(5), 1729. Advance online publication. DOI: 10.3390/ijerph17051729 PMID: 32155789

World Health Organization. (2020). *Coronavirus disease (COVID-19) advice for the public*. Retrieved from https://www.who.int/emergencies/diseases/novel-coronavirus -2019/advice-for-public

Yıldırım, M., & Güler, A. (2020). COVID-19 severity, self-efficacy, knowledge, preventive behaviors, and mental health in Turkey. *Death Studies*, 1–8. DOI: 10.1080/07481187.2020.1793434 PMID: 32673183

Yıldırım, M., Öztürk, A., & Solmaz, F. (2023). Fear of COVID-19 and sleep problems in Turkish young adults: Mediating roles of happiness and problematic social networking sites use. *Psihologija (Beograd)*, 56(4), 497–515. DOI: 10.2298/PSI220412027Y

Yoo, W., & Choi, D. (2019). Predictors of expressing and receiving information on social networking sites during MERS-CoV outbreak in South Korea Predictors of expressing and receiving information on social. *Journal of Risk Research*, 1–16. DOI: 10.1080/13669877.2019.1569105

Yoo, W., Paek, H. J., & Hove, T. (2018). Differential effects of content-oriented versus user-oriented social media on risk perceptions and behavioral intentions. *Health Communication*, 1–12. DOI: 10.1080/10410236.2018.1545169 PMID: 30427203

## KEY TERMS AND DEFINITIONS

**COVID-19:** COVID-19 is an illness caused by a virus called SARS-CoV-2. It typically spreads between people who are in close contact with each other. Preventive measures like wearing masks, washing hands, and social distancing help reduce its spread (World Health Organization, 2020).

**Fake News:** Fake news can be defined as deliberately false or misleading information that has led to significant harm within communities. During disease outbreaks, fake news exacerbates uncertainty and anxiety while perpetuating social stigma associated with the phenomenon (Biradar et al., 2023).

**Preventive Behavior:** Preventive behavior involves actions taken by individuals in response to perceiving a high risk of infection and understanding the severity of a disease. These actions, such as wearing masks and practicing hand hygiene, aim to protect oneself and others from infection during infectious disease outbreaks. Ultimately, adopting preventive behavior helps reduce virus transmission within the community (Dawi et al., 2021).

**Risk Perception:** Risk perception is an individual's personal understanding of how they gather and interpret information about potential public health risks or incidents (Choi et al., 2017; Yoo & Choi, 2019).

**Social Media:** Social media refers to Internet-based platforms enabling rapid information exchange, diverse communication formats, and cross-channel interactions. It allows users to interact, communicate, and share ideas, content, and experiences with others online (Kaplan & Haenlein, 2010).

**Tourist:** Traditionally refers to an individual who journeys away from their usual place of residence and work, spending a minimum of 24 hours in a different location for leisure or business purposes (Dilek & Dilek, 2018).

**Trust:** Trust can be defined as the belief or expectation of people, confirming that the word, commitment, verbal, or written assertion of another individual or group is reliable and can be relied upon (Šuriņa et al., 2021).

# Chapter 8
# The Smart Traveler:
## Impact of Artificial Intelligence on Tourist Behavior

**Swati Sharma**
https://orcid.org/0000-0003-2949-2363
*Amity University, Noida, India*

**Devika Sood**
*Amity University, Noida, India*

**Narendra Kumar**
https://orcid.org/0000-0002-3325-3448
*Amity University, Noida, India*

## ABSTRACT

*Objectives of the Study: The goal of this chapter is to find out the influence of AI on traveler conduct (Gopal et.al 2023), assess how tourism centered AI technology swap tourist aim, goals and ideas (Hoyer et al. 2020). Also to The research aims to recognize the influence of AI on tailored travel, ecological consciousness, and each aspect of the trip itself. Study Method/Design: The current study deploys secondary data and qualitative technique involve content analysis and in-depth interviews. Findings: From the study, it is, highlighted that AI impacts tourist conduct at various period of trip. Moreover, travel gathers abundance of memories, experiences collected by tourist, exploration of new places (Gretzel et al., 2015) On top of that inclusion of AI gives the benefit of smooth AI improves travel experience by making better ways, using less energy, and minimizing waste (Neidhardt et al ., 2015).*

DOI: 10.4018/979-8-3693-3972-5.ch008

## 1. INTRODUCTION

Remarkable transpose are occurring in the lodging and tourism sector due to the usage of AI (Li& Wang, 2022). As per the study by Kong H (2023) highlighted that involvement of automation has provided customized options and robotic service to guest, has changed the overall outlook of the hospitality Industry. By providing humanize services, I has made its own space in this competitive era where tourist can get anything with the blink of an eye.

The goal of the title of the chapter is to show the use of new and improved technology has improved the services offered to the guest, emphasizing at the learning of at every stage of travel. It has multi-folding the profit margin, and boosting the guest experience all basic services that were powered by AI tools made hotels, Airlines, and Hospitality depend on technology for increasing and smoothing their user experiences Bulchand-Gidumal, J. (2023). AI is not just a profit maximizing tool, but also a prominent factor for humanize ideas, but also exposure of friendly, realistic and user and ecological friendly technology.

Wide range of services were provided by involvement of AI such as predictive weather forecasting, room weather changes (Gretzel et al., 2015) to deploying virtual concierge for travel booking, check-in for guest (Xiang &Gretzel, 2010) improving travel occurrence.

Not only this, AI tools keep track of what people are saying on social media, which lets people instantly and accurately figure out how people feel about a brand or any other topic (Li & Wang, 2017). As the technology advances, manages personalized travel bookings, analyses history of traveler which include past experiences, complaint, guest delight bank and any glitches related to guestrooms (Tussyadiah&Pesonen, 2016). Travelling to a new city is no more just a dream of traveler, with the snap of fingers it could be done easily. Prior to tech era, booking and travel itineraries were a heavy load for travel agencies.

Indeed AI has helped in enhancing environmental travel exercise and improves travel experience by making better ways, using less energy, and minimizing waste(Neidhardt et al., 2015). For enquiring about any services, talkbot and robots solve the query within fraction of seconds, operate for the whole day and whole night, reduce the incessant calls to agencies, reduce paper work and increase travel experiences of the guest.

### Research Gaps

1.Existing literature often provides a broad overview of AI in tourism without delving into specific applications and their detailed impacts on tourist behavior.

2. Much of the existing research focuses on developed markets, with less attention given to emerging markets where the impact of AI could be significantly different.

## 2. LITERATURE REVIEW

The table 1 gives the insights on Literature Review on Artificial Intelligence in Travel & Tourism in a chronological overview of key studies and research papers on AI in tourism and hospitality, highlighting the evolution of research in this field over the past few years. Each study contributes to our understanding of the applications, impact, and future directions of AI in the tourism and hospitality industry.

*Table 1. Literature Review on Artificial Intelligence in Travel & Tourism*

| Year | Study/Research Title | Summary/Key Findings |
|------|---------------------|---------------------|
| 2015 | "The Role of Artificial Intelligence in Tourism" (Wang et al.) | Explores the potential applications of AI in various areas of tourism, including recommendation systems, customer service, and predictive analytics. |
| 2016 | "Applying Artificial Intelligence Techniques in Tourism" (Li) | Examines the use of AI techniques such as neural networks and genetic algorithms in tourism-related tasks such as route planning and demand forecasting. |
| 2017 | "Artificial Intelligence and Robotics in the Hospitality Industry" (Almeida et al.) | Investigates the adoption of AI and robotics in the hospitality industry, discussing potential benefits, challenges, and future trends. |
| 2018 | "Personalization in Tourism: A Comprehensive Review" (Gretzel et al.) | Reviews various approaches to personalization in tourism, including AI-driven recommendation systems and personalized marketing strategies. |
| 2019 | "The Impact of Artificial Intelligence on Tourism and Hospitality: A Review" (Zhang et al.) | Provides an overview of the impact of AI on different sectors of the tourism and hospitality industry, highlighting key trends and future prospects. |
| 2020 | "AI Applications in Hospitality: A Review of Current Literature and Future Directions" (Buhalis et al.) | Analyzes recent research on AI applications in hospitality, identifying emerging trends and proposing future research directions. |
| 2021 | "Emerging Trends in AI and Robotics for Tourism and Hospitality" (Xu et al.) | Examines emerging trends in AI and robotics for tourism and hospitality, including the use of chatbots, virtual assistants, and service robots. |
| 2022 | "AI-Driven Innovations in Tourism and Hospitality: A Systematic Review" (Chen et al.) | Conducts a systematic review of AI-driven innovations in tourism and hospitality, synthesizing findings from various studies and identifying gaps for future research. |
| 2023 | Artificial intelligence's impact on hospitality and tourism marketing: exploring key themes and addressing challenges Bulchand-Gidumal, J., William Secin, E., O'Connor, P., & Buhalis, D. (2023). | Presents the challenges faced by Tourism industry by AI |

*Figure 1. Word Cloud created through literature review by Authors*

The above word cloud is generated through literature review and presented as Figure 1 which has maximum frequency of AI Tourism followed by travel behavior and AI powered Hospitality.

## 2.1 Artificial Intelligence in Tourism and Hospitality

AI is a broad category that includes many different technologies and applications that are changing the travel and hospitality sector. The application of AI in this field comprises:

- **Personalized Recommendations:** Artificial intelligence algorithms examine a plethora of data, such as past patterns, client preferences, and behavior, to provide individualized suggestions for lodging, events, and travel locations.
- **Automation of customer service:** AI-powered Chatbots are being utilized more and more to answer questions, make reservations, and address grievances from clients. Installed digital assistant gives quick responses, smoothen reservation facility, provide 24*7 services Buhalis, D. (2020).
- **Predictive Analytics:** Predictive analytics is becoming more and more apparent to business. Allows hotel to provide customized service to guest, implement innovative pricing models, and attract broader range of customer. Solve the queries of guest delight bank of customer, promote the establishment's various family friendly amenities and services. Using data analytics, improve marketing strategies, reach potential guest.
- **Virtual Assistants:** The purpose of voice control in the hospitality industry is to enhance guest convenience and satisfaction by allowing them to use voice

command to control room features like lighting, temperature, and entertaining systems, improving the overall guest experience. Also suggest about the geographical locations visitors request for.

- **Robotic Concierge and Service Robots:**Robots in the hotel industry are becoming more commonplace. Robot is a machine designed to carry out the complex task automatically.Like situated in Nagasaki, Henn-na first hotel employees are robot for storage devices, technology using voice and facial recognition as Connie, robot concierge used by Hilton Hotel used for speech recognition abilities (Weißensteiner, 2018). Similarly travel mate works on anti-collision technology, used to push, pull suitcase of visitor. Robots even satisfy the guest by speaking in their regional language which is an easy way of communication

## 2.2 Artificial Intelligence and Tourist Behavior

In this digital era, has introduced robots and various technologies to comprehend difficult services, reach at the access of the customer within fractions of seconds additionally fulfilling their likes during the stay (Majeed et.al 2021). History of the guest could be easily analyzed and study by using technologies which is AI supported, assist employees to know more about their customer/visitor, improve the services as per the feedback given in the past, make their stay experience better Ma, Siyao. (2024).This technology can even examine huge amount of data and uses STAR report to assess the revenue management and handling in the organization. Additionally reviewing socio-economic statistics, information fetching from social network, online survey all these activities are done by technology nowadays. Not only this, it is useful for procuring information about guest habits, behavior, psychology while booking a room, identify way of staying, number of room nights book and if there is any association between the data that is also searched by AI. Therefore, implementation is boon for the industry stakeholders.

While approaching customer with their package plan, marketing strategies, they personalize the itinerary for the customer as per their suitability, budget, likes, dislikes, exotic locations, also provide services which enhance their experiences by arranging hotel rooms,their meals even historical data managed by AI does all the activities to provide customized memories and exposure (Goljaet.al 2021). With this process, contentment, fidelity of the customer increases who speak good about the hotel, promote them to visit same business and suggest these services among their friends, family, relatives.

In a fast paced world of tourism, understanding tourist behavior and predicting emerging trends are crucial for business, here involvement of AI, a new data era analyze vast amount of data from various sources quickly, identify customer behavior, taste, identify areas of improvement, enhance functional efficiency, promising a future where tourism experience are more customized, seamless and enriching Ma, Siyao. (2024). Adapting new trends, services technology, yields lot of growth and reputation for the organization and stand out firmly in this competitive era in the marketing groups.

Tourism Industry get benefit from artificial intelligence help to manage their operations and activities more effectively. It does the work smoothly and make the communication between host and the customer effectively without any glitch. With resource using effectively, data evaluation has been done (Kong H. 2023).Industries get huge support, increase revenue, reduction in outstanding expenditure as well. Figure 2 explains the Artificial Intelligence in Tourist behavior.

*Figure 2. Artificial Intelligence in Tourist Behavior*

## 2.3 Impact of Artificial Intelligence on Tourist Behavior

Amalgamation of technologies in the industry has influence sightseeing act through various phases of journey (McKercher, B. et.al 2023). Starting from the first stage to the third stage, Artifical Intelligence are modifying expedition so that smoothly communicate with guest Ionescu A-M (2024).This section elaborates on the impact of AI on tourist behavior, supported by citations, author names, and years.

(A) **Pre-Travel Phase-** This is the first period of journey.

(B) Information Search and Planning

- **Personalized Recommendations:** investigate sightseer behavior, pattern, delight bank attitude, perspective, itineraries could be read easily via Artificial intelligence.
- These researchers explored and highlighted in their study that how the modified ideas will go with each customer budget Tussyadiah and Pesonen (2016)
- **Predictive Analytics:** Gretzel et al. (2015) highlighted the pattern of PA in suggesting customized travel itineraries. Their research highlights the efficiency and personalization that AI brings to the travel planning process, estimating tourist likes and wants.

  1. **Personalized Itineraries**

- **AI-Powered Planning Tools:** Xiang and Gretzel (2010) investigated how AI is used in planning travel software. These machines assist in enhancing experience of traveler, by giving a full package deal, based on customer budget and requirements.

(C) **During Travel Phase-** This is the second period of the travel.

  1. **Navigation and Guidance**

- **Real-Time Travel Advice:** Brown et al. (2020) investigated the role of AI in providing real-time travel advice. This is used in increasing customer support services, and enhance their experience.
- **Augmented Reality (AR) and Virtual Reality (VR):** Li and Wang (2017) asserted that AR and VR has opened the doors of restaurant and hospitality Industry. It helps the hotel staff to simplify the booking process by allowing the customer to experience augmented model of room.

  2. **Real-Time Assistance**

- **AI Chat bots and Virtual Assistants:** Smith and Anderson (2018) highlighted that they are expert in handling heavy data, complex interactions. Help business and individual automate individual tasks, cut costs, research and user navigation.

(D) Post-Travel Phase

1.  **Feedback and Reviews**

    *   **Sentiment Analysis:**Leung et al. (2019) using automated senti-
        ment analysis,travel related social network post are posted. It is
        helpful to analyze the text data, involve customer reviews, email,
        and customer support, chat transcript and employees surveys.

2.  **Social Media Sharing**

    *   **Content Analysis:** Neidhardt et al. (2015) explored the usage of
        AI in qualitative analysis and social media monitoring. Their study
        shows that AI can help understand tourist act and likes by examine
        social media content.

3.  **Future Travel Planning**

    *   **Personalized Marketing:**Dwyer et al. (2009) discussed the use
        of AI in personalized marketing strategies. They highlighted the
        potential of AI to enhance customer loyalty by delivering targeted
        promotions and recommendations based on post-travel behavior
        and preferences.

## 3. RESEARCH METHODOLOGY

To conduct this study, Qualitative research has been used by the researcher which
helped in gaining deep knowledge of the feelings of the respondents (Berkwits&
Inui, 1998;Kunjuraman, 2020).Questionnaire were fetched from the parent paper
(Luo& Lam, 2020; Beirman, 2021).Total of 30 participants were taken in the study.
Twenty seven respondents were found valid as their responses were right for the
study (Hennink& Kaiser, 2016). The responses collected were analyzed via Nvivo
software 12.This study employs a thematic analysis approach, examining responses
from 27 travelers who have interacted with AI-powered travel tools. Data was collected through structured interviews and surveys, focusing on their travel planning
experiences, preferences, and the role AI played in shaping their decisions. The
analysis highlights key themes such as personalization, efficiency, trust, and concerns

## 3.1 Research Questions

RQ 1 How has the introduction of AI in the travel industry altered tourist behavior, preferences, and expectations?
RQ 2 How does AI influence tourists' destination choices, accommodation selection, and itinerary planning?

## The study gathered insights using the following key questions:

a.  What factors most influence your choice of destination (e.g., cost, cultural attractions, weather, etc.)?
b.  Have you ever used AI-powered tools or platforms (e.g., chatbots, travel apps) to plan your trips? If yes, which ones?
c.  How do you typically search for travel information (e.g., traditional websites, travel agents, AI-powered apps)?
d.  Do you trust recommendations from AI-based travel platforms? Why or why not?
e.  How does AI influence your choice of accommodation, flights, and activities?

## 4. DATA ANALYSIS

In data analysis all 27 interviews were analyzed through Nvivo 12 to understand the themes and descriptive analysis of the interviews is presented further.

## 4.1. Factors Influencing Destination Choice

Respondents identified several key factors affecting their destination choices, with AI tools playing a significant role in decision-making:

**Cost:** A substantial number of respondents (72%) highlighted cost as the primary factor in selecting a destination. AI-powered platforms that offer cost comparisons and budget-friendly options were highly valued, indicating a shift towards data-driven decisions.

**Cultural Attractions:** Over half of the respondents (56%) emphasized the importance of cultural and historical significance in their travel plans. AI tools that provide detailed insights into local culture and attractions were particularly appreciated for enhancing the overall travel experience.

**Weather:** Weather preferences were cited by 40% of respondents as a major influence. AI-driven weather analysis tools helped travelers predict and plan their trips accordingly.

4.2. Artificial Intelligence in Travel Planning

The majority of respondents provide various highlights given below:

**Usage of AI Tools:**Majority of respondents (88%) were in favor of using technologies like robots, virtual concierge,chatbots for various tourism related services. It depicts more dependence on technology.

**Specific Tools:**Frequently used resources encompassed skyscanner and various other technology for prior luggage weighing, Airbnb for lodging options. Majority of respondents (80%) started using these apps for making their trip easy.

**Preference for AI-Powered Apps:**Respondents (84%) voted that there is more reliance on VacayChatbot, kayak, iplan, Curiosio, which are AI travel app. AI has been a gamer changer in travel.

## 4.3. Trust in AI Recommendations

Regarding confidence in AI-generated travel suggestions:

**Trust in AI**: Eighty percent of respondents said that they trusted AI recommendations because of the machinery credibility, accuracy, impartiality and data driven approach. This shows AI is now a reliable source of travel.

**Concerns**: In-spite of widespread confidence, nearly 32% showed perturb attitude regarding safeguarding of evidences. These worryness showed that there is a need of translucency and factors to be morally taken into account.

## 4.4 Influence on Accommodation, Flights, and Activities

Several facets of travel were discovered to be impacted by Artificial Intelligence.

**Accommodation**: Around sixty eight percent respondents asserted that technology also help in finding accommodation categorized on size, location, clientele, ownership which is a varied choice for different categories of travelers.

**Flights**: Around seventy six percent of respondents were in favor of using skyscanner savvy applications, which provide clients with optimum deals in adequate time of travel.

**Activities:**Chatbots offered by travel companies provide robust security,24*7 customer support, personalized travelling offers, seamless booking, nearly sixty four percent voted in their favor.

## 4.5. Thematic Analysis

After analyzing above data, 3 main themes were emerged. **Figure 3** presents the analysis of Artificial Intelligence Impact on Tourist Behavior

**Personalization:**A remarkable ninety two percent of people who took the survey thoughts AI unique ideas were great. This shows that AI has the commendable ability to critically analyze data regarding customer and discovering their tastes and behavior trends.

**Efficiency:**Around eighty eight percent of respondents strongly believe that Technologies fetch and study heavy load of data, facts, information to provide services within blink of an eye in a real scenario. The increasing popularity of travel solutions driven by AI is largely due their effectiveness Hu, Y.(2023).

**Trust and Privacy**: Although most people voted in favor of AI, still forty percent people surveyed express worry about data privacy and possible biases. This emphasized the two fold difficulty that travel agencies faced; safeguarding confidence while protecting privacy issues.

*Figure 3. Analysis of Artificial Intelligence Impact on Tourist Behavior*

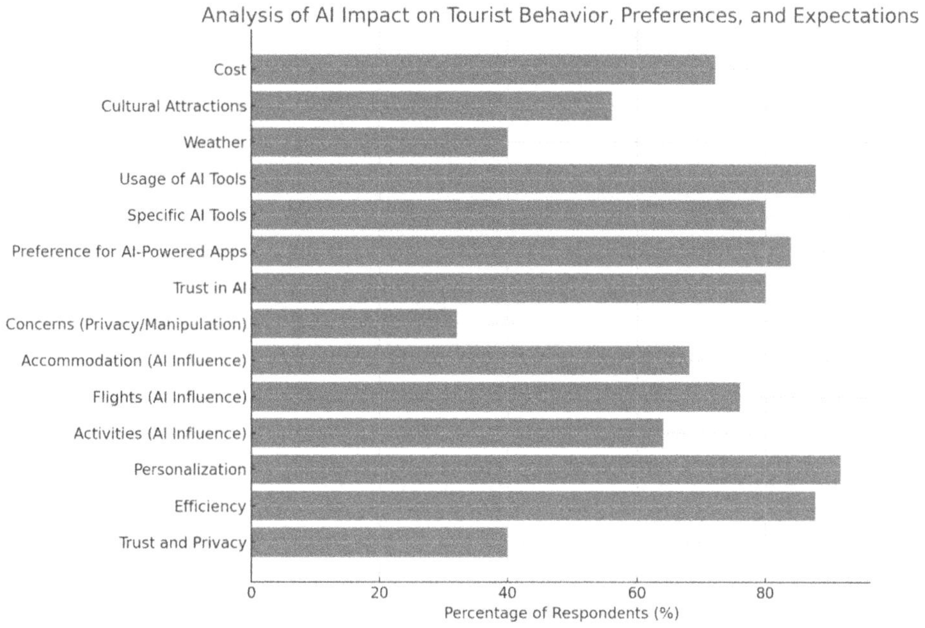

Tabular representation of the thematic analysis of 27 respondents regarding the influence of AI on traveler attitude were presented below. **Table 2** illustrates the analysis of Data with respondent quality and percentage

*Table 2. Analysis of Data with Respondent Quantity and Percentage*

| hemes | Key Insights | Number of Respondents | Percentage |
|---|---|---|---|
| **Cost** | AI tools for cost comparisons and budget-friendly options were valued. | 18 | 72% |
| **Cultural Attractions** | Importance of cultural and historical significance enhanced by AI tools. | 14 | 56% |
| **Weather** | Weather analysis through AI tools influenced destination choices. | 10 | 40% |
| **Usage of AI Tools** | Majority used AI tools like Google Flights, Trip Advisor, and chat bots. | 22 | 88% |
| **Specific Tools** | Commonly used: Skyscanner (flights), Airbnb (accommodation), Google Maps. | 20 | 80% |
| **Preference for AI-Powered Apps** | Strong preference for AI apps over traditional websites and agents. | 21 | 84% |
| **Trust in AI** | AI recommendations trusted for accuracy, unbiased nature, and data use. | 20 | 80% |
| **Concerns** | Privacy and potential AI manipulation were concerns for a few respondents. | 8 | 32% |
| **Influence on Accommodation** | AI personalization based on location, budget, and amenities valued. | 17 | 68% |
| **Influence on Flights** | AI-powered flight comparison tools were influential. | 19 | 76% |
| **Influence on Activities** | AI recommendations for activities and attractions based on interests. | 16 | 64% |
| **Thematic Analysis Personalization** | AI's ability to offer personalized recommendations is highly appreciated. | 23 | 92% |
| **Thematic Analysis Efficiency** | Efficiency in processing data and providing accurate, real-time updates. | 22 | 88% |
| **Thematic Analysis Trust and Privacy** | General trust in AI but concerns over data privacy and potential bias. | 10 | 40% |

# 5. LIST OF OBSTACLES WHILE USING AI
# BY TRAVELERS ARE AS FOLLOWS

Like there are two sides of coin, similarly implementation of AI proved a boon so as curse also which created hurdles while using. Few of the examples are explained below:

**Customers preferences misunderstood:**There were times when AI couldn't read and make proper inferences about their preferences, due to which wrong suggestions were delivered by technology. This has created unsatisfied and angry guest. Like food preference predicted wrong by AI.

**Bots that aren't effective:**Irrelevant responses to customer queries could occur when Chatbots are not properly trained or built. Client satisfaction may decrease as a result of misunderstandings, delay in problem solving approach. Such as customer request for travel itinerary and dialog box doesn't understand anything, will lead to discontentment.

**Privacy and data security concerns:**As AI is responsible for collecting huge amount of data and information about a lot number of guest,there comes an issue of privacy and security of data.This may lead to loosing of goodwill of organization is customer data leaks or any type of misuse happened by the company. Such as delicate data need to be stored properly and under confidential hands, else may lead to loosing of customer as their data become open in public domain.

**Technology exploitation:**In a hurry to bring customized or tailored services to the guest, technology has been used in a heavy amount leads to exploitation, hence loose the personalized touch or hospitality by human as over usage of technology occur in the company. This result to loosing of guest and genuine bond with them. For example, If Hotel deploys robotic concierge or robot for check in and check out then guest will entirely loose human touch.

**Missing Accountability and openness**: It could be challenging for clients to grasp how prices are established when AI algorithms used for revenue management and pricing optimisation lack transparency. Perceptions of injustice or discrimination can arise from this lack of transparency, especially if pricing decisions are not sufficiently justified or explained. For example, customer trust and loyalty could be eroded if a hotel's AI-driven pricing strategy causes large swings in room rates without apparent explanation.

**Unreliable prediction of future demand**: AI supported predictive analysis may sometime go wrong which can cause resources to be overbooked.Businesses in the tourism and hospitality industries may miss out on sales chances and run less efficiently as a result.

This is proved by example such as AI to predict demand to decide how to use its staff and resources and fail to correctly predict its demand, it might not be helpful to meet customer expectations.

## 6. CONCLUSION

Reshaping has been done by Artificial intelligence in the lodging and travel companies, which provide a large number of changes for new discoveries and progress. Whether to talk about tailored recommendations to customized services, in every sphere of life AI is progressing and implementing which is very effective in achieving companies' goals and aim. In this way users wants and needs were totally comprehended by the AI supported system, which give an insight of the client behavior, attitude, perspective and changing trends. Not only this, it has helped in making operations effectively strong and revenue driven which has ultimately satisfied the guest needs and gave an exclusive image of the hotel and travel industry. This AI technology has shape our ways and methods of doing actions easy, quickly, no time bound. This has proven to achieve a memorable package of travel to guest which has satisfied his activities as per their budget. Continuously these services are advancing at a faster pace from travel industry to hotel industry bringing new marketing strategies while selling their services and inventories to their clients.

# REFERENCES

Buhalis, D. (2020). Technology in tourism-from information communication technologies to eTourism and smart tourism towards ambient intelligence tourism: A perspective article. *Tourism Review*, 75(1), 267–272. DOI: 10.1108/TR-06-2019-0258

Bulchand-Gidumal, J., William Secin, E., O'Connor, P., & Buhalis, D. (2023). Artificial intelligence's impact on hospitality and tourism marketing: Exploring key themes and addressing challenges. *Current Issues in Tourism*, 27(14), 2345–2362. DOI: 10.1080/13683500.2023.2229480

Dwyer, L., Forsyth, P., & Spurr, R. (2009). *Economic analysis of tourism*. Channel View Publications.

Golja, T., & Paulišić, M. (2021). Managing-technology enhanced tourist experience: The case of scattered hotels in Istria. *Management*, 26(1), 63–95. DOI: 10.30924/mjcmi.26.1.5

Gopal, A., & Shanmugam, A. (2023). Advancing travel and tourism: embracing the era of artificial intelligence. *YMER Digital.*, 22, 334–341. DOI: 10.37896/YMER22.10/24

Gössling, S., Hall, C. M., & Weaver, D. (2019). *Sustainable tourism futures: A critical analysis of sustainability and development in tourism*. Routledge.

Gretzel, U., Sigala, M., Xiang, Z., & Koo, C. (2015). Smart tourism: Foundations and developments. *Electronic Markets*, 25(3), 179–188. DOI: 10.1007/s12525-015-0196-8

Hall, C. M., & Lew, A. A. (2010). *Understanding and managing tourism impacts: An integrated approach*. Routledge.

Hoyer, W., Kroschke, M., Schmitt, B., Kraume, K., & Shankar, V. (2020). Transforming the Customer Experience Through New Technologies. *Journal of Interactive Marketing*, 51(1), 57–71. Advance online publication. DOI: 10.1016/j.intmar.2020.04.001

Hu, Y., & Min, H. (2023). The dark side of artificial intelligence in service: The "watching-eye" effect and privacy concerns. *International Journal of Hospitality Management*, 110, 103437. Advance online publication. DOI: 10.1016/j.ijhm.2023.103437

Ionescu, A.-M., & Sârbu, F. A. (2024). Exploring the Impact of Smart Technologies on the Tourism Industry. *Sustainability (Basel)*, 16(8), 3318. DOI: 10.3390/su16083318

Kong, H., Wang, K., Qiu, X., Cheung, C., & Bu, N. (2023). 30 years of artificial intelligence (AI) research relating to the hospitality and tourism industry. *International Journal of Contemporary Hospitality Management*, 35(6), 2157–2177. DOI: 10.1108/IJCHM-03-2022-0354

Leung, D., Law, R., Van Hoof, H., & Buhalis, D. (2019). Social media and tourism marketing: A case study of Macau. *Journal of Travel & Tourism Marketing*, 36(1), 1–16.

Li, X., & Wang, X. (2017). The role of big data in personalized recommendation for tourism. *Journal of Destination Marketing & Management*, 6(3), 289–294.

Ma, S. (2024). Enhancing Tourists' Satisfaction: Leveraging Artificial Intelligence in the Tourism Sector. *Pacific International Journal.*, 7(3), 89–98. DOI: 10.55014/pij.v7i3.624

Majeed, A.; Hwang, S.O (2022). Data-Driven Analytics Leveraging Artificial Intelligence in the Era of COVID-19: An Insightful Review of Recent Developments. https://doi.org/DOI: 10.3390/sym14010016

McKercher, B., Prideaux, B., & Thompson, M., The impact of changing seasons on in-destinationtouristbehaviour. Tourism Review. (2023). Towards sustainability and personalization. *Information Technology & Tourism*, 15(4), 319–340.

Neidhardt, J., Werthner, H., & Ricci, F. (2015). The evolution of recommender systems

Richards, G. (2018). Cultural tourism: A review of recent research and trends. *Journal of Hospitality and Tourism Management*, 36, 12–21. DOI: 10.1016/j.jhtm.2018.03.005

Smith, A., & Anderson, M. (2018). AI and machine learning in the travel industry: A research overview. *Journal of Hospitality and Tourism Technology*, 9(2), 155–172.

Tussyadiah, I. P., & Pesonen, J. (2016). Impacts of peer-to-peer accommodation use on travel patterns. *Journal of Travel Research*, 55(8), 1022–1040. DOI: 10.1177/0047287515608505

Weißensteiner, A. A. A. (2018). Chatbots as an approach for a faster enquiry handling processintheservice industry. *Signature (Ramsey, N.J.)*, 12(04).

Xiang, Z., & Gretzel, U. (2010). Role of social media in online travel information search. *Tourism Management*, 31(2), 179–188. DOI: 10.1016/j.tourman.2009.02.016

# Chapter 9
# Chatbots in Hospitality:
## Decoding Tourist Behaviour Among Indian and Filipino Travelers

**Praveen Srivastava**
https://orcid.org/0000-0001-5310-694X
*BIT Mesra, Ranchi, India*

**Lord Jan Rodiris**
https://orcid.org/0000-0003-3936-439X
*Divine Word College of Vigan, Philippines*

## ABSTRACT

*The integration of artificial intelligence (AI) into customer service has revolutionized various industries, with the hospitality sector being a significant beneficiary. Among AI applications, chatbots have emerged as a vital tool for enhancing customer engagement and satisfaction. This chapter explores the role of chatbots in shaping tourist behavior, focusing on a comparative analysis between Indian and Filipino travelers. Utilizing quantitative analysis through SmartPLS (Partial Least Squares Structural Equation Modeling), this seeks to decode the intricate factors influencing tourist behavior and the effectiveness of chatbots in the hospitality sectors of India and the Philippines.*

## INTRODUCTION

Chatbots, powered by artificial intelligence (AI), have become ubiquitous across various industries due to their ability to streamline interactions and improve customer service. Initially adopted in sectors such as retail, banking, and telecommunications,

DOI: 10.4018/979-8-3693-3972-5.ch009

chatbots have proven their utility in handling routine inquiries, providing 24/7 support, and enhancing overall customer engagement (Zumstein & Hundertmark, 2018). Their success in these fields has paved the way for their integration into the hospitality industry, where customer service is paramount.

In the retail sector, chatbots assist customers by offering product recommendations, answering frequently asked questions, and facilitating transactions, thus creating a more efficient and personalized shopping experience (Silva et al., 2023). In banking, they handle tasks such as balance inquiries, transaction histories, and fraud alerts, enabling customers to access vital information without needing to visit a branch or wait on hold for a customer service representative (Mehrolia et al., 2023; Srivastava et al., 2024). Telecommunications companies use chatbots to help customers troubleshoot technical issues, manage their accounts, and schedule service appointments, significantly reducing wait times and improving user satisfaction (Petcu et al., 2016).

The healthcare industry has also begun leveraging chatbots to enhance patient care. These AI-driven assistants can schedule appointments, provide medical information, and even offer preliminary diagnoses based on symptoms described by patients (Hennemann et al., 2017; Verma et al., 2020). This not only improves the efficiency of healthcare providers but also ensures that patients receive timely and accurate information.

Educational institutions are increasingly utilizing chatbots to support students and faculty. They can answer queries about course schedules, campus events, and administrative procedures, thereby easing the burden on support staff and ensuring that students have access to the information they need around the clock (Mohd Rahim et al., 2022). Additionally, chatbots can assist in language learning by providing conversational practice and instant feedback, making the learning process more interactive and engaging. Studies have supported impact of Internet via social media platform and chatbot is a next step in the same direction (Mishra et al., 2022)

In the travel and tourism sector, chatbots offer assistance with booking flights, hotels, and rental cars, as well as providing destination information and travel tips. Their ability to operate 24/7 is particularly valuable for international travellers who may need assistance outside of regular business hours (Melián-González et al., 2021). Furthermore, chatbots can send real-time updates on flight statuses, gate changes, and weather conditions, ensuring that travellers are always informed and prepared (Li et al., 2021).

The hospitality industry, where exceptional customer service is a cornerstone, has seen significant benefits from technology integration (Sinha et al., 2024; Srivastava & Shandilya, 2024). Though metaverse is knocking the door to change the way business is run (Gursoy et al., 2022; Rancati & D'Agata, 2022; Shandilya et al., 2024; Tsai, 2022), e-servicescape is already a debatable topic (Lee & Jeong,

2012; Srivastava et al., 2023; Tri Kurniawati & Yadi Yaakop, 2021) however, most of the hotels currently use chatbots as technology advancement to manage reservations, answer guest inquiries, and provide personalized recommendations for local attractions and dining options (Dash & Bakshi, 2022; Melián-González et al., 2021; Pillai & Sivathanu, 2020). By handling these tasks efficiently, chatbots free up human staff to focus on delivering a more personalized and memorable experience for guests. In the hospitality sector, chatbots are being employed to manage bookings, answer frequently asked questions, assist with check-ins and check-outs, and provide personalized recommendations (Dash & Bakshi, 2022). These virtual assistants enhance efficiency, reduce waiting times, and offer a consistent level of service, contributing significantly to customer satisfaction.

Several factors influence customer satisfaction with chatbots in the hospitality industry. The ability of chatbots to engage in natural, coherent, and contextually relevant conversations is crucial. High interaction quality leads to a more pleasant and satisfying customer experience (Borsci et al., 2022). Customers expect chatbots to resolve issues effectively. The competence of a chatbot in addressing and solving problems is a key determinant of satisfaction. Additionally, prompt responses are essential in the hospitality industry. Chatbots that provide quick and accurate answers significantly enhance customer satisfaction (Nili et al., 2019).

The consistency and dependability of chatbots in providing correct information and services build trust and reliability, which are vital for customer satisfaction The perceived credibility of chatbots, which includes accuracy and trustworthiness of information provided, influences how satisfied customers feel after their interactions (Kim & Chang, 2020).

This study examines the differences and similarities in customer satisfaction with chatbots between Indian and Filipino travellers. Both countries share a growing middle class, an increasing number of tech-savvy consumers, and a thriving hospitality industry. However, there are notable differences in cultural norms, language preferences, and technological adoption rates.

In India, the diverse linguistic landscape and varying levels of technological proficiency across different regions can influence chatbot interactions. Indian travellers might prioritize responsiveness and problem-solving abilities due to the dynamic nature of domestic travel (Behera & Gaur, 2022).

Conversely, the Philippines has a strong English-speaking population and a rapidly growing tourism sector. Filipino travellers may place higher importance on interaction quality and reliability, reflecting their expectations of high service standards in hospitality.

Despite the growing use of chatbots in the hospitality industry, there is a lack of comprehensive studies focusing on their impact on customer satisfaction, particularly through a comparative lens between different countries. This study aims to fill this gap by providing a detailed analysis of how chatbot adoption affects customer satisfaction among travellers in India and the Philippines.

The aim of current study is to analyse the impact of interaction quality, problem-solving abilities, responsiveness, reliability, and credibility on customer satisfaction with chatbots in the hospitality industry. Second, to compare and contrast the satisfaction levels of Indian and Filipino travellers with chatbots. And lastly, to identify any significant differences in the factors influencing customer satisfaction between the two groups.

By addressing these objectives, this study seeks to provide actionable insights for the hospitality industry, enabling more effective implementation and optimization of chatbot services tailored to the unique preferences of travellers from different cultural backgrounds.

## LITERATURE REVIEW

Customer satisfaction with chatbots in the hospitality industry is a multi-dimensional construct influenced by various factors such as interaction quality, problem-solving ability, responsiveness, reliability, and credibility (Dash & Bakshi, 2022). Satisfied travellers are more likely to develop a positive attitude towards the service provider, leading to increased loyalty and repeat business. High satisfaction levels are achieved when chatbots meet or exceed customer expectations, providing a seamless, efficient, and trustworthy service experience that complements the overall hospitality offering and importantly as it behave like human (Melián-González et al., 2021). The construct identified for the present study is based on the available literature and discussion with the expert on this field.

### Interaction

In the hospitality industry, particularly among travellers, the interaction with chatbots plays a pivotal role in shaping customer satisfaction. A well-designed chatbot that can engage users in natural and seamless conversations enhances the overall user experience (Haugeland et al., 2022; Naqvi et al., 2023). Features such as personalized greetings, intuitive dialogue flow, and the ability to understand and respond to user queries in a conversational manner are crucial (Ngai et al., 2021). Effective interaction with chatbots can lead to higher satisfaction levels, as travellers feel more valued and understood, which fosters a positive perception of the service provided by hospitality businesses (Orden-Mejía & Huertas, 2022; Zhu et al., 2023).

The success of a chatbot in this context hinges on several key features. Firstly, personalized greetings set the tone for the interaction. When a chatbot can recognize returning users or access previous interaction histories to offer tailored recommendations or greetings, it creates a sense of familiarity and attentiveness that resonates with travellers (Wang, 2024). This personalization can include addressing guests by their names, remembering their preferences, or suggesting services based on past behaviors, all of which contribute to a more engaging and satisfying experience (Liu et al., 2024).

Secondly, intuitive dialogue flow is essential for maintaining user engagement. A chatbot that can guide conversations naturally, anticipate user needs, and respond promptly to queries without requiring users to repeat themselves or navigate complex menus significantly improves the interaction. The ability to handle multi-turn conversations, where the chatbot can follow the context of previous messages and provide relevant responses, is particularly crucial in creating a fluid and user-friendly experience. This level of conversational intelligence helps travelers feel that they are interacting with a competent and understanding service provider (Um et al., 2020).

This leads to our first hypothesis:

H$_{1:}$ Interaction of chatbot leads to customer satisfaction.

## Problem Solving

Problem-solving capabilities of chatbots are essential for maintaining high levels of customer satisfaction in the hospitality industry (Lei et al., 2021). Travelers often encounter various issues, such as booking errors, itinerary changes, and inquiries about amenities, which require prompt and accurate resolution (Maunier & Camelis, 2013). Chatbots that can effectively diagnose and solve these problems enhance customer trust and satisfaction (Lily Anita et al., 2023). Advanced problem-solving chatbots utilize artificial intelligence to offer quick and relevant solutions, reducing the need for human intervention and thereby increasing efficiency and user satisfaction (Bulchand-Gidumal, 2022).

In a fast-paced environment where travellers expect immediate assistance, chatbots that can diagnose and solve problems efficiently play a crucial role in enhancing customer trust and satisfaction (Naqvi et al., 2023). For instance, when a traveller experiences a booking error, a well-designed chatbot can quickly verify the booking details, identify the issue, and offer a solution, such as rebooking or suggesting alternative options. This quick response helps alleviate potential frustration and reassures the traveller that their concerns are being handled competently (Zhang et al., 2024).

Moreover, itinerary changes, whether due to flight delays, cancellations, or personal reasons, are common scenarios where travellers require assistance. Chatbots equipped with problem-solving capabilities can instantly access relevant information, such as updated flight schedules, alternative transportation options, or changes in hotel check-in times, and provide actionable solutions. This immediacy not only minimizes the stress associated with travel disruptions but also enhances the overall experience by offering seamless support (Saengrith et al., 2022).

Inquiries about amenities, such as requests for room service, information about local attractions, or questions about hotel facilities, are another area where chatbot problem-solving can shine. Advanced chatbots, powered by artificial intelligence, can access comprehensive databases to provide accurate and relevant information instantly. For example, a guest asking about nearby dining options can receive personalized recommendations based on preferences, availability, and proximity, all within seconds. This level of service ensures that guests feel well-cared for and that their needs are met efficiently.

The integration of artificial intelligence in chatbots allows them to continuously improve their problem-solving abilities. Through machine learning, these chatbots can learn from past interactions, becoming better at predicting and addressing common issues before they escalate (Suta et al., 2020). This proactive approach not only reduces the need for human intervention but also increases operational efficiency and customer satisfaction. By handling routine issues independently, chatbots free up human staff to focus on more complex or personalized service requests, thereby enhancing overall service quality (Adam et al., 2021).

Furthermore, the use of AI-driven chatbots in problem-solving aligns with the broader trend towards automation and digital transformation in the hospitality industry. As more businesses adopt these technologies, the ability of chatbots to solve problems quickly and accurately becomes a key differentiator in a competitive market (Vinnakota et al., 2023). Customers are more likely to return to a hotel or service provider that consistently delivers a high level of support, especially when issues arise.

This forms the basis of our second hypothesis:

H$_2$: Problem Solving feature of chatbot leads to customer satisfaction.

## Responsiveness

Responsiveness is a critical construct that significantly impacts customer satisfaction with chatbots (Bulchand-Gidumal, 2022; V. T. Nguyen et al., 2023). Travelers expect swift responses to their queries, especially when dealing with time-sensitive issues like check-in details, reservation confirmations, or travel updates (Hanji et al., 2024; Pillai & Sivathanu, 2020). A responsive chatbot that provides immediate and accurate answers can greatly enhance user satisfaction by minimizing wait times and ensuring that customers' needs are promptly addressed. This immediacy in communication helps in building a reliable and efficient service image for hospitality providers (Klein & Utz, 2024).

A responsive chatbot that provides immediate and accurate answers can greatly enhance user satisfaction by minimizing wait times and ensuring that customers' needs are promptly addressed (Fath et al., 2024). This immediacy in communication is crucial in situations where delays could lead to frustration or missed opportunities, such as last-minute changes to bookings or urgent inquiries about hotel facilities. By offering near-instantaneous responses, chatbots help alleviate the stress associated with travel and provide a sense of reassurance that the service provider is reliable and attentive to the customer's needs.

Moreover, responsiveness in chatbots is not just about speed; it also involves delivering accurate and contextually relevant information (Baabdullah et al., 2022). A chatbot that quickly responds with incorrect or irrelevant information can be more frustrating than no response at all. Therefore, the combination of speed and accuracy is essential in ensuring that the interaction is not only efficient but also meets the user's expectations. This ability to provide timely and precise responses reinforces the perception of the hospitality provider as a trustworthy and competent service provider (Park & Lee, 2023).

The benefits of a responsive chatbot extend beyond individual interactions. Consistent responsiveness helps build a reliable and efficient service image for hospitality providers (Manhas & Tukamushaba, 2015). When customers know they can rely on the chatbot for quick and accurate information, it enhances their overall perception of the brand, leading to increased trust and loyalty. This is particularly important in the hospitality industry, where customer satisfaction is closely linked to brand reputation and repeat business (John & Cheng, 2001).

In addition, responsiveness is closely tied to the overall user experience, influencing how customers perceive the convenience and effectiveness of the service. A seamless experience, where inquiries are handled promptly without the need for escalation to human agents, can significantly improve customer satisfaction and reduce operational costs (Cui & van Esch, 2023). By handling a large volume of routine queries efficiently, responsive chatbots allow human staff to focus on more complex or personalized customer service tasks, further enhancing the overall quality of service.

Furthermore, as the use of mobile devices continues to rise, the demand for responsive, on-the-go support becomes even more critical. Travelers often use chatbots while in transit, during late hours, or from remote locations, where immediate assistance is crucial. A responsive chatbot that meets these needs effectively positions the hospitality provider as a modern, customer-centric organization, ready to meet the demands of today's digitally savvy travelers.

This forms the background of our third hypothesis:

$H_3$: Responsiveness of chatbot leads to customer satisfaction.

## Reliability

Reliability of chatbots is a fundamental factor in achieving high customer satisfaction (Meyer-waarden et al., 2020). Travelers depend on chatbots for accurate and consistent information regarding their travel plans, accommodations, and other related services (Li et al., 2021). A reliable chatbot that consistently provides correct information and functions without glitches instils confidence in users, reducing anxiety and enhancing the overall travel experience (Klein & Utz, 2024). Ensuring reliability through rigorous testing and continuous improvement of chatbot systems is crucial for maintaining customer trust and satisfaction (Pillai et al., 2020).

A reliable chatbot that consistently provides correct information and functions without glitches instils confidence in users. This reliability reduces the anxiety often associated with travel, where unexpected changes or uncertainties can cause significant stress. For example, when a traveller needs to confirm a late check-out or inquire about transportation options, a dependable chatbot that delivers the right information promptly can prevent potential issues and enhance the overall travel experience. The assurance that the information provided is accurate and up to date allows travellers to make informed decisions with ease, contributing to a more positive perception of the service (Nosrati et al., 2020).

Moreover, the reliability of a chatbot is closely linked to its ability to operate smoothly without technical failures or interruptions. In a digital age where service availability is expected around the clock, any malfunction or inconsistency in a chatbot's performance can lead to user frustration and diminish trust in the service provider. Ensuring that chatbots are free from errors, capable of handling high volumes of queries, and consistently responsive is essential to maintaining customer satisfaction (Baabdullah et al., 2022). This requires not only initial rigorous testing but also continuous monitoring and improvement of the chatbot systems to adapt to evolving customer needs and technological advancements

In the context of the hospitality industry, where customer trust and satisfaction are paramount, the reliability of chatbots directly impacts the reputation and success of the business. A chatbot that consistently delivers reliable service can enhance brand loyalty (Vergaray et al., 2023), as satisfied customers are more likely to return and recommend the service to others. On the other hand, a lack of reliability can quickly erode trust, leading to negative reviews and potential loss of business (Aslam et al., 2023).

Furthermore, the process of ensuring reliability involves not just the technical aspects of chatbot design but also the integration of feedback loops that allow for continuous improvement. By analysing user interactions and identifying common issues, hospitality providers can refine their chatbot systems, making them more robust and capable of handling a wider range of inquiries effectively (X. Cheng et al., 2022). This ongoing commitment to enhancing reliability through testing, user feedback, and system updates is crucial for sustaining high levels of customer trust and satisfaction

This leads to our fourth hypothesis:

$H_4$: Reliability of chatbot leads to customer satisfaction.

## Credibility

Credibility of chatbots is crucial in influencing customer satisfaction within the hospitality industry (Jansom et al., 2022). For travellers, the assurance that the information provided by chatbots is trustworthy and accurate is paramount (V. T. Nguyen et al., 2023). Chatbots that offer verified information, cite reputable sources, and transparently handle customer data build a sense of credibility (Lily Anita et al., 2023). When travellers perceive chatbots as credible, they are more likely to rely on them for critical travel-related decisions, thus enhancing their satisfaction with the service provided (Li et al., 2021).

Travelers often seek information on various aspects of their trip, from booking accommodations to understanding local regulations or finding nearby attractions. A chatbot that offers verified information, cites reputable sources, and provides clear, accurate answers helps build a strong sense of credibility (Jyoti & Srivastava, 2008; Xiang et al., 2015). For example, when a chatbot provides details about a hotel's amenities or offers recommendations for dining, the traveller must trust that this information is up-to-date and based on reliable data (Ahmad et al., 2024). The inclusion of citations or references to authoritative sources further reinforces the chatbot's credibility, making it more likely that users will rely on it for important decisions.

Furthermore, the way a chatbot handles customer data plays a significant role in establishing its credibility. In the hospitality industry, where personal data such as payment details, booking information, and preferences are frequently shared, customers must feel confident that their information is being managed securely and ethically (Cheng & Jiang, 2022). Chatbots that transparently communicate their data usage policies, employ robust security measures, and handle sensitive information with care contribute to a greater sense of trust (Przegalinska et al., 2019). This transparency not only builds credibility but also enhances customer loyalty, as travellers are more likely to return to a service they perceive as safe and trustworthy

When travellers perceive chatbots as credible, they are more likely to rely on them for critical travel-related decisions, thus enhancing their satisfaction with the service provided. Whether it's making a last-minute booking, altering travel plans, or seeking recommendations in an unfamiliar city, the perceived credibility of the chatbot directly impacts the traveller's confidence in the service (Jansom et al., 2022). A credible chatbot can serve as a trusted advisor, guiding travellers through their journey with reliable information and support.

Moreover, credibility is also linked to the consistency and professionalism of the chatbot's interactions. A chatbot that consistently delivers accurate, relevant, and well-presented information reinforces its credibility over time (Nguyen et al., 2021). This consistent performance helps build a positive reputation for the hospitality provider, as travellers who have positive experiences with the chatbot are more likely to trust the brand as a whole.

In an industry where customer trust is closely tied to brand reputation, the credibility of chatbots can significantly influence overall customer satisfaction (Huang et al., 2024). By ensuring that chatbots are not only technically proficient but also trustworthy and transparent in their operations, hospitality providers can create a more reliable and satisfying customer experience.

This forms the base of our fifth hypothesis:

$H_5$: Credibility of chatbot leads to customer satisfaction.

## Nationality

The impact of chatbot constructs on customer satisfaction can vary across different nationalities, such as Indian and Filipino travellers. Cultural differences influence expectations and perceptions of chatbot interactions (Srivastava et al., 2024). Indian travellers might prioritize responsiveness and reliability, seeking quick and accurate responses due to the fast-paced nature of their travel needs. Filipino travellers, on the other hand, may place higher importance on interaction and problem-solving capabilities, valuing a more personalized and empathetic approach. Understanding these cultural nuances is essential for designing chatbots that cater effectively to the diverse preferences of travellers from India and the Philippines, ultimately enhancing their satisfaction with the hospitality service. In order to access the role, nationality have on all the above-mentioned relationships, SmartPLS Multi-Group Analysis (MGA) feature is used which provide two different models to assess the difference between two groups.

*Figure 1. Conceptual Model*

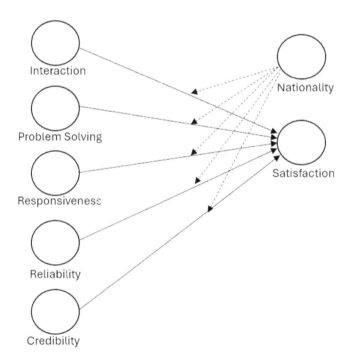

## RESEARCH METHODOLOGY

### Data Collection

An online questionnaire was distributed among travellers from India and the Philippines to gather data on their experiences with a travel chatbot. The questionnaire was carefully designed to ensure that the participants had relevant experiences, with a qualifying question included to confirm that only those who had used the chatbot for their travel-related activities were included in the study. This step was crucial in ensuring the relevance and accuracy of the data collected.

The sampling technique employed was snowball sampling, a method particularly useful for reaching specific populations that may be difficult to access through traditional sampling methods. The questionnaire was initially distributed among a small group of known contacts who had used the chatbot, and they were encouraged to share it within their networks. This approach allowed the study to reach a broader audience while maintaining a focus on individuals who had relevant experience with the chatbot. The questionnaire was shared across various social media platforms, including LinkedIn, Facebook, and WhatsApp, to maximize reach and engagement.

Responses were meticulously collected and screened for completeness and relevance. Initially, a total of 217 responses were gathered, with 88 responses from the Philippines and 125 from India. However, to ensure the integrity of the analysis, the responses were thoroughly reviewed. This screening process involved checking for any incomplete or inconsistent answers, as well as verifying that all participants met the qualifying criteria. After this rigorous screening, 202 responses were deemed useful for analysis, consisting of 85 responses from the Philippines and 117 from India. These responses provided a solid foundation for the subsequent analysis, offering insights into the experiences of travellers from two distinct cultural backgrounds with the travel chatbot.

### Questionnaire Design

The questionnaire was meticulously designed using a 5-point Likert scale, a widely recognized tool in survey research for capturing respondents' attitudes and opinions. This scale ranged from 1 (strongly disagree) to 5 (strongly agree), offering participants a straightforward way to express their level of agreement with various statements regarding their experiences with the chatbot. Each statement was carefully crafted to probe different aspects of the chatbot's performance, such as its problem-solving capabilities, responsiveness, reliability, and overall credibility.

To ensure the reliability and validity of the data collected, the questionnaire was adapted from previously accepted and validated questionnaires in the field. This adaptation process involved reviewing existing literature to identify well-established survey instruments that had been proven effective in similar studies. By using these validated tools, the questionnaire not only maintained a high standard of scientific rigor but also ensured that the questions were relevant and accurately measured the constructs under investigation.

The Likert scale format provided a nuanced understanding of the respondents' experiences, allowing for a detailed analysis of how different factors influenced their satisfaction with the chatbot. The use of a 5-point scale, as opposed to a binary yes/no option, enabled the capture of varying degrees of sentiment, offering richer data for subsequent analysis. This approach was essential for uncovering the subtle differences in perceptions among users, which could then be linked to their overall satisfaction and trust in the chatbot.

## Data Analysis

Smart PLS (Partial Least Squares) was employed as the primary analytical tool to assess both the measurement model and the structural model within the study. The measurement model was rigorously evaluated to ensure the reliability and validity of the constructs, focusing on factors such as indicator reliability, composite reliability, and average variance extracted (AVE). This step was crucial in confirming that the constructs accurately represented the underlying theoretical concepts and were measured consistently across the sample.

Once the measurement model was validated, the structural model was examined to test the hypothesized relationships between the constructs. This phase of the analysis involved assessing the path coefficients, which represent the strength and direction of the relationships between variables. The significance of these relationships was determined through bootstrapping procedures, which provided confidence intervals and p-values for each path in the model. This allowed for a detailed understanding of how various factors, such as chatbot reliability, responsiveness, and credibility, influenced customer satisfaction and trust.

To further explore the potential moderating impact of nationality, a Multi-Group Analysis (MGA) was conducted using Smart PLS. This analysis was instrumental in comparing the path coefficients between the two national groups—India and the Philippines. By doing so, the study was able to determine whether nationality significantly influenced the relationships within the model, offering insights into how cultural differences might affect user experiences with the travel chatbot. The

MGA provided a nuanced view of the data, revealing any significant differences in how respondents from the two countries perceived and interacted with the chatbot.

This methodological approach ensured a robust and comprehensive analysis of the data, allowing for the validation of the proposed hypotheses while also exploring the role of nationality as a moderating factor. The use of Smart PLS and MGA provided a sophisticated framework for understanding the effectiveness of the travel chatbot and highlighted the importance of considering cultural context in the design and deployment of such technologies.

## RESULT

### Measurement Model

The measurement model was evaluated using SmartPLS, focusing on key criteria such as reliability, convergent validity, discriminant validity, and multicollinearity. All constructs demonstrated strong composite reliability and Cronbach's Alpha values, indicating acceptable internal consistency and reliability. The average variance extracted (AVE) values for each construct exceeded the minimum threshold, confirming adequate convergent validity. Discriminant validity was established through the Fornell-Larcker criterion which supported the distinctiveness of the constructs (Fornell & Larcker, 1981). Furthermore, the Variance Inflation Factor (VIF) values were well within acceptable limits, indicating no issues with multicollinearity among the constructs. All items loaded highly on their respective constructs without any cross-loadings, ensuring the distinctiveness and clarity of each construct. As all measures meet or exceed the required thresholds, and no cross-loading issues were identified, the measurement model is validated, and we can confidently proceed to evaluate the structural model. The table below provide details of some of the criteria.

*Table 1. Discriminant Validity*

|       | CRE   | INT   | PSO   | REL   | RES   | SAT   |
|-------|-------|-------|-------|-------|-------|-------|
| CRE   | 0.727 |       |       |       |       |       |
| INT   | 0.433 | 0.749 |       |       |       |       |
| PSO   | 0.081 | 0.318 | 0.732 |       |       |       |
| REL   | 0.190 | 0.379 | 0.236 | 0.691 |       |       |
| RES   | 0.110 | 0.358 | 0.342 | 0.233 | 0.745 |       |
| SAT   | 0.317 | 0.440 | 0.381 | 0.404 | 0.377 | 0.612 |

*Table 2. VIF Value*

| VIF | | | |
|---|---|---|---|
| CRE1 | 1.165 | REL1 | 1.1 |
| CRE2 | 1.129 | REL2 | 1.114 |
| CRE3 | 1.227 | REL3 | 1.065 |
| INT1 | 1.467 | RES1 | 1.179 |
| INT2 | 1.464 | RES2 | 1.335 |
| INT3 | 1.362 | RES3 | 1.192 |
| INT4 | 1.393 | SAT1 | 1.186 |
| PSO1 | 1.134 | SAT2 | 1.217 |
| PSO2 | 1.232 | SAT3 | 1.081 |
| PSO3 | 1.18 | SAT4 | 1.256 |
| | | SAT5 | 1.168 |

## Structural Model

The structural model was rigorously assessed using SmartPLS 4 to elucidate the relationships between the independent variables—Interaction, Problem Solving Responsiveness, Reliability, and Credibility—and the dependent variable, Satisfaction with the Use of Chatbot. This analysis was pivotal in understanding how each of these factors contributes to enhancing customer satisfaction when interacting with chatbots, a crucial element in the hospitality industry's shift towards automated and AI-driven customer service solutions.

The findings from the analysis revealed that all the path coefficients between the independent variables and the dependent variable were statistically significant, underscoring the robustness of the model and the relevance of the selected constructs. Specifically, each construct was found to have a positive impact on customer satisfaction, indicating that improving these factors can lead to a more favorable user experience with chatbots.

Among the examined constructs, Reliability emerged as the most influential factor, with a beta coefficient of 0.224. This finding suggests that customers place a high value on the dependability and consistency of chatbots in providing accurate and reliable information. Reliability's dominant role highlights the critical need for chatbots to function without errors, providing users with trustworthy interactions that meet their expectations.

Following Reliability, Problem Solving Responsiveness was identified as the second most significant predictor of customer satisfaction, with a beta coefficient of 0.204. This indicates that customers greatly appreciate a chatbot's ability to efficiently address and resolve their issues. A chatbot's responsiveness in problem-solving scenarios can significantly enhance user satisfaction by ensuring that customers feel supported, and their concerns are promptly addressed.

Responsiveness, with a beta coefficient of 0.182, was the third most impactful construct. This reflects the importance of a chatbot's ability to respond quickly and effectively to customer inquiries, which is essential in maintaining user engagement and satisfaction. Responsiveness in this context not only pertains to speed but also to the relevance and appropriateness of the chatbot's replies.

Credibility, with a beta coefficient of 0.173, also plays a substantial role in influencing customer satisfaction. This suggests that the perceived trustworthiness and expertise of a chatbot significantly affect how customers judge their overall experience. A credible chatbot can build and maintain customer trust, which is vital for long-term customer satisfaction and loyalty.

Lastly, Interaction, with a beta coefficient of 0.151, while the least impactful among the studied constructs, still significantly contributes to customer satisfaction. This construct reflects the quality of the conversational exchange between the chatbot and the user, including factors such as ease of use, user-friendliness, and the overall interaction experience. Although its impact is relatively lower, improving interaction quality can still enhance the overall satisfaction with chatbot usage.

These findings not only confirm the positive contributions of each construct to customer satisfaction but also provide empirical support for the hypotheses H1, H2, H3, H4, and H5, as originally proposed. The path coefficients and significance levels are comprehensively detailed in Figure 2 and Table 3, offering a clear depiction of the relationships within the model and validating the theoretical framework underpinning this study. These results underscore the importance of optimizing these key constructs to improve customer satisfaction with chatbot technology in the hospitality industry.

*Figure 2. Bootstrapping Result (Complete Model)*

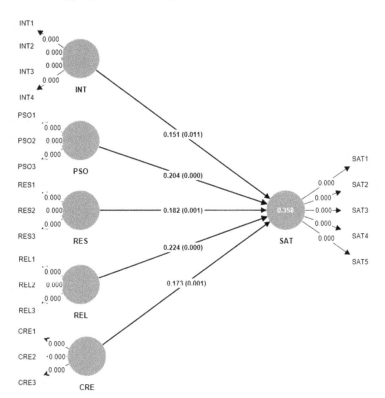

*Table 3. Bootstrapping Result (Complete Model)*

|  | Original sample (O) | Sample mean (M) | Standard deviation (STDEV) | T statistics (|O/STDEV|) | P values |
|---|---|---|---|---|---|
| CRE -> SAT | 0.173 | 0.18 | 0.051 | 3.414 | 0.001 |
| INT -> SAT | 0.151 | 0.15 | 0.059 | 2.559 | 0.011 |
| PSO -> SAT | 0.204 | 0.203 | 0.057 | 3.588 | 0 |
| REL -> SAT | 0.224 | 0.226 | 0.063 | 3.551 | 0 |
| RES -> SAT | 0.182 | 0.187 | 0.057 | 3.189 | 0.001 |

Source: Computed from data

The $R^2$ value for the structural model was calculated to be 0.358, signifying that 35.8% of the variance in customer satisfaction with the use of chatbots can be accounted for by the independent variables: Interaction, Problem Solving Responsiveness, Reliability, and Credibility. This $R^2$ value is an essential metric in evaluating the model's explanatory power and reflects how well the independent variables collectively predict the dependent variable—customer satisfaction in this context.

An $R^2$ value of 0.358 indicates a moderate level of explanatory power, meaning that while the model is reasonably effective in explaining customer satisfaction, there is still a substantial portion of the variance (64.2%) that might be influenced by other factors not included in the model. These could involve additional constructs such as user experience design, chatbot personalization, emotional engagement, or external factors like prior customer expectations and the context in which the chatbot is used.

Despite the moderate $R^2$ value, the significance of the individual path coefficients and their contribution to the model should not be understated. Each independent variable—Interaction, Problem Solving Responsiveness, Reliability, and Credibility—plays a crucial role in shaping customer satisfaction, as demonstrated by their significant positive impact. The $R^2$ value, therefore, complements the path coefficients by providing a broader perspective on the model's overall performance.

In practical terms, this $R^2$ value suggests that businesses and developers aiming to enhance customer satisfaction with chatbots should prioritize improvements in the identified constructs, as these factors collectively account for a significant portion of the customer satisfaction variance. However, they should also remain open to exploring and integrating additional factors that could further increase the model's explanatory power.

The $R^2$ value, along with other relevant model fit indicators, is detailed in Table 4. This table provides a comprehensive overview of the model's ability to explain customer satisfaction with chatbot usage, serving as a key reference point for interpreting the overall effectiveness and potential areas for further research and model refinement.

*Table 4. R square value*

|  | R Square | R Square Adjusted |
| --- | --- | --- |
| Sat | 0.358 | 0.349 |

Source: Computed from data

## Moderation

Additionally, a Multi-Group Analysis (MGA) was conducted to explore whether there were any significant differences in the relationships between the independent variables—Interaction, Problem Solving Responsiveness, Reliability, and Credibility—and the dependent variable, Satisfaction with the Use of Chatbot, among users in the hospitality industry across two distinct cultural contexts: India and the Philippines. This analysis is particularly relevant given the diverse cultural backgrounds and varying expectations that might influence how users in these countries interact with and perceive chatbots.

The MGA was performed using SmartPLS 4, a robust tool for such comparative analysis, which allows for the examination of differences in path coefficients between predefined groups—in this case, Indian and Filipino travellers. To ensure the reliability of the results, the analysis was followed by a bootstrapping procedure with 5,000 sub-samples. Bootstrapping is a statistical technique that involves repeatedly sampling from the data to estimate the distribution of the path coefficients, thereby providing a more accurate assessment of their significance across different groups.

The primary aim of this analysis was to determine whether the strength and direction of the relationships between the independent variables and customer satisfaction differed significantly between Indian and Filipino travellers. Understanding these differences is crucial for tailoring chatbot experiences to meet the specific needs and preferences of users from different cultural backgrounds, thereby enhancing overall satisfaction.

The results of the Multi-Group Analysis are presented in Figure 3 for Indian travellers and Figure 4 for Filipino travellers, providing a visual comparison of the path coefficients for each group. These figures highlight how the influence of each independent variable on customer satisfaction varies between the two countries.

Furthermore, the path coefficients and their corresponding significance levels for each group are detailed in Table 5 and Table 6, respectively. These tables offer a more granular view of the differences identified through the MGA, enabling a deeper understanding of how cultural context influences the effectiveness of various chatbot attributes.

The results of this analysis are instrumental in guiding the development of more culturally sensitive and effective chatbot solutions within the hospitality industry. By recognizing and accounting for the differences in user preferences and expectations between Indian and Filipino travelers, businesses can better tailor their chatbot interfaces, communication styles, and problem-solving approaches to meet the distinct needs of each group, thereby enhancing customer satisfaction and loyalty.

*Figure 3. Bootstrapping Result (Indian travellers)*

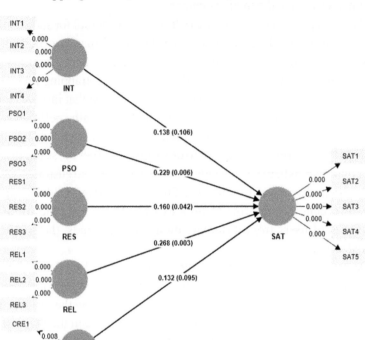

*Table 5. Bootstrapping Result (Indian Travellers)*

|  | Original sample (O) | Sample mean (M) | Standard deviation (STDEV) | T statistics (\|O/STDEV\|) | P values |
|---|---|---|---|---|---|
| CRE -> SAT | 0.132 | 0.152 | 0.079 | 1.67 | 0.095 |
| INT -> SAT | 0.138 | 0.128 | 0.085 | 1.619 | 0.106 |
| PSO -> SAT | 0.229 | 0.231 | 0.083 | 2.765 | 0.006 |
| REL -> SAT | 0.268 | 0.273 | 0.089 | 3.015 | 0.003 |
| RES -> SAT | 0.16 | 0.169 | 0.079 | 2.036 | 0.042 |

Source: Computed from data

*Figure 4. Bootstrapping Result (Filipino travellers)*

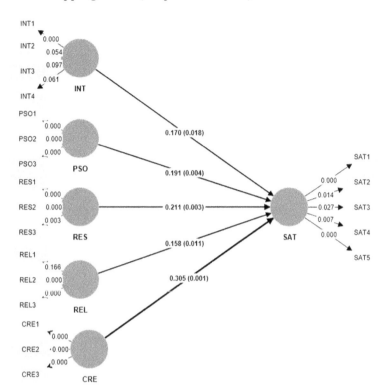

*Table 6. Bootstrapping Result (Filipino Travellers)*

|  | Original sample (O) | Sample mean (M) | Standard deviation (STDEV) | T statistics (|O/STDEV|) | P values |
|---|---|---|---|---|---|
| CRE -> SAT | 0.305 | 0.306 | 0.088 | 3.473 | 0.001 |
| INT -> SAT | 0.17 | 0.193 | 0.072 | 2.366 | 0.018 |
| PSO -> SAT | 0.191 | 0.19 | 0.067 | 2.864 | 0.004 |
| REL -> SAT | 0.158 | 0.158 | 0.062 | 2.534 | 0.011 |
| RES -> SAT | 0.211 | 0.219 | 0.071 | 2.946 | 0.003 |

Source: Computed from data

## Findings

The structural model reveals notable differences in the factors contributing to customer satisfaction with chatbots between Filipino and Indian travellers. For Filipino travellers, Credibility stands out as the most influential factor, with a beta coefficient of 0.305. This suggests that the trustworthiness and reliability of information provided by the chatbot are crucial in enhancing their satisfaction levels. Filipino users highly value the credibility of the chatbot, as it directly impacts their confidence in the information they receive. Following credibility, Responsiveness has a beta coefficient of 0.211, indicating that timely responses from the chatbot also play a significant role in shaping satisfaction. Other important factors include Problem Solving (0.191), Interaction (0.170), and Reliability (0.158), all of which are statistically significant ($p < 0.05$). These results highlight that Filipino travellers place a strong emphasis on the chatbot's ability to provide credible information and quick responses, underscoring the importance of these attributes in driving overall satisfaction.

On the other hand, the response from Indian travellers paints a different picture. For this group, Reliability emerges as the most critical factor, with a beta coefficient of 0.224. This finding underscores the significance of dependable and consistent chatbot performance in satisfying Indian users. Interestingly, Problem Solving (0.229) is also a key predictor of satisfaction, slightly surpassing reliability in importance, suggesting that the ability of chatbots to effectively address user issues is highly valued by Indian travellers. Responsiveness (0.160) remains a significant factor, but to a lesser extent compared to Filipino travellers. However, the constructs of Interaction (0.138) and Credibility (0.132) are the least important for Indian travellers, and notably, these paths are not statistically significant ($p > 0.05$). This contrast indicates that while Indian travellers value consistent performance and problem-solving abilities, they are less concerned with the chatbot's perceived credibility and the quality of interaction, differing from the priorities of their Filipino counterparts.

## Discussion

The findings of this study reveal important insights into how different cultural contexts shape the expectations and preferences of chatbot users. For Filipino travellers, the high beta coefficient for Credibility (0.305) underscores the critical importance of trustworthiness in information delivery. This preference could stem from cultural norms that emphasize reliability and honesty in interpersonal and business interactions. Filipino users appear to value chatbots that provide accurate and reliable information promptly, which can enhance their overall travel experience by reducing uncertainty and building trust. This suggests that chatbots designed for

Filipino users should prioritize features that enhance credibility, such as providing verified information, clear communication, and transparency about data sources.

In contrast, the response from Indian travellers indicates a different set of priorities. The highest beta coefficient for Reliability (0.224) suggests that Indian users place a premium on consistent and dependable chatbot performance. This preference might be rooted in the desire for stability and reliability in services, which can be particularly important in the diverse and often complex travel environments within India. Additionally, the significant beta coefficients for Problem Solving (0.229) and Responsiveness (0.160) indicate that Indian users value chatbots that can efficiently address and resolve issues. This implies that chatbots for Indian travellers should focus on robust problem-solving capabilities and ensure quick, reliable responses to user inquiries.

Interestingly, the lesser importance of Interaction (0.138) and Credibility (0.132) for Indian travellers, with these paths not being statistically significant ($p > 0.05$), suggests that Indian users may be more task-oriented in their interactions with chatbots. They might prioritize practical functionality over relational aspects, possibly due to a higher familiarity with digital interfaces or different expectations from automated services. This difference highlights the need for a more functional and efficiency-driven design for chatbots targeting Indian travellers, as opposed to the more relational and credibility-focused design preferred by Filipino users.

## CONCLUSION

In conclusion, the study highlights the necessity for a nuanced approach to chatbot design, one that takes into account the cultural and contextual preferences of different user groups. For Filipino travellers, chatbots should emphasize credibility and responsiveness, ensuring that the information provided is both reliable and promptly delivered. This can be achieved through features such as verified information sources, transparent communication, and efficient response mechanisms. By focusing on these aspects, businesses can build trust and enhance the user experience for Filipino travellers.

For Indian travellers, the focus should be on ensuring the reliability and problem-solving capabilities of chatbots. This means developing chatbots that can consistently perform well and effectively resolve user issues. Features such as robust troubleshooting protocols, consistent performance metrics, and quick resolution times will be crucial in meeting the expectations of Indian users. By prioritizing these functional aspects, businesses can provide a more satisfactory and reliable service experience for Indian travellers.

These findings suggest that a one-size-fits-all approach to chatbot design is insufficient. Instead, businesses should adopt a culturally sensitive strategy, tailoring chatbot functionalities to meet the specific needs and expectations of different user groups. By doing so, they can enhance customer satisfaction, foster greater loyalty, and ultimately drive better engagement and business outcomes across diverse cultural contexts. This tailored approach not only improves the immediate user experience but also contributes to the long-term success of chatbot implementations in the global market.

## Theoretical Implications

The findings of this study contribute to the existing literature on customer satisfaction with chatbots, particularly in the context of the hospitality industry. The distinct differences in factors influencing satisfaction between Filipino and Indian travelers highlight the importance of cultural and contextual considerations in technology acceptance and usage models. The study reinforces the Theory of Planned Behavior (TPB) and Unified Theory of Acceptance and Use of Technology (UTAUT) by demonstrating that constructs like Credibility, Responsiveness, and Reliability can have varying degrees of influence depending on the cultural background of the users. The significance of these constructs aligns with the notion that users' perceived trust and the effectiveness of technological solutions are critical to their overall satisfaction. This study also adds to the growing body of research that suggests customization and localization of technology are essential for enhancing user experience in diverse cultural settings.

## Managerial Implications

From a managerial perspective, the findings offer valuable insights for companies in the hospitality industry, particularly those deploying chatbots as part of their customer service strategy. For businesses catering to Filipino travellers, the emphasis should be on enhancing the credibility and trustworthiness of chatbots. This can be achieved by ensuring the information provided by the chatbot is accurate, reliable, and up to date, as well as by designing the chatbot to respond promptly to inquiries. Companies should consider investing in AI technologies that can handle complex queries and provide trustworthy responses, as these factors are crucial to maintaining high customer satisfaction levels among Filipino users.

Conversely, for Indian travelers, the focus should be on improving the reliability and problem-solving capabilities of chatbots. Ensuring that the chatbot can consistently perform without errors and effectively address user issues will be key to satisfying this group. Managers should prioritize the development of robust and efficient chatbot systems that can handle frequent interactions without compromising performance. Additionally, while interaction quality and credibility are less critical for Indian users, maintaining a baseline level of these attributes is still necessary to avoid negatively impacting user experience.

Hence, businesses should consider the cultural preferences and expectations of their target audience when developing and implementing chatbot technologies, leading to more personalized and satisfying customer experiences.

## Limitation and Future Scope

Despite providing valuable insights into the differing preferences of Filipino and Indian travellers regarding chatbot satisfaction, this study has several limitations that should be considered.

First, the sample size and demographic diversity within the Filipino and Indian traveller groups may not be fully representative of the broader population. The study's findings are based on a specific cohort of travellers, and variations within each country, such as regional differences, age groups, or travel experience levels, might influence satisfaction factors differently. Future research should aim for a more extensive and diverse sample to enhance the generalizability of the results.

Second, the study relies on self-reported data, which can be subject to biases such as social desirability or recall bias. Participants may have overestimated or underestimated their satisfaction levels or the importance of certain chatbot features. To mitigate this, future studies could incorporate objective measures of chatbot interactions and satisfaction, such as usage logs or performance metrics, to complement self-reported data.

Third, the study's scope is limited to the constructs of Credibility, Responsiveness, Problem Solving, Interaction, and Reliability. While these are critical factors, other potentially influential constructs, such as personalization, user interface design, and emotional intelligence of chatbots, were not considered. Including a broader range of factors could provide a more comprehensive understanding of what drives satisfaction among different user groups.

Finally, the cultural context was inferred from the responses of travellers from the Philippines and India without a detailed exploration of underlying cultural dimensions that might influence their preferences. Future research could explore deeper into cultural theories, such as Hofstede's cultural dimensions, to provide a richer context for interpreting the differences in chatbot satisfaction and to explore how these cultural factors interact with the technological expectations and preferences of users.

# REFERENCES

Adam, M., Weesel, M., & Benlian, A. (2021). AI-based chatbots in customer service and their effects on user compliance. *Electronic Markets*, 31(2), 427–445. DOI: 10.1007/s12525-020-00414-7

Ahmad, M., Naeem, M. K. H., Mobo, F. D., Tahir, M. W., & Akram, M. (2024). Navigating the Journey: How Chatbots Are Transforming Tourism and Hospitality. In Darwish, D. (Ed.), *Design and Development of Emerging Chatbot Technology* (pp. 236–255). IGI Global., DOI: 10.4018/979-8-3693-1830-0.ch014

Aslam, W., Ahmed Siddiqui, D., Arif, I., & Farhat, K. (2023). Chatbots in the frontline: Drivers of acceptance. *Kybernetes*, 52(9), 3781–3810. DOI: 10.1108/K-11-2021-1119

Baabdullah, A. M., Alalwan, A. A., Algharabat, R. S., Metri, B., & Rana, N. P. (2022). Virtual agents and flow experience: An empirical examination of AI-powered chatbots. *Technological Forecasting and Social Change*, 181(May), 121772. DOI: 10.1016/j.techfore.2022.121772

Behera, B., & Gaur, M. (2022). Skill development in India–A literature review. *GIS Science Journal*, 9(1), 1721–1731.

Borsci, S., Malizia, A., Schmettow, M., van der Velde, F., Tariverdiyeva, G., Balaji, D., & Chamberlain, A. (2022). The Chatbot Usability Scale: The Design and Pilot of a Usability Scale for Interaction with AI-Based Conversational Agents. *Personal and Ubiquitous Computing*, 26(1), 95–119. DOI: 10.1007/s00779-021-01582-9

Bulchand-Gidumal, J. (2022). Impact of Artificial Intelligence in Travel, Tourism, and Hospitality. In *Handbook of e-Tourism* (pp. 1943–1962). Springer International Publishing., DOI: 10.1007/978-3-030-48652-5_110

Cheng, X., Zhang, X., Yang, B., & Fu, Y. (2022). An investigation on trust in AI-enabled collaboration: Application of AI-Driven chatbot in accommodation-based sharing economy. *Electronic Commerce Research and Applications*, 54, 101164. DOI: 10.1016/j.elerap.2022.101164 PMID: 35968256

Cheng, Y., & Jiang, H. (2022). Customer–brand relationship in the era of artificial intelligence: Understanding the role of chatbot marketing efforts. *Journal of Product and Brand Management*, 31(2), 252–264. DOI: 10.1108/JPBM-05-2020-2907

Cui, Y., & van Esch, P. (2023). Artificial Intelligence in Customer Service Strategy for Seamless Customer Experiences. In J. N. Sheth, V. Jain, M. E., & A. Ambika (Eds.), *Artificial Intelligence in Customer Service* (pp. 73–97). Springer International Publishing. DOI: 10.1007/978-3-031-33898-4_4

Dash, M., & Bakshi, S. (2022). An Exploratory study of Customer Perceptions of usage of chatbots in the hospitality industry. *International Journal on Customer Relations*, 7(2), 27–33.

Fath, S., Abimanyu, D., & Misbak, M. (2024). Exploring The Relationship Between Responsiveness And Usability And Its Impact On Customer Satisfaction In E-Commerce. *Journal of Management, Economic, and Financial*, 2(4), 72–79. DOI: 10.46799/jmef.v2i4.42

Fornell, C., & Larcker, D. (1981). Evaluating Structural Equation Models with Unobservable Variables and Measurement Error. *JMR, Journal of Marketing Research*, 18(1), 39–50. DOI: 10.1177/002224378101800104

Gursoy, D., Malodia, S., & Dhir, A. (2022). The metaverse in the hospitality and tourism industry: An overview of current trends and future research directions. *Journal of Hospitality Marketing & Management*, 31(5), 527–534. DOI: 10.1080/19368623.2022.2072504

Hanji, S. V., Navalgund, N., Ingalagi, S., Desai, S., & Hanji, S. S. (2024). Adoption of AI Chatbots in Travel and Tourism Services. In Yang, X., Sherratt, R. S., Dey, N., & Joshi, A. (Eds.), *Proceedings of Eighth International Congress on Information and Communication Technology. ICICT 2023. Lecture Notes in Networks and Systems* (pp. 713–727). Springer. DOI: 10.1007/978-981-99-3236-8_57

Haugeland, I. K. F., Følstad, A., Taylor, C., & Alexander, C. (2022). Understanding the user experience of customer service chatbots: An experimental study of chatbot interaction design. *International Journal of Human Computer Studies, 161*(April 2021). DOI: 10.1016/j.ijhcs.2022.102788

Hennemann, S., Beutel, M. E., & Zwerenz, R. (2017). Ready for eHealth? Health Professionals' Acceptance and Adoption of eHealth Interventions in Inpatient Routine Care. *Journal of Health Communication*, 22(3), 274–284. DOI: 10.1080/10810730.2017.1284286 PMID: 28248626

Huang, D., Markovitch, D. G., & Stough, R. A. (2024). Can chatbot customer service match human service agents on customer satisfaction? An investigation in the role of trust. *Journal of Retailing and Consumer Services*, 76, 103600. DOI: 10.1016/j.jretconser.2023.103600

Jansom, A., Srisangkhajorn, T., & Limarunothai, W. (2022). How chatbot e-services motivate communication credibility and lead to customer satisfaction: The perspective of Thai consumers in the apparel retailing context. *Innovative Marketing*, 18(3), 13–25. DOI: 10.21511/im.18(3).2022.02

John, T, B., & Cheng, S.-L. (. (2001). Customer loyalty in the hotel industry : The role of customer satisfaction and image. *International Journal of Contemporary Hospitality Management*, 13(5), 213–217. DOI: 10.1108/09596110110395893

Jyoti, & Srivastava, P. (2008). Introduction to Hospitality Accommodation. In S. C. Bagri & A. Dahiya (Eds.), *Introduction to Hospitality Industry : A Textbook* (pp. 43–68). Aman Publication.

Kim, M., & Chang, B. (2020). The Effect of Service Quality on the Reuse Intention of a Chatbot: Focusing on User Satisfaction, Reliability, and Immersion. *International Journal of Contents*, 16(4), 1–15. https://koreascience.kr/article/JAKO202006763002633.page

Klein, S., & Utz, S. (2024). Chatbot vs. Human: The Impact of Responsive Conversational Features on Users' Responses to Chat Advisors Authors. *Human-Machine Communication*, 8, 73–99. DOI: 10.30658/hmc.8.4

Lee, S., & Jeong, M. (2012). Effects of e-servicescape on consumers' flow experiences. *Journal of Hospitality and Tourism Technology*, 3(1), 47–59. DOI: 10.1108/17579881211206534

Lei, S. I., Shen, H., & Ye, S. (2021). A comparison between chatbot and human service: Customer perception and reuse intention. *International Journal of Contemporary Hospitality Management*, 33(11), 3977–3995. DOI: 10.1108/IJCHM-12-2020-1399

Li, L., Lee, K. Y., Emokpae, E., & Yang, S. B. (2021). What makes you continuously use chatbot services? Evidence from chinese online travel agencies. *Electronic Markets*, 31(3), 575–599. DOI: 10.1007/s12525-020-00454-z PMID: 35603227

Lily Anita, T., Muslikhin, M., Zulkarnain, A., & Wiyana, T. (2023). Enhancing Customer Satisfaction in Hotel Industry Through Chatbot as E-Services Agent and Communication Credibility. *2023 6th International Seminar on Research of Information Technology and Intelligent Systems (ISRITI)*, 14–19. DOI: 10.1109/ISRITI60336.2023.10467873

Liu, S. Q., Vakeel, K. A., Smith, N. A., Alavipour, R. S., Wei, C., & Wirtz, J. (2024). AI concierge in the customer journey: What is it and how can it add value to the customer? *Journal of Service Management*, 35(6), 136–158. DOI: 10.1108/JOSM-12-2023-0523

Manhas, P. S., & Tukamushaba, E. K. (2015). Understanding service experience and its impact on brand image in hospitality sector. *International Journal of Hospitality Management*, 45, 77–87. DOI: 10.1016/j.ijhm.2014.11.010

Maunier, C., & Camelis, C. (2013). Toward an identification of elements contributing to satisfaction with the tourism experience. *Journal of Vacation Marketing*, 19(1), 19–39. DOI: 10.1177/1356766712468733

Mehrolia, S., Alagarsamy, S., Moorthy, V., & Jeevananda, S. (2023). Will Users Continue Using Banking Chatbots? The Moderating Role of Perceived Risk. *FIIB Business Review*, 0(0). Advance online publication. DOI: 10.1177/23197145231169900

Melián-González, S., Gutiérrez-Taño, D., & Bulchand-Gidumal, J. (2021). Predicting the intentions to use chatbots for travel and tourism. *Current Issues in Tourism*, 24(2), 192–210. DOI: 10.1080/13683500.2019.1706457

Meyer-waarden, B. L., Pavone, G., Poocharoentou, T., Prayatsup, P., Tison, A., & Torn, S. (2020). How Service Quality Influences Customer Acceptance and Usage of Chatbots? *Journal of Service Management Research*, 4(1), 35–51. DOI: 10.15358/2511-8676-2020-1-35

Mishra, N., Gupta, S. L., Srivastava, P., Srivastava, S., & Kabir, M. (2022). Student Acceptance of Social Media in Higher Education: An application of UTAUT2 model. *Thailand and the World Economy*, 40(1), 88–108.

Mohd Rahim, N. I., & Iahad, A., N., Yusof, A. F., & A. Al-Sharafi, M. (. (2022). AI-Based Chatbots Adoption Model for Higher-Education Institutions: A Hybrid PLS-SEM-Neural Network Modelling Approach. *Sustainability (Switzerland)*, 14(19). Advance online publication. DOI: 10.3390/su141912726

Naqvi, M. H. A., Hongyu, Z., Naqvi, M. H., & Kun, L. (2023). Impact of service agents on customer satisfaction and loyalty: Mediating role of Chatbots. *Journal of Modelling in Management*, 19(2), 470–491. DOI: 10.1108/JM2-01-2023-0004

Ngai, E. W. T., Lee, M. C. M., Luo, M., Chan, P. S. L., & Liang, T. (2021). An intelligent knowledge-based chatbot for customer service. *Electronic Commerce Research and Applications*, 50, 101098. DOI: 10.1016/j.elerap.2021.101098

Nguyen, D. M., Chiu, Y. T. H., & Le, H. D. (2021). Determinants of Continuance Intention towards Banks' Chatbot Services in Vietnam: A Necessity for Sustainable Development. *Sustainability (Basel)*, 13(14), 7625. DOI: 10.3390/su13147625

Nguyen, V. T., Phong, L. T., & Chi, N. T. K. (2023). The impact of AI chatbots on customer trust: An empirical investigation in the hotel industry. *Consumer Behavior in Tourism and Hospitality*, 18(3), 293–305. DOI: 10.1108/CBTH-06-2022-0131

Nili, A., Tate, M., & Johnstone, D. (2019). The process of solving problems with self-service technologies: a study from the user's perspective. In *Electronic Commerce Research* (Vol. 19, Issue 2). Springer US. DOI: 10.1007/s10660-018-9304-0

Nosrati, S., Sabzali, M., Heidari, A., Sarfi, T., & Sabbar, S. (2020). Chatbots, Counselling, and Discontents of the Digital Life. *Journal of Cyberspace Studies*, 4(2), 153–172. DOI: 10.22059/jcss.2020.93910

Orden-Mejía, M., & Huertas, A. (2022). Analysis of the attributes of smart tourism technologies in destination chatbots that influence tourist satisfaction. *Current Issues in Tourism*, 25(17), 2854–2869. DOI: 10.1080/13683500.2021.1997942

Park, A., & Lee, S. B. (2023). Examining AI and Systemic Factors for Improved Chatbot Sustainability. *Journal of Computer Information Systems*, 1–15. DOI: 10.1080/08874417.2023.2251416

Petcu, R., Ologeanu-Taddei, R., Bourdon, I., Kimble, C., & Giraudeau, N. (2016). Acceptance and organizational aspects of oral tele-consultation: A French study. *Proceedings of the Annual Hawaii International Conference on System Sciences, 2016-March*, 3124–3132. DOI: 10.1109/HICSS.2016.393

Pillai, R., & Sivathanu, B. (2020). Adoption of AI-based chatbots for hospitality and tourism. *International Journal of Contemporary Hospitality Management*, 32(10), 3199–3226. DOI: 10.1108/IJCHM-04-2020-0259

Pillai, R., Sivathanu, B., Zheng, Y., Wu, Y., Pai, C. K., Liu, Y., Kang, S., & Dai, A. (2020). An investigation of how perceived smart tourism technologies affect tourists' well-being in marine tourism. *Sustainability (Switzerland), 18*(8 August), 1–19. DOI: 10.3390/su12166592

Przegalinska, A., Ciechanowski, L., Stroz, A., Gloor, P., & Mazurek, G. (2019). In bot we trust: A new methodology of chatbot performance measures. *Business Horizons*, 62(6), 785–797. DOI: 10.1016/j.bushor.2019.08.005

Rancati, E., & D'Agata, A. (2022). Metaverse in Tourism and Hospitality: Empirical Evidence on Generation Z from Italy. *European Scientific Journal*, 18(34), 122. DOI: 10.19044/esj.2022.v18n34p122

Saengrith, W., Viriyavejakul, C., & Pimdee, P. (2022). Problem-Based Blended Training via Chatbot to Enhance the Problem-Solving Skill in the Workplace. *Emerging Science Journal*, 6(Special Issue), 1–12. DOI: 10.28991/ESJ-2022-SIED-01

Shandilya, G., Srivastava, P., & Jana, A. (2024). Industry Experts and Business Consultants ' Takes on India ' s Readiness for Metaverse: A Review of the Retail Industry. In Singla, B., Shalender, K., & Singh, N. (Eds.), *Creator's Economy in Metaverse Platforms: Empowering Stakeholders Through Omnichannel Approach* (pp. 132–147). IGI Global., DOI: 10.4018/979-8-3693-3358-7.ch008

Silva, S. C., De Cicco, R., Vlačić, B., & Elmashhara, M. G. (2023). Using chatbots in e-retailing – how to mitigate perceived risk and enhance the flow experience. *International Journal of Retail & Distribution Management*, 51(3), 285–305. DOI: 10.1108/IJRDM-05-2022-0163

Sinha, A. P., Srivastava, P., Srivastava, S. K., Asthana, A. K., & Nag, A. (2024). Customer Satisfaction and Loyalty for Online Food Services Provider in India: An Empirical Study. *Vision (Basel)*, 28(3), 327–343. DOI: 10.1177/09722629211034405

Srivastava, P., Mishra, N., Srivastava, S., & Shivani, S. (2024). Banking with Chatbots: The Role of Demographic and Personality Traits. *FIIB Business Review, online fir*(online first). DOI: 10.1177/23197145241227757

Srivastava, P., & Shandilya, G. (2024). Unveiling the Impact of Perceived Smart Tourism Technology on Tourist Satisfaction. In Kajla, T., Kansra, P., & Singh, N. (Eds.), *Multidisciplinary Applications of Extended Reality for Human Experience* (pp. 147–170). IGI Global., DOI: 10.4018/979-8-3693-2432-5.ch008

Srivastava, P., Srivastava, S., & Mishra, N. (2023). Impact of e-servicescape on hotel booking intention: Examining the moderating role of COVID-19. *Consumer Behavior in Tourism and Hospitality*, 18(3), 422–437. DOI: 10.1108/CBTH-03-2022-0076

Suta, P., Lan, X., Wu, B., Mongkolnam, P., & Chan, J. H. (2020). An overview of machine learning in chatbots. *International Journal of Mechanical Engineering and Robotics Research*, 9(4), 502–510. DOI: 10.18178/ijmerr.9.4.502-510

Tri Kurniawati, D., & Yadi Yaakop, A. (2021). The effect of E-Servicescape Dimensions on Customer Trust of Tokopedia E-Store During Covid-19 Pandemic. *Journal of Applied Management*, 19(1), 1–10. DOI: 10.21776/ub.jam.2021.019.01.01

Tsai, S. P. (2022). Investigating metaverse marketing for travel and tourism. *Journal of Vacation Marketing*, 1. Advance online publication. DOI: 10.1177/13567667221145715

Um, T., Kim, T., & Chung, N. (2020). How does an intelligence chatbot affect customers compared with self-service technology for sustainable services? *Sustainability (Basel)*, 12(12), 5119. Advance online publication. DOI: 10.3390/su12125119

Vergaray, A. D., Robles, W. F. P., & Jiménez, J. A. S. (2023). The Impact of Chatbots on Customer Satisfaction: A Systematic Literature Review. *TEM Journal, 12*(3), 1407–1417. https://doi.org/DOI: 10.18421/TEM123-21

Verma, P., Kumar, S., & Sharma, S. K. (2020). e-Healthcare service quality: Consumer satisfaction and its association with demographic characteristics. *International Journal of Health Care Quality Assurance*, 33(6), 413–428. DOI: 10.1108/IJHCQA-02-2020-0030 PMID: 32678536

Vinnakota, S., Dass Mohan, M., Boda, J., Sekuini, J., Mustafa, M., & Madala, H. (2023). Leveraging Artificial Intelligence in the Hospitality Industry: Opportunities and Challenges. *Asian Journal of Social Science and Management Technology*, 5(3), 2313–7410. https://www.researchgate.net/publication/372783951

Wang, P. Q. (2024). Personalizing guest experience with generative AI in the hotel industry: There's more to it than meets a Kiwi's eye. *Current Issues in Tourism*, •••, 1–18. DOI: 10.1080/13683500.2023.2300030

Xiang, Z., Wang, D., O'Leary, J. T., & Fesenmaier, D. R. (2015). Adapting to the Internet: Trends in Travelers' Use of the Web for Trip Planning. *Journal of Travel Research*, 54(4), 511–527. DOI: 10.1177/0047287514522883

Zhang, R. W., Liang, X., & Wu, S. H. (2024). When chatbots fail: Exploring user coping following a chatbots-induced service failure. *Information Technology & People*, 37(8), 175–195. DOI: 10.1108/ITP-08-2023-0745

Zhao, Y., & Bacao, F. (2020). What factors determining customer continuingly using food delivery apps during 2019 novel coronavirus pandemic period? *International Journal of Hospitality Management*, 91(May), 102683. DOI: 10.1016/j.ijhm.2020.102683 PMID: 32929294

Zhu, Y., Zhang, R., Zou, Y., & Jin, D. (2023). Investigating customers' responses to artificial intelligence chatbots in online travel agencies: The moderating role of product familiarity. *Journal of Hospitality and Tourism Technology*, 14(2), 208–224. DOI: 10.1108/JHTT-02-2022-0041

Zumstein, D., & Hundertmark, S. (2018). Chatbots : an interactive technology for personalized communication and transaction. *IADIS International Journal on Www/Internet, 15*(1), 96–109.

# Chapter 10
# From Screens to Streets:
## Volunteered Geographic Information's Impact on Travel Choices

**Munir Ahmad**
https://orcid.org/0000-0003-4836-6151
*Survey of Pakistan, Pakistan*

**Shikha Sharma**
*Vivekananda Institute of Professional Studies, India*

## ABSTRACT

*Geo-tech transforms travel with real-time traffic, weather, and attraction updates. Travelers can personalize plans for safer, more convenient journeys. Volunteered Geographic Information (VGI) empowers them further with user-generated reviews, geotagged content, check-ins, location sharing, social media posts, hashtags, vlogs, collaborative travel itineraries, community forums, and crowdsourced maps. These advancements make travel more accessible, inclusive, and enjoyable for everyone. However, VGI faces hurdles: data accuracy, information overload, privacy concerns, biased reviews, and tech dependence. To address these challenges, improved verification processes, advanced filtering options, offline features, user education on privacy, and AI-driven fraud detection are necessary to enhance the reliability and trustworthiness of VGI in travel planning.*

DOI: 10.4018/979-8-3693-3972-5.ch010

## INTRODUCTION

Digital technology has impacted the world in almost every facet that it touches and has not spared the travel industry. prevalence of digital connectivity and the proliferation of mobile technologies have made a strong impact on the development of planning and navigation for transforming the journey process (Sia et al., 2023; Siuhi & Mwakalonge, 2016). Geo-technology like smart mobiles, GPS, and different travel applications help in sharing updated information on various options available resulting in changes in travel decisions (Jamal & Habib, 2020). Geo-technology has revolutionized travel by providing real-time traffic updates, enabling drivers to avoid congestion and minimize travel time (Gokasar & Bakioglu, 2018). Integrated weather forecasts inform travelers of current and upcoming conditions, enhancing safety and comfort. These technologies also enrich travel experiences by offering information on points of interest and helping discover new places through user-generated content (K. Gao et al., 2020). Additionally, advanced algorithms allow for highly customized travel plans, while features like location sharing and emergency alerts enhance safety. Improved accessibility and inclusivity through detailed information on accessible routes make travel more inclusive, marking a significant departure from the past.

Volunteered Geographic Information (VGI) is defined as the involvement of people who give out geographic information for free and more often collected, processed, and shared by people not as a formal job through the internet and social media (Goodchild, 2007). It may contain everything from pictures and comments which can be associated with the specific geographical coordinates to descriptions of the routes and objects. This reflects the potential of VGI by focusing on the wisdom of the crowd. While a large number of people may provide fragmented knowledge, the collective sum of their experience and information creates a vibrant, ever-evolving knowledge pool. Ideally, this user-generated material can help modify the process of deciding upon a particular travel destination greatly since such insights might not be available through traditional sources.

VGI significantly influences travel choices through various types of user-contributed data. Reviews and ratings on platforms like TripAdvisor and Google Reviews provide insights into quality and experiences, while geotagged photos and videos on social media inspire travel by showcasing destinations visually (Sangkaew & Zhu, 2022; Yalcinkaya & Just, 2023). Check-ins and location sharing highlight popular spots in real-time, and travel blogs and vlogs offer detailed narratives and tips. Crowdsourced maps from OpenStreetMap provide up-to-date route information (Bustamante et al., 2021), and social media posts with hashtags reveal trending destinations (Nautiyal et al., 2023). Community forums like Reddit and Quora may host travel discussions (Monteiro, 2024), while real-time updates on apps like

Waze improve travel efficiency (Li et al., 2020). Collaborative travel itineraries and volunteer-contributed accessibility data further enhance trip planning, making it more informed and inclusive.

The purpose of this chapter is to provide insight into the potential and effects of VGI on travel choices and experiences. The chapter underscores the potential of VGI in enhancing routing decisions, choice of destination, and generating awareness on a particular place, particularly in light of the challenges that go hand in hand with the use of this user-generated geographic data.

## VOLUNTEERED GEOGRAPHIC INFORMATION

VGI is data collected by individuals using mobile devices or other technologies and contributed to a shared database (Goodchild, 2007). It is often generated through citizen science projects or crowdsourcing initiatives. Examples of VGI include location-based social media posts, GPS tracks, and user-generated maps. It is gathered through various methods that leverage the power of technology and community involvement. Some of the methods of VGI data collection are illustrated below.

### Mobile Applications

External data can be provided by applications downloaded on users' mobile phones or tablets. Such apps tend to include features such as files that utilizes GPS, camera, and other fields to input new information. Mobile devices come with inbuilt GPS that allows the user to capture the location coordinates which can be uploaded to the VGI platforms. Photos can be taken by the users of the apps and it is also possible to link the photo with a particular area to give a visual background to various geographic data. By using this feature, the users can feed the app with information such as description, observation, or any measurement that may be about the location.

### Social Media Platforms

Some of the social media websites have some options such as check-in in that enable user to share their location with the followers or the general public. Users may attach geotags to the pictures, clips, or any post they feel like sharing and these reveal the origin of the posts. On some social networks, there is an option to "check in" to some place which can directly contribute to geographic information.

## Citizen Science Projects

Citizen science initiatives usually involve citizens in data collection as well as data analysis. Such projects may be based on a wide range of subjects including: Diversity and abundance of species, clean water, air and noise pollution, and climate change among others. All those who work on citizen science projects often have laid down guidelines and procedures that they should follow with the view of producing quality data. Most citizen science projects help in bringing together members and participants into one group or team.

## Crowdsourcing Platforms

Crowdsourcing geographic data includes website and platforms that offer tools interfaces for the users to contribute some information. Most crowdsourcing platforms promote the use of openness in data curation and crowd-generated and crowd-approved data. Users are capable of uploading or modifying geographical features such as point data, line, or polygon data on these platforms.

Some of the popular VGI platforms include OpenStreetMap, which allows users to collaboratively map the world; Mapillary, a tool for capturing and sharing street-level imagery; and Wikimapia, a crowdsourced map service combining satellite imagery with user-generated information. These platforms harness the power of community participation to create and maintain accurate, up-to-date geographical data.

## OpenStreetMap (OSM)

OSM is a world map that has been created through people's participation; the active participation here means that most of the mapping is done through volunteers. All data that is present on the OSM platform is made available under an open license and can therefore be useful for numerous scenarios. OSM contains several various types of geographical objects, such as roads, various types of buildings, land use, and points of interest. A lot of people use OSM and many active members contribute to updating the map information.

## Waze

Waze is one of the navigation applications that show the best route using the data on traffic situations at the moment. Waze obtains most of its VGI from its users whereby they are able to report on instance traffic accidents, road blocks, among other road hazards. Waze has a dedicated family of committed users contributing to its growth and development of the platform. Moreover, social interaction inside Waze is also well-designed; for instance, users can send messages or be part of groups.

## Mapillary

Mapillary is a VGI platform mainly dealing with collecting and sharing street-level imagery from different parts of the world. It was started in 2013 and allows users to upload photos captured by smartphones, or any other device. The images are analyzed using computer vision to obtain geographical data from objects in the images including roads, buildings, and the environment. The information collected is applied to more precise geographical applications, better route-finding systems and to planning and development of society's physical framework. Using Mapillary's crowdsourcing strategy, it is easy to capture the changes that happen within short periods, hence offering accurate and timely information that is informative to the community and international bodies.

## Wikimapia

Wikimapia can be described as a map service site which has a twofold functionality of a wiki site. Wikimapia was started in 2006 and it allows users to place descriptive text on the satellite images making it look like an annotated map. Contributors can add tags, comments, and descriptions to places, buildings, landmarks, canons, and many other less-standard objects and locations, adding a layer of local knowledge that people often do not get from maps and general landmarks. The model of open editing also means that people are constantly adding more information, developing and gaining new areas. As for the comparison with other free-to-use platforms, Wikimapia is not as popular as OpenStreetMap.

There are several applications of VGI in real life. A few are described below.

## Mapping

VGI has been used in the production of detailed maps, especially of areas that mainstream mapping organizations may neglect to cover. VGI contributions are in areas in which geographical information systems have not been adequately provided particularly in the remote or developing regions to enhance navigation, provision of resources, and disaster management.

### Disaster Response

Through VGI, the level of destruction, areas impacted, and requirements of the victims during natural disasters can easily be established. People can send information regarding events, take and send photos, and monitor the progression of certain disasters to the officials thus enabling government and relief agencies to deploy resources speedily.

### Urban Planning

VGI provides important information regarding the patterns of cities, transport systems, and changes in the usage of land. Through social media analysis, GPS data, and data collected in the framework of various citizen science projects, urban planners can find out where car traffic congestion is most significant, etc., where people spend most of their leisure time, and what new trends in using territory are observed.

### Environmental Monitoring

Some of the environmental changes that have been catered for using VGI include air quality, water quality, and biodiversity. Such factors include the availability of resources that can be leveraged by citizen scientists to gather information through mobile apps and sensors to improve the understanding of the environment problems with a view of enhancing conservation.

### Social and Economic Analysis

VGI can contribute significant data in relation to social and economic processes. Location-based social media research is therefore useful in understanding trends of behavior, social relationships, and business activities. VGI can therefore be applied to monitor the movement of human beings, find areas of poverty, and evaluate the effects of development initiatives.

## METHODOLOGY

This chapter utilizes a literature review approach, examining pertinent academic studies, industry reports, and technical documents. It aims to identify and analyze how geo-technology influences travel decisions, the effects of various types of VGI on these choices, and the challenges posed by VGI in travel planning.

# RESULTS AND DISCUSSIONS

## Geo-Technology and Its Role in Shaping Travel Decisions

Geo-technology has brought about a revolution in the field of travel by offering detailed and up-to-date information that makes traveling safer, faster, and more enjoyable. By incorporating features such as traffic updates and weather conditions, and providing customized travel itineraries, these technologies have made traveling more flexible and customer-oriented than it has ever been. This change to more and more informed and personalized traveling choices is a major departure from the past as such detailed and dynamic information was unavailable earlier.

### Real-Time Traffic Updates

The geo-technology has also provided information on current traffic status as among the important benefits of geo-technology (Gokasar & Bakioglu, 2018; Sia et al., 2023). Online tools like Global Positioning System (GPS) and the applications found in most internet-connected systems, including Google Maps, Waze, etc., constantly track traffic and notify drivers of congestion or hindrances originating from other causes such as a crashes or road blockage. This is because, through this format, travelers can always change their itineraries in real-time, and keep off any risky areas while at the same time sticking to their time of commute. In addition, having the possibility to accept and react to live traffic information is useful to decrease stress and enhance the chances of traveling without so many problems; in this way, rides become less challenging and more planned.

### Weather Information

Hindrances to traveling are some of the things that people face in their day to day lives because of weather conditions. Geo-technology can combine weather conditions in travel-related applications and that can generate alerts to the users about general climate or weather patterns in a route or the destination of a journey (Jamal & Habib, 2020; Sia et al., 2023). Such information is vital when it comes to organizing trips without uncomfortable conditions in a car, especially in climatically questionable periods. The preferably helps travelers to delay or change their travel plans when there is severe weather warning, making it safe and free from any interruption.

## Points of Interest and Attractions

Geo-technology also facilitates the travel experience through points of interest (POIs) and attractions (K. Gao et al., 2020). Travel apps provide reviews, ratings, photos, and detailed information regarding several places that are provided by the user to facilitate other people who want to travel. This data assists in the discovery of unique and unknown tourist destinations, ranging from popular sights to back-water areas. Furthermore, the packages such as the geo-tagged social sites updates, check-ins provide suggestions according to the personal preferences of the traveler in terms of the current location. Thus, travel is made to be more fun and experience-oriented to favour personal tastes.

## Customization of Travel Experience

The incorporation of geo-technology in planning tools makes travel planning advanced and personal. Various route options, such as views or speed, or the type of destination, like historical sites or restaurants, may be recommended or targeted depending on what the traveler prefers. Algorithms take into account users' data and travel preferences and find the most appropriate route and features reflecting the individual wishes of the travelers.

## Enhanced Safety and Convenience

Another area where the use of geo-technology has vast ramifications is safety. Innovations like emergency notification, position reporting, and information on local emergency services increase the safety of tourists. For example, sharing location enables friends and families to monitor the movement of a traveler in real-time and can help him/her in case of an emergency. Some travel apps can also notify users of certain regions that are dangerous or give safety measures towards unknown regions.

## Improved Accessibility and Inclusivity

Geo-technology is also valuable in enhancing the aspects of access and inclusion in travel. Free and well-designed Apps that inform a traveler with a disability on the best routes, accommodations, and attractions to visit make traveling easier for the disabled. Instant information about transport, and options that can accommodate wheelchairs, enables everybody to venture out and find new locations on their own.

## Different Types of VGI for Travel Choices

Volunteered Geographic Information (VGI) encompasses a variety of data types that can significantly influence travel decisions. Some key types of VGI used in the travel context are presented below.

## User Reviews and Ratings

Travelers frequently share their experiences by writing reviews and rating destinations, accommodations, restaurants, and attractions on platforms such as TripAdvisor, Yelp, and Google Reviews. These user-generated reviews and ratings offer a wealth of information that can significantly influence the decisions of other travelers (Bigné et al., 2020; Garner & Kim, 2022; Sangkaew & Zhu, 2022; Yalcinkaya & Just, 2023). Such recommendations tend to describe the standard of service delivered by hotels, restaurants, or tourist attractions in detail. Visitors can read about the cleanliness of a particular hotel room, the extent to which waiters at the hotel are friendly, or the quality of specific food. These insights assist people, who are interested in visiting a particular place, in determining whether its prevailing conditions suit them or not. In addition to recording specific life events, reviews often contain an overall picture of the trip. This can include characteristics like the ambiance of a restaurant, the experience of checking in to a hotel, or the anticipation of an attraction. Lived experiences and concrete descriptions offer a much better picture of what one should expect.

Moreover, ratings are helpful because they enable a traveler to immediately identify the differences between various choices. For instance, if a place receives many high-ranked lodgings and amenities, it may be more popular than another place with low ratings. This comparison data can be rather valuable when one has to decide on what place to go to during the journey. Furthermore, aggregated opinions help build a level of trust and credibility in the reviews. The fact is that a few hundred or a few thousand positive reviews are considered to be more credible than only ten or twenty of them. Such volume of feedback can help persuade potential travelers that they are making the right decision. Additionally, users' comments and ratings can also give actual information regarding the condition of the specific destination or service at the present time. For instance, recent posts can remind people of temporary conditions such as construction at the place of accommodations or changes in the quality of the water during certain months of the year. These points are very useful and enable a traveler to avoid such unpleasant experiences.

## Geotagged Photos and Videos

Using social media applications like Instagram, Facebook, and YouTube, people usually add geotag photos/videos, which, state the place where those particular photos/videos were taken (Nautiyal et al., 2023; Owuor & Hochmair, 2020; Villaespesa & Wowkowych, 2020). By capturing and sharing visuals, geotagged photos & videos give the viewers a glimpse of what they would encounter upon their visit to a particular place. It is much easier to believe what people can see: breathtaking nature, fantastic architecture, unforgettable traditions, and beloved places. Beautiful and appealing images may help traveling individuals get excited about a destination. With the help of a gorgeous snapshot of the seashore at sunset or an inspiring video of a local celebration, such a need starts to emerge. Such visuals provide natural coverage giving real travelers' insights as opposed to official marketing material. This relieves the destination of the glamour often associated with exotic paradises and can make it seem more attainable and within reach. By using geotagged content, one may discover new places and beautiful spots that typically would not be discovered with the help of a regular travel guide. For example, sharing a picture of a specific cascade that no one knew of on Instagram will make it a place of interest.

## Check-ins and Location Sharing

Social media outlets, for instance, Facebook, and Foursquare enable users to tag locations to inform their friends or followers where they are (Chen et al., 2020; Khetarpaul, 2021; Ye et al., 2021). Check-ins are updates regarding places that are visited by individuals. This can let other users know where the current trends are and where would be best to visit. Daily check-ins of a place reveal its popularity and may create an illusion of a highly visited place increasing the chances of attendance by unknown persons. By these check-ins, trending spots cannot lack attention at one point or the other. Some of the ways that are used by friends and family when checking in some places make it act as a recommendation. This is because people are often encouraged by the experience of friends and family to visit certain locations, they know were appreciated by them. Check-ins from the users' network help them discover other places that are not very popular but may be intriguing. For instance, if one of the friends sets the status "checked in" at a particular café or a park that is not very popular, others are likely to follow to possibly discover the places. Check-ins can fulfill the goal of stirring activity and participation with social media. Friends may respond to the check-in, they may ask questions or even post their experiences, thus making the communication forum rich and diverse in travel news and tips.

## Travel Blogs and Vlogs

Travelers' travel diaries involve personal experiences and careful descriptions of the trips, which is very helpful when choosing a place to visit (Chakravarty et al., 2021; He et al., 2022; Irfan et al., 2022). Tours are useful for destinations since those who create blogger and vlogger content typically provide extensive details relating to routes, attractions, accommodations, and local customs. Regarding this, the broad coverage assists those who may be planning on visiting such places to have a clue of what they are likely to encounter. Thanks to the blogs and vlogs that supply more knowledgeable and relatable information and data to the viewers in a more knowledgeable and relatable way through storytelling. It is for this reason that storytelling can be used to share experiences and triumphs as well as set back of a particular destination. Habitually, travel bloggers and vloggers focus on valuable information that can include the following: when is the best time to visit, how much one will spend to get to that specific place and other hidden spots of interest. Such recommendations can be sufficient for organizing a trip. Vlogs, in particular, offer visual insights into destinations. It is rather useful to watch a video of a place, rather than read about it, since this way one gets more of the overall impression of that location.

## Crowdsourced Maps

Platforms like OpenStreetMap rely on user contributions to create and update maps, providing several advantages over traditional maps for tourist attractions (Ahmad, 2023; An et al., 2023; Bustamante et al., 2021; Vaziri et al., 2020). Crowdsourced maps are normally updated by users and are likely to incorporate the most recent information regarding the routes, trails, and other points of interest. This makes them more accurate and reliable for travelers when used to find directions instead of relying on other indicators. People can more easily input features that are often not included in commercially available maps such as small trails, points of interest, and certain characteristics of road and trail networks. These small degrees, especially for experiential adventurers or hiking enthusiasts, can give a more accurate sense of where one is headed. They can contain areas that remain uninfluenced by modern technologies, tourist attractions, and heavily populated areas that are not plotted by GPS maps. This is a great advantage because it increases the number of options that a tourist has concerning the place to go to. The open and shared characteristic of crowdsourced maps helps maintain the idea of unity in the group participating in the map's creation as well as in its utilization. The global community comprises professional individuals, so travelers can access professionals on a single platform in the case of crowdsourced maps such as OpenStreetMap.

## Social Media Posts and Hashtags

Posts on social media platforms like Twitter, Instagram, and TikTok, often accompanied by hashtags, play a crucial role in influencing travel choices (Adamış & Pınarbaşı, 2022; Cheng, 2024; Nautiyal et al., 2023; Yoon & Yoo, 2023). For example, the hashtags like #travel, #wanderlust, #roadtrip combine all the posts that are written about the most popular destinations and those that are gaining popularity among tourists. This is because it enables the users to search and come across new places which are up to date. They help make a collection of posts that involve picture, videos, advice, and other contributions from the community. This vast information is useful if it is going to encourage and educate a would-be traveler. Moreover, social media posts are timely and give accurate information about the destinations, activities, and events took place. Tourists get the chance of knowing what is likely to happen in a specific place at a given time which might affect their intended travel. Furthermore, social media sites provide interfaces to share comments and direct messages in which the users can directly communicate with one another. This engagement helps travelers to put their queries, seek for advice, and get suggestions from other members.

## Community Forums and Q&A Platforms

Online discussion forums and question-and-answer websites like Reddit, and Quora offer a platform for discussions where travelers can seek information (Cheng, 2024; Monteiro, 2024; Norman Adams, 2024). These forums offer the opportunity to ask questions regarding the particular country, the route, things to do and see, or any other travel-related issue. This enables them to seek highly individualized information and advice from those with good firsthand understanding. These include keeping detailed accounts of each responder's experience, providing suggestions that are most likely to be helpful for people in similar circumstances as the responder, and providing tips and information that may not be easily available in travel guides. Moreover. these platforms empower travelers to draw from a pool of ideas from a large community of people. From what one may personally read in the blogs; they get to learn from people's various experiences allowing them to have a better decision-making process when going for travels.

## Real-Time Updates

Some of the navigation apps including Waze, and Google Maps give instantaneous information concerning issues like; traffic congestion, road closure, and incidences of accidents. These updates offer several benefits for travelers and have a greater impact on the tourism industry (Li et al., 2020). It is possible to enhance travelers' situational awareness about their routes to allow them to promptly alter their travel plans to steer clear of threats and obstacles. As such, traffic flow is made easier by the avoidance of congestion or accident scenes hence meaning that the travelers will save lots of time and also experience less stress hence meaning a more efficient way of traveling. Moreover, road conditions and weather conditions that may be life-threatening or even fatal thus may not be encountered because the traveler receives real-time alerts about the conditions of the roads and the other undesirable conditions that may be present on the road.

## Collaborative Travel Itineraries

Several functional applications like Google Docs/Spreadsheet or tools limited to travel coordination allow individuals traveling in a group to collaborate and co-ordinate on itineraries. Several different users can edit the itinerary so that anyone can add recommendations, schedules, and noteworthy places to visit according to the group's preferences. It is possible to plan more detailed travel as every member of the group can contribute and explore more activities that are of interest to each of them. Moreover, some of the features that are provided include the possibility of updating this and any subsequent itinerary as and when the travelers require it during the trip.

## Volunteer-Contributed Data for Accessibility

AccessNow and Wheelmap are some examples of apps that depend on the con-tribution of people in the sharing of highlights about places that can be accessed or not. This type of VGI is crucial for several reasons. People provide information about the accessibility of paths, ramps, and facilities where wheelchair-bound people could travel. Moreover, accessible travel options are often not well-documented in traditional resources. This gap is filled by public contributions so that travelers with a disability can access some form of information. Furthermore, this type of VGI fosters the participation of a larger population since everybody can plan any traveling activity knowing the accessibility of the environments in question for all people.

## Challenges of VGI Use in Travel Choices

### Data Accuracy and Reliability

The information that can be given by users may be incorrect, or simply not updated, which can be an inconvenience for travelers (Q. Gao et al., 2024). Some visitors may input erroneous information about themselves or the location or service they are describing including wrong addresses, wrong descriptions, or wrong coordinates. As mentioned earlier, information in VGI relies heavily on users hence its content might not always be up to date. For instance, an establishment such as a restaurant might close down, but it may still be reported it is open depending on the time that data is collected. For example, A traveler may decide to move to a restaurant through Google Reviews and they find that the restaurant was CLOSED when they got there due to the time which was not updated. Similarly, the issues that are passed to customers in the form of reviews about amenities in hotels may be old thus, when a traveler goes there, they find that such facilities are not obtainable.

To improve data accuracy and reliability implementation of verification processes is required where multiple users can confirm details, such as business hours or location accuracy, before they are considered reliable. Moreover, users need to be encouraged to regularly update information and provide incentives for updating outdated data. Additionally, travelers should cross-check information from multiple sources to ensure accuracy. For Instance, by checking business hours across several platforms like Google Reviews, Yelp, and the business's official website, travelers can ensure they have the correct information.

### Information Overload

The sheer volume of VGI can be overwhelming, making it difficult for travelers to sift through and find relevant information. Some really popular places and services can end up having tens of thousands, if not hundreds of thousands, of reviews and ratings, thus, producing a real cloud of information. Moreover, a lot of times, those who travel require to sift through large chunks of information to come across certain relevant data which may take a lot of time and sometimes the information may not even be quite relevant. For example, popular travel-related sites such as TripAdvisor feature thousands of reviews for a particular hotel making it difficult for one to determine which of the reviews is the most recent or relevant. Similarly, one of the issues that may be observed is that some destinations may receive a lot of excellent or highly negative comments making it difficult for travelers to determine which comments are genuine.

To handle such types of instances, it is suggested to use advanced filtering options on VGI platforms to sort reviews by date, relevance, or rating. Moreover, platforms can provide summarized versions of reviews or highlight the most useful reviews based on user feedback. For instance, TripAdvisor could implement a feature that highlights the most recent and relevant reviews at the top, helping travelers quickly find the information they need. It is also suggested to utilize AI and machine learning to offer personalized recommendations based on the user's preferences and past behavior.

## Privacy Concerns

Sharing location data and personal travel experiences can raise privacy and security concerns (Jain et al., 2021). Posting check-ins or location tags in real-time can expose travelers to potential privacy risks, including unwanted attention or stalking. Travelers sharing detailed experiences and personal stories on public forums or social media might inadvertently reveal personal information that could be misused. For example, checking in at a restaurant on Facebook can disclose a user's current location to a broad audience, potentially leading to privacy breaches. Similarly, bloggers sharing their travel schedules and personal anecdotes may unintentionally provide information that compromises their privacy or security.

To address such privacy concerns, users should be encouraged to utilize privacy settings on social media platforms to control who can see their check-ins and posts. For instance, by adjusting privacy settings on Facebook, users can limit the visibility of their check-ins to trusted friends only. Also, it is suggested that travelers should share their experiences and locations after they have left the site to avoid real-time tracking. Moreover, users are required to be educated on the importance of maintaining privacy and the potential risks of oversharing.

## Potential for Bias

User reviews and ratings can be subjective and influenced by individual biases, which might not reflect the true quality of a service or destination. Reviews are inherently personal and can reflect individual tastes, preferences, and experiences, which may not align with those of other travelers. Moreover, disgruntled customers are more likely to leave negative reviews, potentially overshadowing the positive experiences of others. For example, a restaurant might receive unfairly negative reviews due to isolated incidents like a bad service experience, affecting its overall rating and perception. Similarly, reviews might be influenced by the reviewer's cultural background, leading to biased opinions that may not be relevant to all travelers.

To lessen the effect of such biases, users should be encouraged to read a range of reviews to get a balanced view of the destination or service. Moreover, platforms can also provide context about the reviewer, such as their travel style and preferences, to help others understand potential biases. For instance, Yelp could show an average rating alongside highlighted reviews that represent a range of experiences to give a more balanced perspective. Furthermore, a system should be implemented where reviews from verified and frequent travelers are given more weight.

## Dependence on Technology

Reliance on VGI and digital platforms can create issues in areas with poor internet connectivity or for travelers who are not tech-savvy. In remote or underdeveloped areas, a lack of reliable internet access can hinder the use of VGI platforms, limiting access to real-time updates and user-generated content. For example, a traveler in a rural area with limited internet connectivity might be unable to access live traffic updates or check recent reviews on Google Maps. In addition, travelers who are not comfortable with using digital tools might struggle to leverage VGI effectively, missing out on valuable information. For example, older travelers or those unfamiliar with digital platforms might find it challenging to navigate apps like TripAdvisor or Waze, affecting their travel planning.

To address the technology-related challenges, specialized features should be developed in the travel applications that allow users to download maps, reviews, and other relevant information for offline use. For example. Google Maps offers offline map downloads, which travelers can use in areas without internet access. Moreover, tutorials and user guides should be provided to help less tech-savvy travelers utilize digital tools effectively. Furthermore, travelers should be encouraged to carry traditional maps and guidebooks as backups in areas with poor connectivity.

## Manipulation and Fraud

VGI platforms can be susceptible to fake reviews and manipulated ratings, which can mislead travelers. Businesses or individuals might post false positive reviews to inflate ratings or negative reviews to sabotage competitors. Similarly, some businesses might pay for favorable reviews, undermining the trustworthiness of the platform and deceiving potential customers. Businesses might engage in practices like posting fake positive reviews or hiring services to generate favorable ratings, misleading travelers about the actual quality of the service. Similarly, coordinated efforts to create the illusion of widespread support or disapproval for a place or service through fake reviews can distort public perception.

To handle such types of challenges, verification processes need to be implemented to ensure reviews are from genuine customers, such as requiring proof of purchase or stay. It is also advisable to use AI algorithms to detect and filter out fake reviews and suspicious activities. For example, platforms like TripAdvisor can use AI to detect patterns indicative of fake reviews and flag or remove them accordingly. Further, users should be encouraged to report suspicious reviews and maintain transparency about the review verification process.

## CONCLUSION

Geo-technology significantly enhances the travel experience by providing real-time traffic updates, weather information, and insights into points of interest and attractions. It allows for the customization of travel plans based on personal preferences, ensuring safer and more convenient journeys. The incorporation of VGI enriches travel decisions through user reviews, geotagged content, and crowdsourced maps, offering detailed and up-to-date information. These advancements in geo-technology and VGI collectively contribute to making travel more accessible, inclusive, and enjoyable for a diverse range of travelers.

The advancements in geo-technology have far-reaching implications for travelers and the tourism industry. Real-time updates and personalized travel planning tools help reduce stress and improve the efficiency of travel, potentially increasing satisfaction and loyalty among tourists. VGI platforms enable travelers to make informed decisions based on peer reviews and real-time data, fostering a more interactive and community-driven travel planning process. Additionally, the emphasis on accessibility and inclusivity ensures that travel is more equitable, providing valuable resources for individuals with disabilities. Overall, the integration of geo-technology and VGI enhances the quality and safety of travel, benefiting both travelers and service providers in the tourism sector.

The use of Volunteered Geographic Information (VGI) in travel choices presents several challenges, including data accuracy and reliability issues due to potential erroneous or outdated information. Travelers may face information overload from extensive user-generated content, making it hard to find relevant details. Privacy concerns arise from sharing location data and personal experiences, potentially leading to unwanted attention or stalking. User reviews can be biased, reflecting individual preferences that might not align with others. Dependence on technology can hinder access to VGI in areas with poor internet connectivity or for less tech-savvy travelers. Additionally, VGI platforms are vulnerable to manipulation and fraud through fake reviews and manipulated ratings. To address these challenges, improved verification processes, advanced filtering options, offline features, user education on privacy, and AI-driven fraud detection are necessary to enhance the reliability and trustworthiness of VGI in travel planning.

Future research and development in geo-technology and VGI should focus on further improving the accuracy and comprehensiveness of real-time data. Innovations in artificial intelligence and machine learning could enhance the personalization of travel recommendations, making them even more tailored to individual preferences. Additionally, expanding the scope of VGI to include more diverse and underrepresented voices can provide a broader range of travel insights and experiences. Efforts should also be made to improve the accessibility of travel-related applications, ensuring that they are user-friendly for people with varying levels of digital literacy. Collaboration between tech developers, tourism professionals, and the traveling community will be essential in driving these advancements forward, ultimately making travel safer, more enjoyable, and more inclusive for everyone.

# REFERENCES

Adamış, E., & Pınarbaşı, F. (2022). Unfolding visual characteristics of social media communication: Reflections of smart tourism destinations. *Journal of Hospitality and Tourism Technology*, 13(1), 34–61. Advance online publication. DOI: 10.1108/ JHTT-09-2020-0246

Ahmad, M. (2023). Exploring the Role of OpenStreetMap in Mapping Religious Tourism in Pakistan for Sustainable Development. In J. P. D. M. Vítor, A. G. da R. N. João, L. de J. P. Maria, & A. de M. C. Liliana (Eds.), *Experiences, Advantages, and Economic Dimensions of Pilgrimage Routes* (pp. 23–40). IGI Global. DOI: 10.4018/978-1-6684-9923-8.ch002

An, J., Wan Zainon, W. M. N., & Zainon, W. (2023). An interactive visualization of location-based reviews using word cloud and OpenStreetMap for tourism applications. *Spatial Information Research*, 31(2), 235–243. Advance online publication. DOI: 10.1007/s41324-022-00492-z

Bigné, E., William, E., & Soria-Olivas, E. (2020). Similarity and Consistency in Hotel Online Ratings across Platforms. *Journal of Travel Research*, 59(4), 742–758. Advance online publication. DOI: 10.1177/0047287519859705

Bustamante, A., Sebastia, L., & Onaindia, E. (2021). On the representativeness of openstreetmap for the evaluation of country tourism competitiveness. *ISPRS International Journal of Geo-Information*, 10(5), 301. Advance online publication. DOI: 10.3390/ijgi10050301

Chakravarty, U., Chand, G., & Singh, U. N. (2021). Millennial travel vlogs: Emergence of a new form of virtual tourism in the post-pandemic era? *Worldwide Hospitality and Tourism Themes*, 13(5), 666–676. Advance online publication. DOI: 10.1108/ WHATT-05-2021-0077

Chen, Z., Cao, H., Wang, H., Xu, F., Kostakos, V., & Li, Y. (2020). Will You Come Back/Check-in Again? Understanding Characteristics Leading to Urban Revisitation and Re-check-in. *Proceedings of the ACM on Interactive, Mobile, Wearable and Ubiquitous Technologies*, 4(3), 1–27. Advance online publication. DOI: 10.1145/3411812

Cheng, M. (2024). Social media and tourism geographies: mapping future research agenda. In *Tourism Geographies*. DOI: 10.1080/14616688.2024.2304782

Gao, K., Yang, X., Wu, C., Qiao, T., Chen, X., Yang, M., & Chen, L. (2020). Exploiting Location-Based Context for POI Recommendation When Traveling to a New Region. *IEEE Access : Practical Innovations, Open Solutions*, 8, 52404–52412. Advance online publication. DOI: 10.1109/ACCESS.2020.2980982

Gao, Q., Fu, H., Zhang, K., Trajcevski, G., Teng, X., & Zhou, F. (2024). Inferring Real Mobility in Presence of Fake Check-ins Data. *ACM Transactions on Intelligent Systems and Technology*, 15(1), 1–25. Advance online publication. DOI: 10.1145/3604941

Garner, B., & Kim, D. (2022). Analyzing user-generated content to improve customer satisfaction at local wine tourism destinations: An analysis of Yelp and TripAdvisor reviews. *Consumer Behavior in Tourism and Hospitality*, 17(4), 413–435. Advance online publication. DOI: 10.1108/CBTH-03-2022-0077

Gokasar, I., & Bakioglu, G. (2018). Modeling the effects of real time traffic information on travel behavior: A case study of Istanbul Technical University. *Transportation Research Part F: Traffic Psychology and Behaviour*, 58, 881–892. Advance online publication. DOI: 10.1016/j.trf.2018.07.013

Goodchild, M. F. (2007). Citizens as sensors: The world of volunteered geography. In *GeoJournal*. DOI: 10.1007/s10708-007-9111-y

He, J., Xu, D., & Chen, T. (2022). Travel vlogging practice and its impacts on tourist experiences. *Current Issues in Tourism*, 25(15), 2518–2533. Advance online publication. DOI: 10.1080/13683500.2021.1971166

Irfan, M., Malik, M. S., & Zubair, S. K. (2022). Impact of Vlog Marketing on Consumer Travel Intent and Consumer Purchase Intent With the Moderating Role of Destination Image and Ease of Travel. *SAGE Open*, 12(2). Advance online publication. DOI: 10.1177/21582440221099522

Jain, A. K., Sahoo, S. R., & Kaubiyal, J. (2021). Online social networks security and privacy: Comprehensive review and analysis. *Complex & Intelligent Systems*, 7(5), 2157–2177. Advance online publication. DOI: 10.1007/s40747-021-00409-7

Jamal, S., & Habib, M. A. (2020). Smartphone and daily travel: How the use of smartphone applications affect travel decisions. *Sustainable Cities and Society*, 53, 101939. Advance online publication. DOI: 10.1016/j.scs.2019.101939

Khetarpaul, S. (2021). Mining location based social networks to understand the citizen's check-in patterns. *Computing*, 103(12), 2967–2993. Advance online publication. DOI: 10.1007/s00607-021-01020-x

Li, X., Dadashova, B., Yu, S., & Zhang, Z. (2020). Rethinking highway safety analysis by leveraging crowdsourced waze data. *Sustainability (Basel)*, 12(23), 10127. Advance online publication. DOI: 10.3390/su122310127

Monteiro, S. (2024). Searching for settlement information on Reddit. *International Migration (Geneva, Switzerland)*, 62(3), 100–119. DOI: 10.1111/imig.13261

Nautiyal, R., Albrecht, J. N., & Carr, A. (2023). Can destination image be ascertained from social media? An examination of Twitter hashtags. *Tourism and Hospitality Research*, 23(4), 578–593. Advance online publication. DOI: 10.1177/14673584221119380

Norman Adams, N. (2024). 'Scraping' Reddit posts for academic research? Addressing some blurred lines of consent in growing internet-based research trend during the time of Covid-19. *International Journal of Social Research Methodology*, 27(1), 47–62. DOI: 10.1080/13645579.2022.2111816

Owuor, I., & Hochmair, H. H. (2020). An overview of social media apps and their potential role in geospatial research. In *ISPRS International Journal of Geo-Information* (Vol. 9, Issue 9). DOI: 10.3390/ijgi9090526

Sangkaew, N., & Zhu, H. (2022). Understanding Tourists' Experiences at Local Markets in Phuket: An Analysis of TripAdvisor Reviews. *Journal of Quality Assurance in Hospitality & Tourism*, 23(1), 89–114. Advance online publication. DOI: 10.1080/1528008X.2020.1848747

Sia, P. Y. H., Saidin, S. S., & Iskandar, Y. H. P. (2023). Systematic review of mobile travel apps and their smart features and challenges. In *Journal of Hospitality and Tourism Insights* (Vol. 6, Issue 5). DOI: 10.1108/JHTI-02-2022-0087

Siuhi, S., & Mwakalonge, J. (2016). Opportunities and challenges of smart mobile applications in transportation. [English Edition]. *Journal of Traffic and Transportation Engineering*, 3(6), 582–592. Advance online publication. DOI: 10.1016/j.jtte.2016.11.001

Vaziri, F., Nanni, M., Matwin, S., & Pedreschi, D. (2020). *Discovering Tourist Attractions of Cities Using Flickr and OpenStreetMap Data*. DOI: 10.1007/978-981-15-2024-2_21

Villaespesa, E., & Wowkowych, S. (2020). Ephemeral Storytelling With Social Media: Snapchat and Instagram Stories at the Brooklyn Museum. *Social Media + Society*, 6(1). Advance online publication. DOI: 10.1177/2056305119898776

Yalcinkaya, B., & Just, D. R. (2023). Comparison of Customer Reviews for Local and Chain Restaurants: Multilevel Approach to Google Reviews Data. *Cornell Hospitality Quarterly*, 64(1), 63–73. Advance online publication. DOI: 10.1177/19389655221102388

Ye, Z., Newing, A., & Clarke, G. (2021). Understanding Chinese tourist mobility and consumption-related behaviours in London using Sina Weibo check-ins. *Environment and Planning. B, Urban Analytics and City Science*, 48(8), 2436–2452. Advance online publication. DOI: 10.1177/2399808320980748

Yoon, H. Y., & Yoo, S. C. (2023). Finding tourism niche on image-based social media: Integrating computational methods. *Journal of Vacation Marketing*, 13567667231180994. Advance online publication. DOI: 10.1177/13567667231180994

## KEY TERMS AND DEFINITIONS

**Geo-Technology:** Is a broad term encompassing the technologies used to collect, store, analyze, and visualize spatial data. It includes tools and techniques such as geographic information systems (GIS), remote sensing, global positioning systems (GPS), and online mapping platforms.

**OpenStreetMap:** Is a free, editable map of the world created by a community of volunteers. It is a collaborative project that allows anyone to contribute data, making it a valuable resource for various applications, including mapping, navigation, and analysis.

**Point of Interest (POI):** Is a specific location that is considered significant or noteworthy. It can be a physical location, such as a business, landmark, or natural feature, or a virtual location, such as a website or online community. POIs are often used in mapping and navigation applications to provide users with information about nearby places of interest.

**Spatial Data:** Is information that is tied to a specific location on the Earth's surface. It can include geographic features like points, lines, polygons, and rasters, as well as attributes associated with these features (e.g., population density, land use, elevation). Examples of spatial data include maps, satellite imagery, and GPS coordinates.

**Volunteered Geographic Information (VGI):** Is data collected by individuals using mobile devices or other technologies and contributed to a shared database. It is often generated through citizen science projects or crowdsourcing initiatives. Examples of VGI include location-based social media posts, GPS tracks, and user-generated maps.

# Chapter 11
# Social Media and Its Influence on Travel Decision Making

**Harish Saini**

https://orcid.org/0000-0003-3850-7678

*Lovely Professional University, India*

**Pawan Kumar**

https://orcid.org/0000-0001-7501-3066

*Lovely Professional University, India*

**Rajesh Verma**

*Lovely Professional University, India*

## ABSTRACT

*This chapter critically examines the transformative role of social media in contemporary travel decision-making, situating its analysis within established theoretical frameworks such as the Technology Acceptance Model (TAM), Theory of Planned Behavior (TPB), and Social Influence Theory. Social media platforms—most notably Instagram, Facebook, and YouTube—are explored as pivotal in influencing destination selection, itinerary planning, and the broader experiential dimensions of tourism. The discourse delves into the complex interplay between user-generated content and destination marketing, emphasizing the emergent power dynamics facilitated by social media influencers. Furthermore, the chapter interrogates the psychological constructs of social proof, fear of missing out (FOMO), and identity construction, elucidating their profound impact on tourist behavior. The chapter concludes by identifying significant research gaps, advocating for a nuanced understanding of the implications of social media on sustainable tourism development*

DOI: 10.4018/979-8-3693-3972-5.ch011

## INTRODUCTION

The twenty-first century marks a pivotal era for global tourism, characterized by unprecedented growth fueled by advancements in technology, shifts in work-life balance, and an ever-expanding array of travel destinations. These developments have elevated tourism to one of the fastest-growing economic sectors worldwide, significantly influencing socio-economic structures in both developed and emerging economies (UNWTO, 2022). The sector's contribution to national income, balance of payments, and employment generation across various skill levels has become a critical focus in the economic planning of numerous countries. Consequently, tourism has emerged as a transformative force, reshaping patterns of labor, investment, land use, and taxation, while simultaneously bolstering the capital accounts of nations across the globe (Gössling & Scott, 2018).

With in the developing countries, India stands at the forefront of this global tourism boom, with its tourism sector experiencing substantial growth and playing an increasingly vital role in the national economy. According to the World Travel & Tourism Council, the sector contributed 15.24 lakh crore (US$220 billion), or 9.4% of the nation's GDP in 2017, while supporting 41.622 million jobs, representing 8% of total employment (WTTC, 2022). The sector's growth trajectory is projected to continue at an annual rate of 6.9%, with contributions expected to reach 32.05 lakh crore (US$470 billion) by 2028, accounting for 9.9% of GDP (WTTC, 2023) . This expansion is mirrored by the rise in international tourist arrivals, which surpassed ten million in 2017, reflecting a 15.6% increase from the previous year.

Despite these impressive statistics, there exists a substantial gap in the academic exploration of social media's role in shaping travel decision-making. The advent of digital technologies, particularly social media platforms, has revolutionized the tourism industry, offering travelers unprecedented access to information and the ability to make informed decisions based on peer-generated content (Moro et al., 2016). However, the specific mechanisms through which social media influences travel decisions, nations with a unique cultural and digital landscape, remain under-researched (Buhalis & Sinarta, 2019). This chapter seeks to address this gap by examining the multifaceted impact of social media on travel decision-making, with a particular focus on the tourism sector.

## 2. TOURISM AT A GLANCE

## 2.1 Impacts of Tourism

The establishment or development of a tourism sector comes with a variety of benefits as well as challenges. It is possible to optimise strengths and opportunities while minimising weaknesses and challenges if these influences are recognized at the start of planning. Regarding aspects related to tourism, every location has its own unique challenges and opportunities. The benefits and challenges of tourism are different in each location, and they may shift over time, depending on the mix of tourism and other activities that are taking place in the local and regional context of a given location. The following is a list of prospective benefits as well as challenges to consider. Figure 1 lists benefits and 2 lists challenges of tourism.

*Figure 1. Benefits of Tourism Growth*

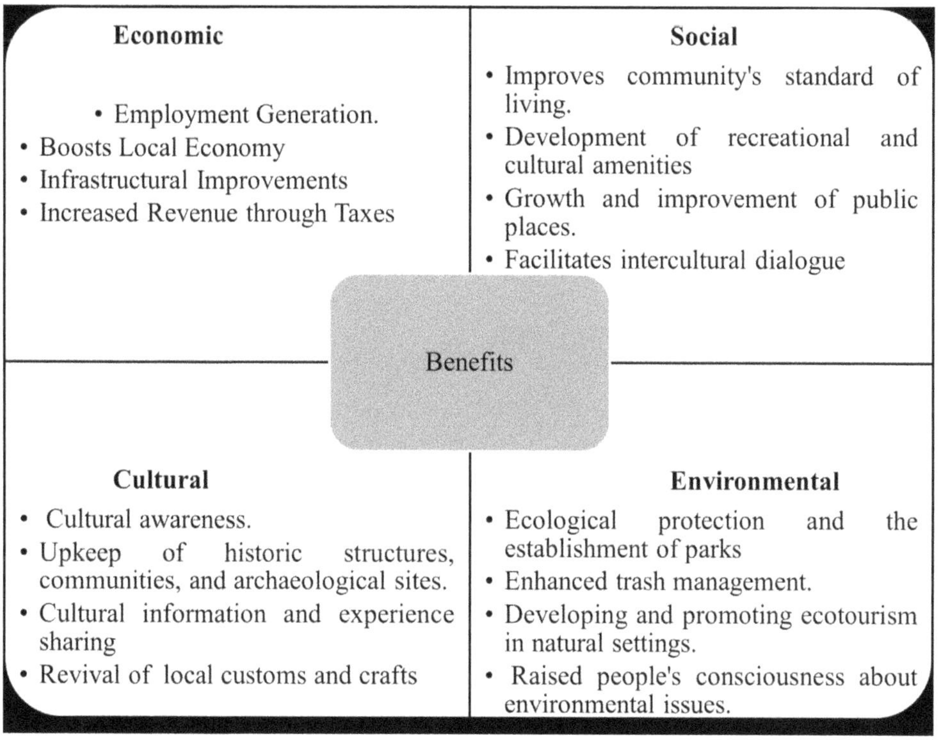

| Economic | Social |
|---|---|
| • Employment Generation.<br>• Boosts Local Economy<br>• Infrastructural Improvements<br>• Increased Revenue through Taxes | • Improves community's standard of living.<br>• Development of recreational and cultural amenities<br>• Growth and improvement of public places.<br>• Facilitates intercultural dialogue |
| **Benefits** | |
| Cultural | Environmental |
| • Cultural awareness.<br>• Upkeep of historic structures, communities, and archaeological sites.<br>• Cultural information and experience sharing<br>• Revival of local customs and crafts | • Ecological protection and the establishment of parks<br>• Enhanced trash management.<br>• Developing and promoting ecotourism in natural settings.<br>• Raised people's consciousness about environmental issues. |

*Source (Authors Compilation)*

*Figure 2. Challenges of Tourism Growth*

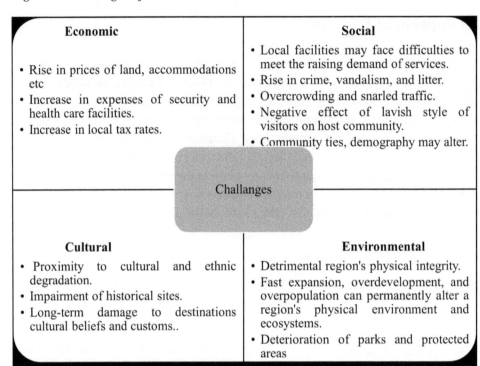

| Economic | Social |
|---|---|
| • Rise in prices of land, accommodations etc<br>• Increase in expenses of security and health care facilities.<br>• Increase in local tax rates. | • Local facilities may face difficulties to meet the raising demand of services.<br>• Rise in crime, vandalism, and litter.<br>• Overcrowding and snarled traffic.<br>• Negative effect of lavish style of visitors on host community.<br>• Community ties, demography may alter. |

Challanges

| Cultural | Environmental |
|---|---|
| • Proximity to cultural and ethnic degradation.<br>• Impairment of historical sites.<br>• Long-term damage to destinations cultural beliefs and customs.. | • Detrimental region's physical integrity.<br>• Fast expansion, overdevelopment, and overpopulation can permanently alter a region's physical environment and ecosystems.<br>• Deterioration of parks and protected areas |

*Source (Authors Compilation)*

## 2.2 Identifying Research Gaps

Despite the evident influence of social media on travel decision-making, several research gaps remain unaddressed. One critical area of inquiry is the differential impact of various social media platforms on distinct segments of the travel market (Gulati, 2022). For instance, while platforms like Instagram and Snapchat are popular among younger travelers for their visual content, older travelers may prefer platforms that offer more detailed information, such as TripAdvisor or Facebook. Understanding these preferences is crucial for developing targeted marketing strategies that effectively reach different demographic groups (Abernethy et al., 2022; De Veirman et al., 2017; Kapoor et al., 2022; Rasul et al., 2020; Thomaz et al., 2017).

Another significant research gap pertains to the role of social media in promoting sustainable tourism epically in developing countries like India. As travelers become increasingly aware of their environmental impact, there is a growing need to explore how social media can be leveraged to encourage eco-friendly travel practices and raise awareness about sustainability issues (Kapoor et al., 2022). This includes examining how social media campaigns can influence travelers' choices in favor of sustainable destinations, accommodations, and activities (Abou-Shouk et al., 2021).

Furthermore, the intersection of social media and cultural tourism presents a rich area for academic exploration. Country's diverse cultural heritage is a major draw for international tourists, and social media plays a pivotal role in promoting cultural tourism by highlighting festivals, historical sites, and traditional practices (Moreno-Manzo et al., 2022; **Xu** et al., 2023). However, the impact of this digital promotion on the preservation and commodification of cultural heritage remains underexplored. Research in this area could provide valuable insights into the balance between promoting cultural tourism and safeguarding cultural integrity (Dey et al., 2020; Xiang et al., 2015)

## 3. THEORETICAL FRAMEWORK AND SOCIAL MEDIA'S ROLE IN TRAVEL DECISION-MAKING

The integration of social media into the tourism industry can be analyzed through the lens of several theoretical frameworks, including the Technology Acceptance Model (TAM), the Theory of Planned Behavior (TPB), and Social Influence Theory. These frameworks provide a robust foundation for understanding how travelers adopt and utilize social media platforms in the context of travel planning and decision-making (Villacé-Molinero et al., 2023; Xiang et al., 2015).

The Technology Acceptance Model posits that the perceived ease of use and perceived usefulness of a technology significantly influence its adoption and use. In the context of tourism, social media platforms such as Facebook, Instagram, and TripAdvisor are valued for their user-friendliness and the wealth of user-generated content they offer, which travelers perceive as highly useful in making informed travel decisions (Chen et al., 2023; Cheung et al., 2021). This perception drives the widespread adoption of social media for travel planning, particularly among younger, tech-savvy travelers who prioritize convenience and accessibility (Ali et al., 2023; Kabadayi et al., 2019).

The Theory of Planned Behavior further elucidates the role of social media in travel decision-making by emphasizing the influence of attitudes, subjective norms, and perceived behavioral control on travelers' intentions and actions. Social media platforms, through the proliferation of reviews, ratings, and recommendations, shape travelers' attitudes toward potential destinations and services (Kumar et al., 2022; Saini et al., 2023). Moreover, the visibility of peer behavior on social media creates subjective norms that can either encourage or dissuade travel-related decisions. The ease with which travelers can access and share information on social media also enhances their perceived control over the travel planning process, reinforcing the intention to use these platforms (Gursoy et al., 2023).

Social Influence Theory complements these perspectives by highlighting the impact of social networks on individual decision-making. In the tourism sector, social media functions as a virtual community where travelers exchange experiences, advice, and recommendations, thereby exerting a significant influence on the travel choices of others within the network (Kaplan & Haenlein, 2010; Yamagishi et al., 2023). This peer influence is potent where collective decision-making and the value placed on peer opinions are deeply ingrained in the culture (Gretzel, 2018; Hudders et al., 2021).

## 3.1 Social Media Influence on Travel Planning

*Figure 3. Social Media Influence on Travel Planning*

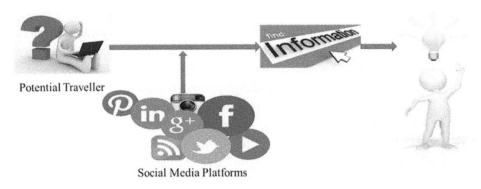

*Source: (Authors Compilation)*

Figure 3 serves as a visual representation of the intricate role that social media plays in the contemporary travel decision-making process. At the outset, the figure with a question mark, coupled with a laptop, symbolizes the initial stage of consumer uncertainty, where the potential traveler is engaged in the early stages of the information search phase. This phase is critical, as it reflects the consumer's cognitive dissonance and the need for external validation or inspiration, which is increasingly sought through digital means. Social media platforms such as Pinterest, LinkedIn, Instagram, Facebook, and Twitter, are emblematic of the multifaceted sources of information available to the traveler. These platforms represent a dynamic ecosystem where user-generated content (UGC) significantly influences consumer perceptions and decisions. The diverse and participatory nature of social media enables the aggregation of a wide array of travel-related content, from peer reviews and testimonials to visual stimuli such as photos and videos. This content, often perceived as more authentic and credible than traditional advertising, plays a pivotal role in shaping travel-related attitudes, beliefs, and behavioral intentions. The information processed from different social media platforms synthesize to form a coherent understanding of their potential travel options. This process is not merely passive but involves an active engagement with the content, wherein travelers evaluate the credibility, relevance, and usefulness of the information presented. The final stage epitomizes the culmination of this decision-making process. Here, the lightbulb is not just a metaphor for an idea but symbolizes the resolution of cognitive dissonance and the formation of a concrete travel decision.

In conclusion figure 3 encapsulates the transition from information uncertainty to informed decision-making, facilitated by the interactive and socially constructed nature of content on social media platforms. The depiction underscores the theoretical underpinnings of the Elaboration Likelihood Model (ELM), where social media serves as both a central and peripheral route of persuasion, ultimately influencing the traveler's intention to finalize their travel decision. This visual narrative aligns with contemporary theories in consumer behavior, emphasizing the evolving nature of information search and decision-making in the digital age. It serves as a powerful tool for understanding the transformative impact of social media on the travel industry, providing a foundation for further academic exploration and empirical validation.

## 3.2 The Role of Social Media in Travel Planning

Social media platforms serve as both information sources and decision-making tools for travelers. According to Gong et al., 2022 and Gulati, 2022, social media has become a significant source of information for travelers, surpassing traditional media in many cases. The interactive nature of social media allows users to access a vast array of user-generated content (UGC), including reviews, photos, videos, and personal recommendations, which significantly influence their travel decisions (Chavez et al., 2020; Fotis et al., 2012).

1. Information Search: Social media platforms provide travelers with access to diverse content generated by other users, including reviews, ratings, and experiences. This user-generated content (UGC) serves as a rich source of information that influences travelers' perceptions and expectations of destinations (Pike et al., 2021). The authenticity and relatability of UGC make it more influential than traditional advertising or official tourism websites (D. Y. Kim & Kim, 2021; Minazzi & Mauri, 2015).

2. Destination Inspiration: Social media platforms like Instagram and Pinterest are visually oriented, making them powerful tools for destination inspiration. Travelers are often inspired by images and stories shared by other users, which can spark interest in new destinations or experiences (Ki et al., 2020). The aspirational nature of social media content encourages users to explore destinations they might not have considered otherwise.

3. Trip Planning and Organization: social media also aids in trip planning and organization. Platforms like Facebook and Twitter allow users to gather recommendations from their network, while travel-specific platforms like TripAdvisor offer detailed reviews and ratings that help in making informed decisions (Donthu et al., 2021). The ease of accessing real-time information on social media contributes to more efficient and informed travel planning.

4. Influence of Social Media Influencers: Social media influencers, who have large followings on platforms like Instagram and YouTube, play a crucial role in shaping travel decisions. Their endorsements, reviews, and recommendations can sway the opinions of their followers, making them a powerful force in the tourism industry (Abidin, 2015). The perceived authenticity and relatability of influencers contribute to their effectiveness in influencing travel decisions.

5. Real-Time Updates and Adjustments: During travel, social media provides real-time updates and information, allowing travellers to adjust their plans. Platforms like Twitter offer up-to-date information on weather, transportation, and local events, while location-based services like Google Maps enhance navigation and exploration (Liu et al., 2022; Ouariti & Jebrane, 2020; Saini et al., 2023). The ability to access real-time information enhances the travel experience and reduces uncertainty.

## 4. THE PSYCHOLOGICAL INFLUENCE OF SOCIAL MEDIA ON TRAVEL DECISIONS

*Table 1. Psychological Influences of Social Media on Travel Decisions*

| Psychological Influence | Description | Impact on Travel Decisions |
|---|---|---|
| Social Proof | The tendency to follow others' actions and opinions. | Positive reviews and popular destinations influence travelers' choices and preferences. |
| FOMO (Fear of Missing Out) | Anxiety about missing out on experiences seen online. | Drives spontaneous travel decisions to avoid missing out on popular or unique experiences. |

continued on following page

*Table 1. Continued*

| Psychological Influence | Description | Impact on Travel Decisions |
|---|---|---|
| Self-Presentation | The desire to curate an idealized image of oneself. | Influences travelers to choose destinations and experiences that enhance their desired self-image |

Source (Authors Compilation)

The psychological impact of social media on travel decisions is profound, affecting travelers' perceptions, motivations, and behaviors. Table 1 shows the psychological influences of social media on travel decisions. Several psychological theories and concepts can be applied to understand this influence.

1. Social Proof and Herd Behavior: Social media amplifies the psychological concept of social proof, where individuals look to others' actions and opinions to guide their own decisions (Lee & Kim, 2020; Masuda et al., 2022). Positive reviews, likes, and shares on social media serve as social proof, encouraging others to visit the same destinations or engage in similar activities. Herd behavior, where people follow the majority's actions, is also prevalent on social media, leading to trends and viral destinations (Donthu et al., 2021; Pop et al., 2021; Seyidov & Adomaitienė, 2016).

2. FOMO (Fear of Missing Out): FOMO is a psychological phenomenon intensified by social media, where individuals feel anxious about missing out on experiences that others are enjoying (Bui et al., 2022; Solazzo et al., 2022). Social media platforms, with their constant stream of curated content showcasing exotic destinations and unique experiences, exacerbate FOMO, driving travelers to make spontaneous travel decisions to avoid missing out.

3. Self-Presentation and Identity Construction: Social media serves as a platform for self-presentation, where individuals curate and share content that reflects their desired identity (Delbaere et al., 2021; Gaenssle & Budzinski, 2021). Travel, being a significant aspect of identity, is often used as a means of self-expression on social media. The desire to construct an idealized identity influences travel decisions, as individuals seek destinations and experiences that align with their self-concept and the image they wish to portray to others (Kim & Fesenmaier, 2017).

4. Expectation vs. Reality: social media can create unrealistic expectations about travel experiences, leading to potential dissatisfaction when the reality does not match the idealized images and narratives portrayed online (Omo-Obas & Anning-Dorson, 2022; Wismantoro et al., 2023). The disparity between expectation and reality can impact travellers' overall satisfaction and their future travel decisions.

# 5. THE IMPACT OF SOCIAL MEDIA ON DESTINATION MARKETING

Destination marketing has undergone a significant transformation due to the influence of social media. Traditional marketing strategies have been supplemented, and in some cases, replaced by social media marketing, which offers unique advantages for reaching and engaging with potential travelers.

1. User-Generated Content (UGC) as Marketing Tool: UGC has become a valuable asset for destination marketers. Authentic content created by travelers, such as photos, videos, and reviews, is often perceived as more trustworthy and credible than traditional advertisements (Kumar et al., 2022; Yuan et al., 2022). Destinations can leverage UGC by encouraging visitors to share their experiences on social media platforms, thus amplifying their marketing efforts through word-of-mouth (WOM) (Akhtar et al., 2019).
2. Influencer Marketing: Collaborating with social media influencers has become a popular strategy for destination marketing. Influencers have the ability to reach specific target audiences and create content that resonates with their followers. By partnering with influencers, destinations can increase their visibility and appeal to new demographics (Abidin, 2015). The authenticity and relatability of influencers make them effective in promoting destinations and experiences.
3. Real-Time Engagement: Social media allows destinations to engage with potential travelers in real-time. Through platforms like Twitter, Facebook, and Instagram, destinations can respond to inquiries, share updates, and interact with travelers during their decision-making process (Sota et al., 2020; Stylos et al., 2021). Real-time engagement enhances customer service and fosters a sense of connection between the destination and potential visitors.
4. Targeted Advertising and Personalization: Social media platforms offer advanced targeting capabilities that allow destination marketers to reach specific demographics based on interests, behaviors, and location (Li et al., 2022; Wu et al., 2022). Personalized advertisements and content tailored to individual preferences can significantly influence travel decisions. The ability to deliver relevant content to potential travelers increases the effectiveness of marketing campaigns.
5. Crisis Management and Reputation: Social media plays a crucial role in crisis management for destinations. Negative incidents, such as natural disasters or safety concerns, can spread rapidly on social media, affecting a destination's reputation (Dellarocas, 2003; Namisango et al., 2019; Wellman et al., 2020). Effective social media management involves monitoring online conversations,

addressing concerns promptly, and communicating transparently with the public to mitigate the impact of negative events.

## 6. SOCIAL MEDIA PLATFORMS AND THEIR SPECIFIC INFLUENCE ON TRAVEL DECISION MAKING

Different social media platforms have unique features and user bases, influencing how they impact travel decision-making. This section explores the specific influence of major social media platforms on travellers. Table 2 depicts the social media platforms and their influence on travel decision-making:

*Table 2. Social Media Platforms and Their Influence on Travel Decision-Making*

| Social Media Platform | Primary Use | Influence on Travel Decisions |
|---|---|---|
| Instagram | Visual content and inspiration | Provides visual inspiration through photos and videos, influencing destination choices and travel trends. |
| Facebook | Social interactions and planning | Facilitates information exchange, recommendations from friends, and event planning. |
| YouTube | Video content and reviews | Offers detailed travel vlogs and reviews, providing in-depth insights into destinations and experiences. |
| Pinterest | Visual discovery and planning | Serves as a digital mood board for saving and discovering travel ideas and inspirations. |
| Twitter | Real-time updates and engagement | Provides real-time information and updates, facilitating interaction with travelers and destinations. |
| TripAdvisor | Reviews and ratings | Offers user-generated reviews and ratings, helping travelers make informed decisions about accommodations and attractions. |

Source (Authors Compilation)

1. Instagram: Instagram, with its emphasis on visual content, is a powerful platform for travel inspiration. The platform's Explore page and hashtags allow users to discover new destinations and experiences through curated photos and videos (Kapoor et al., 2022; Ki et al., 2020). Influencers on Instagram often showcase luxurious and aspirational travel experiences, contributing to the platform's role in shaping travel trends and destination choices.

2. Facebook: Facebook remains one of the most widely used social media platforms, offering a mix of text, image, and video content. It serves as a platform for both inspiration and planning, with features like Facebook Groups, Events, and Marketplace facilitating travel-related discussions and transactions (Molinillo et al., 2019; Tran & Rudolf, 2022). The platform's integration with other ser-

vices, such as booking websites, enhances its role in the travel decision-making process.

3. YouTube: YouTube is a leading platform for travel vlogs and video content, providing in-depth visual insights into destinations and experiences. Travel vlogs offer authentic and immersive perspectives, allowing viewers to virtually explore destinations before making decisions (Djafarova & Rushworth, 2017; Kumar et al., 2022) YouTube's recommendation algorithm also plays a role in guiding users toward content that aligns with their interests, further influencing their travel choices.

4. Pinterest: Pinterest is a visual discovery platform that serves as a digital mood board for travelers. Users create and save "pins" of travel-related content, which can range from destination guides to packing tips (Joseph & Anandkumar, 2021; Saini et al., 2023). The platform's search functionality and curated content make it a valuable tool for travel inspiration and planning, particularly for users seeking unique and niche experiences.

5. Twitter: Twitter's real-time nature makes it a valuable platform for travel updates, news, and customer service. Travelers use Twitter to share their experiences, seek recommendations, and stay informed about developments at their destination (Kiráľová & Pavlíčeka, 2015). The platform's hashtags and trending topics also allow users to discover popular destinations and travel-related discussions.

6. TripAdvisor: TripAdvisor is a travel-specific social media platform that focuses on reviews, ratings, and recommendations. Users rely on TripAdvisor for honest feedback from other travelers, making it a critical resource for destination evaluation and decision-making (Christensen et al., 2024; Türk et al., 2021). The platform's extensive database of reviews and photos helps users make informed choices about accommodations, attractions, and restaurants.

## 7. CHALLENGES AND ETHICAL CONSIDERATIONS

While social media offers numerous benefits for travel decision-making, it also presents challenges and ethical considerations that need to be addressed also refer table 3.

*Table 3. Challenges of tourism*

| Challenge/Ethical Issue | Description | Implications for Travelers and Marketers |
|---|---|---|
| Misinformation | The spread of inaccurate or misleading information online. | Travelers may make decisions based on false or exaggerated information; marketers must ensure transparency |
| Privacy and Data Security | Concerns about the collection and use of personal data by social media platforms. | Travelers should be cautious about sharing personal information; platforms must implement robust security measures. |
| Overtourism | The impact of social media on increasing visitor numbers to popular destinations. | Can lead to environmental degradation and strain on local resources; destinations need sustainable tourism strategies. |
| Cultural Sensitivity | Ensuring respectful and sensitive interactions with different cultures. | Avoiding cultural insensitivity and promoting responsible travel behavior is essential for positive interactions. |
| Artificial Intelligence (AI) | The use of AI in content curation and decision-making, potentially leading to bias and over-reliance. | AI-driven content might reinforce biases or limit exposure to diverse information; marketers must ensure ethical AI use and transparency. |

Source (Authors Compilation)

1. Misinformation and Fake Reviews: The prevalence of misinformation and fake reviews on social media can mislead travellers and impact their decisions negatively. It is essential for users to critically evaluate the credibility of sources and be aware of potential biases (Fedeli & Cheng, 2022). Destination marketers also need to ensure transparency and authenticity in their online content.

2. Privacy and Data Security: Social media platforms collect vast amounts of user data, raising concerns about privacy and data security. Travelers should be cautious about sharing personal information online, and social media companies must implement robust security measures to protect user data (Dube & Nhamo, 2020).

3. Overtourism and Environmental Impact: The popularity of certain destinations on social media can contribute to overtourism, leading to environmental degradation and negative impacts on local communities (Vu et al., 2020). Sustainable tourism practices and responsible travel behaviors are crucial to mitigating these effects and ensuring the long-term viability of popular destinations.

4. Cultural Sensitivity and Respect: social media can sometimes lead to cultural insensitivity, as travelers may inadvertently perpetuate stereotypes or engage in disrespectful behaviors. It is important for travelers to approach different cultures with respect and sensitivity, and for destination marketers to promote culturally appropriate practices (Eichelberger et al., 2021).

# 5. CONCLUSION AND FUTURE RECOMMENDATIONS

Social media has fundamentally transformed the landscape of travel decision-making, offering both opportunities and challenges for travelers, destination marketers, and industry stakeholders. The influence of social media on travel is multifaceted, encompassing information search, inspiration, planning, and real-time engagement. Psychological factors, such as social proof, FOMO, and identity construction, further shape travelers' decisions and experiences. While social media platforms provide valuable tools for destination marketing and engagement, it is essential to address challenges related to misinformation, privacy, overtourism, and cultural sensitivity. By understanding and navigating these dynamics, stakeholders can leverage social media to enhance travel experiences and promote sustainable tourism practices.

As the digital landscape continues to evolve, it is viable for the tourism industry to adapt the implementation of artificial intelligence (AI). Inclusion of AI will not only enhance the positive role of social media in travel decision-making but also to address the complexities and ethical challenges associated with the digital transformation of the tourism industry.

*Table 4. Future recommendations and expected impact of its implications*

| Recommendation | Details | Expected Impact |
|---|---|---|
| **Integrate AI and Machine Learning for Enhanced Content Curation** | Utilize AI and machine learning to curate personalized travel content based on user preferences, past behaviors, and emerging trends. | Ensures travelers receive relevant and high-quality content, improving decision-making efficiency. |
| **Develop a Multi-Layered Verification System for User-Generated Content** | Implement a verification system using blockchain and AI-driven sentiment analysis to authenticate reviews and detect misleading content. | Increases trust in user-generated content, reducing the spread of misinformation and enhancing credibility. |
| **Strategically Utilize Influencers to Promote Sustainable and Ethical Tourism** | Engage influencers who are committed to sustainability to create content that educates audiences on responsible travel and aligns with global sustainability goals. | Encourages ethical travel practices, promotes sustainable destinations, and raises awareness among travelers. |
| **Enhance Data Privacy with Decentralized Identity Solutions** | Adopt decentralized identity solutions like Self-Sovereign Identity (SSI) frameworks to give users control over their data while maintaining security. | Builds greater user trust by protecting personal data and ensuring secure, selective information sharing. |
| **Implement Dynamic, Real-Time Decision Support Systems** | Develop systems that integrate live data feeds (e.g., weather, travel restrictions) with AI and user-generated content to support real-time travel decision-making. | Empowers travelers to adapt plans on-the-go, improving flexibility and enhancing overall travel experiences. |

continued on following page

*Table 4. Continued*

| Recommendation | Details | Expected Impact |
|---|---|---|
| **Foster Interdisciplinary Collaboration for Targeted Marketing** | Collaborate with data scientists, psychologists, and cultural experts to create sophisticated marketing campaigns that consider demographics, psychological profiles, and cultural trends. | Ensures more effective and culturally sensitive marketing, leading to better engagement and conversion rates. |
| **Promote Ethical Use of Social Media Data in Academic and Industry Research** | Establish guidelines for the ethical use of social media data, prioritizing transparency, consent, and anonymization in research and industry analysis. | Contributes to the ethical advancement of research and marketing strategies, protecting user privacy. |
| **Promote Authentic and Reliable User-Generated Content** | Encourage the prioritization of verified authentic user-generated content through platform guidelines and community standards. | Enhances the credibility of content shared on social media, aiding travelers in making informed decisions. |
| **Leverage Influencers for Sustainable Tourism Campaigns** | Collaborate with influencers who advocate for sustainable travel practices to reach and educate a broad audience on eco-friendly travel options. | Drives a cultural shift towards responsible tourism, influencing followers to choose sustainable travel options. |
| **Utilize Social Media for Real-Time Traveler Engagement** | Enhance engagement by providing real-time updates, personalized recommendations, and responsive customer service through social media during all phases of travel. | Improves customer satisfaction and loyalty by offering timely, relevant information throughout the travel journey. |
| **Implement Targeted Marketing for Diverse Demographics** | Develop marketing strategies that target different demographic groups on various social media platforms, tailored to their unique preferences and behaviors. | Increases the effectiveness of marketing campaigns, ensuring they resonate with specific audience segments. |

Source (Authors Compilation)

These recommendations are designed to optimize the role of social media in guiding travel decisions, ensuring that it serves as a reliable, ethical, and influential tool in the tourism industry.

# REFERENCES

Abernethy, B. E., Dixon, A. W., Holladay, P. J., & Koo, W. G.-Y. (2022). Determinants of Canadian and US mountain bike tourists' site preferences: Examining the push–pull relationship. *Journal of Sport & Tourism*, 26(3), 249–268. DOI: 10.1080/14775085.2022.2069147

Abidin, C. (2015). Communicative intimacies: Influencers and Perceived Interconnectedness. *Ada: A Journal of Gender. New Media, and Technology*, 11(8), 1–16.

Abou-Shouk, M. A., Mannaa, M. T., & Elbaz, A. M. (2021). Women's empowerment and tourism development: A cross-country study. *Tourism Management Perspectives, 37*(November 2020), 100782. DOI: 10.1016/j.tmp.2020.100782

Akhtar, N., Kim, W. G., Ahmad, W., Akhtar, M. N., Siddiqi, U. I., & Riaz, M. (2019). Mechanisms of consumers' trust development in reviewers' supplementary reviews: A reviewer-reader similarity perspective. *Tourism Management Perspectives*, 31(April), 95–108. DOI: 10.1016/j.tmp.2019.04.001

Ali, F., Yasar, B., Ali, L., & Dogan, S. (2023). Antecedents and consequences of travelers' trust towards personalized travel recommendations offered by ChatGPT. *International Journal of Hospitality Management*, 114(August), 103588. DOI: 10.1016/j.ijhm.2023.103588

Bui, M., Krishen, A. S., Anlamlier, E., & Berezan, O. (2022). Fear of missing out in the digital age: The role of social media satisfaction and advertising engagement. *Psychology and Marketing*, 39(4), 683–693. DOI: 10.1002/mar.21611

Chavez, L., Ruiz, C., Curras, R., & Hernandez, B. (2020). The role of travel motivations and social media use in consumer interactive behaviour: A uses and gratifications perspective. *Sustainability (Basel)*, 12(21), 1–22. DOI: 10.3390/su12218789

Chen, W. K., Silaban, P. H., Hutagalung, W. E., & Silalahi, A. D. K. (2023). How Instagram Influencers Contribute to Consumer Travel Decision: Insights from SEM and fsQCA. *Emerging Science Journal*, 7(1), 16–37. DOI: 10.28991/ESJ-2023-07-01-02

Cheung, M. L., Ting, H., Cheah, J.-H., & Sharipudin, M.-N. S. (2021). Examining the role of social media-based destination brand community in evoking tourists' emotions and intention to co-create and visit. *Journal of Product and Brand Management*, 30(1), 28–43. DOI: 10.1108/JPBM-09-2019-2554

Christensen, J., Hansen, J. M., & Wilson, P. (2024). Understanding the role and impact of Generative Artificial Intelligence (AI) hallucination within consumers' tourism decision-making processes. *Current Issues in Tourism*, 1–16. DOI: 10.1080/13683500.2023.2300032

De Veirman, M., Cauberghe, V., & Hudders, L. (2017). Marketing through Instagram influencers: the impact of number of followers and product divergence on brand attitude. Https://Doi.Org/10.1080/02650487.2017.1348035, *36*(5), 798–828. DOI: 10.1080/02650487.2017.1348035

Delbaere, M., Michael, B., & Phillips, B. J. (2021). Social media influencers: A route to brand engagement for their followers. *Psychology and Marketing*, 38(1), 101–112. DOI: 10.1002/mar.21419

Dellarocas, C. (2003). The Digitization of Word of Mouth: Promise and Challenges of Online Feedback Mechanisms. *Management Science*, 49(10), 1407–1424. DOI: 10.1287/mnsc.49.10.1407.17308

Dey, B., Mathew, J., & Chee-Hua, C. (2020). Influence of destination attractiveness factors and travel motivations on rural homestay choice: The moderating role of need for uniqueness. *International Journal of Culture, Tourism and Hospitality Research*, 14(4), 639–666. DOI: 10.1108/IJCTHR-08-2019-0138

Djafarova, E., & Rushworth, C. (2017). Exploring the credibility of online celebrities' Instagram profiles in influencing the purchase decisions of young female users. *Computers in Human Behavior*, 68, 1–7. DOI: 10.1016/j.chb.2016.11.009

Donthu, N., Kumar, S., Pandey, N., Pandey, N., & Mishra, A. (2021). Mapping the electronic word-of-mouth (eWOM) research: A systematic review and bibliometric analysis. *Journal of Business Research*, 135(February), 758–773. DOI: 10.1016/j.jbusres.2021.07.015

Dube, K., & Nhamo, G. (2020). Vulnerability of nature-based tourism to climate variability and change: Case of Kariba resort town, Zimbabwe. *Journal of Outdoor Recreation and Tourism*, 29, 100281. Advance online publication. DOI: 10.1016/j.jort.2020.100281

Eichelberger, S., Heigl, M., Peters, M., & Pikkemaat, B. (2021). Exploring the role of tourists: Responsible behavior triggered by the covid-19 pandemic. *Sustainability (Basel)*, 13(11), 5774. Advance online publication. DOI: 10.3390/su13115774

Fedeli, G., & Cheng, M. (2022). Influencer Marketing and Tourism: Another Threat To Integrity for the Industry? *Tourism Analysis*, (April). Advance online publication. DOI: 10.3727/108354222X16510114086370

Fotis, J., Buhalis, D., & Rossides, N. (2012). *Social Media Use and Impact during the Holiday Travel Planning Process BT - Information and Communication Technologies in Tourism 2012*. 13–24.

Gaenssle, S., & Budzinski, O. (2021). Stars in social media: New light through old windows? *Journal of Media Business Studies*, 18(2), 79–105. DOI: 10.1080/16522354.2020.1738694

Gong, X., Liuxiao, X., & Xiao, Z. (2022). A dedication-constraint model of consumer switching behavior in mobile payment applications. *Information & Management*, 59(4), 103640. DOI: 10.1016/j.im.2022.103640

Gössling, S., & Scott, D. (2018). The decarbonisation impasse: Global tourism leaders' views on climate change mitigation. *Journal of Sustainable Tourism*, 26(12), 2071–2086. DOI: 10.1080/09669582.2018.1529770

Gretzel, U. (2018). Influencer marketing in travel and tourism. In *Advances in Social Media for Travel, Tourism and Hospitality* (Issue February). Routledge. DOI: 10.4324/9781315565736-13

Gulati, S. (2022). Social and sustainable: Exploring social media use for promoting sustainable behaviour and demand amongst Indian tourists. *International Hospitality Review*, 36(2), 373–393. DOI: 10.1108/IHR-12-2020-0072

Gursoy, D., Li, Y., & Song, H. (2023). ChatGPT and the hospitality and tourism industry: An overview of current trends and future research directions. *Journal of Hospitality Marketing & Management*, 32(5), 579–592. DOI: 10.1080/19368623.2023.2211993

Hudders, L., De Jans, S., & De Veirman, M. (2021). The commercialization of social media stars: A literature review and conceptual framework on the strategic use of social media influencers. *International Journal of Advertising*, 40(3), 327–375. DOI: 10.1080/02650487.2020.1836925

Joseph, A. I., & Anandkumar, V. (2021). Destination Brand Communication during COVID-19 Pandemic - The Case of Iceland. *International Journal of Hospitality and Tourism Systems*, 14, 44–58.

Kabadayi, S., Ali, F., Choi, H., Joosten, H., & Lu, C. (2019). Smart service experience in hospitality and tourism services: A conceptualization and future research agenda. *Journal of Service Management*, 30(3), 326–348. DOI: 10.1108/JOSM-11-2018-0377

Kaplan, A. M., & Haenlein, M. (2010). Users of the world, unite! The challenges and opportunities of Social Media. *Business Horizons*, 53(1), 59–68. DOI: 10.1016/j.bushor.2009.09.003

Kapoor, P. S., Balaji, M. S., Jiang, Y., & Jebarajakirthy, C. (2022). Effectiveness of Travel Social Media Influencers: A Case of Eco-Friendly Hotels. *Journal of Travel Research*, 61(5), 1138–1155. DOI: 10.1177/00472875211019469

Ki, C. W., Cuevas, L. M., Chong, S. M., & Lim, H. (2020). Influencer marketing: Social media influencers as human brands attaching to followers and yielding positive marketing results by fulfilling needs. *Journal of Retailing and Consumer Services*, 55(April), 102133. DOI: 10.1016/j.jretconser.2020.102133

Kim, D. Y., & Kim, H.-Y. (2021). Trust me, trust me not: A nuanced view of influencer marketing on social media. *Journal of Business Research, 134*(November 2019), 223–232. DOI: 10.1016/j.jbusres.2021.05.024

Kim, J., & Fesenmaier, D. R. (2017). Sharing Tourism Experiencess: The post-trip experience. *Journal of Travel Research*, 56(1), 28–40. DOI: 10.1177/0047287515620491

Kumar, P., Mishra, J. M., & Rao, Y. V. (2022). Analysing tourism destination promotion through Facebook by Destination Marketing Organizations of India. *Current Issues in Tourism*, 25(9), 1416–1431. DOI: 10.1080/13683500.2021.1921713

Lee, S., & Kim, E. (2020). Influencer marketing on Instagram: How sponsorship disclosure, influencer credibility, and brand credibility impact the effectiveness of Instagram promotional post. *Journal of Global Fashion Marketing*, 11(3), 232–249. DOI: 10.1080/20932685.2020.1752766

Li, F., Shang, Y., & Su, Q. (2022). The influence of immersion on tourists' satisfaction via perceived attractiveness and happiness. *Tourism Review*. Advance online publication. DOI: 10.1108/TR-02-2022-0078

Liu, Y., Yu, C., & Damberg, S. (2022). Exploring the drivers and consequences of the "awe" emotion in outdoor sports – a study using the latest partial least squares structural equation modeling technique and necessary condition analysis. *International Journal of Sports Marketing & Sponsorship*, 23(2), 278–294. DOI: 10.1108/IJSMS-12-2020-0232

Masuda, H., Han, S. H., & Lee, J. (2022). Impacts of influencer attributes on purchase intentions in social media influencer marketing: Mediating roles of characterizations. *Technological Forecasting and Social Change, 174*(October 2020), 121246. DOI: 10.1016/j.techfore.2021.121246

Minazzi, R., & Mauri, A. G. (2015). Mobile Technologies Effects on Travel Behaviours and Experiences: A Preliminary Analysis. In Tussyadiah, I., & Inversini, A. (Eds.), *Information and Communication Technologies in Tourism 2015* (pp. 507–521). Springer International Publishing., DOI: 10.1007/978-3-319-14343-9_37

Molinillo, S., Anaya-Sánchez, R., Morrison, A. M., & Coca-Stefaniak, J. A. (2019). Smart city communication via social media: Analysing residents' and visitors' engagement. *Cities (London, England)*, 94, 247–255. DOI: 10.1016/j.cities.2019.06.003

Moreno-Manzo, J., Gassiot-Melian, A., & Coromina, L. (2022). Perceived value in a UNESCO World Heritage Site: The case of Quito, Ecuador. *Journal of Cultural Heritage Management and Sustainable Development*. Advance online publication. DOI: 10.1108/JCHMSD-03-2022-0049

Moro, S., Rita, P., & Vala, B. (2016). Predicting social media performance metrics and evaluation of the impact on brand building: A data mining approach. *Journal of Business Research*, 69(9), 3341–3351. DOI: 10.1016/j.jbusres.2016.02.010

Namisango, F., Kang, K., & Rehman, J. (2019). What do we know about social media in nonprofits? A review. *Proceedings of the 23rd Pacific Asia Conference on Information Systems: Secure ICT Platform for the 4th Industrial Revolution, PACIS 2019, 10*, 27–36.

Omo-Obas, P., & Anning-Dorson, T. (2022). Cognitive-affective-motivation factors influencing international visitors' destination satisfaction and loyalty. *Journal of Hospitality and Tourism Insights*. DOI: 10.1108/JHTI-05-2022-0178

Ouariti, O. Z., & Jebrane, E. M. (2020). The impact of transport infrastructure on tourism destination attractiveness: A case study of Marrakesh City, Morocco. *African Journal of Hospitality, Tourism and Leisure*, 9(2), 1–18.

Pike, S., Pontes, N., & Kotsi, F. (2021). Stopover destination attractiveness: A quasi-experimental approach. *Journal of Destination Marketing & Management*, 19, 100514. Advance online publication. DOI: 10.1016/j.jdmm.2020.100514

Pop, R. A., Săplăcan, Z., Dabija, D. C., & Alt, M. A. (2021). The impact of social media influencers on travel decisions: The role of trust in consumer decision journey. *Current Issues in Tourism*, 25(5), 823–843. DOI: 10.1080/13683500.2021.1895729

Rasul, T., Zaman, U., & Hoque, M. R. (2020). Examining the pulse of the tourism industry in the Asia-Pacific Region. *Umer Zaman.*, 26(1), 173–193.

Saini, H., Kumar, P., & Oberoi, S. (2023). Welcome to the destination! Social media influencers as cogent determinant of travel decision: A systematic literature review and conceptual framework. *Cogent Social Sciences*, 9(1), 2240055. Advance online publication. DOI: 10.1080/23311886.2023.2240055

Seyidov, J., & Adomaitienė, R. (2016). Factors Influencing Local Tourists' Decision-making on Choosing a Destination: A Case of Azerbaijan. *Ekonomika (Nis)*, 95(3), 112–127. DOI: 10.15388/Ekon.2016.3.10332

Solazzo, G., Maruccia, Y., Lorenzo, G., Ndou, V., Del Vecchio, P., & Elia, G. (2022). Extracting insights from big social data for smarter tourism destination management. *Measuring Business Excellence*, 26(1), 122–140. DOI: 10.1108/MBE-11-2020-0156

Sota, S., Chaudhry, H., & Srivastava, M. K. (2020). Customer relationship management research in hospitality industry: A review and classification. *Journal of Hospitality Marketing & Management*, 29(1), 39–64. DOI: 10.1080/19368623.2019.1595255

Stylos, N., Zwiegelaar, J., & Buhalis, D. (2021). Big data empowered agility for dynamic, volatile, and time-sensitive service industries: The case of tourism sector. *International Journal of Contemporary Hospitality Management*, 33(3), 1015–1036. DOI: 10.1108/IJCHM-07-2020-0644

Thomaz, G. M., Biz, A. A., Bettoni, E. M., Mendes-Filho, L., & Buhalis, D. (2017). Content mining framework in social media: A FIFA world cup 2014 case analysis. *Information & Management*, 54(6), 786–801. DOI: 10.1016/j.im.2016.11.005

Tran, N. L., & Rudolf, W. (2022). Social Media and Destination Branding in Tourism: A Systematic Review of the Literature. *Sustainability (Basel)*, 14(20), 13528. Advance online publication. DOI: 10.3390/su142013528

Türk, U., Östh, J., Kourtit, K., & Nijkamp, P. (2021). The path of least resistance explaining tourist mobility patterns in destination areas using Airbnb data. *Journal of Transport Geography*, 94, 103130. Advance online publication. DOI: 10.1016/j.jtrangeo.2021.103130

Villacé-Molinero, T., Fernández-Muñoz, J. J., Muñoz-Mazón, A. I., Flecha-Barrio, M. D., & Fuentes-Moraleda, L. (2023). Holiday travel intention in a crisis scenario: A comparative analysis of Spain's main source markets. *Tourism Review*, 78(1), 18–41. DOI: 10.1108/TR-03-2022-0131

Vu, H. Q., Muskat, B., Li, G., & Law, R. (2020). Improving the resident–tourist relationship in urban hotspots. *Journal of Sustainable Tourism*, 29(4), 595–615. DOI: 10.1080/09669582.2020.1818087

Wellman, M. L., Stoldt, R., Tully, M., & Ekdale, B. (2020). Ethics of Authenticity: Social Media Influencers and the Production of Sponsored Content. *Journal of Medical Ethics*, 35(2), 68–82. DOI: 10.1080/23736992.2020.1736078

Wismantoro, Y., Aryanto, V. D. W., Pamungkas, I. D., Purusa, N. A., Amron, , Chasanah, A. N., & Usman, . (2023). Virtual Reality Destination Experiences Model: A Moderating Variable between Wisesa Sustainable Tourism Behavior and Tourists' Intention to Visit. *Sustainability (Basel)*, 15(1), 446. Advance online publication. DOI: 10.3390/su15010446

World Economic Forum. (2019). The Travel and Tourism Competitiveness Report 2019. *World Economic Forum.*

World Travel & Tourism Council (WTTC). (2022). *Travel & Tourism Economic Impact 2022.* World Travel & Tourism Council.

World Travel & Tourism Council (WTTC). (2023). *Global Economic Impact & Trends 2023.* World Travel & Tourism Council.

Wu, Y.-W., Liao, T.-H., Yeh, S.-P., & Huang, H.-C. (2022). Switching Intention and Behaviors to Wetland Ecotourism after the COVID-19 Pandemic: The Perspective of Push-Pull-Mooring Model. *Sustainability (Basel)*, 14(10), 6198. Advance online publication. DOI: 10.3390/su14106198

Xiang, Z., Wang, D., O'Leary, J. T., & Fesenmaier, D. R. (2015). Adapting to the Internet: Trends in Travelers' Use of the Web for Trip Planning. *Journal of Travel Research*, 54(4), 511–527. DOI: 10.1177/0047287514522883

Xu, H., Cheung, L. T. O., Lovett, J., Duan, X., Pei, Q., & Liang, D. (2023). Understanding the influence of user-generated content on tourist loyalty behavior in a cultural World Heritage Site. *Tourism Recreation Research*, 48(2), 173–187. DOI: 10.1080/02508281.2021.1913022

Yamagishi, K., Canayong, D., Domingo, M., Maneja, K. N., Montolo, A., & Siton, A. (2023). User-generated content on Gen Z tourist visit intention: A stimulus-organism-response approach. *Journal of Hospitality and Tourism Insights*, 34. Advance online publication. DOI: 10.1108/JHTI-02-2023-0091

Yuan, Y., Chan, C. S., Eichelberger, S., Ma, H., & Pikkemaat, B. (2022). The effect of social media on travel planning process by Chinese tourists: the way forward to tourism futures. *Journal of Tourism Futures*, 1–20. DOI: 10.1108/JTF-04-2021-0094

# Chapter 12
# From Search to Stay:
## Mapping the Digital Journey of the Modern Traveler

**Bassam Samir Al-Romeedy**

*Faculty of Tourism and Hotels, University of Sadat City, Egypt*

**Amrik Singh**

https://orcid.org/0000-0003-3598-8787

*School of Hotel Management and Tourism, Lovely Professional University, India*

## ABSTRACT

*This chapter investigates the evolving digital journey of contemporary travelers, focusing on how technology and data-driven insights have reshaped travel experiences. It explores the transition from traditional to digital platforms in travel planning, booking, and in-destination activities, emphasizing the traits of today's tech-savvy travelers. By examining consumer behavior across various groups—including millennials, Gen Z, and business travelers—the chapter highlights the growing significance of user-generated content, mobile-first experiences, and tools for real-time decision-making. It also investigates how travelers engage with digital platforms during the pre-travel phase for research and inspiration, the booking process, and the period before arrival, as well as throughout their trip and in post-travel reflections. Additionally, the chapter critically analyzes the role of data analytics, big data, AI, and machine learning in understanding and forecasting traveler behavior.*

DOI: 10.4018/979-8-3693-3972-5.ch012

## INTRODUCTION

Digital advancements have fundamentally transformed the travel industry, shifting how travelers plan, book, experience, and share their journeys. Traditionally reliant on travel agencies, brochures, and guidebooks, today's travelers increasingly use digital platforms such as search engines, social media, and online booking systems at every stage of their journey (Al-Romeedy & Hashem, 2024; Ivanov & Webster, 2019). These modern travelers are tech-savvy, resourceful, and highly connected, preferring digital methods over traditional ones for making informed travel decisions based on UGC, peer reviews, and influencer opinions. In response, the travel industry has rapidly adapted to meet their expectations for seamless, personalized, and mobile-first experiences (Pirolli, 2018; Neidhardt & Wörndl, 2020).

Over the past decade, the travel industry has experienced a significant shift from traditional to digital platforms, with travelers now using online travel agencies (OTAs), direct booking sites, and comparison websites for trip planning and booking. This digital transformation has democratized travel by providing consumers with greater control and choice, and it has revolutionized the travel experience through technology that offers personalized and convenient services. Modern digital travelers, particularly Millennials and Gen Z, rely heavily on technology for enhanced travel experiences, using online reviews, social media, and mobile apps for instant booking, itinerary management, and personalized recommendations. This trend underscores the growing importance of technology at every stage of the travel journey (Al-Romeedy, 2024a; Tjostheim & Waterworth, 2022; Benckendorff et al., 2019; Wörndl et al., 2021).

The digital journey in travel begins well before the trip, with travelers increasingly relying on search engines, social media, and online platforms for inspiration and information gathering. Online reviews, influencer content, and social media heavily influence travelers' choices, with recommendation algorithms using big data to provide personalized suggestions based on past behavior (Ferrer-Rosell et al., 2023; Cotton et al., 2020). In the booking phase, travelers finalize their trip details using OTAs, direct booking platforms, and comparison sites, with decisions driven by price, convenience, and trust (Anda et al., 2021; Al-Romeedy, 2024b). The pre-arrival phase sets expectations through digital communication, including emails, mobile apps, and social media, and is enhanced by technologies like virtual tours and augmented reality (AR), which help visualize the trip (Tjostheim & Waterworth, 2023; Zhang, 2023). During the trip, travelers continuously interact with digital tools like mobile apps for navigation, real-time updates, and social media sharing, improving their overall experience (Benckendorff et al., 2019; Gaafar & Al-Romeedy, 2024b). Post-travel, the digital journey continues as travelers share their experiences online, influencing future travelers and destination marketing strategies (Choi et al., 2022; Pencarelli, 2020).

Data analytics is essential in mapping the digital traveler's journey. Businesses use big data, AI, and machine learning to predict behavior and personalize offerings, but must also address privacy and consent concerns (Stienmetz et al., 2022; Tjostheim & Waterworth, 2022). Adapting to the digital traveler poses both challenges and opportunities. The digital divide and privacy issues are significant hurdles, but emerging technologies like blockchain, virtual reality, and AI offer innovative ways to enhance the travel experience. Businesses that embrace these technologies will be better positioned in the competitive travel market (Fan et al., 2024; Zhang, 2023; Hsu, 2021; Li, 2023).

The digital journey of the modern traveler is complex, shaped by various digital tools and platforms. Understanding this journey allows tourism businesses to craft personalized, engaging marketing strategies that meet the needs of today's tech-savvy travelers. As the industry evolves, digital experiences and expectations will continue to shape the future of travel.

## Overview of the Modern Traveler's Digital Journey

### The Shift From Traditional to Digital Platforms in Planning and Booking Travel

Over the past few decades, the travel industry has experienced a significant digital transformation, radically changing the way people plan, book, and experience their journeys. This transformation has been fueled by rapid technological advancements, particularly the widespread use of the internet, mobile devices, and digital platforms. Once dominated by brick-and-mortar agencies and printed guidebooks, the industry has shifted to a more dynamic, digital-first model. This evolution has given travelers unprecedented access to information, allowing them to make informed decisions, personalize their experiences, and engage with travel services in ways that were previously unimaginable. The digital transformation in travel is not merely about adopting new technologies; it represents a fundamental rethinking of the entire travel experience to meet the expectations and behaviors of today's travelers (Al-Romeedy, 2024a; Pirolli, 2018).

The move from traditional to digital platforms stands out as one of the most impactful changes in the travel industry. In the past, travelers heavily depended on travel agents, printed brochures, and word-of-mouth recommendations to plan their trips. Booking a flight, reserving a hotel room, or arranging a tour often involved visiting a travel agency or making lengthy phone calls. However, the emergence of OTAs, metasearch engines, and direct booking platforms has revolutionized this process. Today, travelers can plan and book their entire trip from the comfort of their homes using a computer or smartphone (Tjostheim & Waterworth, 2023; Van Nuenen & Scarles, 2021).

Digital platforms have democratized travel planning, offering travelers a vast array of options at their fingertips. They can compare prices across multiple websites, read reviews from fellow travelers, and access detailed information about destinations, accommodations, and activities. This transparency and convenience have led to a major shift in consumer behavior, with more travelers choosing to book online rather than through traditional channels. Additionally, the rise of mobile apps and AI-driven recommendation systems has simplified the process of finding options that match travelers' preferences and budgets, further accelerating the shift towards digital platforms (Rahimi et al., 2020; Cai et al., 2020).

## Characteristics of the Modern Digital Traveler

The modern digital traveler has emerged as a result of the extensive digital transformation, defined by their technological proficiency, self-reliance, and desire for personalized experiences. Unlike previous generations who might have depended on travel agents to organize their trips, today's travelers prefer to manage their own plans, utilizing digital tools to customize every aspect of their journey. These travelers are well-informed, often conducting thorough online research before making any decisions. This research typically involves reviewing UGC such as reviews, blogs, and social media posts, which significantly influence their perceptions and choices.

Today's digital travelers are also highly mobile, relying heavily on smartphones and other devices not only for booking but also for navigating destinations, discovering local attractions, and staying connected with friends and family. They expect seamless, on-demand services that can be accessed at any time and from any place. This includes features such as instant booking, mobile check-ins, real-time flight updates, and personalized recommendations for dining and entertainment. These travelers prioritize convenience, speed, and personalization, and they are more likely to engage with brands that can provide these experiences through digital channels (Gaafar & Al-Romeedy, 2024b).

## Technology's Role in Revolutionizing the Travel Experience

Technology has been the primary catalyst in revolutionizing the travel experience. From the initial inspiration phase to post-travel reflection, technology has become embedded in every stage of the traveler's journey. During the planning phase, search engines, social media, and online platforms offer travelers endless sources of inspiration and information. AI-powered recommendation algorithms assist travelers in discovering destinations and activities that align with their interests, while metasearch engines and OTAs simplify the booking process by aggregating options and providing comparison tools. Throughout the travel experience, technology continues to play a vital role. Mobile apps give travelers access to real-time information, GPS navigation, and services like ride-sharing, dining reservations, and ticket purchases. VR and AR technologies are also enhancing pre-travel expectations by allowing travelers to virtually explore destinations before their arrival. At the destination, digital services such as mobile check-ins, e-tickets, and digital wallets make the travel experience more convenient and efficient. After their journey, technology enables travelers to share their experiences through social media, blogs, and online reviews. This UGC not only influences potential travelers but also provides valuable feedback to travel businesses, helping them refine their services. Furthermore, data analytics and big data are empowering travel companies to gain deeper insights into traveler behavior, allowing them to tailor marketing efforts and improve customer satisfaction.

The digital transformation has dramatically reshaped every aspect of travel, creating a new type of traveler who is more informed, connected, and demanding than ever before. The journey of the modern digital traveler is marked by the seamless integration of technology at every stage, from planning and booking to experiencing and sharing. As technology continues to advance, it is likely to further enhance the travel experience, offering even higher levels of personalization, convenience, and engagement (Pesonen & Neidhardt, 2019; Pencarelli, 2020).

## Consumer Behavior and Preferences

### Understanding the Behavior of Different Traveler Segments in the Digital Space

The digital transformation of the travel industry has led to the emergence of distinct traveler segments, each with specific behaviors and preferences. Recognizing these segments—such as millennials, Gen Z, and business travelers—is crucial for developing targeted marketing strategies and enhancing the customer experience. Millennials, in particular, are digital natives who heavily rely on digital platforms throughout their travel journey, from inspiration to sharing experiences. They are influenced by social media, value personalized and seamless online interactions, and prioritize sustainability, often seeking eco-friendly travel options and transparency from brands about their environmental impact (Choi et al., 2022; Fan et al., 2024).

Gen Z travelers, who are even more digitally immersed than millennials, represent the future of travel. This group is highly active on social media, especially on platforms like Instagram, TikTok, and Snapchat, where visual and short-form content prevails. Gen Z is known for its quick decision-making and desire for instant gratification, making them more inclined to use mobile apps and on-demand services for travel planning and booking. They are also more likely to be influenced by digital influencers and peer recommendations, valuing authenticity and social proof when making travel decisions. Gen Z travelers expect hyper-personalization and are attracted to brands that provide seamless, tech-driven experiences that align with their fast-paced, digitally connected lifestyles. In contrast, business travelers prioritize efficiency, convenience, and reliability. This segment often travels frequently and relies on digital tools to optimize their travel experience. Business travelers commonly use mobile apps to manage their itineraries, check in for flights, book last-minute accommodations, and navigate unfamiliar destinations. They value features like loyalty programs, expedited services, and access to premium amenities, all of which can be managed through digital platforms. For business travelers, time is a critical factor, and they prefer services that offer quick, seamless, and dependable experiences with minimal interruptions.

By understanding the specific behaviors and preferences of these different traveler segments, travel brands can tailor their offerings and marketing strategies accordingly. Addressing the unique needs and expectations of each segment allows brands to build stronger relationships with their customers and enhance their overall travel experience (Van Nuenen & Scarles, 2021; Rahimi et al., 2020; Cai et al., 2020; Hsu, 2021).

## The Importance of User-Generated Content and Peer Reviews in Influencing Travel Decisions

User-generated content (UGC) and peer reviews have become pivotal in the decision-making process for today's travelers. As trust in traditional advertising diminishes, travelers increasingly rely on content produced by their peers—such as reviews, social media posts, and blogs—for authentic and unbiased insights into destinations, accommodations, and activities. UGC, especially in the form of social media content and travel blogs, plays a significant role in inspiring and influencing potential travelers. Visual content, like photos and videos shared by other travelers, often serves as a powerful motivator, helping prospective tourists envision their own experiences and sparking a desire to visit specific destinations. Platforms such as Instagram and Pinterest are particularly influential, as they enable users to discover destinations through visually engaging content, often prompting spontaneous travel decisions.

Peer reviews, commonly found on platforms like TripAdvisor, Google Reviews, and Yelp, are another crucial component in travel decision-making. These reviews offer travelers insights into others' experiences, aiding them in making more informed choices. Reviews typically cover various aspects, including service quality, cleanliness, accuracy of descriptions, and value for money. The perceived authenticity of peer reviews is highly valued, as they are seen as trustworthy sources of information that reflect real experiences, devoid of the biases often present in marketing materials (Al-Romeedy, 2024a; Cotton et al., 2020).

The influence of UGC and peer reviews extends beyond individual decisions; it also shapes broader consumer trends. Positive reviews and compelling UGC can significantly enhance a destination's or business's visibility and reputation, leading to increased bookings and revenue. On the other hand, negative reviews can dissuade potential customers and damage a brand's reputation. Consequently, many travel businesses actively encourage satisfied customers to share their experiences online and respond promptly and professionally to reviews—whether positive or negative.

In an era where consumers are inundated with information, UGC and peer reviews offer clarity and reassurance, guiding travelers toward choices that meet their expectations and preferences. For travel brands, leveraging UGC and maintaining a strong online reputation are essential components of a successful digital marketing strategy (Wörndl et al., 2021; Ferrer-Rosell et al., 2023; Pirolli, 2018; Ivanov & Webster, 2019).

## The Shift Towards Mobile-First Experiences and the Rise of Instant Booking and On-Demand Services

The advent of mobile technology has dramatically altered how travelers engage with travel brands, leading to a pronounced shift toward mobile-first experiences. As smartphones become more integral to daily life, travelers now expect to manage every aspect of their journey through their mobile devices—from researching destinations to booking services and navigating while on the move. Mobile-first experiences are tailored to the demands of contemporary travelers, who prioritize convenience, speed, and accessibility. Mobile apps have emerged as essential tools for travel planning, offering features like flight tracking, accommodation booking, itinerary management, and local recommendations. These apps are designed with user-friendly interfaces and functionalities, allowing travelers to quickly and easily access the information and services they need with just a few taps.

A major advancement in mobile travel technology is the proliferation of instant booking and on-demand services. Travelers are no longer required to meticulously plan every detail of their trip in advance; they can now book flights, hotels, and activities at the last minute, often securing the best available rates. This flexibility is particularly attractive to younger travelers, who prefer spontaneous travel and are less inclined to stick to rigid itineraries. Mobile apps such as Booking.com, Airbnb, and Skyscanner have capitalized on this trend by offering instant booking options and real-time availability updates (Gaafar & Al-Romeedy, 2024a; Neidhardt & Wörndl, 2020).

On-demand services, including ride-sharing apps like Uber and Lyft, food delivery services such as DoorDash and Uber Eats, and concierge services, have also become integral to the travel experience. These services allow travelers to quickly and conveniently access transportation, meals, and other amenities, enhancing their overall travel experience. The ability to access these services instantly, often with the benefit of location-based recommendations, has made mobile devices indispensable for modern travelers. The shift toward mobile-first experiences is further evidenced by the increasing importance of mobile-optimized websites and responsive design. Travel brands that do not provide a seamless mobile experience risk losing customers to competitors who prioritize mobile accessibility. Consequently, optimizing websites for mobile use—ensuring fast load times, intuitive navigation, and secure transactions—has become a crucial aspect of any travel brand's digital strategy.

As consumer behavior and preferences in the digital realm continue to evolve rapidly due to technological advancements and shifting expectations, it is essential for travel brands to understand and cater to the distinct needs and preferences of different traveler segments, from millennials and Gen Z to business travelers. UGC and peer reviews play a significant role in influencing decision-making, while the transition to mobile-first experiences and the rise of instant booking and on-demand services have redefined the travel experience. To remain competitive, travel brands must adapt to these changes, leveraging digital tools and strategies to meet the demands of today's tech-savvy travelers (Li, 2023; Al-Romeedy & Hashem, 2024).

## The Modern Travel Journey

### The Pre-Travel Phase: Search and Inspiration

The pre-travel phase is essential in a traveler's journey, where excitement and curiosity about a potential trip begin to take shape. During this phase, travelers extensively use digital tools like search engines, social media, and online platforms for inspiration and information gathering. Search engines such as Google are pivotal for initial trip planning, helping travelers explore broad queries and discover detailed resources like travel blogs and destination guides. Social media platforms, particularly Instagram, Pinterest, and YouTube, significantly influence the inspiration phase by offering visually driven content, user-generated posts, and virtual glimpses of destinations. These platforms help travelers explore, organize, and refine their travel plans (Pesonen & Neidhardt, 2019; Al-Romeedy, 2024b; Al-Romeedy & Hashem, 2024; Anda et al., 2021).

Online platforms like travel blogs, forums (e.g., TripAdvisor), and booking websites (e.g., Expedia, Booking.com) further contribute to the information-gathering process. These platforms offer a mix of professional content, user reviews, and expert recommendations, providing travelers with a well-rounded perspective on potential destinations. Forums and discussion boards enable travelers to ask questions, share experiences, and gather insights from others who have visited the destinations they are considering.

The integration of search engines, social media, and online platforms offers travelers a wide array of resources to fuel their inspiration and inform their decisions. This digital ecosystem allows travelers to explore destinations from various perspectives, compare options, and form a mental picture of their potential trip before finalizing any plans (Neidhardt & Wörndl, 2020; Ivanov & Webster, 2019).

During the pre-travel phase, online reviews, influencer content, and social media have a significant impact, often acting as the key factors in selecting a travel destination. Modern travelers highly value the experiences and opinions of others, particularly those shared on digital platforms. Online reviews on websites like TripAdvisor, Google Reviews, and Yelp play a crucial role in shaping travelers' perceptions of various destinations, accommodations, and attractions. These reviews provide honest feedback from other travelers, pointing out both the highlights and potential downsides of a location. For many, the quantity and quality of reviews greatly influence their decisions. Destinations with numerous positive reviews and high ratings are more likely to be chosen, while negative reviews can dissuade potential visitors. The credibility of peer reviews lies in the belief that they offer unbiased and genuine insights, making them a trusted resource for travelers seeking dependable information (Gaafar & Al-Romeedy, 2024a; Wörndl et al., 2021).

Influencer content on social media is another major factor in destination selection. Travel influencers, who have garnered large followings by sharing their travel adventures, often set trends and act as reliable sources of inspiration. Their content, usually featuring high-quality visuals and compelling stories, vividly captures the essence of various destinations. Influencers frequently introduce their audience to lesser-known locations or unique experiences, expanding the horizons of their followers. The authenticity and relatability of influencers make their recommendations particularly persuasive, especially among younger travelers who are inclined to follow and replicate the experiences of their favorite influencers.

Social media platforms like Instagram, Facebook, and TikTok enhance the influence of both reviews and influencer content by making it easy to discover and share. A single viral post or popular hashtag can rapidly boost a destination's visibility, attracting the interest of countless potential travelers. The interactive nature of social media allows users to engage directly with content, whether by commenting, sharing, or creating their own posts, which further spreads awareness of a destination. The combination of visual appeal, peer endorsement, and the immediacy of social media creates a powerful tool for influencing destination choice.

Together, online reviews, influencer content, and social media have revolutionized how travelers select their destinations. These digital elements provide a sense of authenticity and social validation, helping travelers make well-informed decisions that match their preferences and expectations (Ferrer-Rosell et al., 2023; Al-Romeedy & Hashem, 2024).

Personalization and recommendation algorithms are pivotal in guiding travelers through the vast online information landscape. These technologies leverage data from past searches, online behavior, and individual preferences to offer tailored suggestions for destinations, accommodations, and activities. Platforms like Google, Amazon, Netflix, and travel sites such as Airbnb and Booking.com use these algorithms to present options aligned with user interests, making the trip planning process more efficient. For instance, if a traveler frequently searches for beach destinations or luxury hotels, algorithms will highlight these preferences in their suggestions. Personalization extends to website experiences and email marketing, where content and offers are customized based on user interactions, enhancing the overall user experience and streamlining the discovery process (Benckendorff et al., 2019; Cotton et al., 2020; Stienmetz et al., 2022; Tjostheim & Waterworth, 2022).

Personalization in travel planning enhances efficiency and enjoyment by presenting options tailored to individual preferences, reducing decision fatigue and increasing booking likelihood. It also strengthens the connection between travelers and brands, fostering brand loyalty. Personalization and recommendation algorithms drive engagement and conversion rates for travel brands by consistently offering relevant suggestions, making travelers more likely to return for future bookings. The pre-travel phase involves dynamic interactions with search engines, social media, and online platforms, where online reviews and influencer content provide trusted insights. Personalization further refines travel choices, creating a seamless and satisfying planning experience (Gaafar & Al-Romeedy, 2024b; Anda et al., 2021).

## The Booking Process: Online Decision-Making

The transition from inspiration to action is a pivotal stage in travel planning, where travelers move from exploring potential destinations to making concrete booking decisions. This phase involves narrowing down options based on personal preferences, budget, and needs, using information gathered from search engines, social media, reviews, and recommendations. Travelers revisit the platforms that initially intrigued them with a focused approach, comparing accommodations, flights, and activities to ensure they receive the best value and experience. The decision-making process relies on detailed information such as pricing, availability, location, amenities, and customer feedback to ensure a satisfying travel outcome (Tjostheim & Waterworth, 2023; Rahimi et al., 2020).

This decision-making process is increasingly facilitated by digital tools that streamline and simplify the booking process. For instance, metasearch engines and comparison websites enable travelers to quickly compare prices across various platforms, filter results according to their preferences, and access real-time availability. These tools provide clarity and confidence in the decision-making process by presenting all available options in an organized manner, thus aiding travelers in making well-informed choices (Zhang, 2023; Fan et al., 2024).

OTAs, direct booking platforms, and comparison websites are central to the online booking process, each offering distinct advantages that impact traveler choices. OTAs like Expedia, Booking.com, and Travelocity provide a comprehensive array of options for flights, hotels, and travel packages, allowing travelers to compare and book multiple components of their trip in one place. The convenience of managing all bookings through a single platform, along with additional perks such as loyalty programs, bundled deals, and last-minute discounts, makes OTAs appealing to many travelers, particularly those seeking efficiency and value (Van Nuenen & Scarles, 2021; Hsu, 2021; Cai et al., 2020).

Direct booking platforms, including hotel websites and airline apps, offer travelers the chance to book directly with service providers. This method is often chosen for the potential benefits of exclusive offers, better rates, or added perks like free upgrades and flexible cancellation policies. Direct bookings can be perceived as more secure and reliable, eliminating intermediary fees and often resulting in more competitive pricing or enhanced customer service. Providers use strategies like price-match guarantees, member-only rates, and personalized offers to encourage direct bookings (Al-Romeedy, 2024a; Neidhardt & Wörndl, 2020; Li, 2023).

Comparison websites like Kayak, Skyscanner, and Trivago aggregate data from multiple OTAs and booking sites, enabling travelers to efficiently compare prices and options. These platforms are especially beneficial for price-sensitive travelers, offering features to filter results by criteria such as price, location, and amenities, thereby enhancing transparency and personalization in decision-making. Key factors influencing booking decisions include price, promotional offers, discounts, and bundled packages, with many travelers prioritizing cost savings. Comparison websites and OTAs play a crucial role by providing tools to find the best deals and ensuring well-informed choices (Gaafar & Al-Romeedy, 2024a; Ivanov & Webster, 2019; Ferrer-Rosell et al., 2023).

Convenience and trust are pivotal in the travel booking process. Travelers prefer platforms that offer a seamless experience, including features like booking multiple trip components in one transaction, real-time availability, and secure payment options. Mobile apps enhance convenience by enabling on-the-go bookings and last-minute decisions, with instant confirmation, easy cancellations, and 24/7 customer support further improving the experience (Al-Romeedy & Hashem, 2024; Wörndl et al., 2021). Trust, established through the reputation of the booking platform, reliable customer reviews, and transparent pricing, is crucial for ensuring travelers feel confident in their bookings. Platforms that provide a reliable and transparent booking process are more likely to gain trust, leading to repeat business and positive referrals, especially for high-value bookings (Tjostheim & Waterworth, 2022; Benckendorff et al., 2019).

Additionally, other factors such as location, amenities, and flexible booking terms (e.g., cancellation policies) also affect booking decisions. Travelers might choose a more expensive option if it offers a prime location or desirable amenities, such as free breakfast or a swimming pool. The flexibility to cancel or modify bookings without penalties can also influence decisions, particularly for travelers who value adaptability.

Overall, the online booking process is influenced by a combination of price, convenience, and trust. The range of available booking platforms—OTAs, direct booking sites, and comparison websites—empowers travelers to make choices that best meet their preferences and needs, guiding them from inspiration to action and enhancing their overall travel experience (Cotton et al., 2020; Stienmetz et al., 2022).

## The Pre-Arrival Stage: Building Expectations

The pre-arrival phase of the travel experience is crucial for building anticipation and managing expectations. Digital communication plays a key role during this period, with emails, mobile apps, and social media serving as primary channels for travel brands to provide essential information and updates. Emails, in particular, are effective for delivering booking confirmations, itineraries, packing advice, and travel warnings, helping travelers prepare and feel confident. Personalized communications, such as tailored emails with specific details like weather updates and local events, enhance the traveler's experience and strengthen their connection with the brand (Pesonen & Neidhardt, 2019; Gaafar & Al-Romeedy, 2024b).

Mobile apps are vital for managing pre-arrival expectations, offering features like booking information, real-time updates, and direct customer service interactions. These apps provide conveniences such as check-in options and digital boarding passes, and use push notifications to remind travelers of important details, reducing stress and enhancing preparedness. Additionally, social media platforms like

Facebook, Instagram, and Twitter allow travel brands to share inspiring content and engage with travelers, addressing queries and generating excitement. Effective digital communication through these channels helps set expectations, build trust, and enrich the travel experience, ultimately contributing to traveler satisfaction (Choi et al., 2022; Fan et al., 2024).

In recent years, digital innovations such as virtual tours and AR have greatly enriched the pre-travel experience, enabling travelers to visualize and explore their destination before arrival. These technologies are crucial in shaping pre-travel expectations, offering travelers a preview of their destination and aiding in detailed trip planning. Virtual tours have gained traction among hotels, resorts, museums, and tourist attractions by providing immersive, 360-degree views of their facilities and surroundings. For instance, travelers contemplating a stay at a hotel can take a virtual tour of the property, examining rooms, amenities, and common areas as if they were physically present. This immersive experience instills confidence in their booking decision by showing exactly what to expect. Additionally, virtual tours help travelers become familiar with a destination's layout and features, alleviating the uncertainty and anxiety often associated with visiting new places (Al-Romeedy, 2024b; Pencarelli, 2020).

AR enhances this experience by superimposing digital information onto the real world, further enriching travelers' understanding and anticipation of their destination. AR apps might enable travelers to point their smartphones at landmarks to instantly access information about their history, significance, and nearby attractions. Some destinations offer AR-enhanced maps or guides that provide real-time navigation and contextual insights as travelers explore. This technology not only improves the pre-travel experience but also deepens travelers' engagement with their destination, making their trip more informative and enjoyable (Anda et al., 2021; Zhang, 2023).

These digital tools are especially beneficial for visual and experiential learners, as they offer a more vivid sense of what to expect compared to traditional brochures or websites. By allowing travelers to virtually experience their destination beforehand, these tools help set realistic expectations, minimize uncertainty, and heighten excitement for the upcoming journey (Tjostheim & Waterworth, 2023; Van Nuenen & Scarles, 2021).

Pre-trip engagement is essential for shaping traveler satisfaction, as it establishes the initial tone for the entire travel experience. When travelers feel engaged and supported before their arrival, they are more likely to approach their trip with optimism and excitement. This engagement can be achieved through various means, including personalized emails, mobile app notifications, and interactive elements such as virtual tours and AR experiences. A major advantage of pre-trip engagement is its ability to alleviate anxiety and uncertainty, which are common feelings leading up to a trip. By offering detailed information, timely updates, and options for travelers to ask questions or request special accommodations, travel brands can address many of the concerns that travelers may have. This support reassures travelers that their needs are being attended to, thereby boosting their confidence in the travel brand and enhancing their overall satisfaction (Rahimi et al., 2020; Al-Romeedy, 2024a).

Pre-trip engagement is crucial for enhancing traveler satisfaction by fostering a sense of involvement and anticipation. Personalized content, such as tailored emails featuring local events or activities, helps travelers connect with their destination and build excitement (Li, 2023; Hsu, 2021). Additionally, digital tools like virtual tours and AR allow travelers to preview their destination, managing expectations and reducing potential disappointments. Effective use of these digital strategies not only prepares travelers but also enriches their experience, contributing to a smoother and more enjoyable journey (Gaafar & Al-Romeedy, 2024a).

## The Travel Experience: On-The-Go Digital Interaction

In the digital age, technology significantly enhances the travel experience through mobile apps, GPS, and social media. Navigation apps like Google Maps and Apple Maps are crucial for accurate directions, real-time traffic updates, and local discoveries, helping travelers explore new areas more effectively (Tjostheim & Waterworth, 2022; Benckendorff et al., 2019; Al-Romeedy, 2024b; Pencarelli, 2020). Additionally, recommendation apps such as TripAdvisor, Yelp, and Foursquare offer personalized suggestions based on user reviews and preferences, aiding in informed decision-making. Social media platforms like Instagram, Facebook, and TikTok enable travelers to share their experiences in real-time and draw inspiration from others, acting both as a personal journal and a source of travel ideas (Stienmetz et al., 2022; Pesonen & Neidhardt, 2019).

The integration of mobile apps, GPS, and social media has transformed travel by making destination exploration more personalized, informed, and socially connected (Anda et al., 2021; Choi et al., 2022). Real-time digital services, such as mobile check-ins and e-tickets, have streamlined the travel process, offering significant convenience by reducing paperwork and wait times, which is especially beneficial for business travelers (Zhang, 2023; Tjostheim & Waterworth, 2023). These technologies also provide real-time updates on flight changes, weather, and local events, enhancing flexibility and reducing stress during trips (Anda et al., 2021; Choi et al., 2022; Tjostheim & Waterworth, 2023; Rahimi et al., 2020). Overall, real-time information and digital tools greatly improve travel convenience, enabling travelers to make informed decisions and adapt to changes more effectively (Al-Romeedy, 2024b; Pencarelli, 2020).

Digital connectivity has profoundly transformed how travelers interact with their destinations and make decisions during their trips. With constant access to information, recommendations, and services through mobile devices, travelers can easily discover new experiences, adjust their plans on the go, and maximize their time at a destination. A major advantage of digital connectivity is the ability to access location-based services and recommendations in real-time. Apps such as Google Maps, TripAdvisor, and Yelp use geolocation to suggest nearby attractions, restaurants, and activities based on the traveler's current location. This is especially beneficial for those who prefer spontaneous exploration rather than sticking to a fixed itinerary. Travelers can use their smartphones to find interesting spots as they travel, making their experience more dynamic and adaptable (Cotton et al., 2020; Gaafar & Al-Romeedy, 2024b).

Additionally, digital connectivity supports more informed decision-making by offering access to a wealth of UGC, including reviews, ratings, and photos. When evaluating whether to visit a particular site, dine at a specific restaurant, or book an activity, travelers can quickly review feedback from other users. This information helps align their choices with their preferences and expectations, minimizing the chance of disappointment. Seeing up-to-date reviews and photos provides reassurance about the current quality of a venue or service before committing. Digital connectivity also keeps travelers informed about local events and activities, allowing them to engage in experiences they might otherwise miss. Event discovery apps and social media platforms often feature information on festivals, concerts, markets, and other local events, enabling travelers to experience the destination more like a local. This real-time awareness enriches the travel experience by adding immersion and cultural depth (Zhang, 2023; Fan et al., 2024).

Furthermore, digital connectivity is crucial for traveler safety and security. Travel apps and services offer real-time alerts about emergencies, health advisories, and travel restrictions, helping travelers make informed decisions about their movements and activities. For instance, during the COVID-19 pandemic, many travelers depended on apps to stay updated on local health regulations, quarantine rules, and testing sites, aiding them in navigating the complexities of travel during a global health crisis (Stienmetz et al., 2022; Pesonen & Neidhardt, 2019; Cai et al., 2020).

## Post-Travel: Reflection and Sharing

The post-travel phase is marked by travelers reflecting on and sharing their experiences through various digital platforms. Social media, blogs, and review sites are key channels for documenting and broadcasting travel memories. Platforms like Instagram, Facebook, TikTok, and Twitter are popular for posting photos, videos, and stories about memorable moments from trips. The visual nature of these platforms, along with features like hashtags and geotags, facilitates the creation and discovery of engaging content, allowing travelers to share their experiences with a broad audience and connect with others (Van Nuenen & Scarles, 2021; Li, 2023; Hsu, 2021).

In the post-travel phase, travelers share their experiences through blogs and review sites, contributing to the broader travel community. Travel blogs provide detailed narratives, practical tips, and personal reflections, often enhanced with multimedia elements like photos and videos. These blogs offer in-depth insights and advice for future travelers. Review sites such as TripAdvisor, Google Reviews, and Yelp allow travelers to leave detailed reviews and ratings for hotels, restaurants, and attractions, influencing future travel decisions with their authentic and personal accounts. This online sharing serves both as a personal record and a valuable resource for others planning their trips (Pirolli, 2018; Al-Romeedy & Hashem, 2024; Wörndl et al., 2021; Tjostheim & Waterworth, 2022).

Post-travel sharing significantly impacts future traveler behavior and destination marketing. Travelers' online content, including social media posts, blogs, and reviews, influences perceptions and decisions about destinations, accommodations, and activities. Positive reviews and engaging photos act as endorsements, motivating potential travelers to visit those locations, while negative feedback can deter them. UGC plays a crucial role in destination marketing; tourism boards and travel brands often leverage favorable UGC in their promotional efforts. Additionally, social media trends, such as "Instagrammable" destinations, can drive rapid increases in visitor numbers, sometimes leading to challenges like overtourism and sustainability concerns (Stienmetz et al., 2022; Fan et al., 2024; Rahimi et al., 2020).

For destination marketing, leveraging the impact of post-travel sharing is crucial. Marketers can analyze shared content to identify prevailing themes, sentiments, and emerging trends. Engaging with this content—through resharing posts, responding to reviews, or partnering with influencers—can boost a destination's visibility and reputation. Effectively utilizing UGC in marketing strategies can help build a robust, authentic brand image that resonates with future travelers (Gaafar & Al-Romeedy, 2024a; Ferrer-Rosell et al., 2023).

Digital platforms are essential for collecting and analyzing post-trip feedback, offering valuable insights that can help businesses enhance their services and overall travel experience. Review sites, social media platforms, and dedicated feedback tools are the primary sources of this data. Platforms like TripAdvisor, Google Reviews, and Yelp are rich sources of post-trip feedback. They allow travelers to leave detailed reviews and ratings, which businesses can analyze to identify common themes and areas for improvement. For example, if multiple reviews highlight issues with room service, a hotel might address this concern to enhance guest satisfaction (Neidhardt & Wörndl, 2020; Ivanov & Webster, 2019).

As well, social media platforms provide another valuable source of feedback through comments, likes, and shares on traveler posts. Travel brands can use social listening and sentiment analysis tools to monitor mentions, gauge public perception, and respond to feedback. This proactive approach helps manage online reputation and build trust with potential customers (Benckendorff et al., 2019; Cotton et al., 2020). Further, post-stay surveys and in-app feedback forms offer direct insights from travelers. These tools ask for ratings on specific aspects of the experience and may include open-ended questions for detailed feedback. The data can be used to benchmark performance, guide improvements, and identify trends. Incentives for survey participation, like discounts on future bookings, can boost response rates and provide a more comprehensive view of traveler satisfaction (Pesonen & Neidhardt, 2019; Al-Romeedy, 2024b).

In addition, advanced data analytics and AI technologies enhance the analysis of post-trip feedback. Machine learning algorithms can detect patterns and correlations between different aspects of the travel experience and overall satisfaction, helping businesses prioritize areas for improvement. Predictive analytics can forecast future trends based on historical data, aiding strategic planning (Anda et al., 2021; Zhang, 2023). The post-travel phase is crucial for influencing future traveler behavior and shaping destination marketing strategies. The content shared online serves as inspiration and validation for other travelers, while feedback collected through digital platforms provides actionable insights for businesses. By leveraging this feedback effectively, travel brands can enhance customer satisfaction, strengthen relationships with their audience, and stay ahead of industry trends (Pencarelli, 2020; Zhang, 2023).

## The Role of Data Analytics in Understanding the Digital Journey

In the digital era, every interaction a traveler has with online platforms—such as searching for a destination, booking flights, or leaving reviews—creates a digital footprint. These interactions produce extensive data that, when analyzed, offer valuable insights into the traveler's journey. Through data analytics, travel businesses can map this journey, pinpointing key moments of engagement, decision-making, and conversion. Understanding the traveler's path from initial interest to post-trip reflection allows businesses to refine their strategies to better meet customer needs. The traveler journey encompasses several stages, including search and inspiration, planning and booking, the travel experience, and post-travel sharing. Each stage generates distinct types of data from various digital touchpoints. For instance, during the search and inspiration phase, data from search engines, social media interactions, and website visits can indicate trending destinations, popular content, and factors influencing travel choices. In the planning and booking phase, data from booking platforms, payment systems, and email confirmations reveals traveler preferences, such as preferred accommodations, budget sensitivity, and booking timing (Choi et al., 2022; Li, 2023; Hsu, 2021).

By analyzing this data, businesses can develop detailed traveler personas and journey maps that highlight common behaviors and preferences. These insights help companies tailor their marketing and services to better align with traveler expectations. For example, if data shows a high demand for eco-friendly accommodations, a hotel chain might highlight its sustainability efforts in marketing campaigns. Similarly, understanding peak booking times can aid businesses in optimizing their pricing strategies and promotions. Real-time data analytics further enhances the ability to track the traveler journey dynamically, allowing businesses to quickly adapt to behavioral changes or emerging trends. For example, if there is a sudden spike in searches for a specific destination, a travel company can adjust its marketing strategies to take advantage of this trend. By continuously monitoring and analyzing data from various touchpoints, businesses can remain responsive to customer needs and preferences, ensuring a more personalized and satisfying travel experience (Gaafar & Al-Romeedy, 2024a; Pirolli, 2018).

Importantly, big data, artificial intelligence (AI), and machine learning are transforming the travel industry by revolutionizing how businesses predict and respond to traveler behavior. These technologies enable rapid processing and analysis of vast amounts of data, uncovering patterns and trends that would be difficult to detect manually. By leveraging these insights, companies can anticipate traveler needs, optimize their operations, and provide more personalized experiences. Big data encompasses the vast quantities of structured and unstructured information generated from diverse sources such as online searches, social media interactions, booking records, and customer reviews. The extensive volume of big data necessitates advanced analytics tools for processing and interpretation. AI and machine learning algorithms are particularly effective at analyzing big data, identifying correlations, and forecasting future behavior based on historical patterns. For instance, machine learning models can examine past booking trends to predict future demand for certain destinations or services. These predictions enable businesses to adjust their inventory, pricing, and marketing strategies to better align with traveler demand. AI-powered recommendation engines exemplify how these technologies predict traveler behavior. By analyzing data from previous searches, bookings, and interactions, AI can suggest destinations, accommodations, and activities tailored to individual preferences. These personalized recommendations not only enhance the travel experience but also boost conversion rates by presenting options that align closely with traveler interests (Al-Romeedy & Hashem, 2024; Cai et al., 2020; Ivanov & Webster, 2019; Neidhardt & Wörndl, 2020).

Machine learning is also pivotal in refining pricing strategies. Dynamic pricing algorithms leverage real-time data to adjust prices based on factors such as demand, competition, and traveler behavior. For example, airlines may use machine learning to predict optimal booking times and adjust fares to maximize revenue while remaining competitive. Similarly, hotels can employ dynamic pricing to offer the best rates at the right times, ensuring high occupancy rates. In addition to marketing and pricing, AI and machine learning enhance operational efficiency and customer service. AI-driven chatbots can provide immediate support by answering common queries, assisting with bookings, and offering personalized recommendations. Predictive analytics can help travel companies foresee potential issues, such as flight delays or overbookings, allowing them to take proactive steps to minimize disruptions and improve the traveler experience. Nevertheless, the use of these advanced technologies must be handled with care, especially regarding the collection and analysis of personal data (Ferrer-Rosell et al., 2023; Al-Romeedy, 2024a).

The application of data analytics, AI, and machine learning in the travel industry introduces substantial ethical considerations, particularly regarding the handling of traveler data. As businesses increasingly leverage personal data to refine their strategies, they must address critical issues related to privacy, consent, and data security. Privacy is a major ethical concern. Travelers provide sensitive personal information, such as names, contact details, payment methods, and itineraries, when booking travel services. While this data can enhance personalization and improve the travel experience, it also raises questions about its storage, protection, and sharing. Data breaches can lead to severe consequences, including identity theft, financial losses, and damage to reputation. Hence, it is crucial for travel companies to adopt stringent data security measures to safeguard traveler information from unauthorized access and cyber threats. Consent is another vital ethical issue. Travelers should be fully informed about what data is collected, its intended use, and any third parties with whom it may be shared. Transparency is key to building trust and ensuring travelers are comfortable with data sharing. Companies must obtain explicit consent from travelers before collecting their data and offer clear, accessible options for opting out. Regulations such as the General Data Protection Regulation (GDPR) in the European Union set strict guidelines for data collection and consent, which businesses in relevant regions must adhere to (Tjostheim & Waterworth, 2022; Wörndl et al., 2021).

Data bias and fairness are additional concerns. AI and machine learning models depend on the quality of the data they are trained on. If the data is biased, it can lead to unfair or discriminatory outcomes. For instance, if a model is trained on data that lacks diversity, it might produce recommendations or pricing strategies that disadvantage certain groups. Travel companies need to ensure their data practices are fair and inclusive by regularly auditing their algorithms to detect and address any biases. Lastly, the issue of data commodification arises as traveler data becomes increasingly valuable. There is a risk that this data could be exploited for profit, potentially at the expense of travelers' rights and interests. Companies must navigate the balance between leveraging data for commercial gain and upholding ethical standards to protect and respect customer information. This includes being transparent about how data is monetized, whether through targeted advertising, data sharing with third parties, or other methods (Cotton et al., 2020; Benckendorff et al., 2019; Stienmetz et al., 2022; Gaafar & Al-Romeedy, 2024b).

## Challenges and Opportunities in the Digital Traveler Journey

The digital transformation in the travel industry has fundamentally altered how travelers engage with destinations, services, and brands. Nonetheless, adapting to the digital traveler introduces several challenges that the tourism sector must address to stay competitive and relevant. One key challenge is the digital divide—the disparity between those with access to digital technologies and those without. Although many travelers today are adept with smartphones, high-speed internet, and digital services, there remains a substantial portion of the global population with limited or no access to these technologies. This gap is particularly evident in rural areas, developing nations, and among older demographics who may be less comfortable with technology. For the tourism industry, this means ensuring that services are accessible and inclusive to all travelers. Companies must balance the needs of tech-savvy travelers who expect seamless digital interactions with those who might prefer more traditional, offline methods (Pesonen & Neidhardt, 2019; Al-Romeedy, 2024b).

Privacy concerns also present a significant challenge in the digital travel landscape. As travel companies increasingly use data to personalize experiences, optimize services, and enhance marketing efforts, the volume of personal information collected—from travel itineraries and payment details to preferences and behavioral data—has expanded. This raises substantial privacy issues, especially given recent high-profile data breaches and growing public concern over data security. Travelers are becoming more wary of sharing personal information and demand greater transparency about how their data is collected, stored, and used. The tourism industry must navigate this by balancing data-driven insights with stringent privacy protections, clear communication about data practices, and adherence to regulations such as the General Data Protection Regulation (GDPR) (Pencarelli, 2020; Choi et al., 2022; Al-Romeedy, 2024a).

The rapid pace of technological change is another challenge, particularly for smaller businesses or those in regions with slower tech adoption. Keeping up with the latest digital tools, platforms, and consumer trends requires ongoing investment in technology, infrastructure, and staff training. For some companies, especially those with limited resources, this can be a significant burden. Furthermore, the fragmented nature of the travel industry, with diverse stakeholders from airlines and hotels to tour operators and local businesses, complicates the standardization of digital experiences. This can lead to inconsistencies in the quality and availability of digital services, affecting the overall traveler experience (Pirolli, 2018; Al-Romeedy & Hashem, 2024).

Despite these challenges, the shift toward digitalization offers substantial opportunities for the tourism industry to enhance traveler experiences and drive growth. The digital transformation of the travel industry has unveiled numerous opportunities to enhance traveler experiences through innovative tools and services. By harnessing technology, travel companies can offer more personalized, convenient, and engaging experiences tailored to the evolving expectations of modern travelers.

A major opportunity lies in utilizing AI and machine learning for delivering customized recommendations and services. AI-driven tools can process extensive data to discern traveler preferences, behaviors, and patterns, enabling companies to tailor their offerings to individual needs. For instance, AI recommendation engines can propose destinations, accommodations, and activities based on a traveler's past choices and current interests. This degree of personalization not only boosts customer satisfaction but also increases the chances of conversions and repeat bookings. Furthermore, AI can automate customer service through chatbots and virtual assistants, providing round-the-clock support and information (Al-Romeedy, 2024b).

Another significant opportunity comes from the integration of mobile technology into the travel experience. Mobile apps have become indispensable for travelers, facilitating everything from flight bookings and hotel reservations to navigation and local recommendations. Managing all aspects of a trip from a single device enhances convenience and streamlines the travel process. Additionally, mobile apps can offer real-time updates on flight delays, gate changes, or weather conditions, helping travelers stay informed and alleviating stress from unexpected disruptions. The use of mobile wallets and contactless payments further simplifies transactions, allowing travelers to make purchases swiftly and securely without the need for cash or physical cards (Fan et al., 2024; Tjostheim & Waterworth, 2023; Gaafar & Al-Romeedy, 2024a; Ferrer-Rosell et al., 2023).

Moreover, AR and VR technologies present exciting possibilities for enhancing both pre-travel planning and in-destination experiences. AR can overlay digital information onto the physical world, offering travelers interactive maps, guided tours, and real-time translations as they explore. For example, an AR app could enable travelers to point their smartphone at a historical landmark and instantly access information about its significance, architectural details, and nearby attractions. Conversely, VR can provide immersive virtual experiences, allowing travelers to explore destinations before they even depart. VR tours of hotels, resorts, or tourist attractions can help travelers make informed booking decisions by giving them a realistic preview of what to expect (Neidhardt & Wörndl, 2020; Ivanov & Webster, 2019; Stienmetz et al., 2022; Gaafar & Al-Romeedy, 2024b).

Blockchain technology also offers a means to enhance security and transparency in travel transactions. Blockchain's decentralized ledger system can securely record and verify transactions, such as bookings, payments, and loyalty points, without intermediaries. This can reduce fraud risks, lower transaction costs, and increase trust between travelers and service providers. Additionally, blockchain can create immutable travel records, providing verifiable proof of journeys and transactions, which can be especially useful for dispute resolution or travel insurance claims (Gaafar & Al-Romeedy, 2024a; Pirolli, 2018).

Lastly, the rise of sustainable travel offers an opportunity for the tourism industry to innovate in alignment with the increasing consumer demand for eco-friendly options. Digital tools can promote sustainable travel practices, such as encouraging public transportation use, supporting local businesses, and reducing waste. For instance, travel apps can feature carbon footprint calculators, suggest green accommodations, or highlight eco-friendly tours and activities. By integrating sustainability into digital travel services, companies can appeal to environmentally conscious travelers and contribute to the preservation of destinations for future generations (Rahimi et al., 2020; Van Nuenen & Scarles, 2021; Al-Romeedy & Hashem, 2024; Cai et al., 2020).

While the digital traveler journey poses challenges like the digital divide, privacy concerns, and rapid technological change, it also presents substantial opportunities for innovation and growth. Embracing digital tools and services can enhance traveler experiences, improve operational efficiency, and meet the evolving needs of today's tech-savvy travelers. The key to success lies in balancing these opportunities with a commitment to inclusivity, privacy, and sustainability, ensuring that the benefits of digitalization are accessible to all travelers and support the long-term health of the industry.

## CONCLUSION AND RECOMMENDATIONS

This chapter explores the profound impact of digital transformation on the traveler's journey, from initial inspiration to post-travel reflection. It highlights the crucial role of digital touchpoints—like search engines, social media, and online booking platforms—in shaping travel planning, booking, experiences, and sharing. The transition from traditional to digital platforms has empowered travelers with access to information, personalized recommendations, and real-time updates, enhancing decision-making. The chapter also underscores the importance of data analytics in improving the digital travel experience through big data, AI, and machine learning, enabling companies to forecast behavior, tailor experiences, and streamline operations. However, it raises concerns about privacy, consent, and data security, which must be addressed to maintain traveler trust. Additionally, the chapter identifies challenges such as the digital divide and the rapid pace of technological change, which can be particularly difficult for smaller businesses. Despite these challenges, there are significant opportunities for innovation, especially in mobile technology, AI, AR/VR, blockchain, and sustainable travel initiatives.

To stay competitive in the rapidly digitizing travel industry, stakeholders such as travel businesses and destination management organizations must enhance the digital journey for travelers. This involves investing in AI, machine learning, and big data analytics to better understand traveler behaviors and preferences, enabling the creation of more personalized experiences that boost customer satisfaction and loyalty. AI-powered tools like chatbots and recommendation systems can significantly improve customer service by offering instant, personalized assistance. With the growing importance of mobile devices in travel, stakeholders should focus on developing mobile applications with features like mobile check-ins, electronic tickets, real-time notifications, and location-based suggestions, while ensuring that websites and booking platforms are mobile-optimized. As data collection advances, it is crucial to prioritize privacy and ethical practices, including strong data security, transparency, and compliance with global data protection laws such as the GDPR. To ensure inclusivity, businesses should address the needs of travelers with limited digital access by providing offline options, digital literacy resources, and simplified interfaces, while also working with local governments to improve digital infrastructure in underconnected areas.

The integration of AR and VR technologies offers new opportunities to enhance both the planning and in-destination experiences for travelers. AR provides interactive, real-time information about destinations, while VR offers immersive previews of travel experiences. Blockchain technology can improve transaction transparency and security, fostering customer trust and streamlining processes such as booking and payments. As sustainability becomes a key concern for travelers, incorporating eco-friendly options into digital services—like promoting carbon offset programs and sustainable accommodations—can attract environmentally conscious consumers and support the industry's long-term sustainability. To address the fragmented nature of the travel industry, stakeholders should collaborate to establish industry-wide standards for digital tools and services, ensuring a consistent and reliable experience across platforms. In summary, embracing technological advancements, addressing ethical issues, and focusing on inclusivity and sustainability can help the travel industry remain competitive and deliver richer, more satisfying experiences for today's digital travelers.

# REFERENCES

Al-Romeedy, B. S. (2024a). Tomorrow's Travel Companion: The Role of Artificial Intelligence in Shaping the Future of Tourism. In Hashem, T., Albattat, A., Valeri, M., & Sharma, A. (Eds.), *Marketing and Big Data Analytics in Tourism and Events* (pp. 162–182). IGI Global., DOI: 10.4018/979-8-3693-3310-5.ch010

Al-Romeedy, B. S. (2024b). Unlocking the Power of Data: Exploring the Dynamic Role of MKIS in Revolutionizing Tourism Marketing. In Hashem, T., Albattat, A., Valeri, M., & Sharma, A. (Eds.), *Marketing and Big Data Analytics in Tourism and Events* (pp. 183–204). IGI Global., DOI: 10.4018/979-8-3693-3310-5.ch011

Al-Romeedy, B. S., & Hashem, T. (2024). From Insight to Advantage: Harnessing the Potential of Marketing Intelligence Systems in Tourism. In Hashem, T., Albattat, A., Valeri, M., & Sharma, A. (Eds.), *Marketing and Big Data Analytics in Tourism and Events* (pp. 80–98). IGI Global., DOI: 10.4018/979-8-3693-3310-5.ch005

Anda, C., Medina, S. A. O., & Axhausen, K. W. (2021). Synthesising digital twin travellers: Individual travel demand from aggregated mobile phone data. *Transportation Research Part C, Emerging Technologies*, 128, 103118. DOI: 10.1016/j.trc.2021.103118

Benckendorff, P., Xiang, Z., & Sheldon, P. (2019). *Tourism information technology*. CABI. DOI: 10.1079/9781786393432.0000

Cai, W., McKenna, B., & Waizenegger, L. (2020). Turning it off: Emotions in digital-free travel. *Journal of Travel Research*, 59(5), 909–927. DOI: 10.1177/0047287519868314

Choi, Y., Hickerson, B., Lee, J., Lee, H., & Choe, Y. (2022). Digital tourism and wellbeing: Conceptual framework to examine technology effects of online travel media. *International Journal of Environmental Research and Public Health*, 19(9), 5639. DOI: 10.3390/ijerph19095639 PMID: 35565033

Cotten, D., Codjoe, J., & Loker, M. (2020). Evaluating advancements in Bluetooth technology for travel time and segment speed studies. *Transportation Research Record: Journal of the Transportation Research Board*, 2674(4), 193–204. DOI: 10.1177/0361198120911931

Fan, D. X., Lyu, J., Huang, Y., Shang, K., & Buhalis, D. (2024, January). Senior Tourists' Digital Travel Experience: A Humanisation Perspective. In *ENTER e-Tourism Conference* (pp. 317–322). Springer Nature Switzerland. DOI: 10.1007/978-3-031-58839-6_34

Ferrer-Rosell, B., Massimo, D., & Berezina, K. (2023). *Information and Communication Technologies in Tourism 2023: Proceedings of the ENTER 2023 eTourism Conference, January 18-20, 2023*. Springer Nature. DOI: 10.1007/978-3-031-25752-0

Gaafar, H. A., & Al-Romeedy, B. S. (2024a). Bridging the Digital Divide: Unleashing the Power of Big Data Analytics for Touristic Destination Promotion. In Hashem, T., Albattat, A., Valeri, M., & Sharma, A. (Eds.), *Marketing and Big Data Analytics in Tourism and Events* (pp. 17–37). IGI Global., DOI: 10.4018/979-8-3693-3310-5.ch002

Gaafar, H. A., & Al-Romeedy, B. S. (2024b). Data Fusion for Destination Success: Exploring the Integration of MKIS and BDA in Marketing Touristic Destinations. In Hashem, T., Albattat, A., Valeri, M., & Sharma, A. (Eds.), *Marketing and Big Data Analytics in Tourism and Events* (pp. 38–60). IGI Global., DOI: 10.4018/979-8-3693-3310-5.ch003

Hsu, S. (2021). The Role of Technology in Transforming the Travel Experience. *International Journal of Business Management and Visuals, ISSN: 3006-2705, 4*(2), 21-27.

Ivanov, S., & Webster, C. (Eds.). (2019). *Robots, artificial intelligence, and service automation in travel, tourism and hospitality*. Emerald Publishing Limited. DOI: 10.1108/9781787566873

Li, S. A. (2023). Revisiting the relationship between information and communication technologies and travel behavior: An investigation of older Americans. *Transportation Research Part A, Policy and Practice*, 172, 103689. DOI: 10.1016/j.tra.2023.103689

Morrison, A. M. (2022). *Hospitality and travel marketing*. Routledge. DOI: 10.4324/9781003292616

Neidhardt, J., & Wörndl, W. (2020). *Information and Communication Technologies in Tourism 2020*. Springer International Publishing. DOI: 10.1007/978-3-030-36737-4

Pencarelli, T. (2020). The digital revolution in the travel and tourism industry. *Information Technology & Tourism*, 22(3), 455–476. DOI: 10.1007/s40558-019-00160-3

Pesonen, J., & Neidhardt, J. (2019). Information and communication technologies in tourism 2019. In *Proceedings of the International Conference*. Springer International Publishing. DOI: 10.1007/978-3-030-05940-8

Pirolli, B. (2018). *Travel journalism: Informing tourists in the digital age*. Routledge. DOI: 10.4324/9781315110738

Rahimi, A., Azimi, G., Asgari, H., & Jin, X. (2020, May). Potential implications of automated vehicle technologies on travel behavior: A literature review. In *International Conference on Transportation and Development 2020* (pp. 234-247). Reston, VA: American Society of Civil Engineers. DOI: 10.1061/9780784483138.021

Stienmetz, J., Ferrer-Rosell, B., & Massimo, D. (2022). *Information and Communication Technologies in Tourism 2022: Proceedings of the ENTER 2022 ETourism Conference, January 11-14, 2022.* Springer Nature. DOI: 10.1007/978-3-030-94751-4

Tjostheim, I., & Waterworth, J. A. (2022). *The psychosocial reality of digital travel: Being in virtual places.* Springer Nature. DOI: 10.1007/978-3-030-91272-7

Tjostheim, I., & Waterworth, J. A. (2023). Tomorrow's Digital Travellers—Who are they? A Study on Travellers' Views on Digital Travel Experiences. In *Advances in Tourism, Technology and Systems: Selected Papers from ICOTTS 2022* (Vol. 1, pp. 381–391). Springer Nature Singapore. DOI: 10.1007/978-981-99-0337-5_32

Van Nuenen, T., & Scarles, C. (2021). Advancements in technology and digital media in tourism. *Tourist Studies*, 21(1), 119–132. DOI: 10.1177/1468797621990410

Wörndl, W., Koo, C., & Stienmetz, J. (2021). *Information and Communication Technologies in Tourism 2021: Proceedings of the ENTER 2021 eTourism Conference, January 19–22, 2021.* Springer Nature. DOI: 10.1007/978-3-030-65785-7

Zhang, Y. (2023). Analysis of the Digital Transformation Development Path for Travel Enterprises. *Ozean Journal of Applied Sciences*, 13(8), 1370–1386. DOI: 10.4236/ojapps.2023.138109

# Chapter 13
# Identity-Driven Tourism Marketing for Millennials:
## Aligning Destination Branding With Values and Self-Expression

**Devika Sood**
https://orcid.org/0000-0001-7007-2905
*Amity Institute of Travel and Tourism, Amity University, Noida, India*

**Swati Sharma**
https://orcid.org/0000-0003-2949-2363
*Amity Institute of Travel and Tourism, Amity University, Noida, India*

**Akshita Tiwari**
https://orcid.org/0000-0002-5167-6794
*Amity University, Noida, India*

## ABSTRACT

*This chapter explores identity-driven tourism marketing, focusing on aligning destination branding with the values and self-expression of millennial travelers to enhance engagement and satisfaction. Millennials prioritize experiences, personal values, and digital connectivity, seeking destinations that resonate with their identities. The chapter integrates self-congruity theory, destination branding, and millennial consumer behavior to analyze travel motivations and preferences. Key concepts like authenticity, sustainability, social responsibility, and digital engagement are highlighted as crucial in creating meaningful connections. The role of social media in facilitating self-expression and community building among millennials is also discussed. Case studies illustrate successful marketing campaigns, demonstrating that aligning destination branding with millennial values is a strategic approach*

DOI: 10.4018/979-8-3693-3972-5.ch013

*to engaging this influential demographic in the digital age.*

## 1. INTRODUCTION

In the contemporary tourism landscape, the millennial demographic represents a significant and influential market segment. Characterized by their emphasis on experiences, personal values, and digital connectivity, millennials seek destinations that resonate with their identities and facilitate self-expression SOFRONOV, Bogdan (2018). By understanding the unique characteristics and preferences of this demographic, tourism marketers can develop strategies that foster a deeper connection between the destination and the traveler, thereby driving loyalty and advocacy (Boston Consulting Group, 2013; Deloitte, n.d.; Eco Africa Digital, n.d.; Noble Studios, n.d.; Wong, n.d.; Bockorny & Westman, 2014).

Millennials, born between 1981 and 1996, are known for their distinct set of values and behaviors that differ from previous generations. They prioritize experiences over material possessions, seek authenticity and meaningful connections, and are highly influenced by digital media. These characteristics have profound implications for the tourism industry, as millennials are not only frequent travelers but also active participants in shaping the travel narrative through social media and online communities (Boston Consulting Group, 2013; Wong, n.d.).

The rise of digital platforms has transformed the way millennials discover, share, and curate their travel experiences. Social media, in particular, plays a crucial role in influencing millennials' travel decisions and expectations (Deloitte, n.d.; Noble Studios, n.d.). Moreover, millennials are known for their commitment to sustainability and social responsibility, preferring destinations and experiences that align with their values (Eco Africa Digital, n.d.). This preference reflects a broader trend towards conscious consumption and ethical travel practices, which is reshaping the tourism industry.

Self-Congruity Theory plays a central role in understanding identity-driven tourism marketing. According to this theory, consumers are more likely to be attracted to brands and destinations that match their self-image. For millennials, who highly value authenticity and self-expression, destinations that align with their personal and social identities are more likely to be chosen. By leveraging this alignment, marketers can create compelling narratives that resonate deeply with millennial travelers (Wong, n.d.; Bockorny & Westman, 2014). This approach involves understanding millennials' desires for authenticity, community, and cultural exploration, and leveraging digital platforms to facilitate meaningful engagement.

Given these dynamics, identity-driven tourism marketing emerges as a strategic approach to connect with millennial travelers. By aligning destination branding with millennials' values and self-expression, marketers can create compelling narratives that resonate deeply with this demographic. Self-Congruity Theory reinforces this approach by emphasizing that consumers are more likely to choose brands or destinations that align with their self-image. For millennials, whose travel choices are driven by authenticity, community, and cultural exploration, destinations that mirror their personal identities create a stronger emotional connection Haddouche, H.(2018). This chapter delves into the theoretical foundations of identity-driven tourism marketing, explores the unique characteristics and preferences of millennial travelers, and presents case studies that demonstrate successful marketing strategies.

## 2. THEORETICAL BACKGROUND

In constructing a theoretical foundation for identity-driven tourism marketing targeted at millennial travelers, several key concepts converge to create a robust understanding of how this generation's unique values and behaviors shape their travel preferences. These concepts, including self-congruity theory, the experience economy, destination branding, and millennial consumer behavior, are essential for developing effective tourism marketing strategies. Each theory offers insights into how marketers can align their messaging, offerings, and branding with millennial travelers' desire for authentic, meaningful, and experience-rich journeys.

### 2.1 Self-Congruity Theory

Self-congruity theory suggests that individuals are more likely to choose products, brands, and experiences that align with their self-concept, leading to greater satisfaction and loyalty (Sirgy, 1982). Applied to millennial travelers, this theory underscores the importance of aligning destination branding and marketing messages with the values, lifestyles, and identities of this demographic. Millennials are known for seeking out travel experiences that resonate with who they are or who they aspire to be. Whether it's choosing a destination that supports sustainability or one that offers culturally immersive experiences, millennials are drawn to places that reflect their personal values and help them express their identity.

Marketers can leverage this by carefully curating the brand identity of destinations to align with the self-concepts of millennials. For example, destinations known for eco-friendly practices, community-driven tourism, or unique cultural experiences can attract millennials who see these values as part of their identity. Self-congruity theory also suggests that by creating marketing narratives that emphasize shared values, destinations can deepen their connection with travelers, fostering loyalty and repeat visits.

## 2.2Destination Branding

Destination branding is the process of creating a unique identity and narrative that sets a location apart from its competitors. Kotler and Gertner (2002) emphasized that for place marketing to be successful, it must focus on building a brand that conveys a clear and appealing message to target audiences. For millennials, whose travel decisions are heavily influenced by a destination's values, story, and perceived authenticity, destination branding must go beyond traditional marketing approaches.

To effectively brand destinations for millennials, marketers must create a narrative that emphasizes the values and experiences this demographic prioritize Dagnew,D. (2014). This includes highlighting eco-friendliness, ethical practices, cultural heritage, and opportunities for self-expression. A successful destination brand for millennials is one that not only captures their attention but also connects with their worldview. For instance, destinations that are committed to sustainability and social responsibility are more likely to attract millennial travelers. This involves not just crafting compelling visual identities or slogans but also ensuring that the branding reflects genuine practices and experiences.

Furthermore, destination branding for millennials should capitalize on digital storytelling. Social media and user-generated content play a significant role in shaping millennials' perceptions of a destination Kabia S. (2023). Authentic and shareable stories, whether told through influencer partnerships, visually captivating content, or community-driven campaigns, can help build a strong destination brand that aligns with millennial values.

## 2.3Millennial Tourist Behaviour

Understanding millennial consumer behavior is crucial to weaving these theoretical elements together in identity-driven tourism marketing. Millennials are digital natives who engage extensively with online communities and rely on social media, peer reviews, and influencer recommendations to make travel decisions. This generation's preference for authenticity, sustainability, and socially responsible experiences makes them selective about where they travel and how they spend their money.

Euromonitor International (2018) identified that millennials are reshaping the travel industry by seeking experiences that are both immersive and aligned with their ethical and social values. This demographic favors travel that allows for meaningful cultural exchanges, supports local communities, and has a minimal environmental footprint. Tussyadiah and Pesonen (2016) further emphasize that platforms like

Airbnb have gained traction among millennials due to their emphasis on local experiences and a sense of belonging, which aligns with this generation's desire for unique, community-driven travel.

Wang and Fesenmaier (2004) explore how millennials actively participate in online travel communities, influencing each other's decisions through shared experiences and content. This digital interaction fosters a sense of community and collective identity among millennial travelers, making them more responsive to marketing that resonates with their shared values and interests.

## 2.4 Integrating Theories for Effective Marketing Strategies

To create a comprehensive and effective marketing strategy for millennials, tourism marketers must integrate these theories into a cohesive approach. The self-congruity theory provides a lens for aligning branding with millennial identities, while the experience economy emphasizes the need for destinations to offer immersive and transformative experiences. Destination branding should strategically highlight values like sustainability, culture, and community engagement, appealing to millennials' ethical considerations and their quest for authenticity.

In practice, this integration could involve crafting destination narratives that emphasize authentic, local experiences while ensuring that these experiences align with millennial values Nur'afifah, O.(2021). For example, a destination might be marketed as an eco-conscious haven where travelers can engage in activities like volunteering in conservation projects, staying in locally owned accommodations, and participating in cultural immersion programs. This narrative can be reinforced through digital channels, leveraging influencer content, peer reviews, and social media engagement to create a brand that resonates with millennial travelers.

Moreover, by understanding millennial consumer behavior, marketers can develop digital-first strategies that tap into the online communities and social networks where millennials are most active. Engaging with this demographic through user-generated content, storytelling, and interactive campaigns ensures that the brand remains relevant and top-of-mind. *Figure1* named "Theoretical Foundations of Identity-Driven Tourism Marketing for Millennials", reflects the key concepts converging in the diagram, such as self-congruity theory, destination branding, millennial consumer behavior.

*Figure 1. Theoretical Foundations of Identity-Driven Tourism Marketing for Millennials*

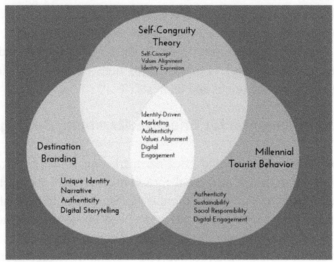

Self-Congruity
Theory
Self-Concept
Values Alignment
Identity Expression

Identity-Driven
Marketing
Authenticity
Values Alignment
Digital
Engagement

Destination
Branding

Millennial
Tourist Behavior

Unique Identity
Narrative
Authenticity
Digital Storytelling

Authenticity
Sustainability
Social Responsibility
Digital Engagement

*(Prepared by the authors)*

Identity-driven tourism marketing for millennials is grounded in understanding the intersection of self-concept, experiential value, brand identity, and consumer behavior. By integrating these theoretical perspectives, tourism marketers can develop strategies that resonate with millennial travelers on a deeper level, creating connections that go beyond transactional relationships. This approach not only enhances engagement and satisfaction but also builds loyalty and advocacy, positioning destinations as the preferred choice for this influential market segment

## 3. METHODOLOGY

The research methodology for this chapter includes a comprehensive literature review & analysis of case studies. The literature review encompasses academic articles, industry reports, and marketing campaigns targeting millennials. Case studies are selected to illustrate successful examples of identity-driven tourism marketing.

# 4. DISCUSSION

The discussion section delves into the implications of identity-driven tourism marketing for millennials, grounding the analysis in relevant theoretical frameworks. It explores how destination marketers can leverage millennials' values, such as sustainability, authenticity, and social responsibility, to create compelling brand narratives. Additionally, the role of digital platforms in facilitating self-expression and community building among millennial travelers is examined, highlighting the importance of social media and user-generated content in modern tourism marketing.

i)  Leveraging Millennial Values

Sustainability: Millennials are increasingly concerned about the environmental impact of their travel choices. Destinations that emphasize sustainable practices, such as eco-friendly accommodations, renewable energy, and waste reduction, are more likely to resonate with this demographic chiopu, A.F.et.al (2016). Marketers should highlight these aspects in their campaigns to appeal to millennials' sense of responsibility. For instance, destinations can showcase their use of solar power, recycling programs, and partnerships with local conservation efforts. By communicating these initiatives clearly, destinations can differentiate themselves and attract environmentally conscious travelers. This aligns with the Triple Bottom Line (TBL) theory, which emphasizes the importance of balancing economic, social, and environmental considerations in business practices.

ii)**Authenticity**: Millennials seek authentic experiences that allow them to immerse themselves in local cultures and traditions. Destinations should focus on offering experiences that provide a genuine insight into local life, such as homestays, cultural workshops, and community-based tourism. Marketing efforts should emphasize the uniqueness and authenticity of these experiences. For example, a destination might highlight a local cooking class where travelers can learn to prepare traditional dishes or a guided tour that explores hidden gems known only to locals. By focusing on authentic experiences, destinations can create memorable and meaningful travel opportunities for millennials. This resonates with McCannell's (1973) concept of "staged authenticity," where tourists seek authentic experiences that are often curated or staged by destinations.

iii) **Social Responsibility**: Millennials are drawn to destinations that demonstrate a commitment to social responsibility. This includes supporting local communities, preserving cultural heritage, and promoting fair trade practices Ketter E. (2021). Marketers should communicate these initiatives clearly to align with millennials' values. Destinations can highlight their involvement in community development projects, cultural preservation efforts, and fair trade practices. For instance, a destination might feature a local artisan market where travelers can purchase handmade goods directly from artisans, supporting local livelihoods and cultural traditions. This aligns with Corporate Social Responsibility (CSR) theories, which emphasize the role of businesses in contributing to societal well-being.

iv) Digital Engagement and Social Media

Visual Storytelling: Instagram and other visual platforms are powerful tools for showcasing destinations and experiences. High-quality images and videos that tell a story can capture millennials' attention and inspire them to travel Gvaramadze, A. (2022a). Marketers should focus on creating visually appealing content that resonates with millennials' aesthetic preferences. This includes using vibrant colors, engaging compositions, and storytelling techniques that evoke emotions and convey the essence of the destination. By crafting compelling visual narratives, destinations can create a strong emotional connection with millennials. This aligns with Keller's (1993) brand equity theory, which posits that strong brands are built on emotional connections and memorable experiences.

v) **Influencer Partnerships:** Collaborating with travel influencers can help destinations reach a wider audience and build trust. Influencers who share authentic experiences and stories can serve as relatable ambassadors for the destination Opute, A (2020). Marketers should select influencers whose values and audience align with the destination's brand. For example, a destination might partner with an influencer who is passionate about sustainability and cultural immersion, ensuring that the content created is authentic and resonates with millennials' values. This aligns with Parasocial Interaction (PSI) theory, which suggests that audiences form one-sided relationships with media figures, influencing their attitudes and behaviors.

vi) **User-Generated Content**: Encouraging millennials to share their own travel experiences can create a sense of community and authenticity. Destinations should facilitate and promote user-generated content through hashtags, photo contests, and interactive campaigns(Noble Studios, n.d.; Eco Africa Digital, n.d.).. This not only provides social proof but also engages millennials in co-creating the destination's narrative. For instance, a destination might launch a photo contest using a branded hashtag, encouraging travelers to share their experiences. The best photos could be featured on the destination's social media channels, creating a sense of community and encouraging further engagement. This aligns with Co-creation theory, which emphasizes the role of consumers in creating and shaping brand experiences.

vii)  Personalization and Technology:

Personalized Experiences: Millennials appreciate personalized travel recommendations and experiences. Destinations can use data analytics and artificial intelligence to offer personalized content and suggestions based on individual preferences and past behaviors (Kishnani, N., & Sharma, V. 2024). For example, a destination's website might use AI to recommend activities, accommodations, and dining options based on a traveler's past preferences and behavior. This level of personalization can enhance the travel experience and make it more enjoyable and relevant for millennials. This aligns with Customer Relationship Management (CRM) theories, which focus on understanding and fulfilling customer needs through personalized interactions.

*Figure 2. Millennial Behaviour Traits depicted through word cloud (Prepared by the authors)*

viii)  **Mobile Technology**: Given the ubiquity of smartphones, destinations should ensure their marketing efforts are mobile-friendly. This includes responsive websites, mobile apps, and location-based services that enhance the travel experience Hausmann, A.et al 2018. For instance, a destination might develop a mobile app that provides real-time information about local events, transportation, and points of interest. The app could also include augmented reality features that enrich the travel experience by providing historical and cultural context at various locations. This aligns with Ubiquitous Computing theory, which posits that technology should be embedded in the environment, enhancing users' experiences in a seamless and unobtrusive manner.

Figure 2 illustrates a word cloud containing various terms related to tourism, social engagement, and modern experiences. The largest word in the cloud is "Social," indicating its significance, while other words like "Sustainability," "Community," "Adventure," "Innovation," "Wellness," "Diversity," "Ethical," and "Authenticity" are also prominent. These words reflect key themes and trends in the travel and tourism industry, focusing on responsible, meaningful, and immersive experiences that emphasize social impact, sustainability, and personalization.

## 5. FINDINGS

The findings reveal that millennials are attracted to destinations that align with their personal values and offer opportunities for self-expression. Destinations that successfully integrate these elements into their branding and marketing strategies are more likely to resonate with this demographic. Key findings include:

i.  **Authenticity and Local Experiences**: Millennials seek authentic experiences that allow them to immerse themselves in local cultures and traditions. Destinations that offer unique, off-the-beaten-path experiences are more appealing. For example, a study by Euromonitor International (2018) found that millennials are more likely to seek out experiences that allow them to connect with local cultures and communities. This suggests that destinations should focus on offering experiences that provide a genuine insight into local life.
ii. **Sustainability and Social Responsibility**: There is a strong preference for destinations that demonstrate commitment to sustainability and social responsibility. Millennials are more likely to choose destinations that have a positive impact on the environment and local communities. A report by the United Nations World Tourism Organization (2018) highlights the growing importance of sustainable tourism practices and their appeal to millennials.
iii. **Digital Engagement**: Digital platforms play a crucial role in allowing millennials to discover, share, and curate their travel experiences. Destinations that leverage social media effectively and engage with millennials online are more successful in building brand loyalty. For instance, a study by Phocuswright (2019) found

that millennials are highly influenced by social media when making travel decisions.

iv. **Personalization and Technology:** Millennials expect personalized travel experiences and seamless digital interactions. Destinations that use technology to enhance the travel experience and provide personalized content are better positioned to meet millennials' expectations. A survey by Skift (2019) revealed that millennials value personalized travel recommendations and are more likely to use technology to plan their trips.

v. **Community and Connection**: Millennials value connections with local people and other travelers. Destinations that facilitate community building and shared experiences are more likely to create lasting impressions. For example, a study by Dr. Brent W. Altman (2017) found that millennials seek travel experiences that allow them to connect with others and contribute to a sense of community.

By understanding and embracing these findings, destination marketers can develop strategies that effectively engage millennials and promote their destinations in meaningful ways. The success of identity-driven tourism marketing lies in aligning with millennials' values, leveraging digital platforms, and creating authentic, personalized experiences that resonate with this influential demographic.

To effectively implement these strategies and integrate marketing in tourism targeted at millennials, destination marketers should consider the following approaches:

vi. **Value Proposition and Branding**: Clearly articulate the destination's unique value proposition that aligns with millennial values. This includes emphasizing sustainability, authenticity, and social responsibility in all marketing materials and campaigns. Branding efforts should create a narrative that resonates with millennials' desire for meaningful and immersive experiences.

vii. **Experience Design and Marketing**: Design and market travel experiences that are immersive, authentic, and meaningful. Highlight unique, off-the-beaten-path experiences that allow millennials to connect with local cultures and communities. Use storytelling and visual content to showcase the destination's cultural heritage, natural beauty, and sustainable practices.

viii. **Digital Marketing and Social Media**: Leverage digital platforms, particularly social media, to engage with millennials. Create visually appealing content, collaborate with influencers, and encourage user-generated content. Use hashtags, interactive campaigns, and social media ads to increase visibility and engagement.

ix. **Personalization and Technology**: Utilize data analytics and technology to offer personalized travel recommendations and enhance the travel experience. Develop mobile apps that provide real-time information, personalized itineraries, and location-based services. Use artificial intelligence to tailor content and recommendations based on individual preferences and past behaviors.

x. **Community Building and Engagement**: Foster a sense of community by creating opportunities for millennials to connect with local people and other travelers. Use social media groups, travel forums, and community-driven events to facilitate interactions. Encourage shared experiences and storytelling to build a loyal community of travelers.

By integrating these marketing strategies, destination marketers can create a cohesive and effective approach that resonates with millennial travelers, enhancing engagement, satisfaction, and loyalty. This holistic approach ensures that the destination not only attracts millennials but also provides them with experiences that align with their values and expectations.


## 6. CASE STUDIES

### 6.1 Airbnb's "Live There" Campaign

Airbnb, the global platform for unique accommodations and experiences, has revolutionized the way people travel by offering a more authentic and immersive experience. The "Live There" campaign is a prime example of identity-driven tourism marketing that resonates with millennials' values of authenticity, community, and self-expression. This case study explores how Airbnb's campaign aligns with millennial travelers' desires and contributes to the brand's success in the tourism industry.

Millennials are known for seeking out unique and meaningful travel experiences that allow them to connect with local cultures and communities. They value authenticity and look for opportunities to live like a local rather than just being a tourist. Recognizing these preferences, Airbnb launched the "Live There" campaign to showcase the unique and immersive experiences available through its platform.

The "Live There" campaign was designed to highlight the transformative power of travel and the authentic experiences that Airbnb offers. The campaign featured a series of videos, social media content, and interactive experiences that encouraged travelers to explore destinations from a local's perspective.

## Key Elements of the Campaign

Authenticity and Local Experiences: The campaign focused on the unique and authentic experiences that Airbnb offers, such as staying in a local's home, participating in local activities, and exploring hidden gems that are not typically found in traditional tourist guides.

Storytelling and Emotional Connection: Airbnb used storytelling to create an emotional connection with millennials. The campaign featured real hosts and guests sharing their personal stories and experiences, which helped to humanize the brand and make the experiences more relatable.

Digital Engagement: Recognizing the importance of digital platforms in millennials' lives, Airbnb leveraged social media, influencer partnerships, and user-generated content to amplify the campaign. This approach allowed millennials to engage with the brand and share their own travel experiences, fostering a sense of community among users.

Sustainability and Social Responsibility: The campaign also highlighted Airbnb's commitment to sustainability and social responsibility, aligning with millennials' values. Airbnb promoted eco-friendly accommodations and experiences, as well as initiatives that support local communities.

The "Live There" campaign was a significant success, resonating with millennial travelers and contributing to Airbnb's growth. Key results include:

Increased Brand Engagement: The campaign led to a significant increase in engagement on Airbnb's social media platforms, with users sharing their own travel stories and experiences.

Higher User Acquisition: The campaign helped to attract new users to the platform, particularly among millennials who were looking for authentic and immersive travel experiences.

Positive Brand Perception: The focus on authenticity, community, and social responsibility enhanced Airbnb's brand perception among millennials, positioning it as a preferred choice for conscious travelers.

Airbnb's "Live There" campaign is a compelling example of identity-driven tourism marketing that effectively aligns with the values and self-expression of millennial travelers. By focusing on authenticity, storytelling, digital engagement, and social responsibility, Airbnb created a campaign that resonated deeply with its target audience. The success of the campaign demonstrates the importance of understanding and embracing the unique characteristics and preferences of millennials in the tourism industry. As the travel landscape continues to evolve, identity-driven marketing strategies like Airbnb's "Live There" campaign will remain crucial for engaging this influential demographic.

## 6.2 Case Study 2: Visit Sweden's "The Swedish Number" Campaign

Visit Sweden, the national tourism board of Sweden, launched the innovative "The Swedish Number" campaign in 2016. This campaign is a prime example of identity-driven tourism marketing that resonated with millennials' values of authenticity, community, and cultural exploration. The campaign aimed to break down barriers between travelers and locals by providing a direct line to Sweden, allowing people from around the world to call and speak with random Swedes. This case study explores how Visit Sweden's campaign aligned with millennial travelers' desires and contributed to the promotion of Sweden as a tourist destination.

Millennials are known for seeking authentic experiences and meaningful connections when they travel. They are interested in immersing themselves in local cultures and having genuine interactions with locals. Recognizing these preferences, Visit Sweden developed the "The Swedish Number" campaign to offer a unique and personal way for potential travelers to connect with Sweden and its people.

The "The Swedish Number" campaign centered around a dedicated phone number (0771-SWEDEN) that people from around the world could call. Each call was randomly connected to a Swede, allowing callers to ask questions, learn about Swedish culture, and even make friends. The campaign was promoted through social media, online advertisements, and partnerships with travel bloggers and influencers.

Authenticity and Local Connections: The campaign provided a direct and authentic way for potential travelers to connect with locals. This unique approach allowed callers to gain insights into Swedish culture and daily life from real people, fostering a sense of authenticity and curiosity about the destination.

Storytelling and Personal Narratives: Visit Sweden encouraged both callers and Swedes to share their experiences on social media using the hashtag #swedishnumber. This user-generated content created a rich tapestry of personal stories and narratives that highlighted the diversity and warmth of Swedish culture.

Digital Engagement: The campaign leveraged digital platforms to reach millennials. Social media played a crucial role in promoting the campaign and sharing stories. Visit Sweden also partnered with travel influencers who shared their experiences of calling the Swedish Number, further amplifying the campaign's reach.

In the contemporary tourism landscape, millennials represent a pivotal demographic whose values and preferences significantly influence travel trends and destination marketing strategies. This chapter has explored the concept of identity-driven tourism marketing, focusing on how destination branding can be aligned with the values and self-expression of millennials to enhance engagement and satisfaction. By leveraging millennials' emphasis on experiences, personal values, and digital connectivity, destination marketers can create compelling narratives that resonate deeply with this influential demographic.

The theoretical foundations of self-congruity theory, experience economy, destination branding, and millennial consumer behavior provide a robust framework for understanding millennials' travel motivations and preferences. These theories underscore the importance of authenticity, sustainability, social responsibility, and digital engagement in creating meaningful connections with millennial travelers (Sirgy, 1982; Pine & Gilmore, 1999; Kotler & Gertner, 2002).

The discussion and findings highlight the critical role of aligning destination branding with millennials' values. Destinations that emphasize sustainable practices, offer authentic experiences, and demonstrate social responsibility are more likely to resonate with millennials (Euromonitor International, 2018; United Nations World Tourism Organization, 2018). Furthermore, digital platforms, particularly social media, play a crucial role in facilitating self-expression and community building among millennial travelers (Phocuswright, 2019; Skift, 2019). By leveraging visual storytelling, influencer partnerships, user-generated content, and personalized technology, destinations can effectively engage millennials and promote their offerings (Wang & Fesenmaier, 2004; Altman, 2017).

The case studies of Airbnb's "Live There" campaign and Visit Sweden's "The Swedish Number" campaign illustrate how these principles can be successfully implemented. Both campaigns demonstrate the power of identity-driven marketing in connecting with millennials on a deeper level, fostering loyalty and advocacy (Tussyadiah & Pesonen, 2016).

## 7. IMPLICATIONS OF THE IDENTITY DRIVEN MARKETING

The theoretical foundations of self-congruity theory, experience economy, destination branding, and millennial consumer behavior provide a robust framework for understanding millennials' travel motivations and preferences. These theories underscore the importance of authenticity, sustainability, social responsibility, and digital engagement in creating meaningful connections with millennial travelers (Sirgy, 1982; Pine & Gilmore, 1999; Kotler & Gertner, 2002).

Armutcu, Tan, Amponsah, Parida, and Ramkissoon (2023) discuss how millennials, who view travel as an extension of their identity, seek experiences that allow them to express who they are or aspire to be. This generation values authenticity, meaningful interactions, and ethical considerations in their travel choices, making them less responsive to traditional marketing and more influenced by content that resonates with their values, especially through digital platforms.

The discussion and findings highlight the critical role of aligning destination branding with millennials' values. Destinations that emphasize sustainable practices, offer authentic experiences, and demonstrate social responsibility are more likely to resonate with millennials (Euromonitor International, 2018; United Nations World Tourism Organization, 2018). Furthermore, digital platforms, particularly social media, play a crucial role in facilitating self-expression and community building among millennial travelers (Phocuswright, 2019; Skift, 2019). By leveraging visual storytelling, influencer partnerships, user-generated content, and personalized technology, destinations can effectively engage millennials and promote their offerings (Wang & Fesenmaier, 2004; Altman, 2017).

The case studies of Airbnb's "Live There" campaign and Visit Sweden's "The Swedish Number" campaign illustrate how these principles can be successfully implemented. Both campaigns demonstrate the power of identity-driven marketing in connecting with millennials on a deeper level, fostering loyalty and advocacy (Tussyadiah & Pesonen, 2016).

In conclusion, identity-driven tourism marketing is a strategic approach that can help destinations effectively engage millennial travelers. By understanding and embracing millennials' values and preferences, destination marketers can create marketing strategies that not only attract this demographic but also create lasting impressions. As the tourism industry continues to evolve, identity-driven marketing will remain a key strategy for success in the digital age (Sirgy, 1982; Pine & Gilmore, 1999; Kotler & Gertner, 2002; Euromonitor International, 2018; United Nations World Tourism Organization, 2018; Phocuswright, 2019; Skift, 2019; Wang & Fesenmaier, 2004; Altman, 2017; Tussyadiah & Pesonen, 2016).

## 8. CONCLUSION

In conclusion, identity-driven tourism marketing is a strategic approach that can help destinations effectively engage millennial travelers. By understanding and embracing millennials' values and preferences, destination marketers can create marketing strategies that not only attract this demographic but also create lasting impressions. As the tourism industry continues to evolve, identity-driven marketing will remain a key strategy for success in the digital age (Sirgy, 1982; Pine & Gilmore, 1999; Kotler & Gertner, 2002; Euromonitor International, 2018; United Nations World Tourism Organization, 2018; Phocuswright, 2019; Skift, 2019; Wang & Fesenmaier, 2004; Altman, 2017; Tussyadiah & Pesonen, 2016).

# REFERENCES

Armutcu, B., Tan, A., Amponsah, M., Parida, S., & Ramkissoon, H. (2023). Tourist behaviour: The role of digital marketing and social media. *Acta Psychologica*, 230, 104025. DOI: 10.1016/j.actpsy.2023.104025 PMID: 37741033

Bogdan, S. O. F. R. O. N. O. V. (2018). Millennials: A new trend for the tourism industry. *Economic Series.*, 18(3), 109–122. Annals of Spiru Haret University. DOI: 10.26458/1838

Boston Consulting Group. (2013). *Traveling with millennials*. Retrieved from https://www.bcg.com/publications/2013/transportation-tourism-marketing-sales-traveling-millennials

Cavagnaro, E., Staffieri, S., & Postma, A. (2018). Understanding millennials' tourism experience: Values and meaning to travel as a key for identifying target clusters for youth (sustainable) tourism. *Journal of Tourism Futures*, 4(1), 31–42. DOI: 10.1108/JTF-12-2017-0058

Dagnew, D. (2014). The Strategic Roles of Social Media Marketing to Build A Strong Brand Equity (The case of selected companies in Ethiopia). 1–87.

Deloitte. (2019). Gen Z and millennial travel: The wanderlust generations. Retrieved from https://www2.deloitte.com/us/en/pages/technology-media-and-telecommunications/articles/gen-Z-and-millennial-travel-the-wanderlust-generations.html

Eco Africa Digital. (n.d.). *How to attract millennials with online messaging for sustainable tourism*. Retrieved on 27th July, 204 from https://www.ecoafricadigital.co.za/sustainable-tourism-online-content-millennials/

Garikapati, V. M., Pendyala, R. M., Morris, E. A., Mokhtarian, P. L., & McDonald, N. (2016, September). Activity patterns, time use, and travel of millennials: A generation in transition? *Transport Reviews*, 36(no. 5), 558–584. DOI: 10.1080/01441647.2016.1197337

Gupta, S., Sufi, T., & Kumar Gautam, P. "Role of Technological Transformation in Shaping Millennials' Travel Behaviour: A Review," *2022 10th International Conference on Reliability, Infocom Technologies and Optimization (Trends and Future Directions) (ICRITO)*, Noida, India, 2022, pp. 1-6, DOI: 10.1109/ICRITO56286.2022.9965175

Gvaramadze, A. (2022a). Digital technologies and social media in tourism, 28–38. DOI: 10.19044/esj.2022.v18n10p28

Haddouche, H., & Salomone, C. (2018). Generation Z and the tourist experience: Tourist stories and use of social networks. *Journal of Tourism Futures*, 4(1), 69–79. DOI: 10.1108/JTF-12-2017-0059

Hausmann, A., Toivonen, T., Slotow, R., Tenkanen, H., Moilanen, A., Heikinheimo, V., & Minin, E. Di. (2018). Social media data can be used to understand tourists ' preferences for nature-based experiences in protected areas, 11, 1–10. DOI: 10.1111/conl.12343

Kabia, S., & Srinivaasan, G. (2023). Role of Smartphones in Destination Promotion and its Impact on Travel Experience. *International Journal of Hospitality and Tourism Systems*, 13, 22.

Keller, K. L. (1993). Conceptualizing, measuring, and managing customer-based brand equity. *Journal of Marketing*, 57(1), 1–22. DOI: 10.1177/002224299305700101

Ketter, E. (2021). Millennial travel: Tourism micro-trends of European Generation Y. *Journal of Tourism Futures*, 7(2), 192–196. DOI: 10.1108/JTF-10-2019-0106

Kishnani, N., & Sharma, V. (2024). *Travel motivation among millennials: Role of social media on tourism in Madhya Pradesh*. SDMIMD Journal of Management., DOI: 10.18311/sdmimd/2024/36424

MacCannell, D. (1973). Staged authenticity: Arrangements of social space in tourist settings. *American Journal of Sociology*, 79(3), 589–603. DOI: 10.1086/225585

Noble Studios. (n.d.). *The rise of AI travel planners: How DMOs can adapt to attract Gen Z and millennial travelers*. Retrieved from https://noblestudios.com/industry/tourism-marketing/ai-travel-planners-dmos/

Nur'afifah, O., & Prihantoro, E. (2021). The Influence of social media on millennial generation about travel decision-making. *Jurnal the Messenger*, 13(3), 238. DOI: 10.26623/themessenger.v13i3.2328

Opute, A. P., Irene, B. O., & Iwu, C. G. (2020). Tourism service and digital technologies: A value creation perspective. *African Journal of Hospitality, Tourism and Leisure*, 9(2), 1–18.

Prahalad, C. K., & Ramaswamy, V. (2004). Co-creation experiences: The next practice in value creation. *Journal of Interactive Marketing*, 18(3), 5–14. DOI: 10.1002/dir.20015

Sacchi, G. (2024). Book Review: Millennials, generation Z and the future of tourism. *Journal of Tourism Futures*, 10(1), 156–157. DOI: 10.1108/JTF-03-2024-302 chiopu, A. F., Pădurean, A. M.,  ală, M. L., & Nica, A. M. (2016). The influence of new technologies on tourism consumption behavior of the millennials. *Amfiteatru Economic Journal*, 18(10), 829–846.

Wong, K. (n.d.). *How millennials and Gen Z transformed tourism marketing.* Retrieved from https://www.linkedin.com/pulse/how-millennials-gen-z-transformed -tourism-marketing-through-kyle-wong

# Compilation of References

Abbasi, A. Z., Tsiotsou, R. H., Hussain, K., Rather, R. A., & Ting, D. H. (2023). Investigating the impact of social media images' value, consumer engagement, and involvement on eWOM of a tourism destination: A transmittal mediation approach. *Journal of Retailing and Consumer Services*, 71, 103231. DOI: 10.1016/j.jretconser.2022.103231

Abboodi, B., Pileggi, S. F., & Bharathy, G. (2023). Social networks in crisis management: A literature review to address the criticality of the challenge. *Encyclopedia*, 3(3), 1157–1177. DOI: 10.3390/encyclopedia3030084

Abell, A., & Biswas, D. (2023). Digital engagement on social media: How food image content influences social media and influencer marketing outcomes. *Journal of Interactive Marketing*, 58(1), 1–15. DOI: 10.1177/10949968221128556

Abernethy, B. E., Dixon, A. W., Holladay, P. J., & Koo, W. G.-Y. (2022). Determinants of Canadian and US mountain bike tourists' site preferences: Examining the push–pull relationship. *Journal of Sport & Tourism*, 26(3), 249–268. DOI: 10.1080/14775085.2022.2069147

Abidin, C. (2015). Communicative intimacies: Influencers and Perceived Interconnectedness. *Ada: A Journal of Gender. New Media, and Technology*, 11(8), 1–16.

Abou-Shouk, M. A., Mannaa, M. T., & Elbaz, A. M. (2021). Women's empowerment and tourism development: A cross-country study. *Tourism Management Perspectives*, 37(November 2020), 100782. DOI: 10.1016/j.tmp.2020.100782

Adamış, E., & Pınarbaşı, F. (2022). Unfolding visual characteristics of social media communication: Reflections of smart tourism destinations. *Journal of Hospitality and Tourism Technology*, 13(1), 34–61. Advance online publication. DOI: 10.1108/JHTT-09-2020-0246

Adam, M., Weesel, M., & Benlian, A. (2021). AI-based chatbots in customer service and their effects on user compliance. *Electronic Markets*, 31(2), 427–445. DOI: 10.1007/s12525-020-00414-7

Ahmad, M. (2023). Exploring the Role of OpenStreetMap in Mapping Religious Tourism in Pakistan for Sustainable Development. In J. P. D. M. Vítor, A. G. da R. N. João, L. de J. P. Maria, & A. de M. C. Liliana (Eds.), *Experiences, Advantages, and Economic Dimensions of Pilgrimage Routes* (pp. 23–40). IGI Global. DOI: 10.4018/978-1-6684-9923-8.ch002

Ahmad, M., Naeem, M. K. H., Mobo, F. D., Tahir, M. W., & Akram, M. (2024). Navigating the Journey: How Chatbots Are Transforming Tourism and Hospitality. In Darwish, D. (Ed.), *Design and Development of Emerging Chatbot Technology* (pp. 236–255). IGI Global., DOI: 10.4018/979-8-3693-1830-0.ch014

Akanfe, O., Lawong, D., & Rao, H. R. (2024). Blockchain technology and privacy regulation: Reviewing frictions and synthesizing opportunities. *International Journal of Information Management*, 76, 102753. DOI: 10.1016/j.ijinfomgt.2024.102753

Akdeniz, A., & Kömürcü, S. (2021). Evaluation of social media accounts of travel agencies: A research on the relations of travel agencies operating in Izmir with social media influencers. *International Journal of Contemporary Tourism Research*, 5(Special Issue), 98–115. DOI: 10.30625/ijctr.956026

Akhtar, N., Kim, W. G., Ahmad, W., Akhtar, M. N., Siddiqi, U. I., & Riaz, M. (2019). Mechanisms of consumers' trust development in reviewers' supplementary reviews: A reviewer-reader similarity perspective. *Tourism Management Perspectives*, 31(April), 95–108. DOI: 10.1016/j.tmp.2019.04.001

Akincilar, A., & Dagdeviren, M. (2014). A hybrid multi-criteria decision making model to evaluate hotel websites. *International Journal of Hospitality Management*, 36, 263–271. DOI: 10.1016/j.ijhm.2013.10.002

Akyol, Z., & Atabey, Z. (2023). Personal Brand Building Process on Social Media: A Review of Twitter Phenomenons. *Afyon Kocatepe University Journal of Social Sciences*, 25(3), 929–944. DOI: 10.32709/akusosbil.1248420

Alaimo, C., Kallinikos, J., & Venegas, E. V. (2020). *Platform Evolution: A Study of TripAdvisor*. Scholarspace.manoa.hawaii.edu. DOI: 10.24251/HICSS.2020.672

Ali, F., Yasar, B., Ali, L., & Dogan, S. (2023). Antecedents and consequences of travelers' trust towards personalized travel recommendations offered by ChatGPT. *International Journal of Hospitality Management*, 114(August), 103588. DOI: 10.1016/j.ijhm.2023.103588

Alkan, Z. (2023). Influencers and Travel Agencies in the Focus of Influencer Communication: An Evaluation of Brand Collaborations. In *Women's Empowerment Within the Tourism Industry* (pp. 203-220). IGI Global.

Alkier, R., Okičić, J., & Milojica, V. (2023). Perceived safety and some other factors in tourist's decision-making process: Findings from Opatija Riviera. *Pomorstvo*, 37(1), 151–159. DOI: 10.31217/p.37.1.12

Al-Romeedy, B. (2024a). Tomorrow's Travel Companion: The Role of Artificial Intelligence in Shaping the Future of Tourism. In Hashem, T., Albattat, A., Valeri, M., & Sharma, A. (Eds.), *Marketing and Big Data Analytics in Tourism and Events* (pp. 162–182). IGI Global., DOI: 10.4018/979-8-3693-3310-5.ch010

Alves de Castro, C., O'Reilly Dr, I., & Carthy, A. (2021). Social media influencers (SMIs) in context: A literature review. *Journal of Marketing Management*, 9(2), 59–71.

Alzaydi, Z. M., & Elsharnouby, M. H. (2023). Using social media marketing to pro-tourism behaviours: The mediating role of destination attractiveness and attitude towards the positive impacts of tourism. *Future Business Journal*, 9(1), 42. DOI: 10.1186/s43093-023-00220-5

Añaña, E., & Barbosa, B. (2023). Digital Influencers Promoting Healthy Food: The Role of Source Credibility and Consumer Attitudes and Involvement on Purchase Intention. *Sustainability (Basel)*, 15(20), 15002. DOI: 10.3390/su152015002

Anda, C., Medina, S. A. O., & Axhausen, K. W. (2021). Synthesising digital twin travellers: Individual travel demand from aggregated mobile phone data. *Transportation Research Part C, Emerging Technologies*, 128, 103118. DOI: 10.1016/j.trc.2021.103118

Andjelic, S., Milutinovic, O., Gajic, A., & Arsic, M. (2024). The influence of traditional and modern communication technologies on consumer attitudes. *Social Informatics Journal*, 3(1), 23–30. DOI: 10.58898/sij.v3i1.23-30

Andrade, S. C., & Mason, H. (2009). Digital Imaging Trek: A Practical Model for Managing the Demand of the Digitally Enabled Traveller. In Pease, W., Michelle, M., & Cooper, M. (Eds.), *Information and Communication Technologies in Support of the Tourism Industry* (pp. 475–498). IGI Global., DOI: 10.4018/978-1-60566-088-2.ch027

Andzani, D., Virgin, D., & Setijadi, N. (2024). Peran media sosial dalam membangun citra destinasi pariwisata yang menarik. [Jurnal Ilmiah Manajemen Bisnis dan Inovasi Universitas Sam Ratulangi]. *JMBI UNSRAT*, 11(1), 188–195. DOI: 10.35794/jmbi.v11i1.53212

An, J., Wan Zainon, W. M. N., & Zainon, W. (2023). An interactive visualization of location-based reviews using word cloud and OpenStreetMap for tourism applications. *Spatial Information Research*, 31(2), 235–243. Advance online publication. DOI: 10.1007/s41324-022-00492-z

Antony, P., & Kannan, R. (2024). Revolutionizing the Tourism Industry through Artificial Intelligence: A Comprehensive Review of AI Integration, Impact on Customer Experience, Operational Efficiency, and Future Trends. *International Journal for Multidimensional Research Perspectives, 2*(2), 01-14. https://www.ch andigarhphilosophers.com/index.php/ijmrp/article/view/115

Any, B., Four, S., & Tariazela, C. (2024). Technology integration in tourism management: Enhancing the visitor experience. [SABDA Journal]. *Startupreneur Business Digital*, 3(1), 81–88. DOI: 10.33050/sabda.v3i1.508

Ao, L., Bansal, R., Pruthi, N., & Khaskheli, M. B. (2023). Impact of social media influencers on customer engagement and purchase intention: A meta-analysis. *Sustainability (Basel)*, 15(3), 2744. DOI: 10.3390/su15032744

Apriyanti, M. E., Subiyantoro, H., & Ratnasih, C. (2023). Focus on local cultural attraction in increasing tourist visits in Central Java Tourism Villages. *Journal Research of Social Science, Economics, and Management*, 2(11), 2645–2653. DOI: 10.59141/jrssem.v2i11.480

Armutcu, B., Tan, A., Amponsah, M., Parida, S., & Ramkissoon, H. (2023). Tourist behaviour: The role of digital marketing and social media. *Acta Psychologica*, 240, 104025. DOI: 10.1016/j.actpsy.2023.104025 PMID: 37741033

Arnesson, J. (2023). Influencers as ideological intermediaries: Promotional politics and authenticity labour in influencer collaborations. *Media Culture & Society*, 45(3), 528–544. DOI: 10.1177/01634437221117505

Asan, K., & Yolal, M. (2022). Travel influencers and influencer marketing in tourism. In *Handbook on Tourism and Social Media* (pp. 365–380). Edward Elgar Publishing. DOI: 10.4337/9781800371415.00037

Aslam, W., Ahmed Siddiqui, D., Arif, I., & Farhat, K. (2023). Chatbots in the frontline: Drivers of acceptance. *Kybernetes*, 52(9), 3781–3810. DOI: 10.1108/K-11-2021-1119

Asri, M. A. Z. M., Ahmad, S. Y., Sawari, S. S. M., & Zakaria, N. F. (2024). Social media influencers and the effect on travel motivation among youth. *journal of tourism, hospitality and environment management (jthem), 9*(36).

Atasheva, D., Sarsenbayev, A., & Kulbayeva, A. (2024). Innovation and Application of Digitalization in the Formation of the Image of a smart hotel. *Eurasian Science Review An International Peer-Reviewed Multidisciplinary Journal*, 2(2), 128–133. DOI: 10.63034/esr-56

Audy Martínek, P., Caliandro, A., & Denegri-Knott, J. (2023). Digital practices tracing: Studying consumer lurking in digital environments. *Journal of Marketing Management*, 39(3-4), 244–274. DOI: 10.1080/0267257X.2022.2105385

Autenrieth, U. (2014). The "Digital Natives" present their children – An analysis of the increasing (self-) visualization of family and childhood in online environments. *Studies in Communication Sciences*, 14(2), 99–107. DOI: 10.1016/j.scoms.2014.12.006

Avci, E., & Bilgili, B. (2020). The effect of the characteristics of the social media phenomenon on the followers' intention to visit a destination. *Journal of Tourism and Recreation*, 2(1), 83–92.

Avcı, İ., & Yıldız, E. (2019). The effects of influencers' credibility, attractiveness and expertise on brand attitude, purchase intention and electronic word-of-mouth marketing: Instagram example. *Kocaeli University Journal of Social Sciences*, 2(38), 85–107.

Avcılar, M. Y., Külter Demirgüneş, B., & Açar, M. F. (2018). Examining the effects of using social media influencers as product endorsers in Instagram ads on attitudes towards the ad and e-wom intention. *Journal of Marketing and Marketing Research*, 21, 1–27.

Awais, M., & Ali, F. (2021). Social Media Exposure and Preventive Behaviors against COVID-19 in Pakistan. *Journal of Media Studies*, 36(1), 23–52.

Azam, M. S. E., Muflih, B. K., & Al Haq, M. A. (2024). Intersection Between Modern Technologies and Halal Tourism: Exploring the Role of Digital Innovation in Enhancing Muslim Travellers' Experience. *The Journal of Muamalat and Islamic Finance Research*, 16-31.

Baabdullah, A. M., Alalwan, A. A., Algharabat, R. S., Metri, B., & Rana, N. P. (2022). Virtual agents and flow experience: An empirical examination of AI-powered chatbots. *Technological Forecasting and Social Change*, 181(May), 121772. DOI: 10.1016/j.techfore.2022.121772

Backaler, J. (2018). *Digital Influence: Unleash the Power of Influencer Marketing to Accelerate Your Global Business*. Palgrave Macmillan. DOI: 10.1007/978-3-319-78396-3

Bae, S. Y., & Chang, P. J. (2021). The effect of coronavirus disease-19 (COVID-19) risk perception on behavioral intention towards 'untact' tourism in South Korea during the first wave of the pandemic (March 2020). *Current Issues in Tourism*, 24(7), 1017–1035. DOI: 10.1080/13683500.2020.1798895

Baker, M. J., & Churchill, G. A. Jr. (1977). The impact of physically attractive models on advertising evaluations. *JMR, Journal of Marketing Research*, 14(4), 538–555. DOI: 10.1177/002224377701400411

Balasubramanian, K., Kunasekaran, P., Konar, R., & Sakkthivel, A. M. (2022). Integration of Augmented Reality (AR) and Virtual Reality (VR) as Marketing Communications Channels in the Hospitality and Tourism Service Sector. In O. Adeola, R. E. Hinson, & A. M. Sakkthivel (Eds.), *Marketing Communications and Brand Development in Emerging Markets Volume II* (pp. 55–79). Springer International Publishing. DOI: 10.1007/978-3-030-95581-6_3

Barbe, D., & Neuburger, L. (2021). Generation Z and Digital Influencers in the Tourism Industry. In Stylos, N., Rahimi, R., Okumus, B., & Williams, S. (Eds.), *Generation Z Marketing and Management in Tourism and Hospitality.*, DOI: 10.1007/978-3-030-70695-1_7

Barbosa, D. P., & Medaglia, J. (2019). Tecnologia digital, turismo e os hábitos de consumo dos viajantes contemporâneos. *Marketing & Tourism Review*, 4(2), 1–33.

Barbu, C. A., Popa, A., & Zaharia, R. M. (2023). The Use of Digital Technologies in Tourism Management. *Ovidius University Annals. Economic Sciences Series*, 23(2), 394–401.

Barragáns-Martínez, A. B., & Costa-Montenegro, E. (2015). Adding personalization and social features to a context-aware application for mobile tourism. In *Hospitality, travel, and tourism: Concepts, methodologies, tools, and applications* (pp. 467–480). IGI Global. DOI: 10.4018/978-1-4666-6543-9.ch028

Barreto, J. J., Rubio, N., Campo, S., & Molinillo, S. (2020). Linking the online destination brand experience and brand credibility with tourists' behavioral intentions toward a destination. *Tourism Management*, 79, 104101. DOI: 10.1016/j.tourman.2020.104101

Barta, S., Belanche, D., Fernández, A., & Flavián, M. (2023). Influencer marketing on TikTok: The effectiveness of humor and followers' hedonic experience. *Journal of Retailing and Consumer Services*, 70, 103149. DOI: 10.1016/j.jretconser.2022.103149

Barykin, S. Y., Kapustina, I. V., Kirillova, T. V., Yadykin, V. K., & Konnikov, Y. A. (2020). Economics of digital ecosystems. *Journal of Open Innovation*, 6(4), 124. DOI: 10.3390/joitmc6040124

Bastrygina, T., Lim, W. M., Jopp, R., & Weissmann, M. A. (2024). Unraveling the power of social media influencers: Qualitative insights into the role of Instagram influencers in the hospitality and tourism industry. *Journal of Hospitality and Tourism Management*, 58, 214–243. DOI: 10.1016/j.jhtm.2024.01.007

Bayuk, M. N., & Aslan, M. (2019). Influencer Marketing. *The Journal of Academic Social Science*, 75(75), 173–185. DOI: 10.16992/ASOS.14033

Behera, B., & Gaur, M. (2022). Skill development in India–A literature review. *GIS Science Journal*, 9(1), 1721–1731.

Belanche, D., Casaló, L. V., Flavián, M., & Ibáñez-Sánchez, S. (2021). Understanding influencer marketing: The role of congruence between influencers, products and consumers. *Journal of Business Research*, 132, 186–195. DOI: 10.1016/j.jbusres.2021.03.067

Benckendorff, P., Xiang, Z., & Sheldon, P. (2019). *Tourism information technology*. CABI. DOI: 10.1079/9781786393432.0000

Bhaskaraputra, A., Sutojo, F., Ramadhan, A. N., & Gunawan, A. A. S. (2022). Systematic Literature Review on Solving Personalization Problem in Digital Marketing using Machine Learning and Its Impact. *IEEE Xplore*, 178–182, 178–182. Advance online publication. DOI: 10.1109/iSemantic55962.2022.9920387

Bhattacharya, A. (2023). Parasocial interaction in social media influencer-based marketing: An SEM approach. *Journal of Internet Commerce*, 22(2), 272–292. DOI: 10.1080/15332861.2022.2049112

Bieser, J. C., & Hilty, L. M. (2018). Assessing indirect environmental effects of information and communication technology (ICT): A systematic literature review. *Sustainability (Basel)*, 10(8), 2662. DOI: 10.3390/su10082662

Bigne, E., & Maturana, P. (2022). Does Virtual Reality Trigger Visits and Booking Holiday Travel Packages? *Cornell Hospitality Quarterly*, 64(2), 193896552211023. DOI: 10.1177/19389655221102386

Bigné, E., William, E., & Soria-Olivas, E. (2020). Similarity and Consistency in Hotel Online Ratings across Platforms. *Journal of Travel Research*, 59(4), 742–758. Advance online publication. DOI: 10.1177/0047287519859705

Bilgin, B. (2023). Influencer Marketing from a Digital Entrepreneurship Perspective. Master's Thesis.

Biradar, S., Saumya, S., & Chauhan, A. (2023). Combating the infodemic: COVID-19 induced fake news recognition in social media networks. *Complex & Intelligent Systems*, 9(3), 2879–2891. DOI: 10.1007/s40747-022-00672-2 PMID: 35194546

Bogdan, S. O. F. R. O. N. O. V. (2018). Millennials: A new trend for the tourism industry. *Economic Series.*, 18(3), 109–122. Annals of Spiru Haret University. DOI: 10.26458/1838

Bognar, Z. B., Puljic, N. P., & Kadezabek, D. (2019). Impact of influencer marketing on consumer behaviour. *Economic and Social Development: Book of Proceedings*, 301-309.

Bokunewicz, J. F., & Shulman, J. (2017). Influencer identification in Twitter networks of destination marketing organizations. *Journal of Hospitality and Tourism Technology*, 8(2), 205–219. DOI: 10.1108/JHTT-09-2016-0057

Borges, A. F., Laurindo, F. J., Spínola, M. M., Gonçalves, R. F., & Mattos, C. A. (2021). The strategic use of artificial intelligence in the digital era: Systematic literature review and future research directions. *International Journal of Information Management*, 57, 102225. DOI: 10.1016/j.ijinfomgt.2020.102225

Borges-Tiago, M. T., Santiago, J., & Tiago, F. (2023). Mega or macro social media influencers: Who endorses brands better? *Journal of Business Research*, 157, 113606. DOI: 10.1016/j.jbusres.2022.113606

Borsci, S., Malizia, A., Schmettow, M., van der Velde, F., Tariverdiyeva, G., Balaji, D., & Chamberlain, A. (2022). The Chatbot Usability Scale: The Design and Pilot of a Usability Scale for Interaction with AI-Based Conversational Agents. *Personal and Ubiquitous Computing*, 26(1), 95–119. DOI: 10.1007/s00779-021-01582-9

Boston Consulting Group. (2013). *Traveling with millennials*. Retrieved from https://www.bcg.com/publications/2013/transportation-tourism-marketing-sales-traveling-millennials

Bozkurt, A. (2023). Using social media in open, distance, and digital education. In *Handbook of open, distance and digital education* (pp. 1237–1254). Springer Nature Singapore. DOI: 10.1007/978-981-19-2080-6_73

Breves, P. L., Liebers, N., Abt, M., & Kunze, A. (2019). The perceived fit between instagram influencers and the endorsed brand: How influencer–brand fit affects source credibility and persuasive effectiveness. *Journal of Advertising Research*, 59(4), 440–454. DOI: 10.2501/JAR-2019-030

Brown, D., & Hayes, N. (2008). *Influencer marketing*. Routledge. DOI: 10.4324/9780080557700

Buhalis, D. (2019). Technology in tourism-from information communication technologies to eTourism and smart tourism towards ambient intelligence tourism: A perspective article. *Tourism Review*, 75(1), 267–272. DOI: 10.1108/TR-06-2019-0258

Buhalis, D., & Cheng, E. S. Y. (2019). Exploring the Use of Chatbots in Hotels: Technology Providers' Perspective. In Neidhardt, J., & Worndl, W. (Eds.), *Information and Communication Technologies in Tourism 2020* (pp. 231–242)., DOI: 10.1007/978-3-030-36737-4_19

Buhalis, D., Efthymiou, L., Uzunboylu, N., & Thrassou, A. (2024). Charting the progress of technology adoption in tourism and hospitality in the era of industry 4.0. *EuroMed Journal of Business*, 19(1), 1–20. DOI: 10.1108/EMJB-11-2023-0310

Bui, M., Krishen, A. S., Anlamlier, E., & Berezan, O. (2022). Fear of missing out in the digital age: The role of social media satisfaction and advertising engagement. *Psychology and Marketing*, 39(4), 683–693. DOI: 10.1002/mar.21611

Buitrago-Ropero, M., Ramírez-Montoya, M., & Laverde, A. (2023). Digital footprints (2005–2019): A systematic mapping of studies in education. *Interactive Learning Environments*, 31(2), 876–889. DOI: 10.1080/10494820.2020.1814821

Bulchand-Gidumal, J. (2022). Impact of Artificial Intelligence in Travel, Tourism, and Hospitality. In *Handbook of e-Tourism* (pp. 1943–1962). Springer International Publishing., DOI: 10.1007/978-3-030-48652-5_110

Bulchand-Gidumal, J., William Secin, E., O'Connor, P., & Buhalis, D. (2023). Artificial intelligence's impact on hospitality and tourism marketing: Exploring key themes and addressing challenges. *Current Issues in Tourism*, 27(14), 2345–2362. DOI: 10.1080/13683500.2023.2229480

Bushara, M. A., Abdou, A. H., Hassan, T. H., Sobaih, A. E. E., Albohnayh, A. S. M., Alshammari, W. G., Aldoreeb, M., Elsaed, A. A., & Elsaied, M. A. (2023). Power of social media marketing: How perceived value mediates the impact on restaurant followers' purchase intention, willingness to pay a premium price, and e-WoM? *Sustainability (Basel)*, 15(6), 5331. DOI: 10.3390/su15065331

Bustamante, A., Sebastia, L., & Onaindia, E. (2021). On the representativeness of openstreetmap for the evaluation of country tourism competitiveness. *ISPRS International Journal of Geo-Information*, 10(5), 301. Advance online publication. DOI: 10.3390/ijgi10050301

Cai, W., McKenna, B., & Waizenegger, L. (2020). Turning it off: Emotions in digital-free travel. *Journal of Travel Research*, 59(5), 909–927. DOI: 10.1177/0047287519868314

Camilleri, M. A., Troise, C., & Kozak, M. (2023). Functionality and usability features of ubiquitous mobile technologies: The acceptance of interactive travel apps. *Journal of Hospitality and Tourism Technology*, 14(2), 188–207. DOI: 10.1108/JHTT-12-2021-0345

Canöz, K., Gülmez, Ö., & Eroğlu, G. (2020). Influencer marketing, the rising star of marketing: A research to determine the purchasing behavior of influencer followers. *Journal of Selçuk University Vocational School of Social Sciences*, 23(1), 73–91.

Cavagnaro, E., Staffieri, S., & Postma, A. (2018). Understanding millennials' tourism experience: Values and meaning to travel as a key for identifying target clusters for youth (sustainable) tourism. *Journal of Tourism Futures*, 4(1), 31–42. DOI: 10.1108/JTF-12-2017-0058

Cavalinhos, S., Marques, S. H., & de Fátima Salgueiro, M. (2021). The use of mobile devices in-store and the effect on shopping experience: A systematic literature review and research agenda. *International Journal of Consumer Studies*, 45(6), 1198–1216. DOI: 10.1111/ijcs.12690

Cepeda-Pacheco, J. C., & Domingo, M. C. (2022). Deep learning and Internet of Things for tourist attraction recommendations in smart cities. *Neural Computing & Applications*, 34(10), 7691–7709. DOI: 10.1007/s00521-021-06872-0

Çetin, F. A., & Öziç, N. (2020). The effect of Instagram influencers on purchasing in integrated marketing communication. *Journal of Business Research*, 12(1), 157–172.

Chaffey, D., & Smith, P. (2022). *Digital marketing excellence: planning, optimizing and integrating online marketing*. Routledge. DOI: 10.4324/9781003009498

Chakravarty, U., Chand, G., & Singh, U. N. (2021). Millennial travel vlogs: Emergence of a new form of virtual tourism in the post-pandemic era? *Worldwide Hospitality and Tourism Themes*, 13(5), 666–676. Advance online publication. DOI: 10.1108/WHATT-05-2021-0077

Chatzigeorgiou, C. (2017). Modelling the impact of social media influencers on behavioural intentions of millennials: The case of tourism in rural areas in Greece. *Journal of Tourism* [JTHSM]. *Heritage & Services Marketing*, 3(2), 25–29.

Chavez, L., Ruiz, C., Curras, R., & Hernandez, B. (2020). The role of travel motivations and social media use in consumer interactive behaviour: A uses and gratifications perspective. *Sustainability (Basel)*, 12(21), 1–22. DOI: 10.3390/su12218789

Cheng, M. (2024). Social media and tourism geographies: mapping future research agenda. In *Tourism Geographies*. DOI: 10.1080/14616688.2024.2304782

Cheng, W., Tian, R., & Chiu, D. K. W. (2023). Travel vlogs influencing tourist decisions: Information preferences and gender differences. *Aslib Journal of Information Management*, 76(1), 86–103. Advance online publication. DOI: 10.1108/AJIM-05-2022-0261

Cheng, X., Zhang, X., Yang, B., & Fu, Y. (2022). An investigation on trust in AI-enabled collaboration: Application of AI-Driven chatbot in accommodation-based sharing economy. *Electronic Commerce Research and Applications*, 54, 101164. DOI: 10.1016/j.elerap.2022.101164 PMID: 35968256

Cheng, Y., & Jiang, H. (2022). Customer–brand relationship in the era of artificial intelligence: Understanding the role of chatbot marketing efforts. *Journal of Product and Brand Management*, 31(2), 252–264. DOI: 10.1108/JPBM-05-2020-2907

Chen, L., Yan, Y., & Smith, A. N. (2023). What drives digital engagement with sponsored videos? An investigation of video influencers' authenticity management strategies. *Journal of the Academy of Marketing Science*, 51(1), 198–221. DOI: 10.1007/s11747-022-00887-2

Chen, W. K., Silaban, P. H., Hutagalung, W. E., & Silalahi, A. D. K. (2023). How Instagram influencers contribute to consumer travel decision: Insights from SEM and fsQCA. *Emerging Science Journal*, 7(1), 16–37. DOI: 10.28991/ESJ-2023-07-01-02

Chen, Z., Cao, H., Wang, H., Xu, F., Kostakos, V., & Li, Y. (2020). Will You Come Back/Check-in Again? Understanding Characteristics Leading to Urban Revisitation and Re-check-in. *Proceedings of the ACM on Interactive, Mobile, Wearable and Ubiquitous Technologies*, 4(3), 1–27. Advance online publication. DOI: 10.1145/3411812

Cheung, W. (2012, June 4). *Trends in Travel Technology*. Handle.net. http://hdl.handle.net/10214/3696

Cheung, M. L., Ting, H., Cheah, J.-H., & Sharipudin, M.-N. S. (2021). Examining the role of social media-based destination brand community in evoking tourists' emotions and intention to co-create and visit. *Journal of Product and Brand Management*, 30(1), 28–43. DOI: 10.1108/JPBM-09-2019-2554

Chilembwe, J. M., & Gondwe, F. W. (2020). Role of Social Media in Travel Planning and Tourism Destination Decision Making. In Ramos, C. M. Q., de Almeida, C. R., & Fernandes, P. O. (Eds.), *Handbook of Research on Social Media Applications for the Tourism and Hospitality Sector* (pp. 36–51). IGI Global., DOI: 10.4018/978-1-7998-1947-9.ch003

Choi, Y., Hickerson, B., Lee, J., Lee, H., & Choe, Y. (2022). Digital tourism and wellbeing: Conceptual framework to examine technology effects of online travel media. *International Journal of Environmental Research and Public Health*, 19(9), 5639. DOI: 10.3390/ijerph19095639 PMID: 35565033

Choo, J., Park, S., & Noh, S. (2021). Associations of covid-19 knowledge and risk perception with the full adoption of preventive behaviors in Seoul. *International Journal of Environmental Research and Public Health*, 18(22), 12102. Advance online publication. DOI: 10.3390/ijerph182212102 PMID: 34831866

Christensen, J., Hansen, J. M., & Wilson, P. (2024). Understanding the role and impact of Generative Artificial Intelligence (AI) hallucination within consumers' tourism decision-making processes. *Current Issues in Tourism*, 1–16. DOI: 10.1080/13683500.2023.2300032

Çınar, K. (2020). Role of mobile technology for tourism development. In *The emerald handbook of ICT in tourism and hospitality* (pp. 273–288). Emerald Publishing Limited. DOI: 10.1108/978-1-83982-688-720201017

Conde, R., & Casais, B. (2023). Micro, macro and mega-influencers on instagram: The power of persuasion via the parasocial relationship. *Journal of Business Research*, 158, 113708. DOI: 10.1016/j.jbusres.2023.113708

Conyette, M. (2015). 21 Century Travel using Websites, Mobile and Wearable Technology Devices. *Athens Journal of Tourism*, 2(2), 105–116. DOI: 10.30958/ajt.2-2-3

Cotten, D., Codjoe, J., & Loker, M. (2020). Evaluating advancements in Bluetooth technology for travel time and segment speed studies. *Transportation Research Record: Journal of the Transportation Research Board*, 2674(4), 193–204. DOI: 10.1177/0361198120911931

Cui, Y., & van Esch, P. (2023). Artificial Intelligence in Customer Service Strategy for Seamless Customer Experiences. In J. N. Sheth, V. Jain, M. E., & A. Ambika (Eds.), *Artificial Intelligence in Customer Service* (pp. 73–97). Springer International Publishing. DOI: 10.1007/978-3-031-33898-4_4

Cunha, M. (2019). The tourism journey, from inspiration to post-travel phase, and the mobile technologies. *African Journal of Hospitality, Tourism and Leisure*, 8(5). https://www.ajhtl.com/uploads/7/1/6/3/7163688/article_1_vol_8_5__2019_portugal.pdf

Ďaďová, I., & Soviar, J. (2021). The application of online marketing tools in marketing communication of the entities with the tourism offer in 2020 in Slovakia. *Transportation Research Procedia*, 55, 1791–1799. DOI: 10.1016/j.trpro.2021.07.170

Dagnew, D. (2014). The Strategic Roles of Social Media Marketing to Build A Strong Brand Equity (The case of selected companies in Ethiopia). 1–87.

Dai, Y., Cheng, X., & Liu, Y. (2023). Information alienation and circle fracture: Policy communication and opinion-generating networks on social media in China from the perspective of COVID-19 policy. *Systems*, 11(7), 340. DOI: 10.3390/systems11070340

Dash, M., & Bakshi, S. (2022). An Exploratory study of Customer Perceptions of usage of chatbots in the hospitality industry. *International Journal on Customer Relations*, 7(2), 27–33.

Das, S. (2021). *Search engine optimization and marketing: A recipe for success in digital marketing*. Chapman and Hall/CRC. DOI: 10.1201/9780429298509

Daugherty, T., Eastin, M. S., & Bright, L. (2008). Exploring Consumer Motivations for Creating User-Generated Content. *Journal of Interactive Advertising*, 8(2), 16–25. DOI: 10.1080/15252019.2008.10722139

Dawi, N. M., Namazi, H., Hwang, H. J., & Ismail, S. (2021). *Attitude toward protective behavior engagement during COVID-19 pandemic in Malaysia: The role of e-government and social media*. 9(March), 1–8. https://doi.org/DOI: 10.3389/fpubh.2021.609716

De Veirman, M., Cauberghe, V., & Hudders, L. (2017). Marketing through Instagram influencers: the impact of number of followers and product divergence on brand attitude. Https://Doi.Org/10.1080/02650487.2017.1348035, *36*(5), 798–828. DOI: 10.1080/02650487.2017.1348035

Deb, S. K., Nafi, S. M., & Valeri, M. (2024). Promoting tourism business through digital marketing in the new normal era: A sustainable approach. *European Journal of Innovation Management*, 27(3), 775–799. DOI: 10.1108/EJIM-04-2022-0218

Dedeoğlu, B. B., Van Niekerk, M., Küçükergin, K. G., De Martino, M., & Okumuş, F. (2020). Effect of social media sharing on destination brand awareness and destination quality. *Journal of Vacation Marketing*, 26(1), 33–56. DOI: 10.1177/1356766719858644

Deegan, O. (2021). # Influenced: The Impact of Influencer Marketing on the Travel and Tourism Industry of Ireland. A qualitative study (Doctoral dissertation, Dublin Business School).

Deiss, R., & Henneberry, R. (2020). *Digital marketing for dummies*. John Wiley & Sons.

Del Vecchio, P., Malandugno, C., Passiante, G., & Sakka, G. (2022). Circular economy business model for smart tourism: The case of Ecobnb. *EuroMed Journal of Business*, 17(1), 88–104. DOI: 10.1108/EMJB-09-2020-0098

Delbaere, M., Michael, B., & Phillips, B. J. (2021). Social media influencers: A route to brand engagement for their followers. *Psychology and Marketing*, 38(1), 101–112. DOI: 10.1002/mar.21419

Dellarocas, C. (2003). The Digitization of Word of Mouth: Promise and Challenges of Online Feedback Mechanisms. *Management Science*, 49(10), 1407–1424. DOI: 10.1287/mnsc.49.10.1407.17308

Deloitte. (2019). Gen Z and millennial travel: The wanderlust generations. Retrieved from https://www2.deloitte.com/us/en/pages/technology-media -and-telecommunications/articles/gen-Z-and-millennial-travel-the-wanderlust -generations.html

Demir, S. (2019). The impact of the perception of memorable tourism experiences across generations on post-purchase behavior. Master's Thesis.

Demirağ, F. (2023). The Impact of Influencer Characteristics on Consumers' Behavioral Intentions. *Dumlupınar University Journal of Social Sciences*, 77, 219–233.

Deng, F., & Jiang, X. (2023). Effects of human versus virtual human influencers on the appearance anxiety of social media users. *Journal of Retailing and Consumer Services*, 71, 103233. DOI: 10.1016/j.jretconser.2022.103233

Deputat, M., Podolian, M., Zhupnyk, V., Terletska, K., & Gorishevskyy, P. (2024). Evolution of information systems and technologies in the hospitality and tourism sector: a historical perspective. *Multidisciplinary Science Journal*, 6.

Dey, B., Mathew, J., & Chee-Hua, C. (2020). Influence of destination attractiveness factors and travel motivations on rural homestay choice: The moderating role of need for uniqueness. *International Journal of Culture, Tourism and Hospitality Research*, 14(4), 639–666. DOI: 10.1108/IJCTHR-08-2019-0138

Dhun & Dangi, H. K. (2023). Influencer marketing: Role of influencer credibility and congruence on brand attitude and eWOM. *Journal of Internet Commerce*, 22(sup1), S28-S72.

Di Censo, G., Delfabbro, P., & King, D. L. (2024). The impact of gambling advertising and marketing on young people: A critical review and analysis of methodologies. *International Gambling Studies*, 24(1), 71–91. DOI: 10.1080/14459795.2023.2199050

Dias, S., & Afonso, V. A. (2021). Impact of mobile applications in changing the tourist experience. *European Journal of Tourism. Hospitality and Recreation*, 11(1), 113–120. DOI: 10.2478/ejthr-2021-0011

Dilek, S. E. (2018). The Changing Meaning of Travel, Tourism and Tourist Definitions. (Unpublished thesis). Batman Üniversitesi.

Dimitriou, C. K., & AbouElgheit, E. (2019). Understanding generation Z's travel social decision-making. *Tourism and Hospitality Management*, 25(2), 311–334. DOI: 10.20867/thm.25.2.4

Dimokas, N., Kalogirou, K., Spanidis, P., & Kehagias, D. (2018, July). A mobile application for multimodal trip planning. In *2018 9th International Conference on Information, Intelligence, Systems and Applications (IISA)* (pp. 1-8). IEEE. DOI: 10.1109/IISA.2018.8633665

Ding, Y., Du, X., Li, Q., Zhang, M., Zhang, Q., Tan, X., & Liu, Q. (2020). Risk perception of coronavirus disease 2019 (COVID-19) and its related factors among college students in China during quarantine. *PLoS ONE, 15*(8 August), 1–13. https://doi.org/DOI: 10.1371/journal.pone.0237626

Djafarova, E., & Rushworth, C. (2017). Exploring the credibility of online celebrities' Instagram profiles in influencing the purchase decisions of young female users. *Computers in Human Behavior*, 68, 1–7. DOI: 10.1016/j.chb.2016.11.009

Dolnicar, S. (2021). *Airbnb before, during and after COVID-19*. The University of Queensland., DOI: 10.14264/ab59afd

Donthu, N., Kumar, S., Pandey, N., Pandey, N., & Mishra, A. (2021). Mapping the electronic word-of-mouth (eWOM) research: A systematic review and bibliometric analysis. *Journal of Business Research*, 135(February), 758–773. DOI: 10.1016/j.jbusres.2021.07.015

Dube, K., & Nhamo, G. (2020). Vulnerability of nature-based tourism to climate variability and change: Case of Kariba resort town, Zimbabwe. *Journal of Outdoor Recreation and Tourism*, 29, 100281. Advance online publication. DOI: 10.1016/j.jort.2020.100281

Dubey, A. K. (2017). Future Technology and Service Industry: A Case study of Travel and Tourism Industry. *Global Journal of Enterprise Information System*, 8(3), 65. DOI: 10.18311/gjeis/2016/15742

Dumbliauskas, V., Grigonis, V., & Barauskas, A. (2017). Application of Google-based Data for Travel Time Analysis: Kaunas City Case Study. *PROMET - Traffic&Transportation, 29*(6), 613–621. DOI: 10.7307/ptt.v29i6.2369

Dwityas, N., & Briandana, R. (2017). Social Media in Travel Decision Making Process. *International Journal of Humanities and Social Science*, 7(7). https://www.ijhssnet.com/journals/Vol_7_No_7_July_2017/24.pdf

Dwyer, L., Forsyth, P., & Spurr, R. (2009). *Economic analysis of tourism*. Channel View Publications.

Eco Africa Digital. (n.d.). *How to attract millennials with online messaging for sustainable tourism*. Retrieved on 27th July, 204 from https://www.ecoafricadigital.co.za/sustainable-tourism-online-content-millennials/

Egbert, S., & Rudeloff, C. (2023). Employees as corporate influencers: Exploring the impacts of parasocial interactions on brand equity and brand outcomes. *International Journal of Strategic Communication*, 17(5), 439–456. DOI: 10.1080/1553118X.2023.2231922

Egger, K. (2019). Bachelor Thesis *Instagram's Impact on Destination Choice in Tourism: A critical perspective*. https://www.kaernten-digital.at/files/content/04-News/Bildung/20201123_Digitalisierungsstipendium%20-%20Online%20Verleihung/EGGER%20Kathrin_Bachelorarbeit.pdf

Eichelberger, S., Heigl, M., Peters, M., & Pikkemaat, B. (2021). Exploring the role of tourists: Responsible behavior triggered by the covid-19 pandemic. *Sustainability (Basel)*, 13(11), 5774. Advance online publication. DOI: 10.3390/su13115774

El Archi, Y., Benbba, B., Kabil, M., & Dávid, L. D. (2023). Digital Technologies for Sustainable Tourism Destinations: State of the Art and Research Agenda. *Administrative Sciences*, 13(8), 184. DOI: 10.3390/admsci13080184

El Archi, Y., Benbba, B., Zhu, K., El Andaloussi, Z., Pataki, L., & Dávid, L. D. (2023). Mapping the nexus between sustainability and digitalization in tourist destinations: A bibliometric analysis. *Sustainability (Basel)*, 15(12), 9717. DOI: 10.3390/su15129717

El Mattichi, F., Elabbadi, A., Hmioui, A., & Barhmi, A. (2024). Exploring Sustainability in Tourism Marketing Through Digital and Social Networks: A Literature Review. *Promoting Responsible Tourism with Digital Platforms*, 213-230.

Ellison, R., 2023. Strategies Behind the Communications: An Analysis of Social Media Platforms and Online Communication Channels Utilized by Agricultural Organizations in Texas.

Elshaer, A. M., & Marzouk, A. M. (2024). Memorable tourist experiences: The role of smart tourism technologies and hotel innovations. *Tourism Recreation Research*, 49(3), 445–457. DOI: 10.1080/02508281.2022.2027203

Erdoğan, M. (2023). The Effect of Phenomenon on the Purchasing Behavior of Generation Z: The Example of Female Students of Istanbul Esenyurt University. *Ordu University Social Sciences Institute Journal of Social Sciences Research, 13*(3), 3033-3050.

Ergun, N., Bayrak, R., & Doğan, S. (2019). A qualitative research on Instagram, an important marketing channel for tourism marketing. *Journal of Current Tourism Research*, 3(1), 82–100.

Ettema, D. (2017). Apps, activities and travel: An conceptual exploration based on activity theory. *Transportation*, 45(2), 273–290. DOI: 10.1007/s11116-017-9844-5

Fan, D. X., Lyu, J., Huang, Y., Shang, K., & Buhalis, D. (2024, January). Senior Tourists' Digital Travel Experience: A Humanisation Perspective. In *ENTER e-Tourism Conference* (pp. 317–322). Springer Nature Switzerland. DOI: 10.1007/978-3-031-58839-6_34

Fanni, S. C., Febi, M., Aghakhanyan, G., & Neri, E. (2023). Natural language processing. In *Introduction to Artificial Intelligence* (pp. 87–99). Springer International Publishing. DOI: 10.1007/978-3-031-25928-9_5

Farid, S., Boudia, M. A., & Mwangi, G. (2023). Revolutionizing Tourism: Harnessing the Power of IoT in Smart Destinations. *Journal of Digital Marketing and Communication*, 3(2), 91–99. DOI: 10.53623/jdmc.v3i2.360

Farkić, J., Isailovic, G., & Lesjak, M. (2023). Conceptualising tourist idleness and creating places of otium in nature-based tourism. *Academica Turistica-Tourism and Innovation Journal*, 15(1), 11–23.

Fath, S., Abimanyu, D., & Misbak, M. (2024). Exploring The Relationship Between Responsiveness And Usability And Its Impact On Customer Satisfaction In E-Commerce. *Journal of Management, Economic, and Financial*, 2(4), 72–79. DOI: 10.46799/jmef.v2i4.42

Fawns, T., Ross, J., Carbonel, H., Noteboom, J., Finnegan-Dehn, S., & Raver, M. (2023). Mapping and tracing the postdigital: Approaches and parameters of postdigital research. *Postdigital Science and Education*, 5(3), 623–642. DOI: 10.1007/s42438-023-00391-y

Fedeli, G., & Cheng, M. (2022). Influencer Marketing and Tourism: Another Threat To Integrity for the Industry? *Tourism Analysis*, (April). Advance online publication. DOI: 10.3727/108354222X16510114086370

Femenia-Serra, F., & Gretzel, U. (2020). Influencer marketing for tourism destinations: Lessons from a mature destination. In *Information and Communication Technologies in Tourism 2020:Proceedings of the International Conference in Surrey, United Kingdom, January 08–10, 2020* (pp. 65-78). Springer International Publishing.

Ferrer-Rosell, B., Massimo, D., & Berezina, K. (2023). *Information and Communication Technologies in Tourism 2023:Proceedings of the ENTER 2023 eTourism Conference, January 18-20, 2023.* Springer Nature. DOI: 10.1007/978-3-031-25752-0

Filieri, R., Acikgoz, F., Li, C., & Alguezaui, S. (2023). Influencers' "organic" persuasion through electronic word of mouth: A case of sincerity over brains and beauty. *Psychology and Marketing*, 40(2), 347–364. DOI: 10.1002/mar.21760

Fornell, C., & Larcker, D. (1981). Evaluating Structural Equation Models with Unobservable Variables and Measurement Error. *JMR, Journal of Marketing Research*, 18(1), 39–50. DOI: 10.1177/002224378101800104

Fotis, J., Buhalis, D., & Rossides, N. (2012). *Social Media Use and Impact during the Holiday Travel Planning Process BT - Information and Communication Technologies in Tourism 2012.* 13–24.

Fung, I. C. H., Tse, Z. T. H., Cheung, C. N., Miu, A. S., & Fu, K. W. (2014). Ebola and social media. *Lancet*, 384(9961), 2207. DOI: 10.1016/S0140-6736(14)62418-1 PMID: 25625391

Gaenssle, S., & Budzinski, O. (2021). Stars in social media: New light through old windows? *Journal of Media Business Studies*, 18(2), 79–105. DOI: 10.1080/16522354.2020.1738694

Gamage, T. C., & Ashill, N. J. (2023). # Sponsored-influencer marketing: Effects of the commercial orientation of influencer-created content on followers' willingness to search for information. *Journal of Product and Brand Management*, 32(2), 316–329. DOI: 10.1108/JPBM-10-2021-3681

Gani, M. O., Roy, H., Faroque, A. R., Rahman, M. S., & Munawara, M. (2024). Smart tourism technologies for the psychological well-being of tourists: A Bangladesh perspective. *Journal of Hospitality and Tourism Insights*, 7(3), 1371–1390. DOI: 10.1108/JHTI-06-2022-0239

Gan, J., Shi, S., Filieri, R., & Leung, W. K. (2023). Short video marketing and travel intentions: The interplay between visual perspective, visual content, and narration appeal. *Tourism Management*, 99, 104795. DOI: 10.1016/j.tourman.2023.104795

Gao, K., Yang, X., Wu, C., Qiao, T., Chen, X., Yang, M., & Chen, L. (2020). Exploiting Location-Based Context for POI Recommendation When Traveling to a New Region. *IEEE Access: Practical Innovations, Open Solutions*, 8, 52404–52412. Advance online publication. DOI: 10.1109/ACCESS.2020.2980982

Gao, Q., Fu, H., Zhang, K., Trajcevski, G., Teng, X., & Zhou, F. (2024). Inferring Real Mobility in Presence of Fake Check-ins Data. *ACM Transactions on Intelligent Systems and Technology*, 15(1), 1–25. Advance online publication. DOI: 10.1145/3604941

Garg, A., & Kumar, J. (2017). The impact of risk perception and factors on tourists' decision making for choosing the destination Uttarakhand/India. *Journal of Tourism and Management Research*, 2(2), 144–160. DOI: 10.26465/ojtmr.2017229490

Garikapati, V. M., Pendyala, R. M., Morris, E. A., Mokhtarian, P. L., & McDonald, N. (2016, September). Activity patterns, time use, and travel of millennials: A generation in transition? *Transport Reviews*, 36(no. 5), 558–584. DOI: 10.1080/01441647.2016.1197337

Garner, B., & Kim, D. (2022). Analyzing user-generated content to improve customer satisfaction at local wine tourism destinations: An analysis of Yelp and TripAdvisor reviews. *Consumer Behavior in Tourism and Hospitality*, 17(4), 413–435. DOI: 10.1108/CBTH-03-2022-0077

Garson, G. D. (2016). *Partial Least Squares: Regression and Structural Equation Models* (3rd ed.). Asheboro: Statistical Publishing Associates.

Gasser, U., & Simun, M. (2010). Digital Lifestyle and Online Travel: Looking at the Case of Digital Natives. In Conrady, R., & Buck, M. (Eds.), *Trends and issues in global tourism 2010* (pp. 83–89). Springer Nature., DOI: 10.1007/978-3-642-10829-7_11

Gedik, Y. (2020). A rising trend in social media: A conceptual evaluation on influencer marketing. *Pamukkale University Journal of Business Research*, 7(2), 362–385.

Ge, J., & Gretzel, U. (2018). Emoji rhetoric: A social media influencer perspective. *Journal of Marketing Management*, 34(15-16), 1272–1295. DOI: 10.1080/0267257X.2018.1483960

Ghaderi, Z., Beal, L., Zaman, M., Hall, C. M., & Rather, R. A. (2023). How does sharing travel experiences on social media improve social and personal ties? *Current Issues in Tourism*, 1–17. DOI: 10.1080/13683500.2023.2266101

Ghaly, M. (2023). The influence of user-generated content and social media travel influencers credibility on the visit intention of Generation Z. *Journal of Association of Arab Universities for Tourism and Hospitality*, 24(2), 367–382. DOI: 10.21608/jaauth.2023.218047.1477

Glenister, G. (2021). *Influencer Marketing Strategy: How to create successful influencer marketing.* Kogan Page Publishers.

Gokasar, I., & Bakioglu, G. (2018). Modeling the effects of real time traffic information on travel behavior: A case study of Istanbul Technical University. *Transportation Research Part F: Traffic Psychology and Behaviour*, 58, 881–892. Advance online publication. DOI: 10.1016/j.trf.2018.07.013

Golja, T., & Paulišić, M. (2021). Managing-technology enhanced tourist experience. *Management*, 26(1), 63–95. DOI: 10.30924/mjcmi.26.1.5

Gong, X., Liuxiao, X., & Xiao, Z. (2022). A dedication-constraint model of consumer switching behavior in mobile payment applications. *Information & Management*, 59(4), 103640. DOI: 10.1016/j.im.2022.103640

Gon, M. (2020). Local experiences on Instagram: Social media data as source of evidence for experience design. *Journal of Destination Marketing & Management*, 19, 100435. DOI: 10.1016/j.jdmm.2020.100435

Goodchild, M. F. (2007). Citizens as sensors: The world of volunteered geography. In *GeoJournal*. DOI: 10.1007/s10708-007-9111-y

Gopal, A., & Shanmugam, A. (2023). Advancing travel and tourism: embracing the era of artificial intelligence. *YMER Digital.*, 22, 334–341. DOI: 10.37896/YMER22.10/24

Gössling, S., Hall, C. M., & Weaver, D. (2019). *Sustainable tourism futures: A critical analysis of sustainability and development in tourism.* Routledge.

Gössling, S., & Scott, D. (2018). The decarbonisation impasse: Global tourism leaders' views on climate change mitigation. *Journal of Sustainable Tourism*, 26(12), 2071–2086. DOI: 10.1080/09669582.2018.1529770

Granell, V. B. (2018). The tourist 3.0 or adprosumer: a new challenge for the law and the economy. *International Journal of Tourism Law Ridetur*, 2(2), 47–73. DOI: 10.21071/ridetur.v2i2.11518

Gretzel, U. (2018). Influencer marketing in travel and tourism. In *Advances in Social Media for Travel, Tourism and Hospitality* (Issue February). Routledge. DOI: 10.4324/9781315565736-13

Gretzel, U., Sigala, M., Xiang, Z., & Koo, C. (2015). Smart tourism: Foundations and developments. *Electronic Markets*, 25(3), 179–188. DOI: 10.1007/s12525-015-0196-8

Gross, J., & von Wangenheim, F. (2022). Influencer Marketing on Instagram: Empirical Research on Social Media Engagement with Sponsored Posts. *Journal of Interactive Advertising*, 22(3), 289–310. DOI: 10.1080/15252019.2022.2123724

Gulati, S. (2022). Social and sustainable: Exploring social media use for promoting sustainable behaviour and demand amongst Indian tourists. *International Hospitality Review*, 36(2), 373–393. DOI: 10.1108/IHR-12-2020-0072

Gulati, S. (2024). Exploring the generational influence on social media-based tourist decision-making in India. *Information Discovery and Delivery*, 52(2), 185–196. DOI: 10.1108/IDD-11-2022-0115

Gulati, S. (2024). Unveiling the tourist's social media cycle: Use of social media during travel decision-making. *Global Knowledge. Memory and Communication*, 73(4/5), 575–595. DOI: 10.1108/GKMC-06-2022-0134

Gümüş, D., & Kızılırmak, I. (2023). The Effect of Recall Marketing on Customer Behavior and Satisfaction. *Yaşar University E-Journal*, 18(72), 380–404.

Gunawan, H., Udin, U., & Rahayu, M. K. P. (2024). Research trends on the impact of digital transformation on the development of the tourism industry: A bibliometric analysis. *Multidisciplinary Reviews*, 7(5), 2024090. DOI: 10.31893/multirev.2024090

Güneş, E., Ekmekçi, Z., & Taş, M. (2022). The effect of trust in social media influencers on pre-purchase behavior: A research on Generation Z. *Turkish Journal of Tourism Research*, 6(1), 163–183.

Guo, P. (2023). Exploring the Effects of Social Media Influencer on Consumers Hotel Decision in China. *Lecture Notes in Education Psychology and Public Media*, 4(1), 1158–1166. DOI: 10.54254/2753-7048/4/2022843

Guo, Q., Mu, L., & Lou, S. (2024). Revolutionizing travel experiences: An in-depth analysis of intelligent booking systems and behavioral patterns. *Intelligent Decision Technologies*, 18(2), 1–18. DOI: 10.3233/IDT-230625

Gupta, S., Sufi, T., & Kumar Gautam, P. (2022). Role of Technological Transformation in Shaping Millennials' Travel Behaviour: A Review. 2022 *10th International Conference on Reliability, Infocom Technologies and Optimization (Trends and Future Directions)* (ICRITO). https://doi.org/DOI: 10.1109/ICRITO56286.2022.9965175

Gürkan, A. S., & Ulema, Ş. (2021). The Effect of Snobism on Tourism Demand: A Research on Instagram Users Living in Nişantaşı. *Journal of Turkish Tourism Research*, 4(4), 3249–3262.

Gursoy, D., Li, Y., & Song, H. (2023). ChatGPT and the hospitality and tourism industry: An overview of current trends and future research directions. *Journal of Hospitality Marketing & Management*, 32(5), 579–592. DOI: 10.1080/19368623.2023.2211993

Gursoy, D., Malodia, S., & Dhir, A. (2022). The metaverse in the hospitality and tourism industry: An overview of current trends and future research directions. *Journal of Hospitality Marketing & Management*, 31(5), 527–534. DOI: 10.1080/19368623.2022.2072504

Gvaramadze, A. (2022a). Digital technologies and social media in tourism, 28–38. DOI: 10.19044/esj.2022.v18n10p28

Haddouche, H., & Salomone, C. (2018). Generation Z and the tourist experience: Tourist stories and use of social networks. *Journal of Tourism Futures*, 4(1), 69–79. DOI: 10.1108/JTF-12-2017-0059

Hair, J. F., Black, W. C., Babin, B. J., Anderson, R. E., & Tatham, R. L. (2006). *Multivariate Data Analysis* (6th ed.). Pearson University Press.

Hair, J. F., Hult, G. T. M., Ringle, C. M., & Sastedt, M. (2014). *A Primer on Partial Least Squares Structural Equation Modeling (PLS-SEM)* (1st ed.). SAGE Publications, Inc.

Hall, C. M., & Lew, A. A. (2010). *Understanding and managing tourism impacts: An integrated approach*. Routledge.

Hameed, I., Mubarik, M. S., Khan, K., & Waris, I. (2022). Can your smartphone make you a tourist? Mine does: Understanding the consumer's adoption mechanism for mobile payment system. *Human Behavior and Emerging Technologies*, 2022(1), 4904686. DOI: 10.1155/2022/4904686

Hamid, R. A., Albahri, A. S., Alwan, J. K., Al-Qaysi, Z. T., Albahri, O. S., Zaidan, A. A., Alnoor, A., Alamoodi, A. H., & Zaidan, B. B. (2021). How smart is e-tourism? A systematic review of smart tourism recommendation system applying data management. *Computer Science Review*, 39, 100337. DOI: 10.1016/j.cosrev.2020.100337

Han, Q., Zheng, B., Cristea, M., Agostini, M., Belanger, J. J., Gutzkow, B., Kreienkamp, J., Leander, N. P., Collaboration, P. (2023). Trust in government regarding COVID-19 and its associations with preventive health behavior and prosocial behavior during the pandemic: a cross-sectional and longitudinal study. *Psychological Medicine* 53(1), 149–159. 9. https://doi.org/DOI: 10.1017/S0033291721001306

Han, D.-I. D., Weber, J., Bastiaansen, M., Mitas, O., & Lub, X. (2019). Virtual and Augmented Reality Technologies to Enhance the Visitor Experience in Cultural Tourism. In tom Dieck, M. C., & Jung, T. (Eds.), *Augmented Reality and Virtual Reality* (pp. 113–128). Springer Cham., DOI: 10.1007/978-3-030-06246-0_9

Han, J., & Chen, H. (2022). Millennial social media users' intention to travel: The moderating role of social media influencer following behavior. *International Hospitality Review*, 36(2), 340–357. DOI: 10.1108/IHR-11-2020-0069

Hanji, S. V., Navalgund, N., Ingalagi, S., Desai, S., & Hanji, S. S. (2024). Adoption of AI Chatbots in Travel and Tourism Services. In Yang, X., Sherratt, R. S., Dey, N., & Joshi, A. (Eds.), *Proceedings of Eighth International Congress on Information and Communication Technology. ICICT 2023. Lecture Notes in Networks and Systems* (pp. 713–727). Springer. DOI: 10.1007/978-981-99-3236-8_57

Hannonen, O. (2022). Towards an Understanding of Digital Nomadic Mobilities. *Transfers*, 12(3), 115–126. DOI: 10.3167/TRANS.2022.120310

Han, X., Wang, L., & Fan, W. (2023). Cost-effective social media influencer marketing. *INFORMS Journal on Computing*, 35(1), 138–157. DOI: 10.1287/ijoc.2022.1246

Harding-Smith, R. 2024. Tourism Australia: an organisation made for crisis. In *Handbook on Crisis and Disaster Management in Tourism* (pp. 295-308). Edward Elgar Publishing. DOI: 10.4337/9781839105388.00025

Hardt, D., & Glückstad, F. K. (2024). A social media analysis of travel preferences and attitudes, before and during Covid-19. *Tourism Management*, 100, 104821. DOI: 10.1016/j.tourman.2023.104821

Harrigan, P., Daly, T. M., Coussement, K., Lee, J. A., Soutar, G. N., & Evers, U. (2021). Identifying influencers on social media. *International Journal of Information Management*, 56, 102246. DOI: 10.1016/j.ijinfomgt.2020.102246

Haseki, M. İ. (2023). *Phenomen Marketing. Accounting and marketing issues in theory and practice*. Crop.

Haugeland, I. K. F., Følstad, A., Taylor, C., & Alexander, C. (2022). Understanding the user experience of customer service chatbots: An experimental study of chatbot interaction design. *International Journal of Human Computer Studies, 161*(April 2021). DOI: 10.1016/j.ijhcs.2022.102788

Hausmann, A., Toivonen, T., Slotow, R., Tenkanen, H., Moilanen, A., Heikinheimo, V., & Minin, E. Di. (2018). Social media data can be used to understand tourists ' preferences for nature-based experiences in protected areas, 11, 1–10. DOI: 10.1111/conl.12343

Hays, S., Page, S. J., & Buhalis, D. (2013). Social media as a destination marketing tool: Its use by national tourism organisations. *Current Issues in Tourism*, 16(3), 211–239. DOI: 10.1080/13683500.2012.662215

He, J., Xu, D., & Chen, T. (2022). Travel vlogging practice and its impacts on tourist experiences. *Current Issues in Tourism*, 25(15), 2518–2533. Advance online publication. DOI: 10.1080/13683500.2021.1971166

Hennemann, S., Beutel, M. E., & Zwerenz, R. (2017). Ready for eHealth? Health Professionals' Acceptance and Adoption of eHealth Interventions in In-patient Routine Care. *Journal of Health Communication*, 22(3), 274–284. DOI: 10.1080/10810730.2017.1284286 PMID: 28248626

Hıra, M., & Karabulut, A. N. (2021). The Effect of Influential Marketing Practices on Brand Equity and Purchase Intention: A Research on Gastronomy Tourism. *International Journal of Contemporary Tourism Research*, 5(2), 116–128. DOI: 10.30625/ijctr.1022806

Holiday, S., Hayes, J. L., Park, H., Lyu, Y., & Zhou, Y. (2023). A multimodal emotion perspective on social media influencer marketing: The effectiveness of influencer emotions, network size, and branding on consumer brand engagement using facial expression and linguistic analysis. *Journal of Interactive Marketing*, 58(4), 414–439. DOI: 10.1177/10949968231171104

Holsinger, B. (2023). *On Parchment: Animals, Archives, and the Making of Culture from Herodotus to the Digital Age*. Yale University Press. DOI: 10.12987/9780300271485

Hovland, C. I., & Weiss, W. (1951). The influence of source credibility on communication effectiveness. *Public Opinion Quarterly*, 15(4), 635–650. DOI: 10.1086/266350

Hoyer, W., Kroschke, M., Schmitt, B., Kraume, K., & Shankar, V. (2020). Transforming the Customer Experience Through New Technologies. *Journal of Interactive Marketing*, 51(1), 57–71. Advance online publication. DOI: 10.1016/j.intmar.2020.04.001

Hsu, S. (2021). The Role of Technology in Transforming the Travel Experience. *International Journal of Business Management and Visuals, ISSN: 3006-2705*, 4(2), 21-27.

Huang, D., Markovitch, D. G., & Stough, R. A. (2024). Can chatbot customer service match human service agents on customer satisfaction? An investigation in the role of trust. *Journal of Retailing and Consumer Services*, 76, 103600. DOI: 10.1016/j.jretconser.2023.103600

Huang, S. S., Shao, Y., Zeng, Y., Liu, X., & Li, Z. (2021). Impacts of COVID-19 on Chinese nationals' tourism preferences. *Tourism Management Perspectives*, 40(July), 1–10. DOI: 10.1016/j.tmp.2021.100895 PMID: 34642624

Huang, W., Bolton, T. A., Medaglia, J. D., Bassett, D. S., Ribeiro, A., & Van De Ville, D. (2018). A graph signal processing perspective on functional brain imaging. *Proceedings of the IEEE*, 106(5), 868–885. DOI: 10.1109/JPROC.2018.2798928

Huang, X. T., Wang, J., Wang, Z., Wang, L., & Cheng, C. (2023). Experimental study on the influence of virtual tourism spatial situation on the tourists' temperature comfort in the context of metaverse. *Frontiers in Psychology*, 13, 1062876. DOI: 10.3389/fpsyg.2022.1062876 PMID: 36687952

Hudders, L., De Jans, S., & De Veirman, M. (2021). The commercialization of social media stars: A literature review and conceptual framework on the strategic use of social media influencers. *International Journal of Advertising*, 40(3), 327–375. DOI: 10.1080/02650487.2020.1836925

Hudders, L., & Lou, C. (2023). The rosy world of influencer marketing? Its bright and dark sides, and future research recommendations. *International Journal of Advertising*, 42(1), 151–161. DOI: 10.1080/02650487.2022.2137318

Hu, Y., & Min, H. (2023). The dark side of artificial intelligence in service: The "watching-eye" effect and privacy concerns. *International Journal of Hospitality Management*, 110, 103437. Advance online publication. DOI: 10.1016/j.ijhm.2023.103437

Hysa, B., Zdonek, I., & Karasek, A. (2022). Social media in sustainable tourism recovery. *Sustainability (Basel)*, 14(2), 760. DOI: 10.3390/su14020760

Icoz, O., Kutuk, A., & Icoz, O. (2018). Social media and consumer buying decisions in tourism: The case of Turkey. *Pasos (El Sauzal)*, 16(4), 1051–1066. DOI: 10.25145/j.pasos.2018.16.073

Ionescu, A.-M., & Sârbu, F. A. (2024). Exploring the Impact of Smart Technologies on the Tourism Industry. *Sustainability (Basel)*, 16(8), 3318. DOI: 10.3390/su16083318

Irfan, M., Malik, M. S., & Zubair, S. K. (2022). Impact of vlog marketing on consumer travel intent and consumer purchase intent with the moderating role of destination image and ease of travel. *SAGE Open*, 12(2), 21582440221099522. DOI: 10.1177/21582440221099522

Ismail, N., & Yusof, U. K. (2023). A systematic literature review: Recent techniques of predicting STEM stream students. *Computers and Education: Artificial Intelligence*, 5, 100141. DOI: 10.1016/j.caeai.2023.100141

Iswari, N. M. S., Afriliana, N., Dharma, E. M., & Yuniari, N. P. W. (2024). Enhancing Aspect-based Sentiment Analysis in Visitor Review using Semantic Similarity. *Journal of Applied Data Sciences*, 5(2), 724–735. DOI: 10.47738/jads.v5i2.249

Ivanova, L., & Vovchanska, O. (2023). Marketing technologies of personalization in tourism based on artificial intelligence. *Business and Management, 39*(4). Advance online publication. Eastern Europe: Economy. DOI: 10.32782/easterneurope.39-4

Ivanov, S., & Webster, C. (2024). Automated decision-making: Hoteliers' perceptions. *Technology in Society*, 76, 102430. DOI: 10.1016/j.techsoc.2023.102430

Ivanov, S., & Webster, C. (Eds.). (2019). *Robots, artificial intelligence, and service automation in travel, tourism and hospitality*. Emerald Publishing Limited. DOI: 10.1108/9781787566873

Iwashita, M. (2019, July). Trend of influencer marketing and future required functions. 20th IEEE/ACIS International Conference on Software Engineering, *Artificial Intelligence, Networking and Parallel/Distributed Computing* (SNPD) (pp. 2-2). IEEE.

Jain, A. K., Sahoo, S. R., & Kaubiyal, J. (2021). Online social networks security and privacy: Comprehensive review and analysis. *Complex & Intelligent Systems*, 7(5), 2157–2177. Advance online publication. DOI: 10.1007/s40747-021-00409-7

Jain, P. K., Pamula, R., & Srivastava, G. (2021). A systematic literature review on machine learning applications for consumer sentiment analysis using online reviews. *Computer Science Review*, 41, 100413. DOI: 10.1016/j.cosrev.2021.100413

Jamal, S., & Habib, M. A. (2019). Investigation of the use of smartphone applications for trip planning and travel outcomes. *Transportation Planning and Technology*, 42(3), 227–243. DOI: 10.1080/03081060.2019.1576381

Jamal, S., & Habib, M. A. (2020). Smartphone and daily travel: How the use of smartphone applications affect travel decisions. *Sustainable Cities and Society*, 53, 101939. Advance online publication. DOI: 10.1016/j.scs.2019.101939

Jansom, A., Srisangkhajorn, T., & Limarunothai, W. (2022). How chatbot e-services motivate communication credibility and lead to customer satisfaction: The perspective of Thai consumers in the apparel retailing context. *Innovative Marketing*, 18(3), 13–25. DOI: 10.21511/im.18(3).2022.02

Jantcsh, J. (2008). Let's Talk: Social Media for Small Businesses. https://ducttapemarketing.com/the-definition-of-social-media

Jiman, J., & Kulal, S. M. (2023, December). Augmented Reality (AR) And Virtual Reality (VR) Applications In Tourism: Embracing Emerging Technologies For Improved Tourist Experiences In Malaysian Tourism Industry. In *International Conference On Digital Advanced Tourism Management And Technology* (Vol. 1, No. 2, pp. 188-199). DOI: 10.56910/ictmt.v1i2.34

Jog, D. R., & Alcasoas, N. A. (2023). Travel decision making through blogs and vlogs: An empirical investigation on how user-generated content influences destination image. *Turyzm/Tourism, 33*(2), 19-28.

John, T, B., & Cheng, S.-L. (. (2001). Customer loyalty in the hotel industry : The role of customer satisfaction and image. *International Journal of Contemporary Hospitality Management*, 13(5), 213–217. DOI: 10.1108/09596110110395893

Joseph, A. I., & Anandkumar, V. (2021). Destination Brand Communication during COVID-19 Pandemic - The Case of Iceland. *International Journal of Hospitality and Tourism Systems*, 14, 44–58.

Juska, J. (2021). *Integrated marketing communication: advertising and promotion in a digital world*. Routledge. DOI: 10.4324/9780367443382

Jyoti, & Srivastava, P. (2008). Introduction to Hospitality Accommodation. In S. C. Bagri & A. Dahiya (Eds.), *Introduction to Hospitality Industry : A Textbook* (pp. 43–68). Aman Publication.

Kabadayi, S., Ali, F., Choi, H., Joosten, H., & Lu, C. (2019). Smart service experience in hospitality and tourism services: A conceptualization and future research agenda. *Journal of Service Management*, 30(3), 326–348. DOI: 10.1108/JOSM-11-2018-0377

Kabia, S., & Srinivaasan, G. (2023). Role of Smartphones in Destination Promotion and its Impact on Travel Experience. *International Journal of Hospitality and Tourism Systems*, 13, 22.

Kadam, S., & Sen, S. (2023, February). Role of E-Business Enabled Smartphones in Creating Smart Travelers. In *2023 International Conference on Computer Science, Information Technology and Engineering (ICCoSITE)* (pp. 933-938). IEEE. DOI: 10.1109/ICCoSITE57641.2023.10127688

Kalinic, C., & Vujicic, M. D. (2022). Social Media Analytics: Opportunities and Challenges for Cultural Tourism Destinations. In Oliveira, L. (Ed.), *Digital Communications, Internet of Things, and the Future of Cultural Tourism* (pp. 385–410). IGI Global., https://www.igi-global.com/chapter/social-media-analytics/295514 DOI: 10.4018/978-1-7998-8528-3.ch021

Kalpaklıoğlu, N. Ü. (2015). The effect of e-wom as a marketing communication element on the choice of tourism products. *Maltepe University Faculty of Communication Journal, 2*(1), 66-90.

Kang, J., Hong, S., & Hubbard, G. T. (2020). The role of storytelling in advertising: Consumer emotion, narrative engagement level, and word-of-mouth intention. *Journal of Consumer Behaviour*, 19(1), 47–56. DOI: 10.1002/cb.1793

Kannan, R. (2024). Revolutionizing the Tourism Industry through Artificial Intelligence: A Comprehensive Review of AI Integration, Impact on Customer Experience, Operational Efficiency, and Future Trends. *International Journal for Multidimensional Research Perspectives, 2*(2), 01-14.

Kaplan, A., & Haenlein, M. (2010). Users of The World, Unite! The Challenges and Opportunities of Social Media. *Business Horizons*, 53(1), 59–68. DOI: 10.1016/j.bushor.2009.09.003

Kapoor, P. S., Balaji, M. S., Jiang, Y., & Jebarajakirthy, C. (2022). Effectiveness of Travel Social Media Influencers: A Case of Eco-Friendly Hotels. *Journal of Travel Research*, 61(5), 1138–1155. DOI: 10.1177/00472875211019469

Kapuscinski, G. (2014). *The effects of news media on leisure tourists' perception of risk and willingness to travel, with specific reference to events of terrorism and political instability* [Doctoral dissertation, Bournemouth University]. Repository of John Kent Institute in Tourism. https://eprints.bournemouth.ac.uk/21778/

Karadeniz, I. (2019). The effect of social media users' perceptions of travel influencer advertisements on attitude and destination choice. Master's thesis, Trakya University, Institute of Social Sciences.

Kaya, A. (2020). Consumption And Perceptual Obsoletion In The Digital Age: A Study Through Social Media Phenomena. *Academic Sensitivities*, 7(13), 169–191.

Keerthana, R., Kumar, T. A., Manjubala, P., & Pavithra, M. 2020, July. An interactive voice assistant system for guiding the tourists in historical places. In *2020 International Conference on System, Computation, Automation and Networking (ICSCAN)* (pp. 1-5). IEEE. DOI: 10.1109/ICSCAN49426.2020.9262347

Keller, K. L. (1993). Conceptualizing, measuring, and managing customer-based brand equity. *Journal of Marketing*, 57(1), 1–22. DOI: 10.1177/002224299305700101

Ketter, E. (2021). Millennial travel: Tourism micro-trends of European Generation Y. *Journal of Tourism Futures*, 7(2), 192–196. DOI: 10.1108/JTF-10-2019-0106

Khang, A., Gujrati, R., Uygun, H., Tailor, R., & Gaur, S. (2024). *Data-Driven Modelling and Predictive Analytics in Business and Finance: Concepts, Designs, Technologies, and Applications*. CRC Press. DOI: 10.1201/9781032618845

Khan, S. W., Shahwar, D., & Khalid, S. (2023). Unlocking the Potential of YouTube Marketing Communication: The Effects of YouTube Influencer Attributes on Millennials' Purchase Intention in Pakistan. *Annals of Social Sciences and Perspective*, 4(1), 65–76. DOI: 10.52700/assap.v4i1.184

Khetarpaul, S. (2021). Mining location based social networks to understand the citizen's check-in patterns. *Computing*, 103(12), 2967–2993. Advance online publication. DOI: 10.1007/s00607-021-01020-x

Khneyzer, C., Boustany, Z., & Dagher, J. (2024). AI-Driven Chatbots in CRM: Economic and Managerial Implications across Industries. *Administrative Sciences*, 14(8), 182–182. DOI: 10.3390/admsci14080182

Ki, C. W., Cuevas, L. M., Chong, S. M., & Lim, H. (2020). Influencer marketing: Social media influencers as human brands attaching to followers and yielding positive marketing results by fulfilling needs. *Journal of Retailing and Consumer Services*, 55(April), 102133. DOI: 10.1016/j.jretconser.2020.102133

Kim, D. Y., & Kim, H.-Y. (2021). Trust me, trust me not: A nuanced view of influencer marketing on social media. *Journal of Business Research, 134*(November 2019), 223–232. DOI: 10.1016/j.jbusres.2021.05.024

Kim, D. Y., Park, M., & Kim, H. Y. (2023). An influencer like me: Examining the impact of the social status of Influencers. *Journal of Marketing Communications*, 29(7), 654–675. DOI: 10.1080/13527266.2022.2066153

Kim, J. H., Kim, J., Kim, S., & Hailu, T. B. (2024). Effects of AI ChatGPT on travelers' travel decision-making. *Tourism Review*, 79(5), 1038–1057. DOI: 10.1108/TR-07-2023-0489

Kim, J., & Fesenmaier, D. R. (2017). Sharing Tourism Experiencess: The post-trip experience. *Journal of Travel Research*, 56(1), 28–40. DOI: 10.1177/0047287515620491

Kim, M., & Chang, B. (2020). The Effect of Service Quality on the Reuse Intention of a Chatbot: Focusing on User Satisfaction, Reliability, and Immersion. *International Journal of Contents*, 16(4), 1–15. https://koreascience.kr/article/JAKO202006763002633.page

Kingsnorth, S. (2022). *Digital marketing strategy: an integrated approach to online marketing*. Kogan Page Publishers.

Kishnani, N., & Sharma, V. (2024). *Travel motivation among millennials: Role of social media on tourism in Madhya Pradesh.* SDMIMD Journal of Management., DOI: 10.18311/sdmimd/2024/36424

Klein, S., & Utz, S. (2024). Chatbot vs. Human: The Impact of Responsive Conversational Features on Users' Responses to Chat Advisors Authors. *Human-Machine Communication*, 8, 73–99. DOI: 10.30658/hmc.8.4

Kocabay, N., & Öymen, G. (2023). Phenomenon Activism: A Research on Environmental Phenomena. *Üsküdar University. Journal of Social Sciences*, 16.

Kong, H., Wang, K., Qiu, X., Cheung, C., & Bu, N. (2023). 30 years of artificial intelligence (AI) research relating to the hospitality and tourism industry. *International Journal of Contemporary Hospitality Management*, 35(6), 2157–2177. DOI: 10.1108/IJCHM-03-2022-0354

Konidaris, A., & Koustoumpardi, E. (2017). The Importance of Search Engine Optimization for Tourism Websites. In V. Katsoni & K. Velander (Eds.), *Springer Proceedings in Business and Economics* (pp. 205–218). Springer Cham; Researchgate. DOI: 10.1007/978-3-319-67603-6_15

Kontopoulou, V. I., Panagopoulos, A. D., Kakkos, I., & Matsopoulos, G. K. (2023). A review of ARIMA vs. machine learning approaches for time series forecasting in data driven networks. *Future Internet*, 15(8), 255. DOI: 10.3390/fi15080255

Köprülü, O., & Turhan, M. (2023). Effects of Influencer Marketing on Consumers' Purchasing Behavior: Bursa Province Example. *Fiscaoeconomia*, 7(2), 1158–1177.

Kostin, K. (2018). Foresight of the global digital trends. *Strategic Management*, 23(2), 11–19. DOI: 10.5937/StraMan1801011K

Krupenna, I. (2022). Marketing digital tools from startup projects in the tourism and travel industry. *Proceedings of Scientific Works of Cherkasy State Technological University Series Economic Sciences*, 67(67), 24–31. DOI: 10.24025/2306-4420.67.2022.278790

Kumar, N. P., Dubey, N. S., & Kumar, A. (2022). A Review on Smart and Intelligent Techniques for Digital Tourism. *International Journal of Scientific Research in Computer Science Engineering and Information Technology*, 8(6), 617–624. DOI: 10.32628/CSEIT228651

Kumar, P., Mishra, J. M., & Rao, Y. V. (2022). Analysing tourism destination promotion through Facebook by Destination Marketing Organizations of India. *Current Issues in Tourism*, 25(9), 1416–1431. DOI: 10.1080/13683500.2021.1921713

Kumar, S., & Sharma, A. (2024). An Era Of Digital Transformation In The Hospitality & Tourism Sector. *Educational Administration: Theory and Practice*, 30(4), 9422–9427.

Kusumawati, Y. A., Lasmy, L., Gasa, F. M., & Renanda, D. G. (2024). Community Development of Tourism Interest Group Malang Regency as an Effort to Optimize Tourism. [SEEIJ]. *Social Economics and Ecology International Journal*, 8(1), 74–81. DOI: 10.21512/seeij.v8i1.11490

Kuzman, B., Petkovic, B., & Milovancevic, M. (2024, July). Information and communication technology in tourism. In *Tourism International Scientific Conference Vrnjačka Banja-TISC* (Vol. 8, No. 1, pp. 75-86).

Labunska, S., Zyma, O., & Sushchenko, S. (2022). The use of information systems as a way to ensure interaction between small and big tourism enterprises. *Access Journal - Access to Science, Business. Innovation in the Digital Economy*, 3(1), 16–28. DOI: 10.46656/access.2021.3.1(2)

Lee, J. J., Kang, K. A., Wang, M. P., Zhao, S. Z., Wong, J. Y. H., O'Connor, S., Yang, S. C., & Shin, S. (2020). Associations between COVID-19 misinformation exposure and belief with COVID-19 knowledge and preventive behaviors: Cross-sectional online study. *Journal of Medical Internet Research*, 22(11), 1–13. DOI: 10.2196/22205 PMID: 33048825

Lee, S., & Jeong, M. (2012). Effects of e-servicescape on consumers' flow experiences. *Journal of Hospitality and Tourism Technology*, 3(1), 47–59. DOI: 10.1108/17579881211206534

Lee, S., & Kim, E. (2020). Influencer marketing on Instagram: How sponsorship disclosure, influencer credibility, and brand credibility impact the effectiveness of Instagram promotional post. *Journal of Global Fashion Marketing*, 11(3), 232–249. DOI: 10.1080/20932685.2020.1752766

Lee, W. K., & Shin, S. R. (2023). Integrated factors affecting intention of COVID-19 preventive behaviors including vaccination in Korea. *Nursing Open*, 10(5), 3424–3431. DOI: 10.1002/nop2.1597 PMID: 36611182

Lei, S. I., Shen, H., & Ye, S. (2021). A comparison between chatbot and human service: Customer perception and reuse intention. *International Journal of Contemporary Hospitality Management*, 33(11), 3977–3995. DOI: 10.1108/IJCHM-12-2020-1399

Lei, S. S. I., Chan, I. C. C., Tang, J., & Ye, S. (2022). Will tourists take mobile travel advice? Examining the personalization-privacy paradox. *Journal of Hospitality and Tourism Management*, 50, 288–297. DOI: 10.1016/j.jhtm.2022.02.007

Leite, Â., Lopes, S., & Rodrigues, A. (2023). Who are Portuguese followers of social media influencers (SMIs), and their attitudes towards SMIs? An exploratory study. *Management & Marketing*, 18(4), 556–576. DOI: 10.2478/mmcks-2023-0030

Leite, F. P., Pontes, N., & Schivinski, B. (2024). Influencer marketing effectiveness: Giving competence, receiving credibility. *Journal of Travel & Tourism Marketing*, 41(3), 307–321. DOI: 10.1080/10548408.2024.2317748

Leung, D., Law, R., Van Hoof, H., & Buhalis, D. (2019). Social media and tourism marketing: A case study of Macau. *Journal of Travel & Tourism Marketing*, 36(1), 1–16.

Li, F., Larimo, J., & Leonidou, L. C. (2023). Social media in marketing research: Theoretical bases, methodological aspects, and thematic focus. *Psychology and Marketing*, 40(1), 124–145. DOI: 10.1002/mar.21746

Li, F., Shang, Y., & Su, Q. (2022). The influence of immersion on tourists' satisfaction via perceived attractiveness and happiness. *Tourism Review*. Advance online publication. DOI: 10.1108/TR-02-2022-0078

Li, J., Hudson, S., & So, K. K. F. (2019). Exploring the customer experience with Airbnb. *International Journal of Culture, Tourism and Hospitality Research*, 13(4), 410–429. DOI: 10.1108/IJCTHR-10-2018-0148

Li, L., Lee, K. Y., Emokpae, E., & Yang, S. B. (2021). What makes you continuously use chatbot services? Evidence from chinese online travel agencies. *Electronic Markets*, 31(3), 575–599. DOI: 10.1007/s12525-020-00454-z PMID: 35603227

Lily Anita, T., Muslikhin, M., Zulkarnain, A., & Wiyana, T. (2023). Enhancing Customer Satisfaction in Hotel Industry Through Chatbot as E-Services Agent and Communication Credibility. *2023 6th International Seminar on Research of Information Technology and Intelligent Systems (ISRITI)*, 14–19. DOI: 10.1109/ ISRITI60336.2023.10467873

Lin, Z., & Rasoolimanesh, S. M. (2024). Sharing tourism experiences in social media: A systematic review. *Anatolia*, 35(1), 67–81. DOI: 10.1080/13032917.2022.2120029

Li, S. A. (2023). Revisiting the relationship between information and communication technologies and travel behavior: An investigation of older Americans. *Transportation Research Part A, Policy and Practice*, 172, 103689. DOI: 10.1016/j.tra.2023.103689

Li, S., Li, Y., Liu, C., & Fan, N. (2024). How do different types of user-generated content attract travelers? Taking story and review on Airbnb as the example. *Journal of Travel Research*, 63(2), 371–387. DOI: 10.1177/00472875231158588

Liu, S. Q., Vakeel, K. A., Smith, N. A., Alavipour, R. S., Wei, C., & Wirtz, J. (2024). AI concierge in the customer journey: What is it and how can it add value to the customer? *Journal of Service Management*, 35(6), 136–158. DOI: 10.1108/ JOSM-12-2023-0523

Liu, S., Aw, E. C. X., Tan, G. W. H., & Ooi, K. B. (2023). Virtual Influencers as the Next Generation of Influencer Marketing: Identifying Antecedents and Consequences. In *Current and Future Trends on Intelligent Technology Adoption* (Vol. 1, pp. 23–39). Springer Nature Switzerland. DOI: 10.1007/978-3-031-48397-4_2

Liu, Y., Duong, H. T., & Nguyen, H. T. (2021). Media exposure and intentions to wear face masks in the early stages of the COVID-19 outbreak: The mediating role of negative emotions and risk perception. *Atlantic Journal of Communication*, 1–14. DOI: 10.1080/15456870.2021.1951733

Liu, Y., Yu, C., & Damberg, S. (2022). Exploring the drivers and consequences of the "awe" emotion in outdoor sports – a study using the latest partial least squares structural equation modeling technique and necessary condition analysis. *International Journal of Sports Marketing & Sponsorship*, 23(2), 278–294. DOI: 10.1108/ IJSMS-12-2020-0232

Li, X., Dadashova, B., Yu, S., & Zhang, Z. (2020). Rethinking highway safety analysis by leveraging crowdsourced waze data. *Sustainability (Basel)*, 12(23), 10127. Advance online publication. DOI: 10.3390/su122310127

Li, X., & Liu, Q. (2020). Social media use, eHealth literacy, disease knowledge, and preventive behaviors in the COVID-19 pandemic: Cross-sectional study on Chinese netizens. *Journal of Medical Internet Research*, 22(10), e19684. Advance online publication. DOI: 10.2196/19684 PMID: 33006940

Li, X., & Wang, X. (2017). The role of big data in personalized recommendation for tourism. *Journal of Destination Marketing & Management*, 6(3), 289–294.

Lou, C., Taylor, C. R., & Zhou, X. (2023). Influencer marketing on social media: How different social media platforms afford influencer–follower relation and drive advertising effectiveness. *Journal of Current Issues and Research in Advertising*, 44(1), 60–87. DOI: 10.1080/10641734.2022.2124471

Loureiro, S. M. C., Guerreiro, J., & Ali, F. (2020). 20 years of research on virtual reality and augmented reality in tourism context: A text-mining approach. *Tourism Management*, 77, 104028. DOI: 10.1016/j.tourman.2019.104028

Lunn, P. D., Belton, C. A., Lavin, C., McGowan, F. P., Timmons, S., & Robertson, D. (2020). Using behavioral science to help fight the coronavirus: A rapid, narrative review. *Journal of Behavioral Public Administration*, 3(1), 1–37. DOI: 10.30636/jbpa.31.147

MacCannell, D. (1973). Staged authenticity: Arrangements of social space in tourist settings. *American Journal of Sociology*, 79(3), 589–603. DOI: 10.1086/225585

Maggiore, G., Lo Presti, L., Orlowski, M., & Morvillo, A. (2022). In the travel bloggers' wonderland: Mechanisms of the blogger–follower relationship in tourism and hospitality management–a systematic literature review. *International Journal of Contemporary Hospitality Management*, 34(7), 2747–2772. DOI: 10.1108/IJCHM-11-2021-1377

Mahmood, Q. K., Jafree, S. R., Mukhtar, S., & Fischer, F. (2021). Social Media Use, Self-Efficacy, Perceived Threat, and Preventive Behavior in Times of COVID-19: Results of a Cross-Sectional Study in Pakistan. *Frontiers in Psychology*, 12(June), 1–10. DOI: 10.3389/fpsyg.2021.562042 PMID: 34220597

Majeed, A.; Hwang, S.O (2022). Data-Driven Analytics Leveraging Artificial Intelligence in the Era of COVID-19: An Insightful Review of Recent Developments. https://doi.org/DOI: 10.3390/sym14010016

Majeed, S., Zhou, Z., Lu, C., & Ramkissoon, H. (2020). Online tourism information and tourist behaviour: A structural equation modeling analysis based on a self-administered survey. *Frontiers in Psychology*, 11, 599. DOI: 10.3389/fpsyg.2020.00599 PMID: 32373008

Malik, A. Z., Thapa, S., & Paswan, A. K. (2023). Social media influencer (SMI) as a human brand–a need fulfillment perspective. *Journal of Product and Brand Management*, 32(2), 173–190. DOI: 10.1108/JPBM-07-2021-3546

Mancinelli, F. (2022). Digital Nomads. In Buhalis, D. (Ed.), *Encyclopedia of Tourism Management and Marketing* (pp. 957–960). Edward Elgar Publishing., https://www.elgaronline.com/display/book/9781800377486/b-9781800377486.digital.nomads.xml DOI: 10.4337/9781800377486.digital.nomads

Mandić, A., Pavlić, I., Puh, B., & Séraphin, H. (2023). Children and overtourism: A cognitive neuroscience experiment to reflect on exposure and behavioural consequences. *Journal of Sustainable Tourism*, 1–28. DOI: 10.1080/09669582.2023.2278023

Manhas, P. S., & Tukamushaba, E. K. (2015). Understanding service experience and its impact on brand image in hospitality sector. *International Journal of Hospitality Management*, 45, 77–87. DOI: 10.1016/j.ijhm.2014.11.010

Manthiou, A., Ulrich, I., & Kuppelwieser, V. (2024). The travel influencer construct: An empirical exploration and validation. *Tourism Management*, 101, 104858. DOI: 10.1016/j.tourman.2023.104858

Manyevere, R. M., & Kruger, M. (2019). The role of social media sites in trip planning and destination decision-making processes. *African Journal of Hospitality, Tourism and Leisure*, 8(5). https://www.ajhtl.com/uploads/7/1/6/3/7163688/article_3_vol_8_5__2019_cut.pdf

Martínez-López, F. J., Anaya-Sánchez, R., Esteban-Millat, I., Torrez-Meruvia, H., D'Alessandro, S., & Miles, M. (2020). Influencer marketing: Brand control, commercial orientation and post credibility. *Journal of Marketing Management*, 36(17-18), 1805–1831. DOI: 10.1080/0267257X.2020.1806906

Martínez-Sala, A. M., Monserrat-Gauchi, J., & Segarra-Saavedra, J. (2019). The influencer tourist 2.0: From anonymous tourist to opinion leader. *Revista Latina de Comunicación Social*, (74), 1344–1365. DOI: 10.4185/RLCS-2019-1388en

Marwick, A., & Boyd, D. (2011). To See and Be Seen: Celebrity Practice on Twitter. *Convergence (London)*, 17(2), 139–158. DOI: 10.1177/1354856510394539

Ma, S. (2024). A Study on the Impact of Influencers on the Tourism Industry in Ningxia, China. *Journal of Social Sciences and Economics*, 3(1), 55–65. DOI: 10.61363/qk9rqv23

Ma, S. (2024). Enhancing Tourists' Satisfaction: Leveraging Artificial Intelligence in the Tourism Sector. *Pacific International Journal.*, 7(3), 89–98. DOI: 10.55014/pij.v7i3.624

Masuda, H., Han, S. H., & Lee, J. (2022). Impacts of influencer attributes on purchase intentions in social media influencer marketing: Mediating roles of characterizations. *Technological Forecasting and Social Change*, 174, 121246. DOI: 10.1016/j.techfore.2021.121246

Maunier, C., & Camelis, C. (2013). Toward an identification of elements contributing to satisfaction with the tourism experience. *Journal of Vacation Marketing*, 19(1), 19–39. DOI: 10.1177/1356766712468733

McKercher, B., Prideaux, B., & Thompson, M., The impact of changing seasons on in-destination tourist behaviour. Tourism Review. (2023). Towards sustainability and personalization. *Information Technology & Tourism*, 15(4), 319–340.

McLean, G., & Barhorst, J. B. (2021). Living the Experience Before You Go . . . but Did It Meet Expectations? The Role of Virtual Reality during Hotel Bookings. *Journal of Travel Research*, 61(6), 004728752110283. DOI: 10.1177/00472875211028313

Mehra, P. (2023). Unexpected surprise: Emotion analysis and aspect based sentiment analysis (ABSA) of user generated comments to study behavioral intentions of tourists. *Tourism Management Perspectives*, 45, 101063. DOI: 10.1016/j.tmp.2022.101063

Mehrolia, S., Alagarsamy, S., Moorthy, V., & Jeevananda, S. (2023). Will Users Continue Using Banking Chatbots? The Moderating Role of Perceived Risk. *FIIB Business Review*, 0(0). Advance online publication. DOI: 10.1177/23197145231169900

Melián-González, S., Gutiérrez-Taño, D., & Bulchand-Gidumal, J. (2021). Predicting the intentions to use chatbots for travel and tourism. *Current Issues in Tourism*, 24(2), 192–210. DOI: 10.1080/13683500.2019.1706457

Mero, J., Vanninen, H., & Keränen, J. (2023). B2B influencer marketing: Conceptualization and four managerial strategies. *Industrial Marketing Management*, 108, 79–93. DOI: 10.1016/j.indmarman.2022.10.017

Meyer, E., & Schroeder, R. (2023). *Knowledge machines: Digital transformations of the sciences and humanities*. Mit Press.

Meyer-waarden, B. L., Pavone, G., Poocharoentou, T., Prayatsup, P., Tison, A., & Torn, S. (2020). How Service Quality Influences Customer Acceptance and Usage of Chatbots? *Journal of Service Management Research*, 4(1), 35–51. DOI: 10.15358/2511-8676-2020-1-35

Mikhailov, S., Kashevnik, A., & Smirnov, A. (2020, June). Tourist behaviour analysis based on digital pattern of life. In *2020 7th International Conference on Control, Decision and Information Technologies (CoDIT)* (Vol. 1, pp. 622-627). IEEE. DOI: 10.1109/CoDIT49905.2020.9263945

Minazzi, R. (2015). *Social Media Marketing in Tourism and Hospitality*. Springer International Publishing., DOI: 10.1007/978-3-319-05182-6

Minazzi, R., & Mauri, A. G. (2015). Mobile Technologies Effects on Travel Behaviours and Experiences: A Preliminary Analysis. In Tussyadiah, I., & Inversini, A. (Eds.), *Information and Communication Technologies in Tourism 2015* (pp. 507–521). Springer International Publishing., DOI: 10.1007/978-3-319-14343-9_37

Mishra, N., Gupta, S. L., Srivastava, P., Srivastava, S., & Kabir, M. (2022). Student Acceptance of Social Media in Higher Education: An application of UTAUT2 model. *Thailand and the World Economy*, 40(1), 88–108.

Mohammed, R. T., Alamoodi, A. H., Albahri, O. S., Zaidan, A. A., AlSattar, H. A., Aickelin, U., Albahri, A. S., Zaidan, B. B., Ismail, A. R., & Malik, R. Q. (2023). A decision modeling approach for smart e-tourism data management applications based on spherical fuzzy rough environment. *Applied Soft Computing*, 143, 110297. DOI: 10.1016/j.asoc.2023.110297

Mohd Rahim, N. I., & Iahad, A., N., Yusof, A. F., & A. Al-Sharafi, M. (. (2022). AI-Based Chatbots Adoption Model for Higher-Education Institutions: A Hybrid PLS-SEM-Neural Network Modelling Approach. *Sustainability (Switzerland)*, 14(19). Advance online publication. DOI: 10.3390/su141912726

Molinillo, S., Anaya-Sánchez, R., Morrison, A. M., & Coca-Stefaniak, J. A. (2019). Smart city communication via social media: Analysing residents' and visitors' engagement. *Cities (London, England)*, 94, 247–255. DOI: 10.1016/j.cities.2019.06.003

Montazeri, A., Mohammadi, S., Hesari, M., Yarmohammadi, P., Bahabadi, H., Naghizadeh, M. R., Moghari, F., Maftoon, F., Tavousi, M., & Riazi, H. (2023). Exposure to the COVID-19 news on social media and consequent psychological distress and potential behavioral change. *Scientific Reports*, 13(15224), 1–10. DOI: 10.1038/s41598-023-42459-6 PMID: 37710006

Monteiro, S. (2024). Searching for settlement information on Reddit. *International Migration (Geneva, Switzerland)*, 62(3), 100–119. DOI: 10.1111/imig.13261

Morakabati, Y., Page, S. J., & Fletcher, J. (2017). Emergency management and tourism stakeholder responses to crises: A global survey. *Journal of Travel Research*, 56(3), 299–316. DOI: 10.1177/0047287516641516 PMID: 29708106

Moreno-Manzo, J., Gassiot-Melian, A., & Coromina, L. (2022). Perceived value in a UNESCO World Heritage Site: The case of Quito, Ecuador. *Journal of Cultural Heritage Management and Sustainable Development*. Advance online publication. DOI: 10.1108/JCHMSD-03-2022-0049

Moro, S., Rita, P., Ramos, P., & Esmerado, J. (2019). Analysing recent augmented and virtual reality developments in tourism. *Journal of Hospitality and Tourism Technology*, 10(4), 571–586. DOI: 10.1108/JHTT-07-2018-0059

Moro, S., Rita, P., & Vala, B. (2016). Predicting social media performance metrics and evaluation of the impact on brand building: A data mining approach. *Journal of Business Research*, 69(9), 3341–3351. DOI: 10.1016/j.jbusres.2016.02.010

Morrison, A. M. (2022). *Hospitality and travel marketing*. Routledge. DOI: 10.4324/9781003292616

Mouha, R. A. R. A. (2021). Internet of things (IoT). *Journal of Data Analysis and Information Processing*, 9(02), 77–101. DOI: 10.4236/jdaip.2021.92006

Mpotaringa, M. C., & Tichaawa, T. (2021). Tourism Digital Marketing Tools and Views on Future Trends: A Systematic Review of Literature. *African Journal of Hospitality, Tourism and Leisure*, 10(2), 712–726. DOI: 10.46222/ajhtl.19770720-128

Mqwebu, B. (2024). Impact of Social Media Influencers on Tourist Destination Choices and Expenditure in South Africa. *Journal of Hospitality and Tourism*, 4(1), 57–68. DOI: 10.47672/jht.1979

Naab, T. K., & Sehl, A. (2017). Studies of user-generated content: A systematic review. *Journalism*, 18(10), 1256–1273. DOI: 10.1177/1464884916673557

Nadanyiova, M., Gajanova, L., Majerova, J., & Lizbetinova, L. (2020) Influencer marketing and its impact on consumer lifestyles. In Forum Scientiae Oeconomia (Vol. 8, No. 2, pp. 109- 120).

Najar, A. H., Wani, I. S., & Rather, A. H. (2024). Impact of Social Media Influencers Credibility on Destination Brand Trust and Destination Purchase Intention: Extending Meaning Transfer Model? *Global Business Review*, ●●●, 09721509241225354. DOI: 10.1177/09721509241225354

Namisango, F., Kang, K., & Rehman, J. (2019). What do we know about social media in nonprofits? A review. *Proceedings of the 23rd Pacific Asia Conference on Information Systems: Secure ICT Platform for the 4th Industrial Revolution, PACIS 2019, 10*, 27–36.

Nandi, S. (2022). Short-term vs long-term influencer marketing campaigns. Available at: https://www.getsaral.com/academy/short-term-vs-long-term-influencer-marketing-campaigns Accessed on: 04.08.2024.

Naqvi, M. H. A., Hongyu, Z., Naqvi, M. H., & Kun, L. (2023). Impact of service agents on customer satisfaction and loyalty: Mediating role of Chatbots. *Journal of Modelling in Management*, 19(2), 470–491. DOI: 10.1108/JM2-01-2023-0004

Nautiyal, R., Albrecht, J. N., & Carr, A. (2023). Can destination image be ascertained from social media? An examination of Twitter hashtags. *Tourism and Hospitality Research*, 23(4), 578–593. Advance online publication. DOI: 10.1177/14673584221119380

Nayyar, A., Mahapatra, B., Nhuong Le, D., & Suseendran, G. (2018). Virtual Reality (VR) & Augmented Reality (AR) technologies for tourism and hospitality industry. *International Journal of Engineering & Technology, 7*(2.21), 156. DOI: 10.14419/ijet.v7i2.21.11858

Nazlan, N. H., Zhang, H., Sun, J., & Chang, W. (2024). Navigating the online reputation maze: Impact of review availability and heuristic cues on restaurant influencer marketing effectiveness. *Journal of Hospitality Marketing & Management*, 33(3), 288–307. DOI: 10.1080/19368623.2023.2246471

Neidhardt, J., Werthner, H., & Ricci, F. (2015). The evolution of recommender systems

Ngai, E. W. T., Lee, M. C. M., Luo, M., Chan, P. S. L., & Liang, T. (2021). An intelligent knowledge-based chatbot for customer service. *Electronic Commerce Research and Applications*, 50, 101098. DOI: 10.1016/j.elerap.2021.101098

Nguyen, D. M., Chiu, Y. T. H., & Le, H. D. (2021). Determinants of Continuance Intention towards Banks' Chatbot Services in Vietnam: A Necessity for Sustainable Development. *Sustainability (Basel)*, 13(14), 7625. DOI: 10.3390/su13147625

Nguyen, V. T., Phong, L. T., & Chi, N. T. K. (2023). The impact of AI chatbots on customer trust: An empirical investigation in the hotel industry. *Consumer Behavior in Tourism and Hospitality*, 18(3), 293–305. DOI: 10.1108/CBTH-06-2022-0131

Nieto-Ferrando, J., Gómez-Morales, B., & Castro-Mariño, D. (2023). Audiovisual Fiction, Tourism, and Audience Studies: A Literature Review. *Review of Communication Research.*, 11, 88–126.

Niininen, O. (2022). *Contemporary issues in digital marketing*. Taylor & Francis.

Nili, A., Tate, M., & Johnstone, D. (2019). The process of solving problems with self-service technologies: a study from the user's perspective. In *Electronic Commerce Research* (Vol. 19, Issue 2). Springer US. DOI: 10.1007/s10660-018-9304-0

Nix, A., & Decker, S. (2023). Using digital sources: The future of business history? *Business History*, 65(6), 1048–1071. DOI: 10.1080/00076791.2021.1909572

Noble Studios. (n.d.). *The rise of AI travel planners: How DMOs can adapt to attract Gen Z and millennial travelers*. Retrieved from https://noblestudios.com/industry/tourism-marketing/ai-travel-planners-dmos/

Norman Adams, N. (2024). 'Scraping' Reddit posts for academic research? Addressing some blurred lines of consent in growing internet-based research trend during the time of Covid-19. *International Journal of Social Research Methodology*, 27(1), 47–62. DOI: 10.1080/13645579.2022.2111816

Nosrati, S., Sabzali, M., Heidari, A., Sarfi, T., & Sabbar, S. (2020). Chatbots, Counselling, and Discontents of the Digital Life. *Journal of Cyberspace Studies*, 4(2), 153–172. DOI: 10.22059/jcss.2020.93910

Novera, C. N., Ahmed, Z., Kushol, R., Wanke, P., & Azad, M. A. K. (2022). Internet of Things (IoT) in smart tourism: A literature review. *Spanish Journal of Marketing-ESIC*, 26(3), 325–344. DOI: 10.1108/SJME-03-2022-0035

Nur'afifah, O., & Prihantoro, E. (2021). The Influence of social media on millennial generation about travel decision-making. *Jurnal the Messenger*, 13(3), 238. DOI: 10.26623/themessenger.v13i3.2328

Ohme, J., Araujo, T., Boeschoten, L., Freelon, D., Ram, N., Reeves, B., & Robinson, T. (2024). Digital trace data collection for social media effects research: APIs, data donation, and (screen) tracking. *Communication Methods and Measures*, 18(2), 124–141. DOI: 10.1080/19312458.2023.2181319

Oh, S. H., Paek, H. J., & Hove, T. (2015). Cognitive and emotional dimensions of perceived risk characteristics, genre-specific media effects, and risk perceptions: The case of H1N1 influenza in South Korea. *Asian Journal of Communication*, 25(1), 14–32. DOI: 10.1080/01292986.2014.989240

Oh, S., Lee, S. Y., & Han, C. (2020). The effects of social media use on preventive behaviors during infectious disease outbreaks: The mediating role of self-relevant emotions and public risk perception. *Health Communication*, 1–11. DOI: 10.1080/10410236.2020.1724639 PMID: 32064932

Ojha, A. C., & Mishra, J. (2018, December). Interest-Satisfaction Estimation Model for Point-of-Interest Recommendations in Tourism. In *2018 International Conference on Information Technology (ICIT)* (pp. 172-177). IEEE. DOI: 10.1109/ICIT.2018.00044

Okonkwo, E. E., Eyisi, A., & Ololo, N. (2015). Social media platforms and their contributions to tourism development and promotion in Nigeria. *Nsukka Journal of the Humanities*, 23(2), 103–117.

Omo-Obas, P., & Anning-Dorson, T. (2022). Cognitive-affective-motivation factors influencing international visitors' destination satisfaction and loyalty. *Journal of Hospitality and Tourism Insights*. DOI: 10.1108/JHTI-05-2022-0178

Opute, A. P., Irene, B. O., & Iwu, C. G. (2020). Tourism service and digital technologies: A value creation perspective. *African Journal of Hospitality, Tourism and Leisure*, 9(2), 1–18.

Orden-Mejía, M., & Huertas, A. (2022). Analysis of the attributes of smart tourism technologies in destination chatbots that influence tourist satisfaction. *Current Issues in Tourism*, 25(17), 2854–2869. DOI: 10.1080/13683500.2021.1997942

Ouariti, O. Z., & Jebrane, E. M. (2020). The impact of transport infrastructure on tourism destination attractiveness: A case study of Marrakesh City, Morocco. *African Journal of Hospitality, Tourism and Leisure*, 9(2), 1–18.

Owuor, I., & Hochmair, H. H. (2020). An overview of social media apps and their potential role in geospatial research. In *ISPRS International Journal of Geo-Information* (Vol. 9, Issue 9). DOI: 10.3390/ijgi9090526

Ozdemir, M. A. (2021). Virtual Reality (VR) and Augmented Reality (AR) Technologies for Accessibility and Marketing in the Tourism Industry. In C. Eusebio, L. Teixeira, & M. J. Carneiro (Eds.), *ICT Tools and Applications for Accessible Tourism* (pp. 277–301). IGI Global. DOI: 10.4018/978-1-7998-6428-8.ch013

Öz, M. (2015). Social media utilization of tourists for travel-related purposes. *International Journal of Contemporary Hospitality Management*, 27(5), 1003–1023. DOI: 10.1108/IJCHM-01-2014-0034

Öztek, M., Yerden, N. K., Çolak, E., & Sarı, E. (2021). A content analysis on the role of social media in phenomenon marketing and the fashion industry. (62), 1053-1077.

Öztürk, O. (2023). A Study to Determine the Relationships Between Phenomenon Stickiness and Its Antecedents. *Business and Economics Research Journal*, 14(1), 123–140.

Ozuem, W., & Willis, M. (2022). Influencer Marketing. In Ozuem, W., & Willis, M. (Eds.), *Digital Marketing Strategies for Value Co-creation* (pp. 209–242). Springer Nature., DOI: 10.1007/978-3-030-94444-5_10

Pahrudin, P., Hsieh, T. H., Liu, L. W., & Wang, C. C. (2023). The role of information sources on tourist behavior post-earthquake disaster in Indonesia: A Stimulus–Organism–Response (SOR) approach. *Sustainability (Basel)*, 15(11), 8446. DOI: 10.3390/su15118446

Paliwal, M., Chatradhi, N., Singh, A., & Dikkatwar, R. (2024). Smart tourism: Antecedents to Indian traveller's decision. *European Journal of Innovation Management*, 27(5), 1521–1546. DOI: 10.1108/EJIM-06-2022-0293

Panchal, A., Shah, A., & Kansara, K. (2021). Digital Marketing - Search Engine Optimization (SEO) and Search Engine Marketing (SEM). *International Research Journal of Innovations in Engineering and Technology, 5*(12).

Pande, L., & Sengupta, S. (2024, April). Digital Commerce and Big Data revolutionizing the tourism industry: A review article. In *2024 IEEE 9th International Conference for Convergence in Technology (I2CT)* (pp. 1-5). IEEE. DOI: 10.1109/I2CT61223.2024.10544348

Park, A., & Lee, S. B. (2023). Examining AI and Systemic Factors for Improved Chatbot Sustainability. *Journal of Computer Information Systems*, 1–15. DOI: 10.1080/08874417.2023.2251416

Parrey, S. H., Hakim, I. A., & Rather, R. A. (2018). Mediating role of government initiatives and media influence between perceived risks and destination image: A study of conflict zone. *International Journal of Tourism Cities*, 1–18. https://doi.org/DOI: 10.1108/IJTC-02-2018-0019

Patel, A., & Jain, S. (2021). Present and future of semantic web technologies: A research statement. *International Journal of Computers and Applications*, 43(5), 413–422. DOI: 10.1080/1206212X.2019.1570666

Paula, M. (2015). Digital Tourism on the Way to Digital Marketing Success. *Holistic Marketing Management Journal, 5*(2), 30–37. https://ideas.repec.org/a/hmm/journl/v5y2015i2p30-37.html

Pawar, V. V., & Pawar, D. (2024). Augmented reality in medical education: Exploring ethical considerations. *Oral Oncology Reports*, 9, 100208. DOI: 10.1016/j.oor.2024.100208

Pencarelli, T. (2020). The digital revolution in the travel and tourism industry. *Information Technology & Tourism*, 22(3), 455–476. DOI: 10.1007/s40558-019-00160-3

Pesonen, J., & Neidhardt, J. (2019). Information and communication technologies in tourism 2019. In *Proceedings of the International Conference.* Springer International Publishing. DOI: 10.1007/978-3-030-05940-8

Petcu, R., Ologeanu-Taddei, R., Bourdon, I., Kimble, C., & Giraudeau, N. (2016). Acceptance and organizational aspects of oral tele-consultation: A French study. *Proceedings of the Annual Hawaii International Conference on System Sciences, 2016-March*, 3124–3132. DOI: 10.1109/HICSS.2016.393

Pham, Q. T., & Tran, T. L. (2014). Customer engagement in a Facebook brand community: An empirical study on travel industry in Vietnam. *2014 IEEE 6th International Conference on Adaptive Science & Technology (ICAST)*, 1–9. DOI: 10.1109/ICASTECH.2014.7068121

Pike, S., Pontes, N., & Kotsi, F. (2021). Stopover destination attractiveness: A quasi-experimental approach. *Journal of Destination Marketing & Management*, 19, 100514. Advance online publication. DOI: 10.1016/j.jdmm.2020.100514

Pillai, R., Sivathanu, B., Zheng, Y., Wu, Y., Pai, C. K., Liu, Y., Kang, S., & Dai, A. (2020). An investigation of how perceived smart tourism technologies affect tourists' well-being in marine tourism. *Sustainability (Switzerland), 18*(8 August), 1–19. DOI: 10.3390/su12166592

Pillai, R., & Sivathanu, B. (2020). Adoption of AI-based chatbots for hospitality and tourism. *International Journal of Contemporary Hospitality Management*, 32(10), 3199–3226. DOI: 10.1108/IJCHM-04-2020-0259

Pirolli, B. (2018). *Travel journalism: Informing tourists in the digital age*. Routledge. DOI: 10.4324/9781315110738

Pizzi, G., Scarpi, D., & Pantano, E. (2021). Artificial intelligence and the new forms of interaction: Who has the control when interacting with a chatbot? *Journal of Business Research*, 129, 878–890. DOI: 10.1016/j.jbusres.2020.11.006

Polat, E., Çelik, F., Ibrahim, B., & Gursoy, D. (2024). Past, present, and future scene of influencer marketing in hospitality and tourism management. *Journal of Travel & Tourism Marketing*, 41(3), 322–343. DOI: 10.1080/10548408.2024.2317741

Pop, R. A., Săplăcan, Z., Dabija, D. C., & Alt, M. A. (2022). The impact of social media influencers on travel decisions: The role of trust in consumer decision journey. *Current Issues in Tourism*, 25(5), 823–843. DOI: 10.1080/13683500.2021.1895729

Pradhan, D., Kuanr, A., Anupurba Pahi, S., & Akram, M. S. (2023). Influencer marketing: When and why gen Z consumers avoid influencers and endorsed brands. *Psychology and Marketing*, 40(1), 27–47. DOI: 10.1002/mar.21749

Prahalad, C. K., & Ramaswamy, V. (2004). Co-creation experiences: The next practice in value creation. *Journal of Interactive Marketing*, 18(3), 5–14. DOI: 10.1002/dir.20015

Prajapat, D. K., & R, D. K. (2024). Revolutionizing Tourism through Technology the Digital Transformation of Travel and Tourism. *International Journal of Research Publication and Reviews*, 5(2), 3643–3648. DOI: 10.55248/gengpi.5.0224.0626

Przegalinska, A., Ciechanowski, L., Stroz, A., Gloor, P., & Mazurek, G. (2019). In bot we trust: A new methodology of chatbot performance measures. *Business Horizons*, 62(6), 785–797. DOI: 10.1016/j.bushor.2019.08.005

Qahtan, S., Yatim, K., Zulzalil, H., Osman, M. H., Zaidan, A. A., & Alsattar, H. A. (2023). Review of healthcare industry 4.0 application-based blockchain in terms of security and privacy development attributes: Comprehensive taxonomy, open issues and challenges and recommended solution. *Journal of Network and Computer Applications*, 209, 103529. DOI: 10.1016/j.jnca.2022.103529

Qin, Y. S., & Men, L. R. (2023). Exploring the Impact of Internal Communication on Employee Psychological Well-Being During the COVID-19 Pandemic: The Mediating Role of Employee Organizational Trust. *International Journal of Business Communication*, 60(4), 1197–1219. DOI: 10.1177/23294884221081838

Rachmad, Y. (2024). *Digital Marketing Theories: From Gimmicks to Loyalty*. PT. Sonpedia Publishing Indonesia.

Rahimi, A., Azimi, G., Asgari, H., & Jin, X. (2020, May). Potential implications of automated vehicle technologies on travel behavior: A literature review. In *International Conference on Transportation and Development 2020* (pp. 234-247). Reston, VA: American Society of Civil Engineers. DOI: 10.1061/9780784483138.021

Raji, M. A., Olodo, H. B., Oke, T. T., Addy, W. A., Ofodile, O. C., & Oyewole, A. T. (2024). Digital marketing in tourism: A review of practices in the USA and Africa. *International Journal of Applied Research in Social Sciences*, 6(3), 393–408.

Rajora, P. (2022). The impact of mobile applications on tourist behavior in national capital region. *International Journal of Research in Finance and Management*, 5(2), 321–328. DOI: 10.33545/26175754.2022.v5.i2d.258

Rajput, A., & Gandhi, A. (2024, March). Influencer Voices: Exploring How Recommendations Drive Tourism Intent. In *2024 International Conference on Automation and Computation (AUTOCOM)* (pp. 586-592). IEEE. DOI: 10.1109/AUTOCOM60220.2024.10486181

Ramirez, E. J., Tan, J., Elliott, M., Gandhi, M., & Petronio, L. (2020, December). An ethical code for commercial VR/AR applications. In *International Conference on Intelligent Technologies for Interactive Entertainment* (pp. 15-24). Cham: Springer International Publishing.

Rancati, E., & D'Agata, A. (2022). Metaverse in Tourism and Hospitality: Empirical Evidence on Generation Z from Italy. *European Scientific Journal*, 18(34), 122. DOI: 10.19044/esj.2022.v18n34p122

Rane, N., Choudhary, S., & Rane, J. (2023, October 31). *Sustainable tourism development using leading-edge Artificial Intelligence (AI), Blockchain, Internet of Things (IoT), Augmented Reality (AR) and Virtual Reality (VR) technologies*. Social Science Research Network. DOI: 10.2139/ssrn.4642605

Rasul, T., Zaman, U., & Hoque, M. R. (2020). Examining the pulse of the tourism industry in the Asia-Pacific Region. *Umer Zaman.*, 26(1), 173–193.

Ray, S., Tawar, S., Singh, N., & Singh, G. (2024). Transition toward Technological Transformation: Challenges of Implementing Virtual Reality and Augmented Reality in the Health Sector. *Journal of Marine Medical Society*, 26(2), 161–164.

Ren, M., & Zheng, P. (2024). Towards smart product-service systems 2.0: A retrospect and prospect. *Advanced Engineering Informatics*, 61, 102466. DOI: 10.1016/j.aei.2024.102466

Ren, W., Zhu, X., & Hu, Y. (2021). Differential effects of traditional and social media use on COVID-19 preventive behaviors: The mediating role of risk and efficacy perceptions. *Journal of Health Psychology*, 27(8), 1861–1874. DOI: 10.1177/13591053211003125 PMID: 33909510

Reverte, F. G., & Solis, D. L. (2019). We Are All Digital Tourists, but Are All Digital Tourists the Same? In de Luna, I. R., Bertran, À. F., Masllorens, J. L., & Cabanillas, F. L. (Eds.), *Sharing Economy and the Impact of Collaborative Consumption* (pp. 263–277). IGI Global., DOI: 10.4018/978-1-5225-9928-9.ch014

Reyna, D., Rivas, Z., Lidia, M., Jaldin, L., Canaviri, B. N., Aguilar, J. P., Fabiola, L., & Ferna, A. M. C. A. (2021). Social media exposure, risk perception, preventive behaviors and attitudes during the COVID-19 epidemic in La Paz, Bolivia: A cross sectional study. *PLoS One*, 16(1), 1–12. DOI: 10.1371/journal.pone.0245859 PMID: 33481945

Rhena, J., Kraugusteeliana, K., & Hamzar, . (2024). Embracing Digitalization in Tourism: Strategic Approaches for Global Competitiveness in the Digital Economy Era. *Indo-Fintech Intellectuals: Journal of Economics and Business*, 4(2), 461–472. DOI: 10.54373/ifijeb.v4i2.1282

Richards, G. (2018). Cultural tourism: A review of recent research and trends. *Journal of Hospitality and Tourism Management*, 36, 12–21. DOI: 10.1016/j.jhtm.2018.03.005

Rivera, E. P., Urioste-Stone, S., Rickard, L. N., Caprara, A., & Estrada, L. N. Tourists and epidemics: how news media cover the risks of Zika virus and chikungunya outbreaks in the Americas. *Current Issues in Tourism*, 1-18. https://doi.org/DOI: 10.1080/13683500.2024.2309164

Rosa, G. (2023). Digital Traveler: The Use of Modern Information Technologies in Passenger Transport. *European Research Studies*, 26(3), 275–288. DOI: 10.35808/ersj/3211

Roscoe, J. T. (1975). *Fundamental Research Statistics for The Behavioral Sciences* (2nd ed.). Holt Rinehart & Winston.

Roy, P., & Jasrotia, A. (2024). An Insight into the Behaviour of Tech-Savvy Millennial Travellers: A Global Perspective. *Tourist Behaviour and the New Normal*, I, 173–184. DOI: 10.1007/978-3-031-45848-4_10

Rubin, G. J., & Wessely, S. (2020). The psychological effects of quarantining a city. *BMJ*, 368, 1–2). https://doi.org/DOI: 10.1136/bmj.m313

Ruiz-Meza, J., & Montoya-Torres, J. R. (2022). A systematic literature review for the tourist trip design problem: Extensions, solution techniques and future research lines. *Operations Research Perspectives*, 9, 100228. DOI: 10.1016/j.orp.2022.100228

Rusdi, J. F., Abu, N. A., Salam, S., Gusdevi, H., Hardi, R., & Nugraha, D. G. (2022, November). An international tourist behaviour on mobile smartphone usage. In *AIP Conference Proceedings* (Vol. 2658, No. 1). AIP Publishing. DOI: 10.1063/5.0106824

Sacchi, G. (2024). Book Review: Millennials, generation Z and the future of tourism. *Journal of Tourism Futures*, 10(1), 156–157. DOI: 10.1108/JTF-03-2024-302

Saengrith, W., Viriyavejakul, C., & Pimdee, P. (2022). Problem-Based Blended Training via Chatbot to Enhance the Problem-Solving Skill in the Workplace. *Emerging Science Journal*, 6(Special Issue), 1–12. DOI: 10.28991/ESJ-2022-SIED-01

Şahin, E. (2020). Self-presentation of popular doctors in personal branding: Practices of using Instagram accounts. In E. Eroğlu, & B. Taşdelen. *Communication Studies and Media Studies in the Digital Age,* (p 42). Education.

Saini, H., Kumar, P., & Oberoi, S. (2023). Welcome to the destination! Social media influencers as cogent determinant of travel decision: A systematic literature review and conceptual framework. *Cogent Social Sciences*, 9(1), 2240055. Advance online publication. DOI: 10.1080/23311886.2023.2240055

Saldamlı, A., & Can, İ. I. (2018). A New Trend in Marketing: Hatırlı Marketing–A Study on Consumers' Accommodation Preferences, 2nd International Future of Tourism Innovation, *Entrepreneurship and Sustainability Congress*, 698-707.

Saldamlı, A., & Özen, F. (2019). The effect of promotional marketing on consumer purchasing decisions in food and beverage businesses. *Journal of Tourism Theory and Research*, 5(2), 327–339.

Sangkaew, N., & Zhu, H. (2022). Understanding Tourists' Experiences at Local Markets in Phuket: An Analysis of TripAdvisor Reviews. *Journal of Quality Assurance in Hospitality & Tourism*, 23(1), 89–114. Advance online publication. DOI: 10.1080/1528008X.2020.1848747

Sano, K., Sano, H., Yashima, Y., & Takebayashi, H. (2024). The effects of temporal distance and post type on tourists' responses to destination marketing organizations' social media marketing. *Tourism Management*, 101, 104844. DOI: 10.1016/j.tourman.2023.104844

Santiago, J. K., & Castelo, I. M. (2020). Digital influencers: An exploratory study of influencer marketing campaign process on instagram. *Online Journal of Applied Knowledge Management*, 8(2), 31–52. DOI: 10.36965/OJAKM.2020.8(2)31-52

Santos, S., Ferreira, S., & Vasconcelos, M. (2024, May). User-Generated Content in Tourism: Could it Impact Brand Equity and Intention to Visit? In *European Conference on Social Media* (Vol. 11, No. 1, pp. 235-242). DOI: 10.34190/ecsm.11.1.2271

Sarıışık, M., & Özbay, G. (2012). A Literature Review on Electronic Word of Mouth Communication and Applications in the Tourism Industry. *International Journal of Management Economics and Business*, 8(16), 1–22.

Sarıoğlu, C. İ. (2023). The Effect of Influencer Source Credibility and Brand Attitude on Purchase Intention. *Journal of Human and Social Sciences Research*, 12(2), 912–937.

Schaefer, C. (2016, June 2). Toward Building a Mobile App Experience to Support Users' Mobile Travel Needs. *Proceedings of the 2016 ACM SIGMIS Conference on Computers and People Research*. SIGMIS-CPR '16: 2016 Computers and People Research Conference. DOI: 10.1145/2890602.2906193

chiopu, A. F., Pădurean, A. M., ală, M. L., & Nica, A. M. (2016). The influence of new technologies on tourism consumption behavior of the millennials. *Amfiteatru Economic Journal*, 18(10), 829–846.

Schneider, H. (2017). Uber and Society. *Innovation in Society*, 55–78. DOI: 10.1007/978-3-319-49514-9_3

Seçer, A., & Boğa, M. (2017). The impact of social media on consumers' food purchasing behavior. *KSÜ Journal of Natural Sciences*, 20(4), 312–319.

Seibel, G. (2021). The impact of influencer marketing on destination choice-A quantitative study among Brazilian and German millennials. *RCMOS-. Revista Científica Multidisciplinar o Saber*, 1(3), 41–150. DOI: 10.51473/rcmos.v1i1.2021.44

Sell, T. K., Boddie, C., McGinty, E. E., Pollack, K., Smith, K. C., Burke, T. A., & Rutkow, L. (2017). Media messages and perception of risk for Ebola virus infection, United States. *Emerging Infectious Diseases*, 23(1), 108–111. DOI: 10.3201/eid2301.160589 PMID: 27983495

Semiz, B. B., & Zengin, E. (2019). Examining The Role Of Social Media Phenomena On The Purchasing Decision Process. B*usiness & Management Studies. International Journal (Toronto, Ont.)*, 7(5), 2325–2347.

Sesar, V., Hunjet, A., & Kozina, G. (2021). Influencer marketing in travel and tourism: literature review. *Economic and social development: book of proceedings*, 182-192.

Setiawan, B., Trisdyani, N. L. P., Adnyana, P. P., Adnyana, I. N., Wiweka, K., & Wulandani, H. R. (2018). The Profile and Behaviour of "Digital Tourists" When Making Decisions Concerning Travelling Case Study: Generation Z in South Jakarta. *Advances in Research*, 17(2), 1–13. DOI: 10.9734/AIR/2018/43872

Seyidov, J., & Adomaitienė, R. (2016). Factors Influencing Local Tourists' Decision-making on Choosing a Destination: A Case of Azerbaijan. *Ekonomika (Nis)*, 95(3), 112–127. DOI: 10.15388/Ekon.2016.3.10332

Shandilya, G., Srivastava, P., & Jana, A. (2024). Industry Experts and Business Consultants ' Takes on India ' s Readiness for Metaverse: A Review of the Retail Industry. In Singla, B., Shalender, K., & Singh, N. (Eds.), *Creator's Economy in Metaverse Platforms: Empowering Stakeholders Through Omnichannel Approach* (pp. 132–147). IGI Global., DOI: 10.4018/979-8-3693-3358-7.ch008

Shariffuddin, N. S. M., Azinuddin, M., Yahya, N. E., & Hanafiah, M. H. (2023). Navigating the tourism digital landscape: The interrelationship of online travel sites' affordances, technology readiness, online purchase intentions, trust, and E-loyalty. *Heliyon*, 9(8), e19135. DOI: 10.1016/j.heliyon.2023.e19135 PMID: 37636344

Sharma, R. (2022). Influence of social media in travel decision making. *REST Journal on Data Analytics and Artificial Intelligence*, 1(3), 42–50. DOI: 10.46632/jdaai/1/3/6

Shin, D. (2020). User Perceptions of Algorithmic Decisions in the Personalized AI System:Perceptual Evaluation of Fairness, Accountability, Transparency, and Explainability. *Journal of Broadcasting & Electronic Media*, 64(4), 1–25. DOI: 10.1080/08838151.2020.1843357

Sia, P. Y. H., Saidin, S. S., & Iskandar, Y. H. P. (2023). Systematic review of mobile travel apps and their smart features and challenges. *Journal of Hospitality and Tourism Insights*, 6(5), 2115–2138. DOI: 10.1108/JHTI-02-2022-0087

Silva, S. C., De Cicco, R., Vlačić, B., & Elmashhara, M. G. (2023). Using chatbots in e-retailing – how to mitigate perceived risk and enhance the flow experience. *International Journal of Retail & Distribution Management*, 51(3), 285–305. DOI: 10.1108/IJRDM-05-2022-0163

Simay, A. E., Wei, Y., Gyulavári, T., Syahrivar, J., Gaczek, P., & Hofmeister-Tóth, Á. (2023). The e-WOM intention of artificial intelligence (AI) color cosmetics among Chinese social media influencers. *Asia Pacific Journal of Marketing and Logistics*, 35(7), 1569–1598. DOI: 10.1108/APJML-04-2022-0352

Singgalen, Y.A., 2024. Understanding digital engagement through sentiment analysis of tourism destination through travel vlog reviews. *KLIK: Kajian Ilmiah Informatika dan Komputer, 4*(6), pp.2992-3004.

Singh, R., Ismail, A., Ps, S., & Singh, D. (2021). Compliance of accessibility in tourism websites: A pledge towards disability. *Journal of Hospitality and Tourism Insights*, 4(3), 263–281. DOI: 10.1108/JHTI-05-2020-0092

Singh, S., Rajest, S., Hadoussa, S., Obaid, A., & Regin, R. (2023). *Data-driven decision making for long-term business success*. IGI Global. DOI: 10.4018/979-8-3693-2193-5

Sinha, A. P., Srivastava, P., Srivastava, S. K., Asthana, A. K., & Nag, A. (2024). Customer Satisfaction and Loyalty for Online Food Services Provider in India: An Empirical Study. *Vision (Basel)*, 28(3), 327–343. DOI: 10.1177/09722629211034405

Siuhi, S., & Mwakalonge, J. (2016). Opportunities and challenges of smart mobile applications in transportation. [English Edition]. *Journal of Traffic and Transportation Engineering*, 3(6), 582–592. Advance online publication. DOI: 10.1016/j.jtte.2016.11.001

Sivarethinamohan, R. (2023, July). Exploring the Transformation of Digital Tourism: Trends, Impacts, and Future Prospects. In *2023 International Conference on Digital Applications, Transformation & Economy (ICDATE)* (pp. 260-266). IEEE. DOI: 10.1109/ICDATE58146.2023.10248691

Smith, A., & Anderson, M. (2018). AI and machine learning in the travel industry: A research overview. *Journal of Hospitality and Tourism Technology*, 9(2), 155–172.

Solazzo, G., Maruccia, Y., Lorenzo, G., Ndou, V., Del Vecchio, P., & Elia, G. (2022). Extracting insights from big social data for smarter tourism destination management. *Measuring Business Excellence*, 26(1), 122–140. DOI: 10.1108/MBE-11-2020-0156

Soltani Nejad, N., Rastegar, R., & Jahanshahi, M. (2024). Tourist engagement with mobile apps of E-leisure: A combined model of self-determination theory and technology acceptance model. *Tourism Recreation Research*, 49(4), 714–725. DOI: 10.1080/02508281.2022.2100194

Son, H., & Park, Y. E. (2024). A deep understanding of influencer marketing in the tourism industry: A structural analysis of unstructured text. *Current Issues in Tourism,* ●●●, 1–11. DOI: 10.1080/13683500.2024.2368152

Sonmez, I. C. (2023). A Different Source of Social Change in Media History Studies: Social Media Phenomena. In *New Media Studies. Language, Image, Phenomena, Technology, Disinformation* (pp. 91–110). Özgür Yayın Dağıtım Ltd. Şti.

Šošić, M. M., Pavlić, I., & Puh, B. (2024, May). Understanding Users' Intention to Use Mobile Apps in Tourism Industry. In *2024 47th MIPRO ICT and Electronics Convention (MIPRO)* (pp. 1053-1058). IEEE.

Sota, S., Chaudhry, H., & Srivastava, M. K. (2020). Customer relationship management research in hospitality industry: A review and classification. *Journal of Hospitality Marketing & Management,* 29(1), 39–64. DOI: 10.1080/19368623.2019.1595255

Srivastava, P., Mishra, N., Srivastava, S., & Shivani, S. (2024). Banking with Chatbots: The Role of Demographic and Personality Traits. *FIIB Business Review, online fir*(online first). DOI: 10.1177/23197145241227757

Srivastava, P., & Shandilya, G. (2024). Unveiling the Impact of Perceived Smart Tourism Technology on Tourist Satisfaction. In Kajla, T., Kansra, P., & Singh, N. (Eds.), *Multidisciplinary Applications of Extended Reality for Human Experience* (pp. 147–170). IGI Global., DOI: 10.4018/979-8-3693-2432-5.ch008

Srivastava, P., Srivastava, S., & Mishra, N. (2023). Impact of e-servicescape on hotel booking intention: Examining the moderating role of COVID-19. *Consumer Behavior in Tourism and Hospitality,* 18(3), 422–437. DOI: 10.1108/CBTH-03-2022-0076

Starcevic, S., & Konjikusic, S. (2018). Why millenials as digital travelers transformed marketing strategy in tourism industry. *Tourism International Scientific Conference Vrnjačka Banja,* 3(1), 221–240. http://www.tisc.rs/proceedings/index.php/hitmc/article/view/12

Stienmetz, J., Ferrer-Rosell, B., & Massimo, D. (2022). *Information and Communication Technologies in Tourism 2022:Proceedings of the ENTER 2022 ETourism Conference,January 11-14, 2022.* Springer Nature. DOI: 10.1007/978-3-030-94751-4

Stoldt, R., Wellman, M., Ekdale, B., & Tully, M. (2019). Professionalizing and profiting: The rise of intermediaries in the social media influencer industry. *Social Media + Society,* 5(1), 2056305119832587. DOI: 10.1177/2056305119832587

Stylos, N. (2019). Technological evolution and tourist decision-making: A perspective article. *Tourism Review,* 75(1), 273–278. DOI: 10.1108/TR-05-2019-0167

Stylos, N., Jiang, Y., & Pergelova, A. (2024). Guest editorial: Marketing via smart technologies in hospitality and tourism. *Journal of Hospitality and Tourism Insights*, 7(3), 1285–1293. DOI: 10.1108/JHTI-07-2024-969

Stylos, N., Zwiegelaar, J., & Buhalis, D. (2021). Big data empowered agility for dynamic, volatile, and time-sensitive service industries: The case of tourism sector. *International Journal of Contemporary Hospitality Management*, 33(3), 1015–1036. DOI: 10.1108/IJCHM-07-2020-0644

Sultan, M. T., Sharmin, F., & Xue, K. (2019). Sharing tourism experience through social media: Consumer's behavioral intention for destination choice. *The Age (Melbourne, Vic.)*, 20(72), 34.

Sultan, M., Scholz, C., & van den Bos, W. (2023). Leaving traces behind: Using social media digital trace data to study adolescent wellbeing. *Computers in Human Behavior Reports*, 10, 100281. DOI: 10.1016/j.chbr.2023.100281

Suraña-Sánchez, C., & Aramendia-Muneta, M. E. (2024). Impact of artificial intelligence on customer engagement and advertising engagement: A review and future research agenda. *International Journal of Consumer Studies*, 48(2), e13027. DOI: 10.1111/ijcs.13027

Šuriņa, S., Martinsone, K., Perepjolkina, V., Kolesnikova, J., Vainik, U., Ruža, A., Vrublevska, J., Smirnova, D., Fountoulakis, K. N., & Rancans, E. (2021). Factors related to COVID-19 preventive behaviors: A structural equation model. *Frontiers in Psychology*, 12(676521), 1–15. DOI: 10.3389/fpsyg.2021.676521 PMID: 34290652

Suryani, W. (2024). New Trends in Consumer and Tourism Marketing Science. In Tarnanidis, T. K., & Sklavounos, N. (Eds.), *New Trends in Marketing and Consumer Science*. IGI Global. DOI: 10.4018/979-8-3693-2754-8.ch015

Suta, P., Lan, X., Wu, B., Mongkolnam, P., & Chan, J. H. (2020). An overview of machine learning in chatbots. *International Journal of Mechanical Engineering and Robotics Research*, 9(4), 502–510. DOI: 10.18178/ijmerr.9.4.502-510

Suzuki, T., Yamamoto, H., Ogawa, Y., & Umetani, R. (2023). Effects of media on preventive behavior during COVID-19 pandemic. *Humanities & Social Sciences Communications*, 10(58), 1–8. DOI: 10.1057/s41599-023-01554-9 PMID: 36818040

Talabi, F. O., & Oko-Epelle, L. (2024). Influence of radio messages on the awareness and adoption of malaria preventive measures among rural dwellers in South-West Nigeria. *Journalism and Media*, 5(1), 271–280. DOI: 10.3390/journalmedia5010018

Tandafatu, N. K., Ermilinda, L., & Darkel, Y. B. M. (2024). Digital Transformation in Tourism: Exploring the Impact of Technology on Travel Experiences. *International Journal of Multidisciplinary Approach Sciences and Technologies*, 1(1), 55–64. DOI: 10.62207/w3vsg352

Tangit, T. M., & Law, R. (2021). Mobile Payments, Chinese Tourists, and Host Residents: Are Destination Stakeholders Prepared to Facilitate Mobile Payments? In *Information and Communication Technologies in Tourism 2021:Proceedings of the ENTER 2021 eTourism Conference,January 19–22, 2021* (pp. 210-215). Springer International Publishing.

Tanti, A., & Buhalis, D. (2017). The influences and consequences of being digitally connected and/or disconnected to travellers. *Information Technology & Tourism*, 17(1), 121–141. DOI: 10.1007/s40558-017-0081-8

Tavana, M., Mousavi, S. M. H., Mina, H., & Salehian, F. (2020). A dynamic decision support system for evaluating peer-to-peer rental accommodations in the sharing economy. *International Journal of Hospitality Management*, 91, 102653. DOI: 10.1016/j.ijhm.2020.102653

Tavitiyaman, P., Qu, H., Tsang, W. S. L., & Lam, C. W. R. (2021). The influence of smart tourism applications on perceived destination image and behavioral intention: The moderating role of information search behavior. *Journal of Hospitality and Tourism Management*, 46, 476–487. DOI: 10.1016/j.jhtm.2021.02.003

Teixeira, R. M., Andreassi, T., Köseoglu, M. A., & Okumus, F. (2019). How do hospitality entrepreneurs use their social networks to access resources? Evidence from the lifecycle of small hospitality enterprises. *International Journal of Hospitality Management*, 79, 158–167. DOI: 10.1016/j.ijhm.2019.01.006

Theocharis, D., & Papaioannou, E. (2020). Consumers' responses on the emergence of influencer marketing in Greek market place. *International Journal of Technology Marketing*, 14(3), 283–304. DOI: 10.1504/IJTMKT.2020.111543

Thomaz, G. M., Biz, A. A., Bettoni, E. M., Mendes-Filho, L., & Buhalis, D. (2017). Content mining framework in social media: A FIFA world cup 2014 case analysis. *Information & Management*, 54(6), 786–801. DOI: 10.1016/j.im.2016.11.005

Tjostheim, I., & Waterworth, J. A. (2022). *The psychosocial reality of digital travel: Being in virtual places*. Springer Nature. DOI: 10.1007/978-3-030-91272-7

Tjostheim, I., & Waterworth, J. A. (2023). Digital Travel – A Study of Travellers' Views of a Digital Visit to Mexico. *Information Technology and Systems*, 1, 185–194. DOI: 10.1007/978-3-031-33258-6_17

Tjostheim, I., & Waterworth, J. A. (2023). Tomorrow's Digital Travellers—Who are they? A Study on Travellers' Views on Digital Travel Experiences. In *Advances in Tourism, Technology and Systems: Selected Papers from ICOTTS 2022* (Vol. 1, pp. 381–391). Springer Nature Singapore. DOI: 10.1007/978-981-99-0337-5_32

Torres-Moraga, E., & Barra, C. (2023). Does destination brand experience help build trust? Disentangling the effects on trust and trustworthiness. *Journal of Destination Marketing & Management*, 27, 100767. DOI: 10.1016/j.jdmm.2023.100767

Tran, N. L., & Rudolf, W. (2022). Social Media and Destination Branding in Tourism: A Systematic Review of the Literature. *Sustainability (Basel)*, 14(20), 13528. Advance online publication. DOI: 10.3390/su142013528

Tri Kurniawati, D., & Yadi Yaakop, A. (2021). The effect of E-Servicescape Dimensions on Customer Trust of Tokopedia E-Store During Covid-19 Pandemic. *Journal of Applied Management*, 19(1), 1–10. DOI: 10.21776/ub.jam.2021.019.01.01

Tsai, C. M., & Hsin, S. P. (2023). The Influence of Influencer Marketing on the Consumers' Desire to Travel in the Post-Pandemic Era: The Mediation Effect of Influencer Fitness of Destination. *Sustainability (Basel)*, 15(20), 14746. DOI: 10.3390/su152014746

Tsai, S. P. (2022). Investigating metaverse marketing for travel and tourism. *Journal of Vacation Marketing*, 1. Advance online publication. DOI: 10.1177/13567667221145715

Tuominen, P. (2011). *The Influence of TripAdvisor Consumer-Generated Travel Reviews on Hotel Performance*. Uhra.herts.ac.uk. https://uhra.herts.ac.uk/handle/2299/7612

Turku, N. (2023). *The consumer perception of short-term and long-term influencer marketing campaigns on Instagram and their effect on consumer brand awareness.* [Master's Thesis, Abo Academy University]. https://www.doria.fi/bitstream/handle/10024/187327/turku_niklas.pdf?sequence=2&isAllowed=y

Türk, U., Östh, J., Kourtit, K., & Nijkamp, P. (2021). The path of least resistance explaining tourist mobility patterns in destination areas using Airbnb data. *Journal of Transport Geography*, 94, 103130. Advance online publication. DOI: 10.1016/j.jtrangeo.2021.103130

Tussyadiah, I. P., & Pesonen, J. (2016). Impacts of peer-to-peer accommodation use on travel patterns. *Journal of Travel Research*, 55(8), 1022–1040. DOI: 10.1177/0047287515608505

Ulusoy, S. (2024). The use of augmented reality (ar) and virtual reality (vr) in tourism marketing. *Bulletin of Dulaty University*, 14(2), 212–225. DOI: 10.55956/XRLV7458

Um, T., Kim, T., & Chung, N. (2020). How does an intelligence chatbot affect customers compared with self-service technology for sustainable services? *Sustainability (Basel)*, 12(12), 5119. Advance online publication. DOI: 10.3390/su12125119

Van Nuenen, T., & Scarles, C. (2021). Advancements in technology and digital media in tourism. *Tourist Studies*, 21(1), 119–132. DOI: 10.1177/1468797621990410

Vanherle, R., Kurten, S., & Rousseau, A. (2023). How social media, news media and interpersonal communication relate to Covid-19 risk perceptions and behaviors. *European Journal of Health Communication*, 4(1), 28–50. DOI: 10.47368/ejhc.2023.102

Vassey, J., Valente, T., Barker, J., Stanton, C., Li, D., Laestadius, L., & Unger, J. B. (2023). E-cigarette brands and social media influencers on Instagram: A social network analysis. *Tobacco Control*, 32(e2), e184–e191. DOI: 10.1136/tobaccocontrol-2021-057053 PMID: 35131947

Vaziri, F., Nanni, M., Matwin, S., & Pedreschi, D. (2020). *Discovering Tourist Attractions of Cities Using Flickr and OpenStreetMap Data*. DOI: 10.1007/978-981-15-5024-2_21

Vecchio, P. D., Mele, G., Ndou, V., & Secundo, G. (2018). Creating value from Social Big Data: Implications for Smart Tourism Destinations. *Information Processing & Management*, 54(5), 847–860. DOI: 10.1016/j.ipm.2017.10.006

Vercic, A. T., & Vercic, D. (2013). Digital natives and social media. *Public Relations Review*, 39(5), 600–602. DOI: 10.1016/j.pubrev.2013.08.008

Vergaray, A. D., Robles, W. F. P., & Jiménez, J. A. S. (2023). The Impact of Chatbots on Customer Satisfaction: A Systematic Literature Review. *TEM Journal, 12*(3), 1407–1417. https://doi.org/DOI: 10.18421/TEM123-21

Verma, P., Kumar, S., & Sharma, S. K. (2020). e-Healthcare service quality: Consumer satisfaction and its association with demographic characteristics. *International Journal of Health Care Quality Assurance*, 33(6), 413–428. DOI: 10.1108/IJHCQA-02-2020-0030 PMID: 32678536

Vila, N. A., Cardoso, L., El Archi, Y., & Brea, J. A. F. (2024). The Role of Digital Technology and Sustainable Practices in Tourists' Decision Making. In *Promoting Responsible Tourism With Digital Platforms* (pp. 36–59). IGI Global. DOI: 10.4018/979-8-3693-3286-3.ch003

Villacé-Molinero, T., Fernández-Muñoz, J. J., Muñoz-Mazón, A. I., Flecha-Barrio, M. D., & Fuentes-Moraleda, L. (2023). Holiday travel intention in a crisis scenario: A comparative analysis of Spain's main source markets. *Tourism Review*, 78(1), 18–41. DOI: 10.1108/TR-03-2022-0131

Villaespesa, E., & Wowkowych, S. (2020). Ephemeral Storytelling With Social Media: Snapchat and Instagram Stories at the Brooklyn Museum. *Social Media + Society*, 6(1). Advance online publication. DOI: 10.1177/2056305119898776

Vinnakota, S., Dass Mohan, M., Boda, J., Sekuini, J., Mustafa, M., & Madala, H. (2023). Leveraging Artificial Intelligence in the Hospitality Industry: Opportunities and Challenges. *Asian Journal of Social Science and Management Technology*, 5(3), 2313–7410. https://www.researchgate.net/publication/372783951

Vinod, B. (2024). Origins of Online Travel Agencies. In *Mastering the Travel Intermediaries* (pp. 329–341). Springer Nature., DOI: 10.1007/978-3-031-51524-8_10

Visser, M., Sikkenga, B., & Berry, M. (2021). *Digital marketing fundamentals: From strategy to ROI*. Taylor & Francis. DOI: 10.4324/9781003203650

Von Mettenheim, W., & Wiedmann, K. P. (2021). The role of fashion influencers' attractiveness: A gender-specific perspective. *Communication Research and Practice*, 7(3), 263–290. DOI: 10.1080/22041451.2021.2013087

Vrontis, D., Makrides, A., Christofi, M., & Thrassou, A. (2021). Social mediainfluencer marketing: A systematic review, integrative frameworkand future research agenda. *International Journal of Consumer Studies*, 45(4), 617–644. DOI: 10.1111/ijcs.12647

Vu, H. Q., Muskat, B., Li, G., & Law, R. (2020). Improving the resident–tourist relationship in urban hotspots. *Journal of Sustainable Tourism*, 29(4), 595–615. DOI: 10.1080/09669582.2020.1818087

Wahlberg, A. A., & Sjoberg, L. (2000). Risk perception and the media. *Journal of Risk Research*, 3(1), 31–50. DOI: 10.1080/136698700376699

Walter, D., Böhmer, M. M., Reiter, S., Krause, G., & Wichmann, O. (2012). Risk perception and information-seeking behavior during the 2019/10 influence A(H1N1) pdm09 pandemic in Germany. *Eurosurveillance*, 17(13), 1–8. DOI: 10.2807/ese.17.13.20131-en PMID: 22490383

Wang, B., Dane, G., & Arentze, T. (2023). A structural equation model to analyze the use of a new multi media platform for increasing awareness of cultural heritage. *Frontiers of Architectural Research*, 12(3), 509–522. DOI: 10.1016/j.foar.2023.02.001

Wang, C., Pan, R., Wan, X., Tan, Y., Xu, L., Ho, C. S., & Ho, R. C. (2020). Immediate psychological responses and associated factors during the initial stage of the 2019 coronavirus disease (COVID-19) epidemic among the general population in China. *International Journal of Environmental Research and Public Health*, 17(5), 1729. Advance online publication. DOI: 10.3390/ijerph17051729 PMID: 32155789

Wang, E. S. T., & Weng, Y. J. (2024). Influence of social media influencer authenticity on their followers' perceptions of credibility and their positive word-of-mouth. *Asia Pacific Journal of Marketing and Logistics*, 36(2), 356–373. DOI: 10.1108/APJML-02-2023-0115

Wang, P. Q. (2024). Personalizing guest experience with generative AI in the hotel industry: There's more to it than meets a Kiwi's eye. *Current Issues in Tourism*, •••, 1–18. DOI: 10.1080/13683500.2023.2300030

Wang, Z. (2010). A preliminary study of the Global Distribution Systems (GDS'). *IEEE Xplore*, 60–63, 60–63. Advance online publication. DOI: 10.1109/ICIME.2010.5478307

Wei, D., Wang, Y., Liu, M., & Lu, Y. (2024). User-generated content may increase urban park use: Evidence from multisource social media data. *Environment and Planning. B, Urban Analytics and City Science*, 51(4), 971–986. DOI: 10.1177/23998083231210412

Weißensteiner, A. A. A. (2018). Chatbots as an approach for a faster enquiry handling process in the service industry. *Signature (Ramsey, N.J.)*, 12(04).

Wei, W. (2019). Research progress on virtual reality (VR) and augmented reality (AR) in tourism and hospitality: A critical review of publications from 2000 to 2018. *Journal of Hospitality and Tourism Technology*, 10(4), 539–570. DOI: 10.1108/JHTT-04-2018-0030

Wellman, M. L., Stoldt, R., Tully, M., & Ekdale, B. (2020). Ethics of Authenticity: Social Media Influencers and the Production of Sponsored Content. *Journal of Medical Ethics*, 35(2), 68–82. DOI: 10.1080/23736992.2020.1736078

Wies, S., Bleier, A., & Edeling, A. (2023). Finding goldilocks influencers: How follower count drives social media engagement. *Journal of Marketing*, 87(3), 383–405. DOI: 10.1177/00222429221125131

Wismantoro, Y., Aryanto, V. D. W., Pamungkas, I. D., Purusa, N. A., Amron, , Chasanah, A. N., & Usman, . (2023). Virtual Reality Destination Experiences Model: A Moderating Variable between Wisesa Sustainable Tourism Behavior and Tourists' Intention to Visit. *Sustainability (Basel)*, 15(1), 446. Advance online publication. DOI: 10.3390/su15010446

Wong, K. (n.d.). *How millennials and Gen Z transformed tourism marketing*. Retrieved from https://www.linkedin.com/pulse/how-millennials-gen-z-transformed -tourism-marketing-through-kyle-wong

Wong, J. W. C., Lai, I. K. W., & Wang, S. (2024). How social values gained from sharing travel experiences influence tourists' satisfaction: Moderated mediation effect of onsite mobile sharing behaviour. *Asia Pacific Journal of Marketing and Logistics*. Advance online publication. DOI: 10.1108/APJML-10-2023-1060

Wong, S. Y., Ong, L. Y., & Leow, M. C. (2024). AIDA-based Customer Segmentation with User Journey Analysis for Wi-Fi Advertising System. *IEEE Access : Practical Innovations, Open Solutions*, 12, 111468–111480. DOI: 10.1109/AC-CESS.2024.3424833

WonSeok, B., DongHwan, C., & Reddy, N. S. (2020). Investigating the effect of creating shared value on the performance of partner companies and social performance. , 20(4), 131-144.

World Economic Forum. (2019). The Travel and Tourism Competitiveness Report 2019. *World Economic Forum.*

World Health Organization. (2020). *Coronavirus disease (COVID-19) advice for the public.* Retrieved from https://www.who.int/emergencies/diseases/novel-coronavirus -2019/advice-for-public

World Travel & Tourism Council (WTTC). (2022). *Travel & Tourism Economic Impact 2022.* World Travel & Tourism Council.

World Travel & Tourism Council (WTTC). (2023). *Global Economic Impact & Trends 2023.* World Travel & Tourism Council.

Wörndl, W., Koo, C., & Stienmetz, J. (2021). *Information and Communication Technologies in Tourism 2021:Proceedings of the ENTER 2021 eTourism Conference,January 19–22, 2021.* Springer Nature. DOI: 10.1007/978-3-030-65785-7

Wren, G. P., & Wygant, J. (2010). Influencing Consumer Decisions Through Personalization. *Proceedings of F 15th IFIP WG8.3 International Conference, ISBN 978-1-60750-576-1*, 152–162.

Wu, E., & Liao, B. Y. (2023). Realization of Vitality Optimization in Traditional Village Human Settlement Environment Supported by Intelligent Sensor Technology. *International Journal of Communication Networks and Information Security*, 15(4), 78–89. DOI: 10.17762/ijcnis.v15i4.6288

Wut, T. M., & Ng, M. L. P. (2024). Virtual reality and augmented reality of tourism research: A review and research agenda. *Journal of Quality Assurance in Hospitality & Tourism*, ●●●, 1–24. DOI: 10.1080/1528008X.2024.2338774

Wu, Y.-W., Liao, T.-H., Yeh, S.-P., & Huang, H.-C. (2022). Switching Intention and Behaviors to Wetland Ecotourism after the COVID-19 Pandemic: The Perspective of Push-Pull-Mooring Model. *Sustainability (Basel)*, 14(10), 6198. Advance online publication. DOI: 10.3390/su14106198

Xiang, Z., & Gretzel, U. (2020). Role of Social Media in Online Travel Information Search. *Tourism Management*, 31(2), 179–188. DOI: 10.1016/j.tourman.2009.02.016

Xiang, Z., Wang, D., O'Leary, J. T., & Fesenmaier, D. R. (2015). Adapting to the Internet: Trends in Travelers' Use of the Web for Trip Planning. *Journal of Travel Research*, 54(4), 511–527. DOI: 10.1177/0047287514522883

Xiao, Y., & Lutz, C. (2024). Wayfarers in Cyberspace: A Temporal Investigation of Digital Nomads Based on Liquid Modernity Theory. *Journal of Travel Research*, 0(0), 00472875231224242. Advance online publication. DOI: 10.1177/00472875231224242

Xie, Q., & Feng, Y. (2023). How to strategically disclose sponsored content on Instagram? The synergy effects of two types of sponsorship disclosures in influencer marketing. *International Journal of Advertising*, 42(2), 317–343. DOI: 10.1080/02650487.2022.2071393

Xu, H., Cheung, L. T. O., Lovett, J., Duan, X., Pei, Q., & Liang, D. (2023). Understanding the influence of user-generated content on tourist loyalty behavior in a cultural World Heritage Site. *Tourism Recreation Research*, 48(2), 173–187. DOI: 10.1080/02508281.2021.1913022

Xu, J., Qu, L., & Zhang, G. (2022). Governing social eating (chibo) influencers: Policies, approach and politics of influencer governance in China. *Policy and Internet*, 14(3), 525–540. DOI: 10.1002/poi3.318

Yalcinkaya, B., & Just, D. R. (2023). Comparison of Customer Reviews for Local and Chain Restaurants: Multilevel Approach to Google Reviews Data. *Cornell Hospitality Quarterly*, 64(1), 63–73. Advance online publication. DOI: 10.1177/19389655221102388

Yamagishi, K., Canayong, D., Domingo, M., Maneja, K. N., Montolo, A., & Siton, A. (2023). User-generated content on Gen Z tourist visit intention: A stimulus-organism-response approach. *Journal of Hospitality and Tourism Insights*, 34. Advance online publication. DOI: 10.1108/JHTI-02-2023-0091

Yang, S.-Y., & Hsu, C.-L. (2016). A location-based services and Google maps-based information master system for tour guiding. *Computers & Electrical Engineering*, 54, 87–105. DOI: 10.1016/j.compeleceng.2015.11.020

Yang, X., Zhang, L., & Zhou, F. (2023). Personalized Tourism Recommendations and the E-Tourism User Experience. *Journal of Travel Research*, 63(5), 1183–1200. Advance online publication. DOI: 10.1177/00472875231187332

Yavuz, D., & Sağlam, M. (2023). Examining the Effect of Phenomenon Characteristics on Repeat Purchase, Word of Mouth Communication and Intention to Pay More. *Süleyman Demirel University Visionary Magazine*, 14(37), 296–313.

Yesawich, P. (2016). The American Traveler: Emerging Lifestyles and Travel Trends.

Ye, Z., Newing, A., & Clarke, G. (2021). Understanding Chinese tourist mobility and consumption-related behaviours in London using Sina Weibo check-ins. *Environment and Planning. B, Urban Analytics and City Science*, 48(8), 2436–2452. Advance online publication. DOI: 10.1177/2399808320980748

Yıldırım, M., & Güler, A. (2020). COVID-19 severity, self-efficacy, knowledge, preventive behaviors, and mental health in Turkey. *Death Studies*, 1–8. DOI: 10.1080/07481187.2020.1793434 PMID: 32673183

Yıldırım, M., Öztürk, A., & Solmaz, F. (2023). Fear of COVID-19 and sleep problems in Turkish young adults: Mediating roles of happiness and problematic social networking sites use. *Psihologija (Beograd)*, 56(4), 497–515. DOI: 10.2298/PSI220412027Y

Yoon, H. Y., & Yoo, S. C. (2023). Finding tourism niche on image-based social media: Integrating computational methods. *Journal of Vacation Marketing*, 13567667231180994. Advance online publication. DOI: 10.1177/13567667231180994

Yoo, W., & Choi, D. (2019). Predictors of expressing and receiving information on social networking sites during MERS-CoV outbreak in South Korea Predictors of expressing and receiving information on social. *Journal of Risk Research*, 1–16. DOI: 10.1080/13669877.2019.1569105

Yoo, W., Paek, H. J., & Hove, T. (2018). Differential effects of content-oriented versus user-oriented social media on risk perceptions and behavioral intentions. *Health Communication*, 1–12. DOI: 10.1080/10410236.2018.1545169 PMID: 30427203

Younis, D. (2024). Social Inclusion portrayal on TikTok and Instagram: The role of social media influencers in promoting mental health literacy, body image and self-esteem. *Journal of Media and Interdisciplinary Studies*, 3(7), 121–140. DOI: 10.21608/jmis.2024.252107.1017

Yuan, Y., Chan, C. S., Eichelberger, S., Ma, H., & Pikkemaat, B. (2022). The effect of social media on travel planning process by Chinese tourists: the way forward to tourism futures. *Journal of Tourism Futures*, 1–20. DOI: 10.1108/JTF-04-2021-0094

Zaim, I. A., Stylidis, D., Andriotis, K., & Thickett, A. (2024). Does user-generated video content motivate individuals to visit a destination? A non-visitor typology. *Journal of Vacation Marketing*, 13567667241268369. DOI: 10.1177/13567667241268369

Zhang, J., & Qiu, H. (2022). Window to the Destination: Tourists' Local Experience via "Online Experiences" on Airbnb Amid the Pandemic. In Stienmetz, J. L., Rosell, B. F., & Massimo, D. (Eds.), *Information and Communication Technologies in Tourism 2022* (pp. 310–315)., DOI: 10.1007/978-3-030-94751-4_28

Zhang, R. W., Liang, X., & Wu, S. H. (2024). When chatbots fail: Exploring user coping following a chatbots-induced service failure. *Information Technology & People*, 37(8), 175–195. DOI: 10.1108/ITP-08-2023-0745

Zhang, T., & Huang, X. (2022). Viral marketing: Influencer marketing pivots in tourism–a case study of meme influencer instigated travel interest surge. *Current Issues in Tourism*, 25(4), 508–515. DOI: 10.1080/13683500.2021.1910214

Zhang, W., Xie, J., Zhang, Z., & Liu, X. (2024). Depression detection using digital traces on social media: A knowledge-aware deep learning approach. *Journal of Management Information Systems*, 41(2), 546–580. DOI: 10.1080/07421222.2024.2340822

Zhang, Y. (2023). Analysis of the Digital Transformation Development Path for Travel Enterprises. *Ozean Journal of Applied Sciences*, 13(8), 1370–1386. DOI: 10.4236/ojapps.2023.138109

Zhao, Y., & Bacao, F. (2020). What factors determining customer continuingly using food delivery apps during 2019 novel coronavirus pandemic period? *International Journal of Hospitality Management*, 91(May), 102683. DOI: 10.1016/j.ijhm.2020.102683 PMID: 32929294

Zheng, K., Kumar, J., Kunasekaran, P., & Valeri, M. (2024). Role of smart technology use behaviour in enhancing tourist revisit intention: The theory of planned behaviour perspective. *European Journal of Innovation Management*, 27(3), 872–893. DOI: 10.1108/EJIM-03-2022-0122

Zhou, L., Qiu, R. T., Wang, S., Liu, A., & Wang, L. (2024). Incidental negative emotions and tourist destination preferences: A choice model during lockdown. *International Journal of Tourism Research*, 26(4), e2722. DOI: 10.1002/jtr.2722

Zhu, J., & Cheng, M. (2021). The rise of a new form of virtual tour: Airbnb peer-to-peer online experience. *Current Issues in Tourism*, 25(22), 1–6. DOI: 10.1080/13683500.2021.2016662

Zhu, Y., Zhang, R., Zou, Y., & Jin, D. (2023). Investigating customers' responses to artificial intelligence chatbots in online travel agencies: The moderating role of product familiarity. *Journal of Hospitality and Tourism Technology*, 14(2), 208–224. DOI: 10.1108/JHTT-02-2022-0041

Zorlu, Ö., & Candan, T. (2023). The impact of social media influencers on destination preferences: A cross-generation comparison. *Journal of Tourism Leisure and Hospitality*, 5(1), 53–61. DOI: 10.48119/toleho.1229922

Zumstein, D., & Hundertmark, S. (2018). Chatbots : an interactive technology for personalized communication and transaction. *IADIS International Journal on Www/Internet, 15*(1), 96–109.

# About the Contributors

**Ahmad Albattat**, is an Associate Professor In Graduate School of Management, Post Graduate Centre, Management and Science University, Shah Alam, Selangor, Malaysia. He is a visiting Professor and external examiner in Medan Academy of Tourism (Akpar Medan). He holds a doctoral degree in Hospitality Management "Disaster and Emergency Planning and Preparedness" from University Sains Malaysia (USM). He worked as an Assistant Professor, Ammon Applied University College, Amman, Jordan. Senior Lecturer and research coordinator in School of Hospitality & Creative Arts, Management and Science University, Shah Alam, Selangor, Malaysia, and Researcher at Sustainable Tourism Research Cluster (STRC), Pulau Pinang, Malaysia. He was working for the Jordanian hospitality industry for 17 years. He has participated and presented research papers in a number of academic conferences held in Malaysia, Taiwan, Thailand, Indonesia, Sri Lanka, and Jordan. He is an active member of Scientific and Editorial Review Board on Hospitality management, hotel, tourism, events, emergency planning, disaster management, human resource for Journal of Tourism Management, Journal of Hospitality Marketing & Management (JHMM), Current Issues in Tourism (CIT), Asia-Pacific Journal of Innovation in Hospitality and Tourism (APJIHT), International Journal of Economics and Management (IJEAM), AlmaTourism, Journal of Tourism, Culture and Territorial Development, International Journal of Tourism and Sustainable Community Development. His latest works have been published in the refereed international journals, conference proceedings, books and book chapters.

**Amrik Singh** is working as Professor in the School of Hotel Management and Tourism at Lovely Professional University, Punjab, India. He obtained his Ph.D. degree in Hotel Management from Kurukshetra University, Kurukshetra. He started his academic career at Lovely Professional University, Punjab, India in the year 2007. He has published 45 Scopus indexed publications. He has published 12 patents and 01 patent has been granted in the inter-disciplinary domain. Dr. Amrik Singh participated and acted as a resource person in various national and international conferences, seminars, research workshops, and industry talks. He has published five books with IGI Global Publication on trending areas such as Food Waste, Solid Waste, Artificial Intelligence in marketing, Mountain Tourism, Virtual tourism, Guest behavior in tourism and hospitality. His area of research interest is accommodation management, ergonomics, green practices, human resource management in hospitality, waste management, AR VR in hospitality, etc. He is currently guiding 8Ph.D. scholars and 5 Ph.D. scholars have been awarded Ph.D. He is PhD thesis external examiner for many national and international universities. He is also editorial team member for Scopus and web of science journals.

***

**Munir Ahmad** is a seasoned professional in the realm of Spatial Data Infrastructure (SDI), Geo-Information Productions, Information Systems, and Information Governance, boasting over 25 years of dedicated experience in the field. With a PhD in Computer Science, Dr. Ahmad's expertise spans Spatial Data Production, Management, Processing, Analysis, Visualization, and Quality Control. Throughout his career, Dr. Ahmad has been deeply involved in the development and deployment of SDI systems specially in the context of Pakistan, leveraging his proficiency in Spatial Database Design, Web, Mobile & Desktop GIS, and Geo Web Services Architecture. His contributions to Volunteered Geographic Information (VGI) and Open Source Geoportal & Metadata Portal have significantly enriched the geospatial community. As a trainer and researcher, Dr. Ahmad has authored over 50 publications, advancing the industry's knowledge base and fostering innovation in Geo-Tech, Data Governance, and Information Infrastructure, and Emerging Technologies. His commitment to Research and Development (R&D) is evident in his role as a dedicated educator and mentor in the field.

**T. Ananth kumar** is working as Associate Professor and Research Head in the IFET college of Engineering(Autonomous),India. He received his Ph.D. degree in VLSI Design from Manonmaniam Sundaranar University, Tirunelveli, India. He received his Master's degree in VLSI Design from Anna University, Chennai, India and Bachelor's degree in Electronics and communication engineering from Anna University, Chennai, India. He has presented papers in various National and International Conferences and Journals. His fields of interest are Networks on Chips, Computer Architecture and ASIC design. He has received awards such as Young Innovator Award, Young Researcher Award, Class A Award – IIT Bombay and Best Paper Award at INCODS 2017. He is the life member of ISTE, IEEE and few membership bodies. He has many patents in various domains. He has edited 6 books and has written many book chapters in Springer, IET Press, and Taylor & Francis press.

**Onur Çakır** received his Bachelor of Science degree in Tourism and Hospitality Management from the Bilkent University in 2007. His professional career in tourism began with internships during high school education and later he worked at international hotel chains such as Dedeman Blue Waters Side, Sheraton Hotel Ankara, Intercontinental Hotel Istanbul and Remington Hospitality Management Orlando between 2001 and 2008. In 2009, he began his academic career as a lecturer at Erzincan University Vocational School of Tourism and Hospitality. He received his MSc in Tourism Management from Sakarya University in 2011, and he completed his PhD in Anadolu University in 2015. Currently, he is working as an Associate Professor in Department of Tourism Management at Kırklareli University. His research interests include tourism and hotel management, sustainable tourism, rural tourism, tourism education, and tourism history.

**Busenur Can** received her bachelor's degree from Balıkesir University, Department of Tourism Guidance, in 2018. He received his master's degree from Kırklareli University, Department of Tourism Management. He continues his doctorate program at Çanakkale Onsekiz Mart University, Department of Travel Management and Tourism Guidance. His research areas are tourism and hotel management, tourism guidance and tourism marketing.

**Shad Ahmad Khan** is serving as Assistant Professor in College of Business, University of Buraimi in Sultanate of Oman. He is an active researcher who has a professional strength in the area of Business Management and Marketing. He has a vast experience of organizing international events like conferences and seminars. His area of interest is Data Sciences, green practices, entrepreneurship, administration sciences and marketing.

**Narendra Kumar** earned his Ph. D. from JS University, Shikohabad, India and currently working as Assistant Professor at Amity Institute of Travel &Tourism, Amity University, Noida. With 23 years of experience in travel & tourism, he has made significant contributions to the area of tourism education. Dr. Kumar has a strong interest in Business travel, tourist behavior and visitor experiences in the field of tourism and has published extensively on related topics. In addition to his academic pursuits, Dr. Kumar is actively involved in helping young graduates of tourism and hospitality domain to help them in establishing their start-ups. He has been invited to speak at numerous conferences and seminars on tourism and related fields and his current research focuses on student mentoring. Dr. Kumar's previous works include one edited book on "Tourist Behavior" published by Apple Academic Press, USA; one book on "Digital Marketing" and one on "Ethical Aspects of Business in Tourism".

**Pawan Kumar** is working as full Professor in the Department of Marketing at Mittal School of Business, Lovely Professional University, Punjab, India. He has 17 years of experience in business academic research .His areas of interest in research include entrepreneurship, marketing, e-commerce, consumer behaviour, social media, technology innovation etc. He is an avid researcher. He is active in Ph.D research supervision and has good number of publications in Q1 and Q2 Journals to his credit in various research papers published Scopus indexed journals namely: The TQM Journal from Emerald, Visions: Journal of Business Perspectives from Sage, International Journal of Business and Globalization, International Journal of Business Information Systems from Inderscience and other national/international journals of repute.

**Mehataj M.** is pursuing a Bachelor of Engineering in Computer Science and Engineering at IFET College of Engineering (Autonomous), Villupuram. Passionate about emerging technologies, Mehataj is working on projects that explore the intersections of Artificial Intelligence, Computer Vision, and real-time communication systems. Her areas of interest include data science, Artificial Intelligence and full-stack development. She is also involved in creating innovative solutions in inclusive communication, combining deep learning and WebRTC for real-time video call interactions.

**Noraihan Mohamad** is a Senior Lecturer at the School of Hospitality and Creative Arts, Management and Science University (MSU). She received her Master of Science and PhD degrees in Media Management from Universiti Utara Malaysia (UUM). Her expertise encompasses Malaysian mass media and new media, media and technology (including social networking), as well as consumer behavior and tourism marketing. In addition to presenting numerous papers at national and international conferences, she has also contributed articles to high-impact journals and chapters in books on media and tourism. Her current contributions to Malaysia's Government include developing the Malaysian National Unity Index 2.0 Study, the Malaysian Family Well-Being Index 2022 Study, as well as the Societal Stress Index Study.

**P. Kanimozhi** is working as Professor and Dean Academics in IFET College of Engineering (Autonomous), Villupuram with 19 years of teaching experience. She got her PhD from Anna University,Chennai and has published more than 17 research papers in IEEE, National and International Journals. Her current areas of interest include Cloud computing security ,Data mining and Blockchainand. Her research area is Data Security and Intrusion Detection in Cloud Environment using LR-OTSFCM and CP-ABE. She is a life member of various societies like ISTE, IAENG etc., She is also the reviewer in 04 reputed International Journals. She has received funds from various agencies like CSIR, ICSSR etc., for organizing awareness programmes on recent trends in Computer Science and Engineering.

**Harish Saini** is Assistant Professor in Mittal School of Business, Lovely Professional University, India. His area of interest include tourism studies.

**Bassam Samir Al-Romeedy** is a motivated Associate Professor at the faculty of tourism and hotels, University of Sadat City - Egypt, and an Accredited external auditor at the National Authority for Quality Assurance of Education and Accreditation – Egypt. I also work as a market research consultant and statistical analyst. Dr. Al-Romeedy has published in premier peer-reviewed journals including Tourism Review, Journal of Tourism and Technology, Journal of Vacation Marketing, Journal of Human Resources in Hospitality & Tourism, Corporate Social Responsibility and Environmental Management, and others.

**Shikha Sharma** is an Assistant Professor at Vivekananda Institute of Professional. She has over 12 years of teaching experience in Marketing Research. She has written many research papers in UGC (CARE), Scopus and ABDC indexed journal. She has done her Digital Marketing course from IIM (Jammu).She has taken workshops on the topics on "Digital Marketing" in institutes of repute. Her areas of teaching include Digital Marketing, Sustainable Consumption, Masstige Marketing and marketing management at the graduate and undergraduate levels. She worked with accreditation compliance at the university and college level.

**Swati Sharma**, Ph.D. is currently working as an Associate Professor with Amity University, India. She holds 18 years of teaching and industry experience. She is Vice- President of Women's Indian Chamber of Commerce and Industry. She is First Indian to receive the Certified Tourism Educator award from Asia Pacific Institute of Events Management. She is the reviewer of Consumer Behavior in Tourism & Hospitality & Inderscience Journals & IGI Global . She has authored & Edited 15 books & published research papers in National & International journals of repute. (IGI Global, Taylor & Francis, Springer, Apple Academy Press, CABI, Edward & Elgar).

**Ridhima Sharma** is an Associate Professor of Management at Vivekananda Institute of Professional Studies-Technical Campus. With a teaching and research experience of 12 years, she has contributed several articles to the journals of national & international repute and have presented papers in national and international conferences apart from authoring books. Her research interest includes Customer Relationship Management & sustainable consumer behavior. She is currently pursuing Post Doc from Amity University, Dubai.

**AnkitShukla** is an Academician and Practitioner in the field of Hospitality. Having intense knowledge of Hotel Industry I have worked in leading International Universities and have worked with multiple nationalities across the globe. I have rich experience in the field of research as well as IPR.

**Devika Sood**, an Assistant Professor at Amity University, Noida, brings over 18 years of corporate experience in the travel and tourism industry, having worked with companies like IndoAsia, Kuoni Travel, and Cox & Kings. Originally from Shimla, she holds a B.Sc. from St. Bede's College, Shimla, a postgraduate degree in Tourism Administration from Himachal Pradesh University, and a Ph.D. in Travel and Tourism from Amity University. With expertise in lead generation, business development, and MICE operations, Dr. Sood is also UGC NET qualified. She has published research in international journals and has extensive experience in behavioral science and soft skills training. A passionate traveler, Dr. Sood embraces change as essential for growth and is committed to preparing her students for the evolving global tourism landscape.

**Praveen Srivastava** is an experienced academician with a demonstrated history of working in the education management industry for more than 20 years. He is skilled in Mendeley (Recipient of Mendeley Advisor Certification), MOOC Courses, Customer Relationship Management and ICT. Authored and edited three books and several journal articles. He is also recipient of "Award of Excellence" by IIT Mumbai for being amongst the top performer of the FDP on "Use of ICT in Education for Online and Blended learning" in 2016. In 2018, IIT Mumbai awarded him with the Top Performer badge in two-week Faculty Development Program (FDP 301X) on "Mentoring Educators in Educational Technology". He was a Mentor in the AICTE FDP (FDP101x and FDP201x) on Pedagogy for Online and Blended Teaching-Learning Process conducted by the IIT Mumbai from August 3, 2017, to September 7, 2017, and from September 14, 2017, to October 12, 2017 respectively.

**Akshita Tiwari** is a dedicated hospitality professional with a passion for learning and expanding her knowledge in the field. She began her hospitality education in 2014 with a Bachelor's in Hospitality and Hotel Administration from IHM, Faridabad, and went on to complete her Master's in Hospitality Administration with a specialization in Human Resource Management from IHM, Pusa, New Delhi in 2019.In pursuit of her interest in hospitality and a desire to deepen her knowledge, she joined the Ph.D. in Hospitality at Amity School of Hospitality, Amity University, Noida, in January 2020.. Dr. Tiwari is currently a faculty member at Amity School of Hospitality, Amity University, Noida, Uttar Pradesh, where she teaches Front Office Operations and Management to Bachelor's in Hotel Management students and Master's in Hospitality students.

**Rajesh Verma** is Sr. Dean & Professor of Strategy at Mittal School of Business in Lovely Professional University, Punjab, India. His research & teaching interests entail areas like Business Models, Strategic Management & Political Marketing.

# Index

Milton Keynes UK
Ingram Content Group UK Ltd.
UKHW030659161024
449742UK00008B/108